Gavin Evans was born in London in 1960. He grew up mainly in South Africa where he tried his hand at boxing, worked as a campaigning journalist and threw himself into the underground politics of the African National Congress. Since returning to London in 1993, he has written on politics, health and sport for the *New York Times*, *Esquire*, *Playboy*, *Men's Health*, the *New Statesman*, the *Daily Mail* and the *Guardian*, and is a boxing correspondent for the BBC World Service. His biography of Naseem Hamed, *Prince of the Ring*, was published in 1996.

DANCING SHOES
IS DEAD

A Tale of Fighting Men in
South Africa

Gavin Evans

BLACK SWAN

DANCING SHOES IS DEAD
A BLACK SWAN BOOK : 0 552 999326

Originally published in Great Britain by Doubleday,
a division of Transworld Publishers

PRINTING HISTORY
Doubleday edition published 2002
Black Swan edition published 2003

1 3 5 7 9 10 8 6 4 2

Set in 11/13pt Melior by
Kestrel Data, Exeter, Devon.

Black Swan Books are published by Transworld Publishers,
61–63 Uxbridge Road, London W5 5SA,
a division of The Random House Group Ltd,
in Australia by Random House Australia (Pty) Ltd,
20 Alfred Street, Milsons Point, Sydney, NSW 2061, Australia,
in New Zealand by Random House New Zealand Ltd,
18 Poland Road, Glenfield, Auckland 10, New Zealand
and in South Africa by Random House (Pty) Ltd,
Endulini, 5a Jubilee Road, Parktown 2193, South Africa.

Printed and bound in Great Britain by
Clays Ltd, St Ives plc.

To Joan and the memory of Bruce: you are not to blame

Contents

Acknowledgements

A few words of gratitude to some people featured in the pages that follow: to my London family – Pat, Tessa and Caitlin, who give meaning to my life far beyond anything reflected here – you've been so wonderfully supportive and helpful. To my South African family – Joan, Karen, Michael, Khusta and Bridget – you are, of course, a central part of this tale and have helped me write it in all sorts of ways, huge and small. And to my friends who have lent me their names (especially, Tony, Maxine, Mark, Alan and Brett) and also those whose identities are so lightly encoded (particularly Wanda, Rosa, Leon and the Boulders tripper): without your assent it would have been impossible and I'm sorry if this has caused too much trouble.

I also want to say thank you to a few people who are not mentioned by name but helped in important ways: John Perlman, Thabiso Thema, Steve Kahanovitz, Ronald Harwood, Helen Falconer and the volunteers of the Crouch Hill Community Centre.

Many people connected to the world of South African boxing gave of their time and themselves over the last few years and in particular, Thulani Malinga, Mercy Morake, Stephen Mayisela, Phyllis Baronet, Rodney Berman, Mzi Mnguni, Mike Segal, Johnson Tshuma, Jacob Matlala, Jacob Mofokeng, Elias Tshabalala, Harold Volbrecht, Brian Mitchell, Bert Blewett, Theo Mthembu and Dumile Mateza.

I am especially grateful to those with a direct role in the publication of this book – my agent Clare Alexander, who proposed the germ of the idea, steered it into proposal form and then somehow managed to sell it; John Saddler, who took the chance; my editors Alison Tulett, who gently coaxed it into shape, Sarah Westcott, who completed the process, Aelred Doyle, who did it again for Black Swan, and Emma Dowson in London and Stephen Johnson and Laura Boon in Johannesburg, whose efforts helped to make this edition possible.

Thank you all.

Prologue

KILLING TIME AT SUN CITY

Sun City, South Africa, November 1985. The prelude to a knockout is one I know well. It's that moment of anticipation before the kill, when you know what's coming and become utterly transfixed with the thrill of seeing it through. It's the kind of 'closure' my strange sport feeds on – integral to its rationale – and I am certainly not immune to the feeding frenzy. But this one is different. It is beginning to feel horribly wrong.

It's the fourth fight between the hardened white Johannesburg lad Brian Mitchell and the skinny black man from Soweto with a body full of burn scars, Jacob 'Dancing Shoes' Morake. They've had some good scraps in the past – two wins for Brian, one for Jacob – but the gap has been widening and this time it's apparent from the start that Mitchell, the ambitious and determined son of an alcoholic ex-fighter, has outgrown Morake, the part-time boxer whose purse money feeds a large extended family.

'Dancing Shoes' does his dancing thing – up on his toes, jabbing and moving, but Brian is superior in every department – stronger, quicker, more accurate, a harder puncher, more resilient. With each round this dominance is more apparent and by the tenth the fight is no longer a fight but rather a sustained beating. My flatmate Maxine, who is sitting a few rows back, rushes forward to ask me: 'Why are they letting this go on? It's so one-sided. Why don't they stop it?'

'Fucking Snowball,' I reply, giving the half of the answer that doesn't require a fuller account of Morake's courage or his trainer's quixotic hope of a miracle – a cut eye, a lucky punch, a low blow. My verbal shorthand refers to what seemed to me the referee's callous disregard for the safety of a victim. The third man tonight is one Colonel Wally Snowball, a grey-eyed Murder and Robbery cop and a regular feature in the ring when black men fight whites. Perhaps he's having an off night, or maybe it's just that his job involves a daily dose of the kind of brutality that can make men immune to the suffering of others. Whatever, to me he seems so transfixed by Mitchell's brutal dominance that he hovers without intervening, looking like he wants to see just a little more.

In the eleventh round Dancing Shoes is dropped and when he hauls himself to his feet he is battered about the head. He drags his feet to his corner at the bell, his face lumpy and those hideous childhood burn scars that cover two thirds of his upper body making it appear even more vulnerable than current reality would suggest. But it's the eyes that are the real give-away. He needs the sparse pickings from these fights – his day job as an insurance clerk can't quite stretch far enough to feed, clothe and shelter his ill mother, his brothers and sisters, his fiancée and baby son, but those tired eyes say it's just too much. He tells his corner he doesn't really want to continue. He knows he has nothing left to offer, and that three minutes is an awfully long time when you're exhausted and in pain and faced with a still-fresh pair of 24-year-old fists. 'Just one more round, Jacob,' they plead, not wanting a stoppage defeat on his record. And so he comes out wearing a look of desperate resignation, for the last round of his life.

Brian Mitchell, a professional who knows his job extremely well, pounces, bouncing hard punches off Jacob's unprotected head. Jacob falls heavily, rises slowly and is clearly in no condition to continue. He can no longer defend himself, let alone fire back. I mutter, 'Stop the fucking fight,' but I should be screaming it with all the air in my lungs because for reasons known only to himself Colonel Snowball is about to wave Brian Mitchell in for a final duckshoot. Three heavy, unanswered punches and Dancing Shoes falls as if shot, his head audibly banging against the canvas-covered ring floor.

I rush forward to the ropes as Snowball counts, and see the victim lying prostrate, stiff, with shallow breath and glazed eyes, and I mutter to my girlfriend, Pat, who has been beside me in the front row at ringside: 'He's dying. Morake's going to die.' And then: 'This is gonna be my first ring death.' Most of the Sun City crowd senses this too, and there is a sudden change in the atmosphere. Everyone goes silent. The whites, even the few who'd been raucously chanting racist slogans a few minutes earlier, are suddenly subdued. They've been given what they were yelling for – 'Kill him, Brianie' – but do they really want it?

The blacks are stunned too, but I sense they also want revenge. Or maybe I'm just projecting my own sense of injustice about the fight's conclusion, marrying it with everything else going on in South Africa and in my life: the State of Emergency, my recent spell of detention without trial, the assassinations of trusted comrades, the torture, the massacres and so much else. Anyway, right here, right now, there's another fight to come, another black versus white fight – the big one – and my thoughts are interrupted by a booming announcement.

'Ladies and gentlemen, a really big hand for Charles the challenger – a truly gallant loser. Charles the *challenger*.' With his smarmy grin ring announcer Naidoo is letting us know that despite appearances everything-is-going-to-be-all-right, that this is the summer of 1985 and we are here at Sun City to be *entertained*, to have the *time of our lives*! and we shouldn't let anything get in the way – not even the sight of a waif-thin man having an oxygen mask strapped onto his face after absorbing a sustained battering courtesy of a superior opponent and a transfixed referee. This is Sun City, where nothing gets in the way of fun, fun, fun. The seats are comfy, the lights are bright, the loudspeakers are booming, there's more to come and then there's gambling to be done. Never mind that the dying man's name is not Charles the Challenger but Jacob Morake, Jacob 'Dancing Shoes' Morake. Never mind that his family is about to become destitute because he is their only provider. Never mind anything. This is an undercard fight, dammit – and there are contractual obligations to be fulfilled.

'And now, ladies and gentlemen,' Naidoo continues, 'could you please be upstanding for the visiting Australian cricket team – all the way from Australia,' and the unofficial squad of boycott-breaking mercenaries haul themselves upright, waving lazily before plonking themselves down again. 'Tonight we have a *galaxy* of boxing stars at ringside,' the announcer continues and proceeds to give the treatment to each of the local notables as the stretcher carrying Dancing Shoes is borne from the ring.

With that burnt black body conveniently out of the way, the white section of the crowd begins to relax again. There's a sense of relief – one less thing to think about and the beaming Mr Naidoo is helping them forget. 'I would now like to announce the winner of the Isuzu *bakkie* competition,' he says, with Dancing Shoes dying.

It's not just me. I can feel the black anger and resentment in the bleachers silently bubbling and boiling away. Someone will have to pay. Someone else will get hurt tonight. It is time for the main event.

1

MUHAMMAD, JOE AND JESUS

Kalk Bay, Cape Town, May 1966. We're sitting at a table near the window of a beachside tearoom. My older brother, Michael, my mother Joan and my baby sister Karen are here, but the conversation is monopolized by the men and all but the most insistently curious of children. The dads include my father, Bruce, and two of his Anglican clergymen friends.

The background to their conversation is this: they have just read in the *Cape Times* that Cassius Clay has carved up Henry Cooper in six rounds. Cooper dropped Clay three years earlier, and somewhere in the hopeful mind of my ex-boxer dad there existed a faint hope that Our 'Enry would do it again. Not a racial thing – my father's childhood sporting heroes were black men: Joe Louis ('greatest heavyweight ever, son') and Sugar Ray Robinson ('finest boxer, pound for pound, of all time'). More a question of what is familiar and what isn't.

South Africa is enduring a stiff Calvinist time warp and even political liberals like Bruce have yet to absorb the spirit of the Western 1960s – unless you count jibes about mop-top hairstyles, gleaned from Beatles bubblegum cards. 'Shims' he calls them, an amalgam of she and him; his little joke. In May 1966 this is uncharted, threatening territory, and this Clay is part of it. He's disrespectful of his elders. He's rude. He demeans his opponents. He's a polarizing force and, darn it, he converted to become a *Mohammedan*, a *Black* Muslim he calls himself. To the Reverend Bruce Read Evans – born a Jew, raised an atheist, and then, after a Pauline epiphany, an evangelical Anglican minister – this isn't quite on. 'Clay's parents called him Cassius and that's his name,' he says, forgetting, it would seem, that I'm already on my third name change (from Gavin to Hopalong Cassidy at three, to Johnny at four, and finally, under paternal duress, to Mark at five). Forgetting, too, his commendable permissiveness in accepting these bewildering re-creations. Of course, familiarity breeds contentment and in time my father will make earnest attempts to square it all – buying *Simon and Garfunkel's Greatest Hits* along with the Seekers and Satchmo, getting his heart beat up at François Hardy concerts, quoting *Eleanor Rigby* in his sermons, and, along the way, allowing himself a little admiration for Ali Muhammad, as he calls him, and a little amnesia on prior impressions. But in May 1966 we are still a few years from that moment.

'We really need a Joe Louis or a Rocky Marciano to give him a good hiding and put him in his place,' Bruce says. He is given to talking of 'good hidings' although for Michael and me he seldom delivers worse than the threat of such fearful consequences (and an occasional, much-resented hair tug or ear pull). I'm halfway through my first year at primary school, where beatings are already the order of the day, but this time the 'good hiding' statement confuses me. I wonder why this man with a strangely compelling name inspires such strong feelings from apparently reasonable adults like the assembled clergymen, and I inquire why this Joe or that Rocky don't volunteer for the job. After a collective chuckle, Bruce provides an instant lesson in the recent history of the heavyweight division, with once again the assurance that Joe at least could have done it 'in his prime'.

I am not sure why this moment stuck, when so many others faded, and I wouldn't swear an oath on the date and detail, but this was its essence: my first boxing memory. Over the next three years Muhammad and his sport hovered in the background, competing with John Wayne, the Hardy Boys, the Battle of Britain, and the little worlds of boys together. The firm figure of my father was the connection. He was the inspiration, the norm, the standard. His story seemed so full of majesty and mystery. Where he led, I did my best to follow, and boxing was one of the zones he claimed for himself.

His own father, Roy, was a tall, lean and unnaturally strong motor-racing driver and car dealer of Welsh–Irish extraction who'd fought in the First World War. I don't know much of him* except that he had a quiet authority and that his early demise had a devastating effect on his family. He crashed his racing car into an escaping female convict during the South African Grand Prix and punctured a lung. This trauma, combined with his thirty years of smoking, led to an early, painful, blood-coughing death from lung cancer when my father was 14.

Bruce's mother, Lilly, who died a decade later, was a

---

*His family arrived in Johannesburg in the late nineteenth century, claiming Jonathan Swift among their forebears.

tiny, extremely smart Jew, born in London to parents who escaped anti-Semitism in Warsaw and emigrated to England in the early 1890s and on to Cape Town in the 1900s.* Lilly became a staunch political liberal and at the age of 18 the first female science graduate from the University of Cape Town. She raised her three children as secular, atheist Jews. Her second son, Bruce – tall, sallow skinned, black haired, dark eyed, with a hooked Semitic nose broken several times from boxing – grew up with an artistic bent, an inquiring mind, an exceptionally strong will and a naive inclination to see the very best in other people, and in himself.

My mother, Joan Erlangsen, was the second child of Arthur, a Danish South African who worked for a tobacco company and died of cigarette-assisted heart disease when Joan was in her twenties, and Blanche, an English South African farmer's daughter who smoked twenty a day for seventy years and died in her

---

*Lilly's parents, the Peppers, or Pfefferblums as they were called before the English renamed them, were an inquisitive, intellectual family. One cousin, Paul Erlich, was a physicist who discovered an early cure for syphilis (and later won the Nobel prize for his work on cancer); her father, Adolph, was a merchant with an obsession for photography; her mother, Eva, an English teacher, Zionist campaigner and suffragette (Bruce loved the tale of Lilly – the second of three children – standing by Eva's side as she chained herself to the rails outside Buckingham Palace). After a decade in London Adolph was told by his doctor that his bad chest would benefit from sunshine, but their decision to emigrate again was also influenced by Eva's fervent opposition to vaccination. They took advantage of the assisted passages offered to white people and sailed to Cape Town where Eva continued campaigning for Zionism while Adolph made money from selling ostrich feathers, then ran a pub and, finally, after a fit of conscience about encouraging working men to blow their pay packages on liquor, sold it at a loss and turned to his true love, photography.

sleep in her nineties.* Blonde, fair-skinned, blue-eyed Joan was sharp and perceptive but raised to undervalue her own intellectual prowess. Her brother studied architecture in London. She, too, wanted to go to university but was told the money was spent and this was an extravagance for girls, so instead she studied pre-school education and became a nursery-school teacher and, along the way, a born-again Christian.

In their early twenties, when they both lived in Johannesburg, Bruce pursued Joan, but she was more interested in his unsaved soul than his boxer's body and she steered him towards a debate with her Christian mentors. Bruce fiercely defended his atheist corner, but floundered when asked if he'd ever read the New Testament. He accepted the challenge, read all night, saw the light, and, just like that, became a believer. He was not a mild man and in no time he felt called to abandon his business career and enter the ministry. My mother eventually accepted his marriage proposal, after which he followed the advice of his

*I never met Arthur, but his family were gentle people, the elders among them retaining their quaint Danish accents. Blanche – Granny to us – was our only living grandparent. One of six children, raised on a sheep farm in Kimberley that was raided by the Boers during the Anglo-Boer war (which ended when she was three), she lived in Hillbrow, Johannesburg when we were children. We loved her annual visits. She smelled of cigarettes and the first sniff provided proof that Christmas was coming. She was a twinkle-eyed, patient granny who could laugh at herself and seemed to enjoy life's little pleasures. We were particularly amused by her antipathy to Afrikaners – for instance, joining her in the wilder excesses of ridicule as we were dragged off to the Paul Kruger museum – but late in life, when she saw it as a choice between the Afrikaners and the blacks, she plumped for the enemy she knew. Still, by then she was already 80-plus, so we let it pass and would always accept her invitations to 'join me for a joint' – we enjoyed that one too, even if it was the culinary variety.

church and left South Africa for an evangelical Anglican theological college in north London while she studied at a Bible college on the other side of town. He became a curate in Redhill, where Michael was born in 1958, then a minister who worked among businessmen in the City, where I was born in 1960, before being 'called' to Cape Town, where Karen was born in 1965.

The Jewish side to my father's upbringing was a significant part of my childhood. It was something I was always aware of – at least from the time as a little boy when I asked why his penis looked different, and he explained that as a Jew he'd been circumcised by the rabbi at seven days old, but that it wasn't really essential for us. His Jewish heritage came out in all sorts of little ways – the Yiddish names and phrases he invoked from his mother, his Abe jokes, his carefully pressed yarmulke and most significantly his strong sense of Jewish exceptionalism. My earliest memories of war stories were from my father telling us what the Nazis did to the Jews – who must have included his relatives – and from this we were taught that any hint of anti-Semitism was not to be tolerated. He also explained to us why he would never buy a Volkswagen or any other German car, although he relented in later life, recognizing that Germans and Nazis weren't synonymous. His evangelicalism carried with it the belief that those who didn't accept Christ as their personal saviour were hell-bound, but he couldn't quite swallow this for his fellow Jews. We were regularly reminded that the Jews were God's chosen people and that God had a special plan, involving special grace, for them. We were reminded that we were immensely privileged to have a share of this bloodline. He delighted in talking about Lilly's intelligence, wit and

22

kindness and he clearly adored her. 'You would have loved her,' he often said to me. Our Jewish relatives were the only ones we saw on his side, and a little to my retrospective surprise his Christianity never seemed to create family tensions. Privately he talked of himself as a 'completed Jew' – a phrase I'm sure would sound obscene to many Jews – but he never proselytized with the cousins and aunts and they seemed to accept him for what he was, or what he'd become.

If Jewishness was a substantial subtext to our heritage, its central theme was Christianity. Aside from all it imparted about morality, destiny, salvation and purpose of life, the church served as an extended family which reinforced and complemented our own, nuclear unit – on the one hand as a baby-sitting and farming-out service to allow for my parents' meetings, conferences and long-distance travels, and on the other as a refuge for waifs and strays who were struggling to cope with life and would stay for days, weeks, months and sometimes years, as well as for a bewildering variety of Christian teachers and travellers.

While Jesus and his disciples were never absent from our table, the secular world was occasionally allowed to creep in, especially when the visiting pilgrims were taking a break. My father's pre-Christian years were a particular source of fascination. In between the Bible stories, family prayer and talk of conversion and redemption, we learnt bit by little bit of his childhood and early adult years and these tales were so much more beguiling than the talk of the soul-saving English curate on his fixed-wheel bicycle. I was always ready for his vignettes of youthful derring-do – the times when as a 14-year-old he nicked Lilly's car and drove around Johannesburg (only to crash it when reversing it back into the garage); his school truancy (with girls, in a boat, on Zoo Lake); how he volunteered for the commandos after school ('they wanted men who knew how to fight – boxers and wrestlers') and then went AWOL to meet his girl (before being demobbed for medical school); his few years as what he quaintly called 'a ladies' man' (no further elaboration offered or requested) who cruised around in open-topped sports cars (until my mum put an end to it).

But more than all this, I harvested his fond memory for stories about his fighting days, in the ring and out, and I built in my mind a model of courage, skill and fortitude. He would tell of 'training behind closed doors' to spar with black boxers 'because it was forbidden in those days, son'. I hung on those words, 'behind closed doors' – the illegality, the defiance, the romance of it all. He signed up for ballroom dancing 'to improve my footwork – because to box, you must learn to dance'. He boxed bravely (but lost) against the Olympic gold medallist, Gerald Dreyer. He competed in 'the 1948 Olympic trials' (though sub-sequent interrogation revealed it to be no more than the Transvaal amateur finals, 'which amounted to the Olympic trials'). Once as a youth he tackled a burglar who had broken into his home, and took a slug in the shoulder for his troubles. 'I was a boxer so I didn't hesitate to confront him but not even a boxer can defend himself against a gun,' he helpfully explained. If not a boxer, then no-one, I reasoned, and was enchanted.

He had two favourite stories, both of which im-pressed me immensely. The first involved Alf James, a quick-witted, quick-fisted product of a Jewish

24

orphanage who became the South African professional lightweight and welterweight boxing champion. Alf arrived at my father's school, King Edwards, to conduct an exhibition while training to fight England's big-hitting, big-drinking Eric Boon. Seventeen-year-old Bruce was then a school prefect and cadet officer known to be a young man who could hold his own. He was therefore volunteered to spar with 27-year-old Alf and as a person of considerable self-confidence and physical courage Bruce didn't hesitate, and sailed in full of bravado. 'I caught him coming in – I suppose he wasn't concentrating' – a modest little rider – 'and down he went – in front of the whole school.' A paternal smile, a shake of the head, a relived memory. 'I felt tremendous.'

'What happened next, Dad?'

'Oh, of course he got up and made me pay – dropped me actually – but I finished on my feet.'

Many years later the raffish, kind, charming old conman and former jailbird Alf – by then 71 years old – would pass briefly through my life, teaching me how to counter a lax jab with a lead right cross, but that's another story. At the time I developed a precise picture of Alf and my father in that school gym with all those boys watching and it offered me a beguiling image of what I wanted to become – a good man, a dashing man, a brave man capable of dropping professional boxing champions in front of my admiring friends.

His second tale had to do with nobility in the guise of the boxer, with a subtext I've never quite been able to shake off despite my claims to logical thought: that one should never back down from a fight. He was cycling downhill near his childhood home in Berea, Johannes-burg when three 'Afrikaner thugs', 'Nazi Afrikaners',

25

'Ossewabrandwag types' (the pro-Nazi wartime terror group) put a broomstick through his front spokes. When he had scraped himself up from his mangled bicycle they came for him. He rose to his feet. 'I'll fight the strongest of you,' he challenged. The biggest Nazi swaggered forward, slipping his fingers into a knuckle duster, 'and I gave him a real hiding, a boxing lesson – jab, jab, jab, right cross – he didn't know what hit him.' But then the anti-Semites revealed their moral turpitude. 'They threw sand in my eyes so that I couldn't see and then all three of them jumped on me and beat me up. They kicked me like donkeys.' This had great significance for him, and unlike other tales it was limited to a single version. Perhaps more than any other event in his youth it fuelled his hatred of Nazis and Afrikaner nationalists and encouraged his political liberalism, but for me it was all about the marvels of boxing as a form of self-defence against anything but sand. Sand and bullets.

Like eight-year-old boys the world over, my imagination was constantly fed by Westerns and war movies, while martial pursuits of one kind or another were taking over more innocent territory. Hide and seek was being edged out by cops and robbers, tennisette bowed to judo, the capgun of the cowboy was giving way to the products of the amateur gunsmith – catapults, bows and arrows and cracker guns that fired iron balls down greased pipes. Once, during a holiday war with some Afrikaner lads, Michael – calm, brave and practical – staved off a stick attack on our friend Peter by grabbing my catapult, pulling the bands back as far as they would go, and firing a stone at the forehead of the charging Nico, who dropped, stunned. His parents complained. My father demanded an explanation. 'He was hitting Peter and calling him a *rooinek'* – redneck limey – 'Dad,' we said. Bruce Evans thought for a moment and I think the memory of that spoke in the wheels and his Jewish roots surfaced once again. 'OK, but next time just use your fists,' he said.

But most of these wars took place in my mind, where they were transformed into something heroically physical. I was David with the sling cutting down Goliath. I was Rooster Cogburn with the six-shooter. I was Joe Hardy landing an uppercut on the chin of a no-good. I would cut and chop and shoot and charge at trees and flowers that were really heads and bodies, and bottles and tins that were really, well, just bottles and tins. My daily conversational contribution tended to involve the shortest route to a thousand variants of the who-would-win debate – lion or tiger, bull terrier or bulldog, crocodile or shark, lynx or wolf, anaconda versus reticulated python, T-Rex against a stegosaurus, you or Mr Myburgh, Dad? I would press my father, the source of all useful information on such points. 'Wouldn't a karate man beat a boxer? A black belt, hey? They can kick and kill a man with one neck chop.'

'Oh no,' my father would insist. 'Kicking is for asses. By the time he's kicked a boxer would either catch his foot or knock him out before he regains his balance.'

So boxing was the finest form of self-defence, and it was also a gentlemanly pursuit, apparently suitable even for born-again Christians who took the word of the Lord literally. 'Did you ever use it for attack, you know, like starting a fight, Dad?' I once asked. His answer was more restrained. 'Only once, and then it was provoked,' and under further inquiring provocation he explained: 'When I was a third-year student at Wits, this chap kept taunting me, trying to provoke me, calling me names, so I warned him a couple of times. Then he did it again on the main steps, and I turned around and gave him a swift one-one-two – two jabs and a right cross. Knocked him out cold and he never worried me again. He was asking for it though.' He paused for a second, noticing the inspired light in my eyes, and felt compelled to add a rider: 'Of course, that was before I was born again.'

My blind faith in all things emanating from the wisdom of Bruce Read Evans was enough for me, and boxing was certainly part of it. My mother's stories were rather lower on hyperbole, usually with herself as the foil. When she faked a cold to get out of class, her teacher produced a huge sheet and ordered: 'Blow!' When she slid down the drainpipe to get out of school, her headmistress was waiting at the bottom. When cousin Marcia took her galloping across the veld, Marcia ended up laughing at Joan's black and blue bum. It was all a bit self-deprecating, lacking that paternal quality of thrilling, grandiose resonance.

In contrast to the heroic past and hard-driven present of my father, the world of my mother seemed anodyne – soft, safe, secure – and when you're a boy you can't quite appreciate the immense value of softness, safety and security. Such gifts were not really worthy of admiration or even focus. They were just absorbed. She was the constant, the day to day or hour to hour, the unexotic. She gave and gave and I took and took, without offering much in return that I can recall. It was her place to give and mine to take, I thought. When I was five and Michael seven she slapped our bums for parading around the bathroom chanting 'bare botties, bare botties' and we responded by plotting in the bathtub a kissing boycott – from which our father was

28

naturally exempt. Today this piece of calculated collective action seems strangely, curiously cruel, but the stand-off was absolute and lasted over seven years. The end more or less coincided with the violent conclusion to my mother's role as a dispenser of discipline – on the day Michael shook back and won. After that a closer relationship slowly and tentatively emerged, although it took me another decade to discover her sense of humour, intelligence and emotional strength. But at the age of nine I had no desire to be a mummy's boy. It was physical strength I admired, and my father, the son of the racing driver who could pull out long carpentry nails with his fingers, my father the tall, dark man of physical courage, my father the former boxer, was the available role model.

But this is not quite enough to explain the mania to come. Obsession – like its kissing cousin, fetish – is highly personalized by nature, even if its characteristics are worthy of generalization. An ostensibly similar set of environmental stimuli can produce wildly different results in two individuals because here one is talking about the minutiae of social catalysts as well as chemical reactions. Michael, for instance, never developed more than a passing regard for boxing. He was obsessed with cricket, and I trailed in his wake, as a junior member of the Western Province Cricket Club, watching every test, provincial and club game on offer. In summer we batted on the back lawn. When it rained we played the carpet games 'cricket at Lord's' and 'continuous cricket'. In winter we'd swap cricket for rugby and soccer, using our season tickets for Saturday excursions to Newlands, and on Friday nights we would watch the likes of Geoff Hurst and Bobby Moore breaking the international sporting boycott to play in whites-only football. In this sense we were no different from most other white, South African schoolboys our age – devoted to sport, and close to oblivious to the fact that the players were all white and the crowds segregated.

We were both born in England but before I reached my second birthday our parents felt called by God – via the medium of an invitation from a Cape parish – to return home. Joan, who was having a trying time raising two children in a tiny, steep-staired flat in Westminster in a time of peasouper fogs when clothes were hand-washed and rack-dried, was delighted with this call. Bruce was less sure, partly because his work with businessmen was stimulating, but also because of his distaste for apartheid. He supported the liberal-ish Progressive Party, whose sole member of parliament was his heroine, Helen Suzman, but I think the idea that he could make a difference, and that Jesus wanted him to make this difference, helped him to answer the call, as did the specifics, which meant relocation to a thirsting-to-thrive evangelical church in the leafy middle-class suburb of Kenilworth, Cape Town. They arrived, however, to discover a final-hour change of plans and found themselves instead in a small church in the 'coloured' area of Diep River, which was in the process of being ethnically cleansed by a government who regarded it as a 'brown spot' and wanted to make way for more whites.

The residents of Diep River were uprooted from their homes, most of them dumped in a desolate area twelve miles away called Mannenburg, which would soon become one of the roughest gang-infested townships in the country. The dislocation of families and the disruption of settled communities had a devastating effect on these people, and much of my father's early ministry involved dealing with the fall-out from this brutality. The misery was multiplied by the flood of 1962, which robbed many of the remaining coloured residents of their possessions, and the personal consequences were frequently dire. Soon after the flood my father was alerted by a terrifying scream from the railway line down the road. Ten years earlier he had given up his medical studies at the end of his third year after witnessing his first amputation, which made him vomit.* He was not ready for what was to come. One of the coloured parishioners, a teenager jilted by her boyfriend and no doubt further confused by the break-up of her community, dived in front of a train. But instead of killing her, the train chopped off her legs at the thigh and my father, the first on the scene, had to press the pressure points to slow the blood flow, and then place the legs in the ambulance. The woman survived to become a church worker. My father had nightmares for years to come.

My own first memory is of pulling a kettle of boiling water over my almost two-year-old body and being rushed to hospital. My reward was a new coloured pen from the nurse for each visit. But the rest of my recall from my early life is wonderfully sublime: staring for what seemed like hours at a mirror in my parents' room, trying to sit on a train that doubled as my second birthday cake, watching the firemen coax our cat, Smoky, down from a tree, returning stray balls to the school children next door.

*He later told me he had only studied medicine to please his mother. I think the reaction to the amputation was the final sign that the gap between Lilly's dreams and his own revulsion could not be bridged.

By the time I was old enough to absorb a bigger picture, we had finally said goodbye to Diep River, moving to a large, old house in Kenilworth from where our points of cultural reference were more Home Counties than homelands. It was a world modelled on collective colonial memory, and this is what came to seem normal – the jacarandas, gum tree and willows in the garden, the smell of hydrangeas, the long winter rains, the bonfires made by suburban gardeners, the vegetable cart pulled by a dray horse, the steamroller that blew real steam. We grew up with warm tales from Beatrix Potter, A.A. Milne, Kenneth Grahame and Enid Blyton, which conjured up images of little children with button-down coats playing exotic games like conkers or else tobogganing down snow-covered slopes, re-emerging into cosy, log-fire homes with endless cups of tea or warm Bovril. It was a safe, faraway world benignly ruled by eccentric and proud adults. When I read my children the old stories, I still feel vicariously nostalgic for this imaginary world, and in those early days it seemed tantalizingly close. The only toboggans were for the sand dunes, but there was an English vicarage feel to our days – summer-morning teas with the Thursday Wives in their floral frocks, Youth Fellowship evenings in our lounge with 'our young people', the gatherings of clergymen with English and Welsh accents, hanging their musty-smelling black cassocks in the entrance hall and shuffling into my father's study, while we boys enjoyed the freedom of the hedgerow suburbs on our bicycles.

Africa? Pardon? There was a great deal else happening in our little southern African world at the time, but we absorbed no more than a dim image of events beyond the safe hum of tree-lined life within the planet's most beautiful city. The world of Mannenburg, let alone the African townships of Langa, Nyanga and Guguletu, was a continent or two away and it barely touched us in any way we could recognize. Like most white South African children our only contact with black people was with domestic workers, which in our case meant Maria – a rotund, jovial, endlessly kind and extraordinarily patient woman. Maria was a victim of the Diep River forced removals, which coincided with the death of her husband and the discovery of a terminal illness in her fourth child. For over five years she came to work for our family as a char, and remains one of the few people from my childhood I still visit. I had not yet discovered the difference between 'African' and 'coloured' but from Maria's manifest goodness I drew an incipient prejudice that most people with brown skins were kinder and warmer than most people with pink skins and in time this would spread to my view of black sportsmen and black boxers in particular. We knew from our parents that Maria had a hard time, but that was about the limit of our social awareness.

Political consciousness arrived in tiny, news-related bites. For instance, one of my first radio memories was a special news item on Radio South Africa in 1966.* It was announced that a tapeworm-inspired Greek madman (who might actually have been a coloured communist who was less than totally insane) stabbed to death the Dutch-born madman who fathered apartheid, Hendrik Verwoerd. It was extremely exciting, especially since our next-door neighbour, an opposition MP, provided an 'eyewitness' account on the

*The very first was sitting on the floor in the lounge, listening to Churchill's funeral in 1965.

news bulletin. My father, whose work gave him ongoing contact with the coloured churchgoers driven from their homes under the Verwoerd-enforced Group Areas Act, made sure there was no mourning in our house. 'Verwoerd was evil,' he said, before adding that the new man, the beetle-browed alcoholic and former Nazi Second World War intern Balthazar 'Jackboot John' Vorster, was 'even worse'.

This input rubbed up against the mild terror of Rondebosch, our boys' state school, built in the late Victorian era and, like most South African schools of that kind, modelled on a version of Eton, with white shirts, striped ties and thick melton blazers for boiling the little boys in the African sun, and, of course, regular beatings. There we were told of Verwoerd's greatness, and what a sad day it was. But we knew better. As we proceeded through the ranks, we were given endless lessons on the noble Great Trek and on the courage of Boers against those greedy Brits and those treacherous Zulus, but it never quite washed for Michael and me.

Outside this regime we were free – on rainy days to hoover up Classic Comics, or to squeeze into the Saturday-morning double features at our local bioscope, but in the main ours was an outdoor, physical world. Our bikes took us to and from school, eight miles a day, and far beyond, while our occasional family outings invariably involved the mountains or the sea, and our afternoons were filled with pickup games of rugby, cricket and soccer, or swimming pools or Cub camps, building treehouses, chasing each other in games of red rover and cops 'n' robbers, playing *toktokkie* on neighbourhood doors, pea-shooting passing cars, erecting roadblocks and romping with our succession of dogs. It was a boys' world, one from which girls like Karen were excluded. She operated on another plane of existence, moving to rules and rhythms untouched by ours.

By 1969, however, I was beginning to see myself as a bit outside this Boy's Own loop – starting to seek and discover little areas of difference, finding them a source of both worry and contentment. I came from a family of tall men – a 6 foot 1 father, a brother who eventually passed 6 foot 3 and a pack of robust cousins – yet I was the second smallest in my class, and not too delighted about it either. There were other things too. I had chosen my own name; I spent many hours talking to myself in worlds of my own creation, or somebody else's; at the age of eight I had been 'born again' at a Christian camp but had kept it to myself – wary of the behavioural expectations that would follow from revelation; and for the previous three years (and the following five) I had served time as a vegetarian 'on principle' (refusing to eat meat, fish or chicken) after seeing netted yellowtails being killed by fishermen. By nine I was starting to search for ways to express my incipient sense of oddness – a feeling exacerbated when my brother informed me that 'anything you can do, I can do better'.

'I'm a better actor,' I pleaded.

'But I don't want to act.'

'I can rollerskate, you can't.'

'*Ja*, but rollerskating's for girls.'

If I had to accept Michael's supremacy in the areas that counted – ball games – my early life-struggle involved restraining any attempt by my parents to give official recognition to his superior status. Anything he was allowed – me too. It was my sole triumph against him until he reached eleven and joined the Scouts, who wouldn't have me yet. The fallout from this random fact clinched my thirty-year connection with the world of professional boxing, whose start I would like to blame on Ali, though really that wouldn't be fair. If I were to name a single catalytic culprit it would have to be Joseph Louis Barrow. Well, Joe, the Second Kenilworth Scouts, Springbok Radio and a Jewish Anglican clergyman father.

My campaign one late winter Friday night in 1969 was to stay up until Michael came home at 11 p.m. I was very firm on this point with our babysitter, Miss Findley, and I would not take no for an answer. This led me to an intimate acquaintance with night-time radio. I sat defiantly at the kitchen table, staring at our big oblong wireless with Miss Findley scurrying around me, until she faded from view and the pictures from the world of Springbok Radio took on vivid form.* Friday-night listening started at 7.30 with *Squad Cars*, a dramatized tribute to the South African police. 'They prowl the empty streets at night, waiting, in fast cars and on foot, facing danger at every turn . . . They protect the people of South Africa; these are the men of *Squad Cars*.' Next there was a drab quiz programme called *100,000 To Go!*, which had contestants boning up on a biography of their choice. If they made it to the end they would earn 100,000 cents – 1,000 Rand (then £500) – for their efforts. On this August evening, a few months before the moon landing and Woodstock, a dour middle-aged man with a monotonous voice chose

*Television was still six years away – mainly because the government was worried there weren't enough Afrikaans programmes and that English would therefore become dominant.

the life of Joe Louis, and I sat at the kitchen table utterly transfixed. When the contestant fell at the penultimate stage, the Brown Bomber story required closure, and this started me searching and asking and eventually doing. It would lead to the moment when I could say to Michael, trembling, 'You can beat me in everything – except a fight' – a claim never fully tested. But more importantly it unearthed an alternative existence and a new sense of meaning. I was no longer to be just the odd little vegetarian, or the minister's son, or Michael's little brother, or Karen's middle brother. I was the boxing boy.

Joe Louis, conveniently, had been my father's inspiration, so I sucked him dry on this glorious subject. He offered me vivid accounts of the visiting British boxers of his era – Freddie Mills, Eric Boon, Bruce Woodcock – and I took it all in with uncritical relish, but it was Joe I really wanted. I latched on to Joe and delighted in what he seemed to represent. I took a personal share-ownership in the official version of this man's tremendously triumphant, pathetically sad life, the version cleaned of the drug, alcohol and sex addictions, the wife-beating and the mental illness. It was enough that he caught up with Billy Conn – 'he can run but he can't hide' – rose from the floor to carve up Two-ton Tony Galento, and, as I would put it to anyone patient enough to listen, '*literally* took the head off Max Schmeling', second time around. This extraordinary victory was portrayed to me and then by me as a vindication of liberalism, a triumph over Nazism and proof that Louis was the greatest heavyweight of all time. To top it all, Joe gave it all up along with his hard-won purses to fight the good fight against Hitler – 'We'll win, not because God's on our side, but because we're on God's side.' Soon after I discovered him, Joe Louis was admitted to a mental hospital suffering from paranoid delusions, and I was terribly upset. Impossible. Louis couldn't be nuts. I refused to believe it and when Joe was released and went on to referee the second Joe Frazier–Jerry Quarry fight I felt relieved and vindicated.

I had never seen a boxing match and had yet to experience the thrill of its brutal uncertainty, its sense of unknown destination, its marvellous capacity for improvisation and surprise. For me, then, it was enough to soak up the written word on the sport's history. I cancelled my subscriptions to *Tiger* and *Jag* and replaced them with a subscription to the British weekly, *Boxing News*. My pocket money was saved for monthly doses of Nat Fleischer's *Ring* magazine. I became a regular correspondent to the letters pages of such publications, sending little polemics from 'Mark Evans, aged 11¾' on why a boxer would lick a martial artist or why Bob Fitzsimmons was the greatest light heavyweight of all time and why our very own Pierre Fourie deserved to be the number-one contender. I even acquired a sad British pen-pal, an adult with whom I would swap notes on fights between boxers and wrestlers, karate men and the like. My school orals were all on boxing, I clipped the newspapers for every reference to my sport and stuck them in scrapbooks, and I scoured the Wynburg public library for boxing books, and in time these taught me far more than I sought.

From *Noble and Manly*, a history of the British National Sporting Club, I learnt of the deep racism of the British establishment. From Denzil Batchellor's biography of Jack Johnson, I discovered the Ku Klux

Klan and lynchings. In Dave Anderson's *Sugar Ray* I came across American military segregation during the Second World War. In *Lionel Rose, Australian* I encountered oblique hints about the genocide committed against Aborigines. And my early sense of the American 1960s was drawn from all the Ali books I managed to find. Malcolm and Martin, the Nation of Islam, the Vietnam War and the War at Home, *motherfuckers* and *cocksuckers* – I discovered all of this and so much more via Muhammad and his biographers. These, however, were nuggets acquired in passing, on the way to the essence: the written accounts of the great fights, and eventually their ancient images from fight films my father would treat me to, held at cinemas in the city and the suburbs.

1969 began with our no-nonsense teacher, Miss Bierman, taking us to visit her dad, the chief of the navy, but the year of Woodstock changed direction when the beaded, thonged Miss Moore took over, placing our desks in circles and encouraging us to write free verse. I was one of her favourites – too shy to be a pet but still encouraged, and I loved it. Her friend the botanist and poetry enthusiast Mr Kenyon encouraged my acting and told me I could go all the way if I wanted, and I was delighted with this discovery because after I retired, undefeated, as heavyweight champion of the world I could become the next Laurence Olivier. I proceeded to spend many hours listening to and then reciting my father's 78rpm records of Olivier's Hamlet, and fiercely rejected my father's claim that Lord Larry was a homosexual. But my Cape spring wasn't to last. The year of Altamont arrived and Miss Moore left. Mr Kazner caned me for wiggling my ears in class, and Mr Holmes caned me for not getting my homework signed, and Mr Pocock beat the whole class for making too much noise. A boy called Wyness let loose a prolonged shriek. Mr Pocock led him into the lighting room and re-emerged several minutes later. 'He had a boil on his bum. Should've told me. I would have hit the other cheek.' I refused to cry but my schoolwork went into freefall and I lived in perpetual terror, biting my nails, licking my lips, pissing in my bed twice after terrifying dreams of being sentenced to hell, and constantly praying that I would be spared the next caning. My academic work, and interest, went into a prolonged decline.

But it wasn't all gloom by any means. My youth coincided with a period of reawakening after the repressed Verwoerdian era of the South African Sixties. The dead hand of oppression was starting to slacken and little openings were created in unexpected areas. Interspersed with the bubblegum on the radio were snatches of what we fondly called the 'underground', and in its wake came a variety of alien cultural influences which the state struggled to understand or control. Joe Louis may have been a catalyst, but Muhammad Ali welded it all together for me. There were no serious contenders when it came to naming a defining figure, even if Ali did not quite fit many of the dimensions of the peace and love decade. He began his return against Jerry Quarry in 1970 and I was ready for him. For my classmates I was a walking encyclopedia on anything to do with Ali, his profession and his view of the world. I told them Joe Frazier would beat Ali because I knew from boxing history that two fights was not enough after three years away, and when this proved correct, my standing soared, my sense of self swelled and my head cleared itself of unrelated thoughts. In this way, amid the buzzing of the lawn-mowers, the barking of the dogs and the heaven and hell in my pre-teen head, a new world was emerging with boxing firmly at centre stage.

I recall precisely what I was doing when, say, the Watergate scandal broke, the Mai Lai massacre was exposed or when I first heard *Imagine* – but it was the boxers, and particularly the black American heavy-weight boxers, who framed the first half of my second decade. Sitting in the stratosphere was Muhammad, and then below him the polyester fighting men, lesser gods without higher callings, but splendid neverthe-less. In my eclectic way, I was happy to worship all of them and to slot my future identity into their images. I would buy a pink Cadillac and chunky gold jewellery like Joe Frazier and a five-acre mansion like George Foreman, and most of all I would stand up for my principles like Ali. I would have preferred sharing Ali's skin colour too. I bought a poster, 'Black is Beautiful – White is White', and placed it next to Muhammad's ridiculously handsome photographic image in my first act of conscious political identity.

My prime ambition in life was to emulate the Greatest. To get there I had to learn how to box. I also had to grow up to be Ali's size, 6 foot 3, 212 pounds, which I felt was the optimum for a heavyweight champion of the world. My father reassured me that, come puberty, I had every chance of shooting up to his six foot-plus, though he also insisted that the only way I would make my dreams come true was to work at it. He erected a small ring in our garage, drilled a hole through my bedroom carpet to erect a punch ball, and bought me my first pair of gloves.

He then set about teaching me, and occasionally Michael and I would spar together. After a few months he declared I was ready for the next step, and so on Friday nights I was driven to the YMCA in down-at-the-heel Long Street, in Cape Town's city centre, to box.

Our cosy family had moved to a big church house with a rambling forestry garden in the once mixed but now whites-only suburb of Wynberg, where my father was appointed rector of a parish of five churches. But the appearance of opulence was not quite the reality. The church was rich in property but poor in cash and my father's income seemed derisory – less than that of any of the fathers of children in my neighbourhood or school – which meant that when it came to clothes, cars, toys or pocket money I felt nobly short-changed. This created a mixture of admiration and contempt for wealth – the former expressed in gold-chained dreams of my boxing future, the latter in festering little resentments about the present: the products of fee-paying schools, the suburbs they inhabited, the swimming pools in their gardens. Even at state-funded Rondebosch there were many points of enviable comparison: their dads drove spanking new, carpeted, automatic Zephyrs, Zodiacs and Valiant Rebels; mine drove a manual, metal-floored, second-hand Cortina, and for a while, when he was hit by the medical bills from a long bout of encephalitis, we had to manage without a car. My parents dutifully paid their tithes to God and we followed suit, handing over a tenth of our pocket money; their parents spent their savings on hotelled holidays. In this way I somehow acquired a not exactly accurate self-image of being part of the Godly poor. We would surely make it through the eye

of the needle, but I was less certain about our neighbours.

I was rather taken aback to find that for the YMCA
boxers such fine distinctions of privilege went un-
noticed. I was a *larney*, a boy who spoke posh, and
I also rapidly discovered that even in the white
community there was a long way down the financial
scale to fall from our comfortably cash-strapped
suburban existence. The YMCA boxers were mostly
rough boys who had no interest in my theories on
boxing and my opinions on the history of the game or
any other subject. They just wanted to fight and fool
around. Several were Afrikaners so conversation in
English was limited, except with the older lads who
seemed amused by my quaint ways and would tease
and indulge me. Soon I grew to love the place –
the rickety staircase leading up two grand stairway
flights to a large, open room with dirty, splintering
floorboards and a permanent aroma of congealed sweat.
Combined with the sawdust of the heavy bag and
the leather of the gloves and the speedball and the
medicine balls, this became the smell I identified with
my sport.

The boxing itself was a crude introduction to my
dislike of taking pain and my middle-class, Jesus-boy
caution about dishing it out. It took me several months
to get used to hitting other boys in the face, and several
years to learn not to turn away or close my eyes when
facing up to a head blow. It gradually dawned on me
that my below-par ball skills were replicated when it
came to the reflexes and timing required in this sport.
Still, I was getting fitter, running every morning with
my dog Brutus past the Wynberg military camp, around
the park and home to pick up the paper and scour it for

boxing news, and then to do my sit-ups and push-ups and pound my bedroom speedball.

I learnt much from my two years in the YMCA boxing club. I discovered for the first time that some Afrikaners could be nice, although like all people with racist sensibilities I restricted this observation to the exceptions – the ones who belonged to my club and cheered when I fought. And I picked up many other things in passing during my Friday-night visits to that gym. Like lust, for example. I'd been tipped off by my parents about the mechanics of sex a few years earlier (after Michael and I innocently brandished the word 'fuck' – a present from our neighbour, Rael), but until now it had been vague theory. My first memory of a self-aware, inspired erection came from the gym. More specifically, from observing one of the young mums sitting in a shiny purple miniskirt, watching us with her legs crossed and a little smile, smoking a cigarette while painting her long nails. I was facing the front, doing group push-ups, which became awkward when the call came to roll over for sit-ups, but I couldn't stop staring.

After two months Reg, the head trainer, decided I was ready for my first amateur fight – a large amateur tournament held in Rugby, a poor white peninsula suburb. I was ten but they filled in a form saying I was twelve (the minimum age), and I silently apologized to Jesus for going along with this deception, even though I reassured him it was not my invention. That done, I proudly pulled on the black club vest my mother had dutifully dyed, the baby-blue satin trunks Reg handed to me and finally my blue sneakers and was sent behind the curtains of the school hall to weigh in. I was a little alarmed to discover that the other boy was a genuine 12-year-old, four pounds heavier, half a head taller and having his fourth fight, but I also knew something he didn't: I was going to be heavyweight champion of the world.

Coming out from the green corner and forgetting all I had been taught, I fought my little heart out, and after three flailing, utterly exhausting two-minute rounds, I thought I'd done enough to win. The scores were added and to my ecstatic delight I was declared the victor. I shot my hand up before the referee could raise it, beaming in triumph. A minute later, however, as we were leaving the ring, there was a second announcement. 'Sorry, ladies and gentlemen, there is a mistake. The winner, red.' I'd been robbed, and knew now that unlike Sugar Ray Robinson it was impossible for me to go through my amateur career undefeated. I rushed to the toilet, locked the door and blubbed my heart out – the last time I would cry, other than through the vicarious emotions safely and regularly released in the cinema or reading myself to sleep, until my father died twenty-two years later.

For my next fight, in a provincial novice tournament, my opponent was no bigger and no more experienced than me, and I won easily, knocking him around the ring with ecstatic glee. It was the start of a lose–win–lose–win pattern that continued throughout my stop–start amateur career. I went on to reach the finals and my father and brother came along to watch me getting dropped twice and stopped in the third by a barrel-chested pubescent who looked several divisions larger than me. I was relieved when the referee stepped in. 'You need to do more push-ups, son' was my father's considered verdict, and so I did, and this time I didn't cry.

* * *

My class teacher in 1971 was Carl Olsen. When I first heard his name I was intrigued because Carl 'Bobo' Olson once beat Randy Turpin to become middle-weight champion of the world. But this was Carl 'Arl throw you with the duster' Olsen, a wiry little grease-ball with a collection of sticks and planks, all called Suzie-Q. Once he bent me over a desk and whipped me on my naked thighs with a long bamboo cane for the offence of whispering in class, leaving angry welts that lasted for days. With some boys his propensity for violence seemed even less restrained. 'Fetch us a plank,' he'd order, and we'd all rush out for a prize two-by-four, which he'd proceed to break on the bum of a Jewish lad every single woodwork class. He seemed to enjoy the sight of this boy screaming, clutching his buttocks, bouncing around the room and then up the little flight of stairs as if propelled by some inner force. We hated it, feared it and loved it too – the watching, the surviving, the taunting – proudly displaying our wounds in the gym showers afterwards, or admiring those of our chums.

Carl Olsen's taste for violence was not restricted to the cane and the plank. In one PE session this little sadist called me to the front and then called up one of the three Jewish boys in our class, a lad not much bigger than me called Ivan. 'Rart, Effans, you lark to talk boxing hey, let's see what yous can do,' he sneered after lacing on our boxing gloves. Ivan had never been whacked in the face before, so one combination did it. Next he chose Colin, another Jewish boy, bigger and an A-team rugby player. He was quick and athletic, but had also never boxed. A right cross drew blood from his nose and for the rest of the round he ran and I chased. I felt guilty, but proud too.

After these ego-boosting triumphs I decided to add boxing to my playground armoury, which up to then had relied on my green belt in judo. A year later a big rugby A-team wing called Erasmus began to taunt me. I was a lowly C-team hooker who, for one game, was promoted to the B-side and therefore had to face him in practice. He stiff-arm tackled me, so I punched him. We met behind the bicycle sheds in the playground and before I could get going he lifted me off the ground. When I wriggled loose there was only one remaining solution – two jabs and a right cross. Blood spurted from his nose; he turned away and burst into tears as I stalked off beaming. At the age of twelve I was sure I had what it took: heavyweight champion of the whole wide world. I had never felt better.

But I was soon to discover that courage has more to do with the shape of the mind than the shape of the body. In any event, I was hardly well endowed in either territory. Having briefly thought of myself as the Jack Russell of the playground, I was doomed to confront the woeful discovery that I was actually a roll-on-my-back Labrador puppy.

The first clear sign came late in my final year of junior school. Having seen off Erasmus, I decided I was untouchable, and this cock-a-hoop illusion led to a phase of low-level rule breaking. One of the sorties involved leading my friends Pay and Goldschmidt in a plot to disrupt a break-time choir session by switching off the lights and chanting insults at the fat choir-master, but I was spotted running from the scene of the crime by a telltale chorister and hauled into the headmaster's office. 'Who else was there?' the boss demanded, and my bravado evaporated in the face of a certain six of the very best. I could have said no-one or 'I'm not telling you, sir – I stand by my friends' and taken the extra consequences. Instead, I spluttered: 'Pay, sir,' thinking for a nanosecond that I'd done well to save Goldschmidt. I was then given the humiliating mission of calling Pay, who naturally did not appreciate the trade-off. We each received four lashes, and I walked away, my bum stinging and my head swimming with the realization of my mortifying gutlessness. I continued to hang out with Pay, and cheered as this scientist's son constructed homemade guns with silencers, hydrogen–oxygen bombs which brought the police knocking and huge gas balloons which carried our messages of immortality, but my cowardice haunted me. Fifteen years later, when being assaulted and threatened by the security police while in detention, I had a vivid flashback to this incident and refused to name names – not out of strength or courage but more out of the terror of humiliating myself once again: a lesson well learnt.

Nature finished the job. I was now the smallest and one of the youngest in my year, and in terms of the race to manhood, a late starter. So while the 13-year-old bodies of my classmates were starting to pump out testosterone, my 12-year-old body lingered, and then did the job too slowly. I fretted that my lack of stature might be a product of an infant spell of rickets, itself a product of an allergy to milk and of London peasouper smogs, or perhaps it was my defiant vegetarianism, or maybe some genetic throwback – Lilly had barely made five foot. Or worst of all, something hormonal. While I waited in desperate hope of a satisfying leap in stature, the physical gap grew from barely manageable to intimidating. I was no longer sure that my combination of judo and boxing could bridge it.

At the age of thirteen, when I was still several months from puberty, I meekly allowed a bigger boy called Greeff, who had succumbed in an earlier playground fight, to get away with a push and threat, and too late remembered my father's stories about never backing off. I also started to divert my eyes when Erasmus passed. But my biggest hate and fear was Garth, a strong, well-built pole-vaulter and a star of the judo team who was a year or so older than me. I avoided him and he ignored me, but he regularly picked on weaker boys – taunting, pushing, punching, throwing. One of my classmates was an uncoordinated, pompous and effete theatre-designer's son called Alexander. He was just the sort of victim designed for Garth, who made a regular point of humiliating him. While crossing paths on the stairs one morning Garth elbowed Alexander and laughed in his face. This time the victim didn't hesitate – he just turned around and punched Garth in the ear with everything he possessed. Garth collapsed in agony and shame, writhing on the ground before dissolving into bleating tears, 'He went for my ear, he went for my ear.' I was delighted at the bullyboy's pathetic demise, but also deeply ashamed that Alexander had found the courage I lacked. The dream of being heavyweight champion began to fade.

One summer's day I went canoeing with my friend David, who implored me to grow out of my childish thing for bubblegum music and tune into the alternative music scene. He offered to help me along this essential road and I promptly tore down my Jackson Five posters and absorbed the likes of Neil Young, the late Beatles and the early Strawbs. Under the guidance of Henry, our art teacher, I became an enthusiast for anything and everything that fell under the artistic banner of modernism. Through Craig, a literature teacher, I binned my Alistair Macleans and plugged into Jane Austen, Oscar Wilde and the aesthete's mantra that all art is quite useless. From Solly, my lisping guidance teacher, I was inspired by Roger McGough and the idea of becoming an angry young man. By chance I discovered Anthony Burgess's *A Clockwork Orange* and read it over and over between the covers of my textbooks. And like teenagers the Anglo world over, I competed with my chums in doing Monty Python imitations, imagining we were funny and clever and unconventional.

It was also a time of nascent political revival, and this began to excite me. My early forays centred on the enemy of my enemy. Republicanism was one of the platforms of Afrikaner nationalism and this prompted my spell of allegiance to all things associated with Empire and Crown. I was delighted to have been born in England and when Mr Brand preached of the crimes committed by the Britons against the Boers I posted Union Jacks on the board and took to devouring books like *Tom Brown's Schooldays* while learning Churchill's speeches by heart. I felt immense personal satisfaction about D-Day, the Great Escape and the Wooden Horse, and even welled up with pride when watching movies on the Royal Family. I recall being particularly excited watching a newsreel of Ken Buchanan dancing with Princess Anne after they both won British sports star awards, and I persuaded 8-year-old Karen to include this detail in her class oral on the princess.

In 1973 the police beat up protesting students on the steps of Cape Town's cathedral and, to justify this assault, put out thousands of bumper stickers saying, 'If you don't like the police, next time you're in trouble try calling a hippie.' I realized then that I supported the students and the hippies and I despised the heroes of *Squad Cars*, and I gradually shelved England and started thinking more about home. I began to hate the ruling National Party more actively, tearing down their election posters when no-one was looking and arguing for aggressive liberalism with my friends. This also affected my attitudes to sport. I couldn't stop myself roaring with delight when the radio commentator announced that our Arnie Taylor had lifted the world bantamweight title by knocking out Romeo Anaya in the fourteenth round but I switched my support from the Springboks to the Lions at the start of their 1974 rugby tour, and announced to my friends that Peter Hain – the exiled South African anti-tour leader – had a point.

But there was also God to think of. In the wake of the faux-freaks came another American import, the Jesus People, with their hippie looks, their coffee bars and their hell-obsessed, dark and light message. 'I have a vision. I have a vision. I have a vision that the Lord has great plans, great plans, great plans, brothers and sisters, great plans for Cape Town this year, great plans for miracles – if we heed his word,' a flaxen-haired, guitar-playing 18-year-old pontificated and oh how we believed. It was my first sortie to the Upper Room coffee bar in suburban Medowridge and there was much talk of demons and the devil, of the Book of Revelation, which, we were told, predicted the coming of the anti-Christ from the Soviet Union, and then the Second Coming and millenarian redemption, and inevitably this was tailored for the local market. 'If my people humble themselves and pray I will heal their land' said the new Jesus People bumper sticker (conveniently omitting the biblical caveat, 'and turn from their wicked ways') and there was indeed much praying, most of it in unintelligible languages.

I too was drawn to speak in tongues. 'Why do you two look so joyless?' Danoon, an older teenager, asked of Michael and me during our third trip to the Upper Room. And when no suitable explanation was forthcoming we were informed we needed to be 'baptized in the spirit', and with that were ushered into a back room, where we sat cross-legged on scattered cushions and raised our arms. Danoon began: 'Shubbabubbabee, shubbabubbabee, shubbabubbabee, shubbabubbabee,' and in no time we too were babbling away. When I doubted the validity of that experience, I had another try, another baptism in the spirit from which more gobbledegook flowed uncertainly, only to peter out again.

By then my parents too had hooked up with the charismatic movement that swept through both high and low church, linking Anglicans with Pentecostals, Catholics with Protestants, and the 'gifts of the spirit' flowed accordingly. Tongues and interpretations of tongues and healings a-plenty. My father developed a huge stomach ulcer requiring an operation. A laying-on of hands and it was gone – no trace, the specialist couldn't understand it when it no longer showed on the X-ray. Our friend Flikkie, a polio victim, had one leg shorter than the other. At a healing service it seemed to grow and she no longer limped. Brutus, my dog of little faith, suffered from eczema, which left his back raw. It seemed incurable but after a laying-on of hands the hair grew instantly and for the rest of his long life he never suffered again. And there were devils too – demons and ghosts from hell. Our next-door neighbour's house was haunted – locked windows flying open, the noise of footsteps and heavy breathing on the stairs with no-one there, and so my father went along to exorcise it, and the ghosts left.

There was a war out there and we were in the firing line – powerful stuff, which even now makes me raise an eyebrow whenever the likes of Richard Dawkins protest too loudly at talk of worlds beyond their perception. Certainly, then, it was far too big to question intellectually. My inherited beliefs seemed irrefutable – there was no space for alternatives, no middle road, no permissible deviation, and so, after the flirtation with the counter-culture came the counter-revolution. Uncertainty in the form of guilt descended and boxing was its most expendable target because by then it had become the most dispensable of my interests. I began to feel it was getting in the way of my relation with Jesus. Bible verses and stories leapt forth to confirm this revelation – Abraham obeying God's testing diktat to roast Isaac; Jesus telling his followers to drop all, hate their fathers even; 'you shall have no other gods but me'. I prayed that God would take away my addiction to boxing, and it came to pass.

God works in mysterious ways, however, and so it was that he permitted a perverse Cupid to do the trick. For a while girls in general had been objects of romantic desire rather than lust – fuelled by movies like *Melody*, *Love Story* and *Jeremy* and books like *Jane Eyre* – and I'd endured a silent crush on one girl for six years. Then a new girl arrived on the scene at our 'Contact' Jesus-jumping youth group. From my first glimpse, when she walked into the room, I fell for her big eyes, brown hair, large mouth and uninhibited smile. She was about the same age as me, but with her near-adult body she looked and acted far older, and was dating older boys, oblivious to my fantasy world. She fascinated me in a way that was utterly over-whelming. I couldn't really talk to her; I had no idea what to say, and when I tried my voice became stilted and I spoke too quickly out of fear of silence until my words made no sense, and my ears would heat up and I would trail off and look down, and become conscious of every movement in my face and body. So mostly I just watched, listened to her deep voice and watched some more, and found everything she did and said to be just perfect. I knew she was untouchable but that made it even more intoxicating – every moment spent in her presence was a thing of splendour and I went to great lengths to contrive more of these moments, just for another glimpse because she was lovely. With this girl absorbing my waking moments, inadvertently tempting me to peep during prayers and to find excuses to pass her home, boxing slid even further from view.*

The other side of boxing's demise was physical. My confidence in my potential prowess as an alpha male fighting lad had its final denting through an incident that seemed trifling to my parents but to me appeared as something of momentous significance. In June 1974

*Many years later we ended up working for the same newspaper group, and she joined me in watching a Sugarboy Malinga fight, but in the 1970s Muhammad Ali just couldn't compete.

I was a cheeky early pubescent on holiday with my family in Durban, staying in a little flat owned by a Christian couple. I was in the middle of reading *The Assassins*, a novel on errant hippies by Elia Kazan, and contrary to that turncoat film director's intention, I identified with their defiance. I had recently turned 14 and the scales of parental, and particularly paternal, wisdom were finally beginning to fall from my eyes. I was starting to question the judgements of my father more openly, second-guessing his opinions and missives, to reveal a mild dose of doubt.

Bruce, who had lost his own father at the same age, was a kind, loving and gentle person, but he was also an imposing paterfamilias when aroused. No doubt he was feeling confused and challenged by the obstreperous effects of my impending adolescence – something he'd never had the opportunity to show to his Dad – and one afternoon he lost it for a few seconds. He lashed out with the old one-two, and then three-four-five-six with his fists – not particularly hard but certainly in anger. I covered up until his flurry subsided and then turned around and walked away. Others might have reacted to this without blinking, but for me that warm sense of home and family as a safe cocoon instantly evaporated.

I didn't cry. I didn't complain. I said nothing and seethed – against my father for losing control, against my mother for her failure to intervene, against myself for being humiliated. My resentment against my father would not go away. I hated him for it. Loved him and hated him, and wanted to punch him and kick him, and to be embraced by him, and the doubts flooded in. It was innocence lost, never to be regained. I reminded him of this incident seventeen years later and although he barely recalled the details, he was mortified, humbly apologizing after a remorsefully sleepless night. At the time, though, I felt demeaned by the evidence that for all my boxing I was just a weak little boy, one who longed to be big enough and strong enough to beat up his dad, and small enough still to love and be loved without complication.

In 1975 my father was elected Bishop of Port Elizabeth. While Michael stayed behind in Cape Town to complete his schooling, I moved city with Karen and my parents. The day before I was due to start school Brutus got into a fight with our new next-door neighbour's dog, Caesar, and true to history the usurper got the upper hand. Our neighbour's son, a first-team rugby wing, leapt the fence and proceeded to lay into Brutus with a large stick. My father reciprocated, raised his guard, assumed the stance, and said to the rugby player: 'Drop that stick, son, or I'll knock your block off.' I was mortified with embarrassment and arrived at the new school with a fear of being victimized for the sins of the father.

Grey High School was, like Rondebosch, a state institution but this one was 120 years old, named after a British colonial governor. It fancied itself as the town's premier establishment for moulding solid citizens out of white boys. It prided itself on its rugby teams, its large boarding house full of farmers' sons (with the seniors permitted to cane the juniors), and its compulsory cadet corps, run by Citizen Force officers who doubled as teachers and taught us to shoot and salute as we marched around in our khaki cadet uniforms before being sent to camps where we played a game called Nats and terrorists. When I arrived there the school was headed by an aged Baptist beater fallen among humanitarians, who had managed to assemble a collection of teachers so incompetent that the exam results were among the worst in town. He retired and was replaced by a less genial, less forgiving little German, whose first words to the school were: 'Zis school is not a democracy', after which the school snapped to attention.

On my debut day at this new institution I received a rope whipping from a chain-smoking gym teacher for the sin of not drying my feet after showering, and that set the tone for the next couple of years. I felt contempt for all that Grey represented but I combined this with a determination to make my mark regardless. My girl-gazing experience as much as anything prodded me into a phase of conformity. I gave up vegetarianism along with all other palpable insignia of oddness and made a bid to fit in wherever I could find a suitable slot. I desperately wanted to pass as normal. I was now in mid-puberty, with my voice newly broken and my hair turning strangely coarse and curly, but still I felt it best to steer wide of the farmers' sons, who seemed bigger, rougher and hairier than those at Rondebosch. I made a strategic decision: go easy on confrontation. Instead I threw myself into the Christian Union, never mentioned the subject of boxing, and tried to get noticed through middle-distance running, public speaking and poetry writing.

My initial take on white Port Elizabeth was of the mindless boredom reflected in its soporific, colloquial newspapers. Its self-conception was of the Friendly City; outsiders called it the Windy City and knew it for its beachfront dolphinarium, its good waves and its equal division between English and Afrikaners in public life. But it was at the centre of a parallel existence, and both reflected and defied its bland 1820-settler, picket-fenced provincial image. Most astonishing for me was its large and surprisingly open white male gay subculture, amply represented by my school's pupils and teachers – several of them openly out at a time and place where such candour seemed rash. I soon discovered, with a mixture of horror and delight, that the devil wasn't restricting his work to the heathens. My mother once told me that those closest to God were tempted the most, and Satan certainly tried hard with the church and its ministers, without preference for creed or denomination. They fell like ten-pins. At one youth camp our family friend – a local preacher – gave us all a stern warning: 'Don't let yourself get led into temptation. If you go alone with your girlfriend up Table Mountain, I guarantee you she won't come back a virgin.' Guarantee? I had no idea what he was getting at – I was still a year away from even a decent snog – but a while later this robust father of three left the church after his wife caught him out in the act of resuming a prolonged affair with one of his flock. He was followed by a family-man Baptist minister who, after being convicted for impregnating a 15-year-old schoolgirl, declared in mitigation: 'Your honour, King David also failed.' Then came a pair of Anglican ministers – one convicted for carnal acts with schoolboys; another caught soliciting young men on the beach. Both left the country, claiming the security police had set them up. And one evening, while surreptitiously sitting at my father's desk reading one of his books on sex, I found a letter from a distraught parishioner from an Anglo-Catholic church in the city centre, who complained the priest was systematically buggering the choirboys.* And so it went, the gap between appearance and reality widening the more I discovered.

It was all tremendously thrilling stuff – the thought that the devil was doing his damnedest coming at a time when I was being saturated with Jesus, full of intrigue, mystery and lots of muttering. It made me feel easier about my own early acquaintance with the carnal world, or rather the world of my carnal imagination, inspired by magazines, or record covers, or by my parents' female friends, relieved in the shower and never admitted or discussed. Soon I was wrapping myself in sexual fantasy – small stories for exam breaks or showers, longer ones for bedtime – and I wasn't quite sure what Jesus would make of it. It certainly wasn't a subject I raised with him in my bedside 'sorry, Jesus' prayers because I knew what was to come. Yes, God would one day bring into judgement my 'every secret thing', but I couldn't help myself, or didn't want to, and with this realization prayer became no more than a duty of conscience while the boring mumble of 'tongues' was consigned to the past.

This mix of fantasy and discovery transformed Port Elizabeth into a place of fascination. I soon discovered this sleepy town embraced a thriving drug culture through which dagga was finding its way into our school. This, in turn, plugged into an uncertain, rather confused white counter-culture, publicly represented by a thriving folk music scene that was nationally renowned. I was drawn to it, but it also began to worry

---

*Years later, when researching a *Playboy* story on the sordid affairs of the apartheid cabinet minister John Wiley, I learnt this priest was at the centre of a paedophile ring.

me that it was all so exclusively white. Very few in the Four Winds Folk Club or the gay bars or the surfer beaches, let alone the rest of white Port Elizabeth, made much effort to discover what was happening beyond the white people's highway, and they would remain in this state of numbed oblivion until the consumer boycotts a decade later forced them to peer over their fences.

The black side of this 600,000-strong city was the epicentre of the reawakening mass political revolt in South Africa. In the 1950s its townships had been organized by the ANC under the leadership of a brilliant communist intellectual, Govan Mbeki,* and from then on it became regarded as the 'engine of the struggle'. One of the young black consciousness leaders, Barney Pityana, who was Steve Biko's deputy, came to our house every week to see my father, staying on for lunch, and on those days I made sure I was home. Shortly after Biko's death my father helped him to escape into exile in Britain. Other leaders, like Desmond Tutu, were also regular visitors, and I absorbed their words, and was exposed to ideas and information alien to the segregated world around me. This was reinforced by occasional visits to the townships, which exposed me to the gap between white and black living experiences and sharpened my sense of the injustice of apartheid. Port Elizabeth was also the training headquarters of the increasingly brutal security police, who periodically made threats against my father, and devised various bizarre and unsuccessful schemes to try to frame him falsely in

*Who sired the country's future president and went on to spend twenty-two years on Robben Island.

criminal activity, get others to spy on him and intimidate him into silence.

At about the same time my father introduced me to Norm, an ex-con with deep ties in the black boxing world. 'My son's a boxer, as I used to be,' my father announced proudly, and so he arranged that Norm take me under his wing. We did not have a television, so I would go to Norm's house to watch the major fights and he would break the law by taking me to Port Elizabeth's black townships of Kwazakheli and New Brighton, where we were treated as guests of honour and taken to meet the boxers in their changing rooms. Once again I fell for the smell and taste of the game. Not yet in love, but certainly a reawakened intrigue. My prayed-for release from the game had not lasted long.

The usual bill-header was the superb black South African bantamweight champion, Chris 'Kid' Dlamini. At that stage the titles were still segregated between black and white, and Dlamini was regarded rightly as the nonpareil of his division. I loved to watch his economic style and flowing fighting rhythm and adopted him as my local hero. In 1975 he killed an opponent in the ring and I took on the faith that Chris was invincible. Eventually, fighting on his home turf in 1976, he lost his title to the Mdantsane student political activist Mzukisi Skwiyiya, only surviving the distance because the arena was plunged into darkness at a crucial moment. My brother-in-law, Mkhuseli Jack, recalled the fight a quarter of a century later: 'Hey, we couldn't believe it – we were sitting there with our mouths open, watching this novice kid from Mdantsane beating up our Chris badly – really hurting him. He looked like stopping Chris, so some of my friends switched off the lights in the ninth round.'

Dlamini had a ten-minute rest and survived to lose the decision. Skwiyiya, however, never got to benefit from his brilliant victory. A few months later this University of Fort Hare student was detained by the security police and spent several months in detention without trial and with torture, before fleeing into exile in Lesotho, where he joined the ANC.* My outrage at his treatment and my exposure to the township world of Chris Dlamini inspired me further, renewing my interest in boxing while feeding my emerging political passion.

Until then I had successfully kept boxing from my classmates – fearing the consequences – but one lunchtime in late 1976, two days after watching Dlamini knock out a lightweight, I mentioned to a chum where I'd been, describing the scene with animated enthusiasm. He asked if I'd ever boxed. 'Ah, not really – I mean I tried it once as a child, but nothing much.' He suggested we go to the gym to spar, and although he was far bigger, he was not very sporty, so I agreed. We fished out the gloves from the gym storeroom and, as I'd expected, it was an easy job: jab and move, jab, move and jab. I assumed it would go no further – it was unlikely he would boast of getting knocked around by a smaller boy – but in our last minute an enormous farmer's son, Moolman, and his skulking friend Ferreira spotted us and watched, calling me by my nickname. 'Fuck it, who would have known? Barney's a boxer,' said Moolman. '*Ja*, but they're both *moffies*,' said Ferreira, as they stalked off.

Within days the story had done the rounds and I was

*Skwiyiya died in a car accident in Lesotho, still undefeated as a professional.

called upon to referee a boxing match between the first-fifteen eighth man and the second team prop. A crowd of about seventy boys gathered in the gym, and I got carried away with my refereeing duties, making it clear that I enjoyed an intimate acquaintance with the intricacies of the rules. When it was over some of the crowd started shouting for me to box, and then a squat, swaggering, insecure sports star called Andy stepped up and challenged. He was a social poser whom I disliked and I thought I might just be able to handle him, but I also knew that this would invite more serious threats from the larger, harder boarders who despised me for being a public speaker, a Christian and a bishop's son. I worried that these challenges would not be restricted to the gym and that it would get out of control. I hesitated for a second and then, descending back into cowardice, reached my decision with an obsequious smile. 'I'm no boxer, just your humble referee for the day.' I walked back to class thinking *You gutless coward* and returned to my previous status – the runner, the aesthete, the debater, the Christian, but definitely not the fighter.

My years of frightened conformity finally drew to a close during my last year at school. The catalyst was a caning from an inept vice-headmaster for a display of mild insolence towards a little mop-topped, platform-heeled braggart of a class teacher we called Noddy, and my resentment turned into hatred. I was almost 17 years old, president of the Grey Union and a prefect, and I thought I was beyond being beaten. Yet I had to bend for four with the long bamboo cane, and then say, 'Thank you, sir,' otherwise four more. This time I walked away without showing the pain, feeling utter contempt for all they represented. My gaze turned towards the antidotes. Every day my friend Greg would return from lunch stoned after sharing a spliff with friends, smiling at Noddy during the afternoon classes. I admired him immensely for this. Another friend, Grant, a Sex Pistols devotee, was expelled for vandalizing the cars of teachers, and I regretted that I lacked the balls to follow his glorious example.

'You're a Jesus freak,' Grant reminded me, 'but I guarantee you, you'll be smoking dagga and talking revolution as soon as you leave here. I can see it in your eyes.'

'Doubt it,' I said, but I knew he was right. I began to fret over my co-option into the school establishment, knowing that I couldn't justify my role as a prefect and that I didn't believe in any of the school's archaic values designed for training boys to be children for ever. In class I began to advocate views that worried my Christian Union fellow-travellers – Abortion on demand! Legalize dagga! Black majority rule now! And at home I would sit for hours at my desk or on my bed, unable to absorb a single sentence of my textbooks, and retreat into my imaginary worlds of sexual fantasy. Then I would turn contemplative, listening to Joni Mitchell's *Hejira* or Pink Floyd's *Animals* or Bruce Springsteen's *Born to Run* and ruminate over things like the meaning of modernism in art and architecture and, more and more, the need for revolution in South Africa.

I completed my matric exams, campaigned for Dr Van Zyl Slabbert's quasi-liberal Progressive Party in the 1977 white general election, and then, after our man lost to a *swart gevaar* – black danger – racist, decided there was no future in parliamentary opposition. The next day I started a hitchhiking tour around the country with my friend Vernon and his mandolin. On another cross-country hitchhiking trip I met up with an old Cape Town chum who, on his way to starting his compulsory military service, introduced me to the throat-searing joys of dagga smoked through a broken bottle neck. My world was changing fast and the freedom of it all, the sense of personal liberation, was utterly intoxicating.

The last semblance of my father's authority evaporated in a stand-off in his study on the subject of drinking, and this time I did not back down. *Touch me and I'll fight you*, I thought to myself, but I was too scared to say it aloud, and he wisely held back from trying to enforce his will. I was now in glorious control of my own destiny, released from the censure of teachers and beatings and parental authority. I was 17 and I was free and it felt magnificent.

Much of this fresh new existence was focused on the Land of the Free. If boxing had introduced me to American history and values, the deal was clinched by music and the printed word. My new aim was to find a shortcut to take me to this wild promised land of Steinbeck, Hemingway and Springsteen and so, as the year ended, I packed my bags to depart for the small university town of San Marcos, Texas to become a Rotary Exchange student.

It was at this point the carnal and the devotional finally ran up against each other, and there could really only be one winner. This was no Stephen Dedalus experiencing a reverse epiphany after a spell of intense devotion. It was more of a kind of strategic decision to go it alone for a bit, along 'sorry, God, but maybe I'll return some day' lines. My teenage years had been filled with the exclamation marks in the testimonies of the saved. 'I am a sinner! I was under the grip of

Satan but the Lord rescued me from drugs/alcohol/debauchery/homosexuality!' 'Praise the Lord! Hallelujah!' Suddenly, having left the immediate censure of the home, this was thrown into question. I began to feel the salvation business lacked symmetry without the prior fall. My father had been rescued from atheism and open-topped sports cars, but what had I been saved from? I was silently 'born again' at eight and had stayed true to the fine line ever since. And more than this, the crashing tedium of the church was becoming intolerable, and the prospect of continuing, impossible. I lacked any desire to bring others to Christ. I wanted to pursue lust, smoke mounds more dagga and try out a few new ideas. Hell was terrifying enough but heaven seemed so, so boring. I was in need of some serious 'backsliding', and my Texan year was the time and the place. This small thought broke the Gideon's wall of hidden doubt, and finally the niggling questions were allowed to leave their cages, and within a month I was a confirmed agnostic.

And so it was that I spent a year liberated from any higher allegiance. My new-found freedom of thought and action was invigorating, but also perplexing. For seventeen years I had grown up with the idea of a pre-eminent purpose in life and a clear destination and then, rather hurriedly, I divested myself of this reassuring certainty. Life suddenly had no inherent meaning beyond living, no innate morality, no pre-ordained future. Inevitably I settled on existentialism, stifling those midnight despairs about the blank everlasting – the thought of perhaps being no more one day – and doing my best to discover the here and now.

The problem was that the here and now in America wasn't quite what I was after. It was late-1970s disco

America, moving inexorably to the political right, and it exasperated me. I was after hope and glory, the feel of a cause, the shared passion of a movement, the sense of moving forward, the security of a community of revolutionaries – all things the church had once offered. Instead I moved backwards in time to the vicarious pleasures of more heroic American eras. In the south-west corner of Texas, I became infatuated with bohemian idealism, following the train from pre-First World War Greenwich Village, to the Spanish Civil War volunteers and the Parisian émigrés, to the San Francisco beat boys, and from there to an even more concentrated passion for everything emanating from the 1960s, from the freedom marchers to psychedelia and beyond, reading the histories, recreating the experiences – first as tragedy, then as farce, as Marx would have it – and most of all buying the records. I didn't just taste it and move on; I devoured it, and if I am to be honest, have yet to fully digest it. It hardly bears mentioning that the Sixties were over by the time I turned ten.

In this spirit I hitchhiked through twenty-five of the states in the company of various foreigners as well as a Montana heir, a gun-toting hippie outlaw and several out-and-out crazies. Along the way I developed deep affections for Texas country, New York punk, New Jersey rock 'n' roll and Jamaican reggae and enjoyed my first fleeting, fumbling experiences with hard Colombian drugs and soft Texan women, or was it the other way around? In between trips I worked for three months, fifty-five hours a week, on a construction site, had a bit part in a movie called *Piranha*, lived on a ranch where I learnt to ride a bull and rope a steer, went from high school to university, and read Marx's

Das Kapital, Mao's *Little Red Book* and biographies of Biko and Malcolm X.

Boxing was still edging its way back in – first through watching Muhammad Ali lose to Leon Spinks, then rediscovering the man through Malcolm's story, and from there to a fresh range of American fighting men. The idea of emulating Ali was long forgotten – I had stopped growing half an inch short of 5 foot 8 – but still, I wanted another go at it, making a brief comeback through a makeshift Mexican gym, to which a friend who was a Golden Gloves lightweight champion introduced me. I worked out in a converted garage with a bunch of Hispanic high-school boxers, trained by an old Tex-Mex motor mechanic. They seemed intrigued by the enthusiasm of this long-haired boy with the funny 'British' accent and I loved the way they hung loose, letting it all flow so naturally. At the end of my first session I came away proud and happy with my knuckles bleeding from whacking the heavy bag. But the moment didn't last long. The Golden Gloves champion moved to Michigan; I moved to a ranch and lost contact with the gym, instead trying my hand at wrestling and karate. But I was certainly back in the martial groove, searching for fights on the television schedules, taking bets on them with my friends, seeking out co-conspirators.

It was the Ali–Spinks return that sealed it for me, more for idiosyncratic reasons than for anything that happened in the ring. I was unable to afford the price of a ticket to the fight in New Orleans and settled for the idea of watching at the 'pad' of a new hippie chum. Pony-tailed, shaggy-bearded, 23-year-old Joseph discovered me giving a speech at the university about the need for divestment from South Africa and befriended me, revealing himself as one who had tuned in and turned on as a 15-year-old in 1970. He helped me buy a secondhand guitar and introduced me to a record collection full of Summer of Love classics. Together we'd hang out at San Marcos's acid rock club, talking drugs, radical politics and Sixties culture. I was open to any invitations along these lines, so we agreed we'd get stoned and watch the Ali fight together. The night before the fight, he phoned: 'Why not come round for a smoke and some beer tonight?' After three albums, six beers and two double-blade spliffs he homed in.

'Tell me, have you ever slept with a man?' he asked after some small talk about a folk icon who cut both ways.

'No,' I replied, recoiling in shock.

'Would you like to? Would you like to sleep with me?'

'No,' I said, horrified.

My only direct experience with anything homo-sexual happened six years earlier at the walk-in house of horrors at Cape Town's Maynardville fair. Michael and his friend Steven went first and I followed, but as I reached the end of the dark maze a rough-looking man hiding behind one of the styrofoam monsters jumped on me from behind and dragged me into a sandpit. He pinned me down and began trying to kiss me, but I struggled and said, 'Hey! Hey! What you doing?' I tried to get loose but he felt too strong. At that moment Michael and Steven came back to look for me, wondering why I hadn't emerged, and my brother said: 'Are you OK?' The man looked up and I wriggled loose and ran to them, after which the man disappeared. We all decided it was a bit strange since no-one else had been accosted, but I soon forgot about it, and it took a couple of years before I realized what it was about. I thought about this again when Joseph propositioned me and felt afraid.

'Can I go home? I'd better be going. I want to go home. I'm going home – now,' I said.

In excruciating silence, he drove me home in his battered Volkswagen Beetle, and from then on whenever I saw him I would look the other way. I was shocked that he had thought of me in this light. Was it that I was still so boyish? Girlish perhaps? The idea troubled me. It troubled me so much that I wanted to box again, to throw punches. The day after the incident I felt I could not possibly watch Ali with Joseph, so I secured the keys for the student television den and, alone, whooped and punched the air with unrestrained delight as the aged Ali outboxed the confused Leon for the final victory of his glorious career, ending with Howard Cosell pontificating to a soundtrack of Bob Dylan's *Forever Young* as for one last time, in the fifteenth round of his final victory, Muhammad Ali rose on his toes and danced to victory.

Joseph aside, it was a year of tasting and feeling, and part of this eclectic dabbling involved my first excited forays into political activism. I became involved in the anti-apartheid divestment movement at the University of Texas in Austin and delivered regular speeches on the need for revolutionary change in South Africa. I had already run into trouble with the Texas Rotarians because of my hitchhiking and cannabis-smoking, but now I fell out with a fellow South African Rotary student – a pompous private schoolgirl who seldom removed her kudu-crested Rotary uniform. The final hurdle to open hostility was surmounted when we were asked to design posters about our country to adorn a parade bus in San Antonio. Mine was a hackneyed image of a pair of black hands breaking out of chains, with the slogan, 'South Africa: the struggle continues regardless'. Hers was a seaside tableau under the heading, 'South Africa: Land of Fun and Sun'. After this, she reported my activities to my Port Elizabeth Rotary Club and then tipped off a US-based group called the Friends of South Africa, which was a front for South Africa's CIA (then called BOSS – the Bureau of State Security). This in turn prompted a series of reports in the South African press, including a back-page spread in the *Sunday Times* entitled 'Bishop's son in Rotary storm!' and condemnatory editorials from the Afrikaans papers.

From then on I vainly suspected that all my letters home were scoured by enemy agents and took to signing them 'Abbie Hoffman', 'Jerry Rubin', 'Lawrence Ferlinghetti', 'Angela Davis' and the like. Years later I learnt that the spooks had indeed become hooked at this premature point, filling files with informer reports, details of my letters and long-distance calls, travel plans ('financial problems may prevent his planned trip to Cuba'), reports on left-wing academics I associated with and even my reading habits ('stated the book *Biko* included outstanding material and the book *Socialism* by Michael Harington influenced his political thought processes'). The Port Elizabeth security police did their bit by daubing the walls of the Bishop's House with hammer and sickle insignia, followed by a series of malicious calls. 'This is Dr Stewart from Conradie Hospital,' one call began at a time my father was away in Namibia. 'Your husband has been in a terrible car accident. He's with us, but even if he makes it he will remain a vegetable.' My mother phoned my brother to rush to Conradie, and when my father wasn't there, and no Dr Stewart was on staff, he contacted all the other Cape hospitals, only to find he was safe and sound in Windhoek – a little security branch joke. They also encouraged Rotary South Africa to try to order me back to Port Elizabeth, although when I refused to comply Rotary meekly backed down, frightened of an international incident.

This sense of being watched and wanted – enhanced by letters of support from my brother's political friends and the likes of Desmond Tutu – made me feel noble and significant, and in no time the thrill of it all became irresistible. I was studying drama at Southwest Texas State University with the idea of auditioning at RADA to become a future British Dustin Hoffman. I had written to my father's London-based playwright cousin, Ronald Harwood, who graciously replied that he could help arrange an audition, but when this direction seemed set, I backed off. I was just too hooked on the thrill of political defiance and the sense of purpose and community that flowed from it, and therefore felt compelled to give up the idea of acting. The final impetus was a letter from my brother, who by then was a second-year student, well immersed in campus radicalism: 'You'll get to the end of your life and all you'll be able to say is that you've entertained a few people,' Michael's letter concluded. 'Come home and join the struggle.' I walked outside into the late-afternoon Texan ranchland sunlight and decided my role in life was to become a revolutionary.

2

ACCIDENTS OF HISTORY

Observatory, Cape Town, February 1979. The smells
and sounds of my beautiful old town were enough for
the moment. I was back home and I was in love with
home all over again, and while love is seldom blind, it
lacks perspective.

Cape Town was Cape Town for ever, a bimbo of
a city so overwhelmed by the marvels of its own
geography – dissected by a range of mountains,
surrounded by a warm sea and a cold one, and carpeted
in its own unique vegetation – that it retained a reassuring illusion of permanence. For all their churning
and burning the people and their buildings seemed
incidental to the grand geological plan.

That was my take on it, anyway, and still is most
of the time, despite the human evidence, although I
suppose I should hastily add that within a few months
of being back in this city I loved, after spending many
hours interviewing squatters for a migrant-labour
research project, assisting a trade union based in
the coloured townships and *jolling* at jazz events in the
older African townships, I understood the folly of

taking this facile emotional sense of belonging too far as an objective perspective.

I was hardly ignorant by then of the most palpable human dimension of my lovely city's loveless recent past: that its coloured majority were callously frog-marched out of their homes in the 1950s and 1960s to be resettled in sandy, windswept ghettos to make way for more whites, with terrible consequences in terms of human misery. Most of the gangs that today control the city's prostitutes, drug dealers, clubs, prisons, taxi ranks and housing allocation have their roots in the application of this sordid Group Areas policy. But while the coloureds were battered with the right hand they were propped up with the left. The peninsula was declared a 'coloured labour preference area', meaning that black Africans could only get jobs in categories not taken by whites or coloureds.

If you were black there were (and still are) few worse cities in South Africa – you either lived in a desperately deprived township, trying to scrape by on a menial job, with few legal rights and a constant obligation to display your pass book to any cop or official who might demand it, or you lived in a muddy or dusty squatter camp, probably with no job, certainly with no rights, with your corrugated-iron shanty home liable for periodic bulldozing. If you were coloured you were caught in the middle of a hierarchy of colour: identity, life prospects and legal rights set by arbitrary means, including such innovations as the 'pencil test': if the pencil remained in your frizzy hair, you were classified African, third class; if it fell you were safe – coloured, second class. For some this meant identification with the black-led struggle; for others, a strain of anti-black racism no less virulent than among the city's poor whites, and for many it meant a bit of both, with allegiances changing according to the shifting balance between fear and hope. But if you were white you had the pick of all the loveliness. You were led to believe you owned the mountains and beaches, your free schools came with acres of well-watered fields, you travelled first class on the trains and if you had any sense you worked at a leisurely pace and made time for all that sun and scenery. It was, for most of us whites, the good life.

This wasn't new to me. I'd read the history, and soon saw enough of the misery and desperation, and sometimes the triumph too, to gain at least a superficial appreciation of what it signified, and yet I could never escape the sense of my city as benign, beautiful and wonderfully wild. If you live on the edge of an ocean you are constantly confronted by an untameable savannah. Live under a mountain and you grow accustomed to another kind of savage mystery. Combine these in a city as apparently genteel as Cape Town, especially its suburban enclaves with their alien pines and oaks framing majestic views, and your vistas are filled with this juxtaposition of natural wildness and urban tranquillity, and it becomes part of the norm. In my childhood Cape Town's magnificence was what was – the everyday, the expected. It took a spell of exile before I appreciated just how exceptional it really was.

I now live in London, the city of my birth – have done for almost a decade – and I am constantly exhilarated and enthralled by it, and occasionally appalled too. Yet for all London's vigour and fascination, its deep history, and its beauty too – and my home-owning, school-tripping, dog-walking, park-jogging existence within it – Cape Town retains its status as home. When I smell sage or rosemary I am pulled back to the *fynbos* vegetation on the mountains. Jacaranda or jasmine sends me to my suburban childhood gardens. The smell of curry takes me past the Malay stores, Christmas shopping in the city bowl. I still dream of Cape Town most nights and it remains the place that makes most sense to me in the light of day, the one that framed my earliest notions of normality, the town that feels just right, that tugs every sensory cue from my childhood memory, and is therefore endlessly forgiven. It was with this feeling that I made my elated return in February 1979. I was home again and I never wanted to leave.

A month earlier I slept my final night in America in a shelter for destitute youths in Harlem, after spending my last dollars on an ounce of cannabis, which I stuffed in my deodorant stick and smoked two days later while hitchhiking from London to Oxford. A week on I arrived at Jan Smuts airport in Johannesburg to be whisked off to what felt like an interrogation room, where for an hour or so my luggage was searched, some of my political literature confiscated and I was inanely questioned, causing me to miss my connecting flight to Port Elizabeth. After a year in the land of the brave this little interference in my freedom of movement puffed up my sense of mission, and when I finally arrived, cowboy hat in hand, looking and sounding suitably absurd with my Kicker boots, shoulder-length locks and the traces of an accent that spoke too loudly of the American south-west, I felt defiant and ready to struggle to liberate South Africa.

The next night I joined a friend in vandalizing my

old school on a stoned binge, then berated my local Rotary club at one of their luncheons, and finally resolved to hotfoot it to Cape Town, where student politics was spiciest. Early one afternoon I hitched a lift out of Port Elizabeth and then jumped a goods train to Mossel Bay, where a couple of junior policemen put me up for the night after driving up and down the main drag, taking pleasure in *skrikking kaffirs* – scaring 'niggers' – with their blue flashing light and loud-hailer. I finally hitched the last leg to Cape Town and was disgorged outside the Valkenberg mental hospital in Observatory as the warm summer's sun was descending.

I lugged my overladen backpack down the road, stopping to adjust the straps outside the gateposts leading to a large white building. I looked up and noticed a small sign saying, Liesbeek Park Boxing Club. 'I will return,' I said to myself, aloud, and continued walking. I passed the Hartleyvale football ground, crossed the highway and absorbed the competing aromas of bubbling cabbage stew, incense, dagga and curry from little terraced houses on narrow streets, and from the distance I could hear Neil Young singing *Thresher* through a cheap loudspeaker. I paused to take in a game of street cricket played between barefoot children and ragged-trousered students, smiled at a greasy-haired young woman in overalls changing the gaskets on a motorbike, and stroked the ears of a mongrel who came to say hello. And finally I made it to the front door of an address my brother had given me. *I will return*, I thought again, *but not quite yet*.

My new home was part of a terraced row in Bedford Street, overlooking the Lion Match factory, in lower-middle-class Observatory: all rack renting with peeling paint and porous roofs, but always with an oblique view of Devil's Peak. There were eight of us in six rooms, with rotten floorboards in the habit of caving in, a persistent population of evil rats competing for our precious vegetable co-op supplies, sacks of Kupagani soya mince, powdered milk and chicory coffee. It was bohemian heaven on flaky earth and I loved it.

The day I arrived Mike, a Lebanese Catholic communist who was the unofficial leader of the commune, inquired why I felt it necessary to acquire a small bedside mat for my room. 'Will it make you more effective in the struggle?' he wondered. I confessed this consideration hadn't quite crossed my mind. '*Ja*, you see, effectivity is the only criteria,' he informed me. A few days later Georgie, a nursing sister who doubled as an aspirant revolutionary, explained our place in the nation's class structure. 'You can always tell by the toilet paper people use. The bourgeoisie use soft double-ply, of course and the African working class use newspaper.' Where did that put us, I wondered. 'Petty bourgeois – lower-middle-class if you like,' she said with resignation. 'We use rough single-ply.'

This austere philosophy, which I instantly embraced, was both romantic and convenient, not least because I had no money. I had not asked for, nor received, a cent from my parents since leaving home – they had none to give – and therefore I had to pay my fees for my degree in economic history and African politics as well as my board and lodging. This came through part-time jobs, like selling marble coating for the houses of aspirant working-class whites and coloureds, and controlling the parking for a local circus (while creaming off a generous share of the profits). This, in turn, made me feel nobler than those white lefties whose fees and marginally less austere existences were financed through parental handouts. I despised the students with chars and cars paid for by Daddy. It made me feel better about myself.

Other lifestyle questions were soon impressed upon me. On day one on campus I mentioned that one of the students I encountered 'seems like a nice chick'. Which met with an instant response from Clare, my brother's girlfriend: 'She's not a chick – she's a *woman*.' Goddit. On day two I idly remarked that while I was perfectly comfortable with the fact that the *women* did not shave their legs, I wasn't, um, quite so sure about the armpits thing. Georgie lifted her arms above her head and wondered why I found her 'lovely, soft armpit hair' anything other than utterly delightful. 'Feel it,' she instructed. I did, and instantly corrected myself, and decided that female body hair, wherever and whenever it appeared, oh, and yes, certainly, an absence of make-up, was part of the badge of genuine, non-sexist commitment, and quite lovely too. I was an eager learner, and soon an eager preacher too.

Our house had a shifting mixture of inmates over the next two years, racially, politically and socially: radical Catholic activists who first exposed me to life in the black townships; student bohemians like my old school friend Vernon, who would bring home his musician chums to jam the night through; two socialist feminist nurses; a depressed genius of an alternative engineer; a pair of art students – one who astounded the rest of us by taking on a high-school punk guitarist boyfriend, the other, today a gay performance artist, then in the process of creeping out of the closet; and a couple of sexy goodtime girls. The younger of this goodtime pair, Maggie, brought home her boyfriend Nong, a former

ANC recruit who, we later discovered, had been 'turned' (recruited through blackmail) by the state's National Intelligence Service. Maggie left the house after failing her exams, and when I phoned to visit her at her new place she pleaded for me not to come. 'Nong thinks we had a scene,' she whispered, while I thought, *If only*. But Maggie was insistent. 'He has a knife and he says he's going to kill you.' I never saw her again. The elder goodtimer, Bella, a drum majorette fallen among student radicals, moved into my bed following an alleged rat attack, and after a five-minute pause gently placed my hand on her breast – 'Just for comfort,' she said, after which things moved quickly. Which in turn raised the ire of Ari, a male student leader with similar designs on me. In a state of pique he refused to give Bella a lift home from a city centre Scratch dance club. Bella hitchhiked, and was gang-raped, with the subsequent result that both of us, having resumed our nightly liaison after a less than respectable break, had to rush off to hospital with 105 degree temperatures, cured by stiff shots of penicillin.

We also attracted a regular supply of stay-over visitors of various descriptions – like Cyril, the toothless coloured community organizer, who sold us stolen bicycles and radios when not organizing the masses (and ended up as a respected criminologist); and Shepherd, the dedicated African student leader who would write earnestly accomplished revolutionary poems on our blackboard and expose us to an Africa we knew only rhetorically; and Vuyani, the township layabout who just hung out for the free food and smokes and whatever else he could filch, and why ever not?

Then there were squatters, who simply arrived or

were brought in like stray dogs by one or another communard. They came from all over the world, and from just around the corner. Like Frank and Steff, two rural coloured vagrants we found living under the station bridge with their nephew. Georgie brought them home for three days that turned into three months, until reality intervened when Frank started beating up Steff. One morning Frank returned home with my bicycle chain covered in congealed blood. 'Thanks, hey, my bra,' he said, handing it back to me. 'I killed an *ouk*' – man – '*lekker*' – nicely – 'with it.' We could just about live with this, but when Frank suggested Steff earn her keep by cleaning our house, this was too much. We very politely asked them to leave.

So, you get the picture: lots of social posturing, occasional snatches of sex and some skewed glimpses of what we thought was 'the real world'. None of these reality checks was allowed to get in the way of the new religion, and the rhetoric fluttering in its wake. I desperately needed it to fill the vacuum left by Christianity and I swallowed it with Marxian garnish, convinced myself that my intellectual indigestion was no more than some passing existential wind. I came to believe with the shrill, unquestioning faith of a hallelujah convert and yet, despite my pose as a dedicated struggler and theorist of the struggle, in those eager early student days I was really no more than a weekend warrior of the dark political arts. I did my thing on various student committees, joined the protests, carried out agit-prop tasks for strike support committees, read my Marx, Lenin, Althusser and Poulantazas diligently, pretended to read my Germaine Greer and Sheila Rowbotham, and made token common cause with an African future by trying to learn

Xhosa. But all this was balanced with conventional student pursuits – all-nighter exam crams certainly, but more commonly activities like sleeping on the beaches, hitchhiking the sub-continent, flirting with the city's jazz, punk and reggae scenes, playing poker and smoking *zol*. When the meetings were over we would rush out to catch some obscure title at one of the foreign film festivals at the cut-rate Labia, or an experimental play at the Space, where the boards were trod by eminent South Africans like Henry Goodman and Richard E. Grant (or Richard Esterhuys, as his parents called him, in the days before he reinvented himself as an Englishman).

It certainly felt like the best of times and it was in this spirit that I rediscovered my old chum, boxing, for what I thought would be just another little slice of fun. I would slip out of earnest Women's Movement lectures on topics like the 'triple oppression' of South African women ('class, race *and* gender') or Students for Social Democracy seminars on, say, modes of production in the homelands, to seek out a television set to watch the big fights, like Kallie Knoetze getting beaten up by Big John Tate, or Leon Spinks' demise at the bionic hands of Gerrie Coetzee. And so I began to toy with the idea of keeping my hand and eye in once more.

I soon acquired a couple of personal sparring partners who would meet me in the university gym for a few rounds with the sixteen-ounce gloves. My squat, powerful friend Moeketsi had boxed with professionals in the Transkei, and would knock me around, dropping me occasionally when I became too cocky. Then there was a bigger lad called Andy, an off-beam former karate boy who had never boxed before, and I was delighted to find I could handle him. But Andy disappeared from the campus left scene, years later admitting to my brother that the security police had recruited him by threatening him with a drugs prosecution, after which he had left university to sign up for an army killer unit.

Next I joined the university boxing club, a loose collective containing a mixture of novices and amateur veterans. The best of them included an elegant coloured bantamweight, Mike Tissong – a scion of one of South Africa's premier black boxing families who went on to become a radical political correspondent for the *Sowetan* – and a beefy, amiable redhead called Eric Atmore, the Western Province and South African Universities heavyweight champion, who came from Woodstock, on the wrong side of the white Capetonian tracks. Aside from his considerable prowess and power as a boxer, Eric was a warm-hearted radical social democrat who would help out the rest of us pencil-necked Marxists when the going got rough. I once watched a provincial rugby player called Ginsberg mocking two members of the Women's Movement. 'On your backs, chicks, on your backs,' he chanted, to the barking amusement of his mates. Eric yanked him to his feet and said: 'Are you going to apologize now, or am I going to make you?' Ginsberg grovelled. A week later we were involved in protest against an honorary degree awarded to the Inkatha leader, Mangosuthu Buthelezi. When the chief's thugs moved in on us, grabbing our placards, Eric served as a one-man defence squad, bumping them out of the way whenever they attacked. We organized a protest against the notorious 'Rhodesian' defence chief, General Peter Walls, who was due to give a speech on campus. A pair of oversized 'Rhodies' in their all-weather shorts launched a pre-emptive strike, grabbing our banners and posters and marching off. My brave but skinny friend Vernon blocked their way, and just as they were about to rip him apart, Eric arrived, gripping the larger of the two around the neck and lifting him off the ground before asking: 'Are you going to turn and run, or am I going to have to fuck you both up right now?' They ran.

The following day my own pumped-up bravado outpaced my meagre supplies of bravery and I was the one doing the running. When the generalissimo made his speech, Vernon, his friend Will and I went beyond the call of duty, using a loudhailer to heckle him from outside a window at the back of the hall. We were in full cry when I looked down and noticed a posse of enormous bruisers wearing T-shirts decorated with pictures showing wide-eyed little blacks fleeing in terror from enormous, armed white men, carrying the legend, 'The Rhodesians are Coming'. One of them carried an iron bar. I did not need a second glance before taking to my heels, sprinting to the sanctuary of the library. Vernon and Will remained intrepidly defiant, only to be rescued by an administration official who arrived on the scene just in time. Once again, I felt shame for my loss of physical courage, and decided that if I couldn't face up to these nasties, I had no place in a boxing ring. For the next two months I stayed away from the ring.

In any event I had more pressing concerns. The day after I had arrived in Cape Town, Vernon and I made our way to watch a gushing film on the life of one of my musical heroes, the blues singer Leadbelly. He brought along some student friends, and afterwards we went around to one of their homes to listen to music and smoke dagga. I liked them all and was particularly enchanted by one woman – I'll call her Wanda. She seemed so warm, so interested and interesting and friendly that I took to her immediately. *She's lovely*, I decided, without any further designs. Over the next few months I saw her now and then and always came away feeling good about the world, thinking about how open and unpretentious she was, and how happy she made me feel. We both ended up being elected to a student council and began seeing each other daily, giggling at meetings, going to the beach, studying in the library, visiting each other's homes, relishing each other's company, gossiping, joking, just getting off on being together.

About six months after our first encounter, it dawned on me that a day spent without Wanda was a day wasted, that other options – like boxing, politics even – were not quite so sublimely wonderful and that every quirky little thing she did was enchanting. From there it was a quick leap to the discovery that I might just be falling a teeny little bit in love. The implication of this rather sudden realization delighted and frightened me, as it had nothing in common with the frantic crushes and frightened flirtations of my recent past. *What if she doesn't feel the same? If I tell, won't it all evaporate? It will spoil this precious thing we have. It will become awkward and stilted. I will lose a friend in a vain bid to gain a lover. As a feminist it's her call to initiate the action if she feels the same, isn't it? Surely it's worth waiting a few days longer for the big opening.*

My housemates looked on indulgently, saying little to me and, I later learnt, much to each other, until Vernon finally asked: 'Are you into her knickers yet?' I replied, burning inside, 'Naah, just friends.' I kept quiet, forever on the verge of blurting it out, and then not quite finding the words or the moment. Finally, after a sleepless night, I decided the time had come. I would say it, I would, I would: 'Um, actually, I'm quite into you.' I had it all worked out. But the intended weekend of confession and absolution was interrupted.

I was about to discover that histories are created not only by great social forces, but also by little leaps of chance. The cliché about the fluttering of a butterfly's wings in Berlin setting off hurricanes in Brazil has its way of translating into human interaction: an extra vote here, a stray bullet there, a fortuitous illness the next place, and unpredictable changes of immense and lasting significance are unleashed. Luck seems even more pertinent when it comes to individual histories. The meshing of nature and early nurture may set the base but every moment bolts of lightning and bites of snakes are altering lives. We can amble along at the expected pace and then suddenly, without warning, find ourselves hostages to fate in ways we can never anticipate. A little mistake can vanish into nothing or resound into a thousand tragedies. My life, and its relationship with boxing and with politics and with love, was a case in point.

Jimmy, the left-wing son of an Afrikaner farmer from the Northern Transvaal, and one of my younger lecturers in African government, organized a trip to his old university town of Maseru in Lesotho – the idea involving an academic conference on southern Africa and probably some chats with ANC types, with a little mission on the side to bring home a young black comrade. I was not on the conference list and spent the previous night with Vernon, piecing together a household photographic montage. But a couple of students dropped out and Jimmy asked my brother, Michael, to assist him in making up the numbers. And so Vernon and I joined Michael, his girlfriend Clare and five other students in Jimmy's group. I hesitated when the last-minute invitation arrived – I had this love thing to declare – but this was only two days away; another excuse to stall.

There was one tiny detail that slipped through the net. At the precise moment we were pulling away in the university kombi, our Maseru conference hosts were desperately trying to get through to Jimmy on the phone to inform him that the event had just been cancelled. Someone delayed passing on the message until it was two minutes too late, and so we left in ignorance of the awful futility of our journey. In the late-morning sunshine we drove onto the freeway, feeling flushed with the prospect of adventure.

At this point, time slows; memories become vivid. They are repeated over and over and over again, never forgotten.

We each take turns driving, an hour or so at a time. At the end of my spell I pull over to get petrol. Jimmy and the others are drowsy: 'How do you feel about doing another hour?' he asks. 'OK,' I say, not wanting to appear lazy or weak. We're running late so Jimmy directs me to a shortcut along a bumpy gravel road, which he says will get us all the way to a suitably obscure border post before nightfall if we move quickly. 'Go faster man, we're running late,' a student called Nathan says from the back seat, and I obey, eager to please.

There's a bend in the road, and suddenly the firm gravel transforms into a sea of loose stones and sand, and the kombi begins to swim. Michael, sitting beside me in the front, says, 'Are you OK?' Time slows to a crawl. I turn the wheel into the skid without braking. This is what I must do. I'm not panicking. I can handle this. But it has no effect. The kombi drifts across the bend, swimming with no grip until the front left wheel hits a ditch and we roll in slow motion, stopped only by the poles of a barbed-wire fence. The kombi has no seatbelts and I am thrown forward over the steering wheel. I feel a ripping in my back, but no pain. There is glass all around me. A fence pole is positioned behind my neck, passing through one broken window and out the other, bracing the kombi in position. I realize it has missed my head by a centimetre, no more. Salvation has been secured by the absence of seatbelts – fancy that. I am relieved. I notice the barbed wire is attached to my back. My blue denim press-stud Texan shirt is torn and I'm bleeding, but still no pain. Anyway, I'm alive; I've been saved. I climb out of the window. I'm feeling lucky. No seatbelts.

Some of the others are already standing, shaken and hurt – whiplash, back pain, bruises, shock, but we're all remarkably calm. Shocked-calm. 'Where's Jimmy?' Derrick asks, and suddenly Will springs to action, flying through the Freestate veld with his long hair waving behind him shouting, 'I'll find a farmer.' Then I see Jimmy, lying unconscious on the ground ten metres away. He's been thrown out of the passenger window.

The farmers arrive. Big, burly, kindly Afrikaners. '*Jussus, jong*, this is the fifth bad crash we've had on this corner so far this year,' one of them remarks, shaking his head. 'We gotta get them to do something about this loose sand.' I'm standing there, bleeding, hearing their words but thinking only of the woman I've left behind, wanting Wanda there with me, wishing

I'd stayed, when Vernon puts his arm around me. 'Hey, man, we're all with you. It wasn't your fault. Don't blame yourself, OK?' I feel grateful, but why should I blame myself? Derrick, his back in spasms of pain, says: 'I just want you to know, I don't blame you.' 'Thanks,' I say, but I think, *Why should anyone blame me? It's just chance. The turn of the dice. I didn't ask to drive. I wasn't being reckless.*

A slow hour passes. An ambulance skids up from the opposite direction and we are rushed to a surgery to be stitched up. The anaesthetic doesn't seem to take, but I don't mind. I want the pain. Jimmy is in a coma, we're told. We don't know if he'll make it – probably not. We join him at Bloemfontein hospital. His parents arrive – ageing Afrikaner farmers, looks of deep pain and worry on their haggard faces. I want to run, to hide but I greet them – show embarrassed concern – but I don't say sorry. We're all in this together. There's no individual guilt. I just happened to be driving. It's all the confluence of circumstance. It could have been anyone. I didn't ask to drive. 'Hey, man, I could, like, really do with, like, a Valium now,' Nathan says to me. *Arsehole*, I think to myself. *What have you got to worry about?*

We are transferred to the Bloemfontein Bishop's house. My father phones. 'Now more than ever before you need to come back to Jesus, son. You need forgiveness. You need to ask Jesus for forgiveness and give your life to him again.' I slam the phone down. Michael phones him back, angry. He accuses my father of trying to use a tragedy for his own religious ends. *Yes, yes, you tell him, Michael,* I think. Why should I need forgiveness? Why should I feel guilt? I feel better. I go to sleep. My wound opens, and when I wake the bishop's sheets are covered in blood.

And then time returns to its normal uneven, blotchy pace. The course of events becomes muddled. Memory plays tricks and refuses to move in straight lines. What did I think about on the flight home? I don't recall. It's gone. Here things are clear, there murky. Only glimpses remain. But some still seem as vivid today as they were in 1979. More so, with the voyeur's perspective of hindsight, repeated over and over and over again.

Like this one: the back of my shirt is torn and still covered in congealed blood – in the last-minute rush of my late inclusion I had forgotten to take a change of clothing. I become aware of this when walking to the terminal at D.F. Malan airport, and I'm glad of it. It says, *Hey, I've also been hurt, you know*. There to meet me is my rough-diamond housemate, Mike. At this point my memory cross-references to another event a year earlier, the day after I bought that press-stud Texan shirt. I've been badly kicked by a horse, winded for what seems like a dying hour. There's a blackening hoofmark on my solar plexus. I stagger back to the roping paddock, where rancher Sam asks me what's happened. I tell him. 'Yup. Now off you go, boy. Catch that horse – now.' And so, terrified, but even more afraid of my cowardice and his disapproval, I retrace my steps, catch the wilful creature and ride him back. 'When you fall, son, you always get right back on,' he explains. 'That's the Texan way.' Next track: Mike hands me the keys of Boris's off-white Anglia, presumably with the horseman's logic in mind. 'We're going to the beach, and you're driving.' It's not what I want. 'Hey, actually, rather not,' I say. 'Drive,' he says, with a kind smile. And then I think of Wanda again. I want to see her so very much. But no, no, I'm the driver. I appreciate the logic. We're going to the beach first and I'm driving. Back in the saddle. Won't take long. Won't mention it.

The beach passes. Bakoven? Camps Bay? Clifton? That's it, Clifton. Yes, yes, it's coming back. I lie there with the sun beating on my stitched back until I fall asleep and I dribble while I dream and the sea starts to wash over me, huge spring-tide waves looming and crashing, and I can't move, and I feel myself drowning gently, and then – I don't know. Memory returns outside the front door of the Bedford Street commune.

I'm moving quickly now, towards the railway line, walking with purpose in the direction of Wanda's front door. I'm halfway there, just before the bridge, looking down to step off the pavement when I see it: the beach sand on my feet and legs. *Fuck-shit, fuck-shit, fuck-shit. How will this look? I've just survived a terrible accident that left Jimmy in a coma and I've fucked off to the beach instead of visiting her, that's how it looks. What will she think?* I start brushing off the evidence with hurried strokes but the sand holds its grip. I look up and there she is, Wanda, walking with her quick, determined little steps in my direction. She has come to see me. She looks at my legs, remarks about the sand, says something about me going to the beach first. She says it lightly but I think I can see hurt in her eyes. I so want to explain – it's not like that, it's like this, really, but I can't because, well, there's nothing to explain, because we're only friends and what's a beach trip between friends? The remaining details are forgotten. All I remember is that the sand has stuck, wires have been crossed, distance created, barriers erected, metaphors mixed.

And then the memory video switches off again, and time meanders. It acquires the added value of retrospection. What was that all about? What happened? Wanda asks me how I feel about it, but I stonewall – all I know is I don't want to talk about it. I want to go back to normal. I want to be absolved. I want it not to have happened. The police arrive, I show them my driver's licence, they ask a few questions, and say I have no charges to face. Then Jimmy wakes up, paralysed from the chest down, we are told. Michael and I immediately write him a letter, and soon we receive a typed one back. He sounds confused and yet strangely grateful for our correspondence. What next?

I walk the line again. *This time I'll say it, I will, I will*, I think. It's a warm night with a full moon, but the house of Wanda is dark. It's late. I knock and knock and knock again and then some more, but there's no-one at home. Why? Where could she be at midnight? I trudge back, not wanting to think my fears. I arrive home to Bedford Street, feeling morose. My housemate Georgie sits beside me on the old sofa in the kitchen. 'Um, I thought you should know,' she says in a bad-news-breaking tone. 'It's best if you hear it now, from me. She's just started sleeping over at St Michael's Road, with Joshua. I'm sorry. I think they just got it together last night.' I feel too sick to speak.

When clear thought returns, I blame this on the accident – a kind of punishment, if not from God then surely from fate. No, no, I don't believe in such rubbish, I'm a historical materialist – it's just bad luck, that's what. Shit happens. Planets collide. Meteors fall. The dice rolls. You move on. You move on.

And so, my guilt is throttled. I desperately convince myself it could have happened to anyone – wrong place, wrong time. Hey, I didn't ask to drive. *But you could have said no to that second hour*. I was being careful. *But you could have driven slower*. They asked me to move it. *But you were at the wheel*. My mind was sharp. *But you shouldn't have stayed up the night before*. I don't want to think about it. I don't want to think.

Time leaps again, and the legal wheels start moving. Jimmy's attorney, smelling of booze, asks for help. I'm happy to give anything they need. 'Did you have a licence?' he inquires, as he packs away his reel-to-reel tape. Yes, I did. 'Thanks for your help,' he mumbles. 'I really appreciate it.' And then I squeeze it from my head. I try to forget until one day a letter arrives from the same attorney, demanding I find a way of acquiring this document and that paper from the university files, and if I do this to his satisfaction they won't take any further action against me. They won't sue me. Sue *me*? No, no, you've got it wrong. I was helping you. I'd be happy to help some more but not through threats. I tell them I don't respond to blackmail. And then another attorney knocks on my door and serves me papers, and I go to the legal aid office where I find the much-beaten vagrant Steff, asking for money to divorce Frank. She tells me she's free at last.

My money comes through, and I wait, feeling torn between the desire for vindication and the still-stifled guilt, until I receive another call, this time from my lawyer. The case has been dropped. Why? 'They based their claim on the false perception that you didn't have a driver's licence.' Relieved and guilty, I write to Jimmy again. Can I come and visit you? Don't worry, it's not necessary, he replies, adding that we will both have to live with the consequences. *Both?* But of course he's right. Because although it takes me many years to admit to the feelings of guilt and self-centred remorse, the effort of hiding them leads to another application of the law of unintended consequences – pushing me further into politics, further from love and sealing my pact with the world of boxing.

One response is to dive deeper into the struggle. White student politics through most of the 1970s drank from the residues of Paris '68 and Hell No We Won't Go and was sustained by the adrenaline of the symbolic protest. But at the turn of the decade the rapid emergence of trade unions and civic and youth organizations in the black communities, the liberation of Zimbabwe and the regeneration of the ANC changed all this. It was the era of Reagan and Thatcher in the West, but in South Africa it was a decade of impending liberation in which student politics became less frivolous and more connected to the political world off-campus, with its focus on tight organizational discipline rather than loose counter-cultural gesture. The leaders who emerged were more stolid and less flamboyant – ambitious young men and women whose conversion to leftism took them from their perches as earnest school prefects, Zionist youth leaders and young Christian evangelists to new lives of order, hierarchy and mission. They despised counter-cultural frivolity, cast out or re-educated other sinners such as 'ultra democrats', adventurists, liberals and dilettantes, and admired the top-down order of what Lenin called 'democratic' centralism. It was therefore a suitable time to rein in my flirtation with bohemia and to adopt the sterner ethic of committed committee comrade.

My fresh batch of friends were fellow students who wore similarly severe hairshirts, many of them, I later discovered, harbouring persistent little inner monsters of their own. We found in the political community a substitute for families recently left behind, and jostled and made up accordingly. We believed with the shrill certainty of the fundamentalist convert. We swallowed whole this glorious socialist future built through the praxis of the masses, guided by the immutable science forged by Marx and honed by Lenin and led by the African working class. Their struggle was our struggle; we followed their lead and adopted their songs, symbols, their heroes and villains as our own. We were sailing with the historical tide, we had the wind behind us, we were part of the movement. We became very close in this way.

Boxing was my premier diversion – suddenly promoted in status. I wanted it, I needed it. Early in the New Year of the new decade I knew the time had come at last. I crossed the railway line with no right turns and trotted off to make my first acquaintance with the Liesbeek Park Boxing Club. With the Mexicans in Texas and the students in the university gym I was just having a laugh but now it was more serious. My motivation was to punch and to be punched, to get this thing I was feeling out of my body, and when I returned home, my knuckles bleeding from hitting the heavy bag, I did indeed feel just a little better. I had become reacquainted with the giving and getting of pain and I wanted more.

The white, working-class world of the boxing club was a million miles from the student communes on the other side of Liesbeek Parkway – rough, racist and dedicated to fighting rather than struggling. But for all that I felt at home immediately, or comfortable anyway – as long as these two worlds kept their safe distance apart. Whatever their views on the country and the universe, I liked these motley protagonists for what they were. As I was later to conclude about every boxing gym I entered, this collection of men and boys had nothing in common with, say, a barking rugby squad on the make, with its alpha-male, packdog mentality, nor with the quasi-spiritual, sensei-worshipping drill squad of the martial arts dojo. They were just a disparate bunch of wideboys, misfits, outcasts and ragamuffins – all hard, but seldom swaggeringly macho. The boxing club became my niche, my little bit of rough, untouched and unreachable by the struggle.

Our trainer, George le Roux, was a plump, genial man steeped in the family history of the white version of the amateur sport, and he had assembled a crop of twelve seniors and twenty juniors, including two of his sons (one of them, Boetie, ended up as the warder of my friend Chris who was later jailed for his ANC activities). The best of his seniors was an ambitious trainee engineer called Jan, who held the provincial featherweight title. On my second outing in the gym I sparred with him and went all out. 'Jesus, Jan, he's catching you – take it serious, *jong*,' George shouted. Jan slipped the next jab, stepped inside and let loose a one-two combination, a thing of beauty with the right connecting with the edge of my chin as I reached forward. I'd been dropped several times before, but for the first time I found myself on the floor without memory of the journey down, or the next few seconds. I rose, shook my head and continued, knowing what it was like to be knocked out – not particularly painful but a little confusing.

My other regular sparring partners were Dirk, a quick, friendly light welterweight, and Gert, a lean, hard-hitting but slow welterweight. Then there was the elusive, chain-smoking lightweight Claude, whose brown skin, missing front teeth and accent suggested he hailed from the rougher areas of the coloured Cape Flats, but who managed to get himself registered for boxing purposes as white. Until 1992 there was the rigid colour bar in the amateur game, enforced by the sport's right-wing, military- and police-based Pretoria establishment, but in the more liberal Cape blind eyes were turned.

George was also willing to turn a blind eye, with the occasional half-knowing nudge, wink or shrug, in my direction. As a soft-faced student in a den of hardy railway workers and mechanics, I was regarded as an oddity, and was given a more generous leeway than my mediocre boxing skills warranted. Soon after my arrival George told me he'd seen my picture in the paper, participating in a student march (part of a week-long class boycott in protest against the state's brutal treatment of striking Ciskei students). 'I'm sure it wasn't me,' I spluttered. '*Ja*, it was you – I know what you *ouks* are up to.' He laughed about this and never held it against me. Two weeks later, a small batch of Free Mandela pamphlets fell out of my dungarees pocket as I was undressing to shower. I quickly stooped to retrieve them, stuffed them back and no-one said a word.

Some time later George noticed a tattoo of a flying swallow on my thigh – a creation by Tattoo Jim of Salt River via a bet with a chum (which I'd celebrated with him, Wanda, a bottle of whisky and almost enough dagga to loosen the tongue – almost, but not quite). Staid, quizzical George examined it carefully, shook his head and then smiled with knowing resignation. 'Tell me, Evans – are you one of those who go to Sandy Bay [a nudist beach]?'

'Occasionally,' I replied, thinking nothing of it. Swimming, sunbathing and hanging out without clothes on were an integral and almost obligatory part of the summer milieu I moved in. But George nodded again. '*Ja*, one of those, I thought so,' he said with another resigned smile and another shrug. I could not work out the connection between the tattoo and Sandy Bay, but a few minutes later, horrified, I decided that he might just have suspected I was gay. I was mortified but it was too late to correct him, so my response was to train and fight harder.

After six weeks I was deemed ready for my first fight – in the rough edge of the white suburb of Goodwood. George was surprised to find me coming in as a light welterweight when I should have been no more than a lightweight and probably could have boiled down to featherweight. Part of my problem was dagga, which I was still smoking regularly despite my austere political pretensions. Late-night munchies were the enemy of weight-watching and the scales condemned me. The result was that my opponent was not only more experienced – his eighth senior fight – but was also far taller and bigger.

For most of the day I felt edgy, and this general sense of foreboding became more specific as I pulled on my dark blue satin trunks and light blue club vest. The idea that pain and humiliation were a few hours away grew more frightening, bringing back memories of that long wait before an after-lunch caning in my school years. As I watched my opponent get off the scales, I began to feel queasy and my stomach rumbled. I kept saying to myself – literally whispering it: 'You stupid fuck. What are you doing here? What the fuck are you doing? This is definitely the last time.' I was struck by the absurdity of my position: waiting for a fight against a hard man in Goodwood, in the care of people who knew nothing about me, when I could have been with friends who had become a kind of second family, talking shit around the kitchen table, getting stoned listening to the Jam, the Clash, Joe Jackson and Elvis Costello, or beach *braaing* in Clifton.

Finally, I was gloved up, warmed up by punching at George's open hands and ushered into the ring. The bell rang, and just like my first fight as a junior, I forgot all I'd been taught and rushed in frantically. When I finally settled, I realized that despite being bigger and fitter than me, the opposition wasn't that hot. I thought I won the first two rounds but in the third my exhaustion took over and I spat out my gumshield, gulped in huge draughts of stale air, and fought in retreat, extremely relieved when the final three-minute bell tolled. A minute later the decision was announced. '*Die wenner*, Liesbeek Park – *groen.*' My hand was raised and I smiled with happy relief, but history repeated itself. There was a protest from my opponent's camp and an addition error was apparently discovered, or so they later claimed. The decision was reversed. But this time I didn't really care. This was not about becoming a Sugar Ray any more; those dreams were long forgotten. What mattered was that I'd come through my first senior fight without losing face. I was a boxer once more.

Early in 1980, a week after that first fight, I was part of a group of twelve activists caught by the police while handing out 'Free Nelson Mandela' and Freedom Charter pamphlets to coloured factory workers. We were detained for seven hours and then charged for distributing banned literature, but we were eventually acquitted on the technicality that the Charter was not genuinely banned because it had appeared in a state-sanctioned Afrikaans history textbook.

Soon afterwards one of my regular missions to 'score' at the Salt River railway station went wrong. Three members of the drug gang rushed me in an attempt to steal Bella's motorbike, and I only managed to shake them off by opening the throttle. A week on, while hanging out in Bo Kaap with a group of friends after another score, a white Cortina pulled up and two men leapt out, swearing at us about a stolen stash or something. Thinking they were cops we surreptitiously hid the dagga in a hedge. One of the men pulled out a 9mm pistol and started waving it around, pointing it at our heads, screaming at us, threatening to blow our brains out. Eventually we managed to convince the men that it really was a case of mistaken identity. 'Sorry, hey – wrong *ouks*,' the deflated gunman said, and with that they raced off again, looking for someone else to terrorize.

The combination of these scrapes, my increasing political profile following our arrest and trial, and the stern line against dagga from the severe, hard-drinking student political establishment meant that I refrained from scoring or keeping my own stash, with the result that my dagga consumption declined significantly. I was also adapting to a lifestyle of dedication – primarily to politics but also to my body. I began running and cycling with serious intent, riding my bicycle around the peninsula or jogging among the pines of Newlands Forest and the mountain paths of Devil's Peak, past the kudu, duikers, wildebeest and zebras, getting high on the endorphins and on the evocative beauty of the Cape, sweating the kilos off my body, pushing the pain out of my head.

Shortly before the next amateur tournament, my intended opponent pulled out and instead I was thrown in with an experienced campaigner who was four inches taller than me and held the senior provincial lightweight title. 'I've watched him before and there's only one way you can beat him, Evans,' said Jan. 'Stick to him like Bostick, man, and go for his body. I swear, he doesn't like it there. Really crack him in the solar plexus, hey, bang those ribs, work him over.' I figured I had absolutely no chance, but, assured he was all skill and no power, I felt less terrified than before. There was no humiliation in a novice like me losing to a provincial champion, so what the hell.

I watched Roberto Duran outpoint Sugar Ray Leonard on the club television and decided Duran would be my model. In an extremely inept imitation of the Hands of Stone, I charged out, bundled my man into the ropes and began to belt his body with everything I had. Every time he prised loose I took a few light punches and closed the gap again, giving him no room to punch or move while working his stomach and ribs, but by the end of the round I was finished. For all my running in the mountains, I had nothing left. I spat out my gumshield, refused to put it back and swallowed huge gulps of water. The tension and the three minutes of effort left me stranded and when the bell rang for the second round I was still in a state of exhaustion.

The provincial champion began picking me off with his jab and sneak right crosses – pop, pop, pop. My nose was leaking blood, my left eye swelling but I was beyond caring, relieved he was neglecting my body. After a minute or so I began to hope the referee would rescue me, but then the lad stepped in closer, perhaps tiring himself, and with my last exhausted effort I landed one more reflex punch to his midriff. It was not particularly beefy – I was too weak by then – but to my astonishment he folded, grabbed the top strand of the ropes and began retching. The referee tried to persuade him to return, but he shook his head. I was the winner on a technical knockout, even though I could hardly stand myself. When the tournament was over, I had recovered enough to present the flowers to the prize-giving aunty. I gratefully accepted my obligatory cheek kiss, and trotted away with my little winner's trophy. An hour later I hauled it out of my tracksuit pocket with understated pride and displayed it to my bemused housemates, who were drinking cheap red wine and chicory coffee at the kitchen table.

In late 1980 I was among a group of seven left-wing students who toured the newly liberated Zimbabwe as part of an Africa Society research project on the country's 'transition to socialism'. We drove up in a university kombi in a spirit of heightened anticipation and discovery, with the idea of producing a publication on the country's first year of freedom. After a fort-night of inspiring meetings with still-revolutionary Zimbabwe cabinet ministers, party leaders and rural cadres, I was invited to visit Comrade Peter, an old friend who was now an Harare-based exile. He was a former trade union activist who commanded my respect, trust and loyalty. When he phoned, asking me to make an excuse to leave the group for a few hours one night, I willingly obliged.

We drove off in a battered old sanctions-era Renault through the tree-lined Harare suburbs and then pulled over in a deserted side street where he began to talk, observed by a more senior comrade sitting silently in the back seat. He meandered for a while, asking about our group and its mission, and then homed in on the subject of the ANC and its future plans, until finally he popped the question: 'Comrade Gavin' – pause – 'we would like to recruit you to the African National Congress.' Another pause while he watched me absorb the impact. 'Are you prepared to work in the ANC underground?'

There was no pause for thought from my side. Naturally I said yes without a moment's hesitation or doubt. I had been chosen: Hallelujah! At that moment I thought my decision was the mark of courage – doing my patriotic bit. I was being called, honoured, and I was answering the call. Now I see it a little differently. It was about many things; some to do with my hatred for the consequences of white rule, sure, but most involving excuses not to look inwards. It offered a platform for self-importance and in this sense was a marvellous way of confirming the self and escaping from its doubts at the same time through the willing absorption into something nobler and greater. I was certainly inspired by anger about the scale of injustice and inequality I saw around me and by a fervent desire to change it, but the conceit of high-minded altruism doesn't quite cover it. It was also about proving myself, building a positive self-image, finding meaning, certainty and direction after the abandonment of Christianity, and perhaps too a response to the accident and to seemingly unrequited love.

I was delighted to be a member of this supposedly select band and secretly thrilled with the prospect of adventure (although I would have fervently denied any accusation of the terrible political crime of adventurism at the time). I did not even think of the potential consequences, which were rather severe. The ANC was banned in 1960 and remained that way for the next thirty years. In 1980 the going rate for mere membership was up to ten years in jail, after a stretch of solitary confinement, torture and endless interrogation sessions to force a confession out of you or to turn you into a state witness. It was worse if you were black, obviously: the torture and beatings would be more vicious and sustained, your cell would be smaller, your food worse, your chances of being killed through the assaults and the electric shocks that much higher (over a hundred detainees died this way, with official causes listed as 'slipping on soap in the shower' and the like). And if you were black and linked to the ANC military wing, Umkhonto we Sizwe, it could be worse: they would take you away for a few days of torture and then offer you the choice of death, usually through further torture, or cooperation. Cooperation went way beyond spilling the beans on your comrades and extended to joining a police killer network directed against your former comrades. In this way hundreds of ANC cadres were 'recruited' into the ranks of the Askari police death squad. Hundreds more were recruited by financial inducement and then sent with scant training and porous cover stories to infiltrate the ANC, which usually caught them out. And I suppose I should add that it was easier for whites that way around too: a white agent of apartheid caught by the ANC might well have a horrible time, but was less likely to end up dead than a black one.

Anyway, silently basking in my own self-importance I pretended to have a severe bout of flu the next day, and stayed behind while the rest of the group went to visit a farm that was run by former guerrillas. Comrade Peter arrived as soon as they drove off and provided a few hours of instant training in communications and counter-surveillance techniques and rather suddenly I found myself thrown into a Le Carré world of dead letter boxes, secret drops and concealed messages. I said goodbye to my ANC mentor minutes before the group arrived back. 'Remember, you can't mention this to anyone – not even your lovers – never,' he said as he drove off and suddenly I felt very alone.

I had no lover then but I certainly had a love of gossip and a hatred for keeping secrets. I was bursting to tell one person in particular, a handsome, intelligent, resolute young woman – I'll call her Rosa – for whom I had developed an attraction strong enough to grow a thin crust over my love-hurt of the previous year. She was bright, tough, dedicated and courageous, and, I thought, refreshingly free of weak-headed sentiment. Through our shared passion for political struggle and theory we became close friends. The thought occurred to me that if only I could let her know that I'd been selected for this new revolutionary role, it would tip the balance into revolutionary romance. I pondered this option but resisted, saying nothing as we made our way from Victoria Falls to Lesotho where we spent a few days on a farm run by a pair of hippies. We watched the second Leonard–Duran fight on their tiny television set, awoke to the offer of morning spliffs and then made our way to a Hugh Masekela and Miriam Makeba concert. I was beginning to relax again but when Rosa and I hitchhiked together to the surfing beaches of Cape St Francis, it dawned on me for the first time that I was being trapped by my accumulation of secrets. I wanted an outlet; a way of expressing the things I was carrying inside me every day but couldn't or wouldn't mention.

The turning point came when Rosa chose my close comrade Leon as her lover. This time I was disappointed and hurt but I didn't quite implode like the year before with Wanda. I felt I was tougher, that my defences were better constructed, and I would not repeat the mistakes of 1979. I confessed my feelings to her – 'Um, I'm quite into you, actually' – and, to my delight and a little to my surprise, we remained friends, closer than before. This was the way to go then: tell it straight every time, you feel better. This new stab of pain was bearable if I could rationalize it into a long-term plan. I decided I would merely divert my focus for a while – for as long as it took – and until then I'd take it on the chin, bide my time, swallow my blood, wait my chance, create openings and exploit them, go the distance if necessary, but get the result.

In any case I did not feel quite so alone this time. The camaraderie fostered through the juxtaposition of comradely politics and communal living forged close friendships, some of them still flourishing. In particular I had a new best friend to commiserate with – generous, vulnerable Liverpool-supporting, *NME*-devouring Tony, with his overgrown bush of an Afro and his wild beard and his sparkling, dancing, hopeful eyes, forever twinkling with new ideas and fresh angles on the old and the tired. He was a former Haboniem Zionist leader reborn among anti-Zionist Marxists and was now ready to become an all-or-nothing revolutionary (with sidelines in film festivals and video games). Today he is a senior writer with Time Life in New York and we remain close. At the time, the two of us became inseparable, drawing manic inspiration from each other. But even the closest friendships were compromised by the accumulation of secrets. Top of these for me (or so it felt at the time) were my newly acquired underground commitments involving monthly reports, sent in various guises to Zimbabwe, which tended to conflict with my open political activities and required me to sneak off at late hours to compose reports on untraceable typewriters.

Early in the year I was briefly detained again as the representative of a large group of students who refused to move from a picket line while protesting against the detention of meat workers during their strike. We were charged, convicted and fined. Soon after, I became a national representative of the Wilson Rowntree strike support committee, which had me making speeches in African townships around the country, dropping off pamphlets at various struggle homes in the coloured townships of the Western Cape, and generally feeling important. My life was changing in other ways too. We were evicted from our Bedford Street communal house after the landlord discovered we were 'harbouring blacks and coloureds' and so I formed a new student house – in an old brothel, periodically visited by johns and former hookers. I also had a new girlfriend, whom I treated with callous disregard for several months until, after laughing together over the television coverage of the Royal wedding, I glibly told her that actually I didn't really love her. Is it Rosa, she asked. 'Nah,' I lied.

I didn't have the women I wanted but I had my politics and I had my boxing. Whenever the demons in my head grew too noisy, I would jog off to the gym to bounce around its sagging wooden floorboards and suck in the smell of stale sweat that dragged me back to my boyhood days in the YMCA club. In this way I became an errant boxer, fighting occasionally, losing as much as winning. George would regularly implore me to fill a place on an amateur bill, and occasionally, when there was no student meeting or trade union-supporting trip in the way, I would oblige. He asked me to take a slot in a provincial tournament late in 1981. 'Evans, I know you're not so fit, but in the first round at least you've got an easy opponent. You'll beat this *ouk*, no hassle, but remember, hey, you got to make light-weight.'

My next seven days were spent with my brother, his girlfriend and Rosa at a beachside cottage – not the ideal training environment. Over the final two days I tried starving myself by taking diet pills, and from the evidence of the bathroom scale I made it. When I reached the venue, I hadn't touched a morsel for 24 hours and was feeling weak with a dodgy tummy. Then my weight was announced – five grams over the 60-kilogram limit. Dirk, who came in lighter than expected, took my place and won as he pleased. I was forced to take on the hardest-looking light welterweight I'd ever come across, or at least that was the way he appeared when I first set eyes on him as he stepped onto the scale. He weighed 3.4 kilograms more than me but looked several weight divisions bigger – five centimetres taller, with immense shoulders, a barrel chest and tight, bulging biceps. *Oh, shit, shit, shit*, I said to myself, and George rubbed it in after Dirk's easy victory over his opponent. 'You see what you could have had? Simple stuff, hey,' he said, shaking his head with a when-will-you-ever-learn look. 'Now see what you've got yourself.'

Jabbing and moving seemed to work for a minute or

two until he found his range and began unleashing heavy hooks to my ribs and stomach. One of them dropped me for a short count, and when I went to my corner I was dispirited, weak and exhausted from the tension of concentrating on avoiding punches. South African amateurs did not wear head guards in those days, and with eight-ounce fighting gloves hard blows to the head tended to produce results. In the second he caught me with a heavy right hook to the temple and I went down again, this time rising unsteadily at the count of six. My legs felt uncertain and there was no fight left in me. I was hoping for deliverance and after six more unanswered punches to my head, chin and mouth, the referee mercifully stopped it. I was relieved to get out of there, but embarrassed too, knowing that my sorry performance had been completely lacking in confidence, courage or conviction. I coughed blood for a week, the cuts inside my mouth, which always bothered me, became infected and took over a fortnight to heal, and my body and face ached for several days. Without much evidence to prove it, I had always fancied that my boxing might supplement my pulling power, but clearly this was becoming ridiculous.

I dug myself even deeper into politics, getting elected to the university's students representative council, popping off to student national council meetings, stepping up my underground vigilance, studying my Lenin, Luxemburg and Gramsci more intensely but less critically, and shutting out my many doubts, just as I had done about Christianity a few years earlier. One summer's night, while suffering from a bronchial fever, I was feverishly seduced into what became a casual, year-long romance with a tough, garrulous, conspiratorial Johannesburger – part Jewish princess, part revolutionary ragamuffin. Her lack of inhibition and disdain for courtship rituals were just what I thought I required. I convinced myself that relationships were really about the here and now, about fun, and most of all about uninhibited sex. For the time being, this suited us both. We had no worries. This love business? Hah! Bourgeois sentiment.

But the illusion was not to last. At the end of the year, the ANC instructed me to return to Harare with proposals for potential recruits. Leon – my friend and Rosa's lover – joined me for the trip without being told of its underlying purpose. I liked Leon. He was brainy, studious and eccentric, utterly dedicated to revolutionary ideals, apparently immune from sentimentality, and, uncommon for a male activist, extremely practical. He was a boffin in the emerging world of personal computers, an ambitious cook with a taste for fine wines and a comrade with an impressively wide range of intellectual and experiential pursuits. Leon was deemed outstanding fodder and enthusiastically recruited. Together we received intense training in counter-surveillance, encoding and decoding, invisible inks, concealment, debugging and the theory of what was called Military and Combat Work. Just before we departed after our two-week crash course, we were asked to suggest a third member of an ANC underground unit we were instructed to form. We looked at each other. 'Rosa,' we both said together.

'Hmm,' said Comrade Peter. 'She sounds really outstanding but, you know, we usually discourage the idea of lovers being in the same unit.' He thought about it for several seconds. '*Ja*, these things can go horribly wrong but I suppose that if you can assure me it won't interfere with your ANC work, I will have to take your word for it.' We gave our word, and we believed it. Next he asked us for the name and address of a safe house to be used for sending reports and underground literature. I thought for a second and I knew what I was about to say had an ulterior motive. 'I have a friend who's been out of politics for two years and she's just moved into a new house in Observatory,' I volunteered. 'Her name's Wanda.'

Several white student leaders at the time were obeying their military call-ups under the rationale of 'strategic participation' – two years of heads-down military service, supposedly in exchange for decades of dedication – but the ANC underground leaders felt this was causing huge damage to non-racial solidarity and was undercutting their attempts to foster white resistance to the military. One of our instructions was to push the 'line' that no activist should serve in the army (unless sent there as an ANC spy) and at the same time initiate an anti-war movement. I was delighted by this mission – I'd always felt sick seeing comrades meekly donning enemy uniforms, and besides, it was a chance to kick at the Johannesburg student leaders I despised. And so, after hitchhiking home and being detained for some light interrogation on the South African side of the Zimbabwe border, we returned to Cape Town flushed with missionary zeal.

I wasted no time in delivering our message of military abstention with didactic impatience. Its content was swallowed by most but not by everyone. In particular, followers of 'the Leader' – an archetypically messianic Johannesburg activist whose high-profile decision to obey his military call-up was blindly defended by his uncritical followers – viewed this new line as a personal attack on him and fiercely resisted. A bitter and prolonged factional war was sparked and soon burnt out of control, picking up the fuel of new disputes along the way and soon leaping beyond student politics and finding its way into the wider resistance milieu and beyond. I can't pretend all these subsidiary disputes were totally lacking in significance* but most were niggling debates about pinhead angels, magnified into wars between principalities and powers.

Today there is a feeling of *What was that all about?* It seems trifling and even amusing but at the time it felt deadly serious and inevitably it followed the path of all things serious and became intensely personal. For me, the worst of the bile was produced by a strangely duplicitous lad, also a minister's son, later a psychologist, who made a consistent point of throwing imagined dirt at me – whispering small personal lies about whom I was sleeping with and why, and big political lies about whom I was serving. I despised him intensely and imputed his sins onto his comrades, and no doubt they had equally valid furies against me and mine, and in this way the bitterness spread out of control with each half wishing plagues and pestilence on the other. Soon we had an 'informer' in their camp; later the informer's brother reversed the favour with interest, and so it went: a prolonged family dispute made more bitter by the sense of betrayal that comes from the slight loosening of tight ties, producing a classic exposition of Freud's theory of the narcissism of the small difference. With my flatmate and me on

*For instance, we had a bitter little scrap about state witnesses in political trials – 'we' argued fiercely for a firm line against them; some of 'them' argued for greater flexibility.

different sides, we both moved out. I settled into a box room in a new commune started by my friend Tony, but I was seldom home. Politics, intrigue and bile became all-consuming.

Meanwhile our underground unit flourished – for a few months, anyway – putting out regular reports, always meticulously coded and concealed, secretly distributing banned literature, spotting potential new recruits to be sent to Zimbabwe for crash courses and carrying out various other underground tasks along with our student and trade union activities. But this too began to fray at the edges. First the factional battles took their toll, exposing those of us pushing the ANC underground lines, and we began to suspect signs of surveillance. Then one bright summer's morning, Wanda, who had agreed to her postbox role without asking any questions about its source, popped around with a load to deliver and a message of caution. One of the parcels, not properly wrapped, tore apart, disgorging its load of banned literature on the post office floor. All eyes turned from the newly unwrapped copies of *Mayibuye!* and *Sechaba* to Wanda. She casually scooped up the fallen load, trotted off and delivered it to me at my door without complaint and only the gentlest word of warning: 'I think you should ask your friends to wrap it better next time,' she whispered. I nodded guiltily but I was horrified at the potential implications for her safety and immediately complained to the ANC in Harare, demanding that Wanda's name be removed from the safe address list, although they continued to send material to her address.

I then received an urgent coded missive to travel to Botswana forthwith. I dropped what I was doing, flew to Gabarone and then hitchhiked to the Mahalapi Hotel fifty miles from the border, where I was supposed to meet Comrade Peter. But there was no-one there and after I had been hanging around for eight hours an off-duty Botswana policeman became suspicious, and it took some feverish lying to get myself out of a diplomatic incident. I slept in a mud hut and hitch-hiked back the next morning, departing via an obscure border post and then hiking home to Cape Town to report the disaster to my two comrades. It eventually turned out that the courier had forgotten to include the last line of the coded message, 'telegraph coded reply confirming arrival'. I became paranoid about my Botswana trip, fearing that my 'legend' about assisting a former girlfriend with an abortion there just wouldn't hold up under prolonged interrogation.

A week after I returned from Botswana we hit another crisis. The ANC encouraged us to 'cultivate' high-school students for future attention – presumably under a catch-'em-while-they're-young rationale. One 16-year-old was a particularly keen learner and after a few months I followed up on an ANC prompt, en-couraging her to suggest friends who might show similar interest – 'Just to send them student publi-cations and stuff, you know.' She went beyond the call of duty, handing over a long list, and we promptly sent this to Harare, cautioning the ANC to do no more than keep it for future reference. A month later, however, our protégée came to me in panic. 'All those people on the list I gave you have been sent these heavy ANC pamphlets, and some of their parents have called the police, and I think they're blaming me,' she said. I assured her I had no idea how the names got into ANC hands – 'I think I lost the list in the *Varsity* office. Sorry.

114

I wanted to send them each a copy of the paper' – and we quickly sent a coded message to ditch the high-school plan forthwith. We dropped our protégée, and nothing more came of it.

Finally, a week after my twenty-second birthday, all this intrigue and the intensity of the relation between Leon, Rosa and me led to a changing of the guard in the bedroom. I was a close friend of Leon's, I had lured his willing soul to the clutches of ANC and he trusted me, but when Rosa kissed me I didn't look back. There was no guilt or hesitation. Saying no to Rosa was not an option I contemplated. Our underground unit, Leon's well-being, our friendship – these would just have to roll with the punches. It was *my* chance now, and that was that. Except it wasn't quite, because after a spell in the cold, Leon was back, leaving me distraught, and then it was my turn again and so on, until our little cell could barely contain all the madness and rage inside it.

In mitigation I should say we were by no means alone in this. The practice of two boys sharing one girl was becoming a norm in our circles, although the converse would never have been tolerated. To rub it in, amid all this bed-hopping confusion the female majority revolted, accusing the male minority of dominating debate: we boys were too obsessed by the contents of our bookshelves and we needed some chop-chop feminist re-education. They formed themselves into consciousness-raising groups, while we, at their insistence, were herded into parallel men's group structures, where we smoked dagga and talked with earnest animation about our obsessions and conquests, seldom forgetting to pass the most salacious details to our inquisitive and demanding lovers. What the hardmen of the Liesbeek Park Boxing Club would have made of all this, I can't even imagine, but that was part of the charm of keeping my different worlds apart.

Then there were worlds within worlds – alternative universes. With one errant lover in Cape Town and a ragamuffin princess in Johannesburg, and insanity all around, I felt compelled to see Wanda again. Even without the postbox rationale, I just couldn't stop myself from visiting her. It was, as ever, my favourite way to spend a late afternoon in autumn, or any other time, come to think of it. It was still my happiest place to be. After a while I ceased making excuses and one rainy evening I finally dislodged my confession in a lucid dagga haze. 'Um, actually, I was into you all those years ago,' I volunteered, and felt immense, clear-headed relief that I'd finally been able to say it. 'I know,' she said, in a voice so kind. 'Your housemates told me – afterwards. You know, I was also *into* you,' she said. 'But why didn't you tell me then?' It was a question we both asked – wires crossed, telephone broken, sand stuck.

We went out together to see Nina Hagen and Hazel O'Connor in a punk double-feature that night but the following evening I was back, and after another spliff I announced, eyes down: 'Actually, you know, the other thing I really wanted to say last night was that I was *still* into you – I mean, I still am, you know, like, seriously into you.' But it was too late: our lives had moved in different directions – too late for her anyway. For me, well, perhaps not quite *Love in the Time of Cholera* but for far too long I just couldn't quite let go, couldn't let go of anything, and I was left to wonder what might have been.

Still, it was never too late at the gym. George le Roux was delighted to have me back and gave me the task of leading his son Boetie and the other juniors in their workouts. I felt a bit embarrassed about this – I wasn't worthy. I sensed I was being given special treatment – as the sole university student, the token member of the bookish middle-classes, the boyish oddity. There was a parallel with the political world I was moving in. Much as we denied it at the time, in retrospect a kind of colonial ethos was at work, particularly within the ANC. As a white recruit I was part of a small band of the chosen who were treated as a little bit special, almost as a pampered elite. We were nurtured, listened to and given access to senior leaders in a way that I'm not sure all black recruits at our level could expect. It was a dynamic bound to cause future resentment but under the all-embracing cloak of non-racialism such feelings were kept mute for another decade.

In any event, at the gym, as in the political ring, I was doing my bit to show I was worth all this attention. When it wasn't my innings in the love triangle I would spend my nights listening to Miles Davis's trumpet or Abdullah Ibrahim's piano and then run hard, some-times for hours on end, winding through my old childhood haunts – up Wynburg Hill and down into the dreamlands of the Constantia Valley until the rising of the morning sun. My legs seemed to move without effort, up and down the hills, and at times I felt like I was dream-running, free from pain and effort, talking to myself, aloud.

I was far fitter than before and came in close to featherweight for my next fight – this one against a heavily tattooed drug-squad policeman. I politely greeted him at the weigh-in, smiled and tried to make small talk. 'Fuck off, cunt,' he replied. He was bigger than me – taller, broader shouldered although with skinnier legs – but this time I felt virtually free from fear. I was angry and wanted to hurt him – for calling me a cunt, for being a pig, for busting drug users, for Rosa, for Wanda, for myself.

He took me by surprise when the bell rang, rushing out and catching me flush and then raining crude blows on my head as I covered up. I realized that unless I did something soon the referee would stop the fight. 'Jab, Evans,' George and Jan both yelled from my corner, and so I jabbed – harder and longer and more accurately than ever before, and soon his mouth was bleeding. Every time he came in I would bang in my left jab. I had not yet mastered the left hook off the jab and I was standing in the old English style, the angle too acute for my right cross to be more than a finishing weapon, but the jab was enough to pick off this drug-squad tough. I had found my range, and it was working.

In the second round I resumed my one-armed display until he came in, dipped low and whacked me with all he had, flush in the groin. It was deliberate and well aimed and, despite my protective though rather loose-fitting cricket cup, I went down in agony. The referee warned him, but after ten seconds he ordered me to resume hostilities. I clinched, the referee barked 'Break!' and again the policeman fouled, hitting me on the break, this time hard on the nose, which started to leak blood.

I flopped down in my corner at the bell, sore, tired and thirsty. 'Drink!' said George. I drank. 'Spit.' I spat. 'Now drink and swallow.' I gulped. 'OK, spit out your gumshield and fight without it. You need the air.' It plopped out. 'He's also tired, man. I swear, you can do it! Go for him, Evans.' For this last round I came out using the jab merely for probing. As he moved to my left, I launched the hardest, straightest right cross I'd ever thrown. It landed smack on the side of his jaw as he was coming in and dropped him heavily. I retreated quickly to my corner, forgetting the neutral corner rule, and George was ready. 'Get him, Evans. Now!'

My exhaustion lifted when he groggily rose at the count of nine and I rushed across the ring and hit him again with a lead right. He grabbed and clung on, and I lost it, shouting: 'You fuck! You fuck! You fuck!' The referee stopped the fight and gave me a stern warning about profanity for what seemed like at least ten seconds. He looked like he was contemplating a disqualification but then he ordered us to get it on again. 'Jump on him,' shouted Jan, and I leapt. Slugging wildly but probably hitting more than missing, I trapped him on the ropes and he took too many un-answered punches, and the referee pulled me off. As my hand was raised, this young drugs cop glared at me, and the referee glared back at him, and I felt utterly elated.

The policeman tried to start it up again in the parking lot, and I said, 'Let's do it,' knowing I was surrounded by Jan, Dirk, Gert and Claude, who told him to go fuck himself or they'd beat the shit out of him. He backed off. I returned home that night, my nose still clotted with my blood, my balls still aching, with my little trophy to display, as proud as could be. It might not have impressed anyone else, but, hey, it impressed me.

It seemed a fine note on which to end my fighting career, and I never again boxed competitively, although I would make occasional toe-dipping returns to the sparring ring just to feel and smell it again. George pleaded for a change of mind, to take part in this or that tournament, but I would always make my excuses. 'I'm feeling sick,' 'I've got an exam.' I felt I had nothing left to prove and by this stage I was too caught up in politics to train regularly. I began to drift and soon lost touch with my trainer.*

As my 1982 staggered to a close, I made a decision based on what seemed then like paradoxical logic. I announced to my comrades that I would resettle in Johannesburg, attributing the move to altruistic political grounds. By then I had confided in my mature and sensible brother, Michael, who was a full-time employee of the National Union of Students and whose recruitment to the ANC I had facilitated a few months earlier. He undertook to motivate the idea of my departure to the movement's underground leadership and they gave it their go-ahead, partly because they were worried about the sanity of our unit and the state attention its activities might have been drawing, but also because they thought I might be useful in furthering their organizational aims over there. My real reason, however, had very little to do with politics. Rosa and Leon had finally parted ways and I figured

---

*Ten years later, when I was boxing correspondent for the *Sunday Times* and contributing editor to *Boxing World*, George wrote a gushing letter about me to the magazine, praising my prowess, fighting spirit and punching power. Of course, I had no illusions, but I felt grateful for this praise, which certainly did my reputation in the sport no harm. A week after his letter appeared in print, I understood what it was really about. He phoned me at home: 'Hey, Gavin, remember me – George le Roux,' and it turned out he was now training professionals in our old gym – mostly blacks this time – and wanted some publicity. I said I'd do my best if his lads made an impression, and I meant it. None of them cut it then, but over the next decade he persevered to become one of Cape Town's leading professional trainers.

that if I hung around I too would get the sack sooner or later – quite understandably, because the jealous pair of us had become too much for one woman. The idea of living in the same city and working in the same organizations without being with her was too much for me. Better to get out when the going was good, to leave before getting the final drop. And as for Wanda, well, better to dream on from afar.

So rather than face down my agonies all the way to the sure conclusion of lip-biting defeat, I ran in the hope of being able to fight another day. Rosa and I hitchhiked across the country – our first lift with an ex-cop who had resigned after seeing Steve Biko's dying body – and then spent five days hiking down the Transkei coast, and finally back home to Cape Town for a last sad, blissful fortnight together. Blissful for me, anyway.

It was February 1983 when I said goodbye to the mountains, the *fynbos* and the sea, the friends and lovers and the unrequited loves, dispirited and without confidence in my future, and headed for a metropolis that permanently smelled of petrol and housed half of the country's professional boxers.

3

WHITE-HOPING WITH DIAMOND WAYNE AND THE BOKSBURG BOMBER

Central Johannesburg, September 1984. 'Listen!' a smirking, boyish, half-familiar face from the office demands. 'I've heard you're into boxing: OK, so tell me, who was the first *ouk* to drop Ali? The *first*, hey.'

The first, hey? Well now, I'm no good at factual questions under interrogation, and after a spell in a pugilistic wilderness I'm feeling a little rusty on history, but this time the pressure is mild – a beaming face, pushed too close to mine, wanting an instant answer. 'Aaah, shit, I know it, I know it,' I begin. 'Not Henry Cooper in '63. No, no. Before then. Must have been Doug Jones, I s'pose. I dunno.'

'Not Cooper, you say?' the face says, closing in. 'I'll bet you on Jones. Twenty Rand.'

Cooper came second; I know that, so I fall for it. 'OK. *Ja,*' and we shake on it. It's the first bet I've taken since, oh, early secondary school at least, and I'm feeling childish. Within seconds a *Rand Daily Mail* phone is dialled and Bert Blewett, editor of *Boxing World*, is called at his Durban flat. 'Hey, Bert, it's me. Listen, I've got a bet with this *ouk* Evans in the office. Who was the first to drop Ali?' And too late I remember – shit, not Jones, the soft-hitting light heavy who held Ali to a disputed decision in '63, but Sonny Banks, the hard-hitting light heavy who caught him clean in '62. When the receiver is passed to me, a slightly embarrassed Bert is forced to confirm it.

I have no idea how my connection with boxing was unearthed by my colleague-interrogator, but I recall I wasn't the one to take the initiative, which would fit, given my subsequent discoveries about the motives of the man-child I'll call Diamond Wayne. In any event it was a fortunate moment for my relation with the game – if fortune and boxing can be said to co-exist – because at that point, twenty months after leaving Cape Town, the prosaic world of *my* sport was in danger of drowning under the deluge of my freshly invigorated political activism. Instead Wayne saved it. Wayne pulled me back, or at least I followed willingly until I no longer had need for him.

Half-handsome, six feet tall with a soft nose and impudent face that told of childhood prolonged, he was someone more utterly devoted to the immediate gratification of his senses, and less inclined to consider the cost, than any putative adult I'd met before. In this sense, despite his impossibly boastful egotism and his wild inclination for invention, Wayne possessed a certain charm. He lived in a state of child-like oblivion to the notion that the universe was larger than his own desires. Wayne's inner world was not in the habit of being harvested for self-analysis, and he seemed happily devoid of even the slightest hint of introspection, guilt, self-doubt or moral confusion, and yet he was not without the guile and cunning of a tactical thinker. He possessed an enormous capacity for devious design, and was capable of a kind of callously casual immorality that I found intriguing in the sense that it was little different from the capriciousness of a six-year-old, and therefore more open to indulgence than from someone more obviously grown up.

I never made the effort to discover where all this came from. He told me his father was a doctor, his mother the winner of a glamorous granny competition – of this he was proud – and the man-boy would regularly genuflect in their direction, but it was to the world of bent cops, illicit diamond dealers, thugs, murderers and professional fighting men he was drawn. Here lay his true vocation.

He was a junior reporter in his early twenties, same as me. Unlike me he was completely lacking in any sense of decorum for rank, age or station. I found this amusing. It was not simple defiance, which might have been admirable. He was indeed a stickler for conventions that suited, and there was nothing courageous about it either. It was more that Wayne had no clue how he was coming across to the world. He simply presumed the camaraderie of anyone he wasn't fighting. From a lowly fellow reporter like me, to an editor, a senior cop, a gangster, a boxing champion – no-one was too big or small for Wayne to walk in on, to harangue, to boast at. He operated without embarrassment.

Looking back, there was a great deal about Wayne that should have made me take flight – and the more I learnt of his criminal friends and cop connections the worse it appeared – but none of this registered yet. Of more concern was his effect on me – the way he brought out my own child, and pulled me back to a time when I would get hot and bothered over whether a Great White had the beating of an Orca, or whether Joe Louis could have done the job on Jack Johnson – a habit, I should add, I have yet to see off.

We first met soon after my arrival at the *Rand Daily Mail*, where my maiden job was to follow ambulances and report on night crime. This involved sending bottles of whisky to the emergency services in return for tip-offs whenever anything interesting happened – often arriving before the police or ambulances made it. I became accustomed to doorstepping mothers of suicide, murder and drowning victims, and peering through the gaps in imploded vehicles to see blood spurting out of eyesockets. This worried me, or at least I thought it should, but for Wayne it was neither here nor there. His amorality and bravado entertained me, and even when I discovered his boasts of physical prowess were not quite matched by the performance I remained intrigued. I also found him useful. He supplied me with tickets to the fights I wanted to see. In this way I suppose I could say that the renewed upward trajectory of my boxing thing owed more than it should have to what seemed like a chance interaction with a sociopathic oddball.

A catch-up history then: I arrived in Johannesburg in 1983 with all my belongings in the back of a comrade's car, feeling utterly alone and sensing I'd made a terrible mistake. I moved into a house in Berea, near central Johannesburg, with three older comrade friends, with the aim of completing an honours dissertation and nine law courses. Because of previous security police attention, the ANC asked me to work alone for a while and maintain a low profile, which I interpreted as doing nothing. I ceased despatching coded reports because I no longer trusted the security of our communications system, and began hanging out with friends who had moved beyond the fringes of politics, winding my way around the streets of Johannesburg on an ancient Honda motorcycle I purchased with the remaining profits of a stint as a university tutor. Eventually an ANC courier contacted me, bearing an angry coded instruction to get back to business, and so, reluctant but also relieved to have been restored to my sense of mission, I began to carry out the little tasks assigned.

But there was not much joy in it. I missed my Cape Town connections, I longed for the smell of the sea and the view of the mountains and I pined for love's past. I later came to a grudging appreciation of the vibrancy of Johannesburg's insistent, pulsating rhythm, but at the time it felt remorseless and I regretted my move. I would sit at my desk, daydreaming about the past or the future, finding it impossible to work without powerful chemical stimulants.* When exams arrived I would provide doctor's certificates in my desperation to postpone the inevitable.** Whenever I had an excuse I would hitchhike home to Cape Town, forever

---

*I started with Obex and settled on a prescription drug called Reactivan, until, after several years of using it for exams and long-distance travel, I noticed that aside from side-effects like temporary impotence, I was developing 'tolerance', requiring more and more for the same effect. I then gave it up.

**I would feign gastroenteritis attacks, until one of my professors noticed I'd had six such exam attacks in a row. I then moved on to claiming motorbike accidents by scraping my elbow along the tarmac.

inventing characters, personal histories and accents for myself – the army boy, the foreigner and, of course, the boxer. After returning from one of these journeys, this time as a delegate to the national launch of the UDF (the semi-legal, ANC-backed mass movement), the security police raided our house. I was alone and the officer-in-charge pinned me against the wall and began throttling me, demanding cooperation. But remembering past humiliations, I refused, and was carted away in handcuffs and then released that evening following some light interrogation. After that I saw no point trying to maintain a low political profile and returned to the business of open activism.

The next morning I was part of a student group attacked by a band of pro-apartheid students, and this time, feeling braver than usual after my throttling experience, I didn't run, and started punching back with conviction. I felt sufficiently exhilarated by the in-consequential results of this fifteen-second experience to start seeking out the local amateur boxing clubs. I also acquired a secret diversion from the competing worlds of the law and politics. Each day, while return-ing from campus, I would pass a large Hillbrow bookstall called Estoril Books which stocked inter-national boxing magazines. I could never resist, and without deviation would spend a precious hour reading them from cover to cover until a manager chased me off. There was also a professional boxing gym en route, and I began to hang out there, becoming a familiar presence. I liked the reassuring feel of the place and felt myself getting sucked back in.

I had just turned 23 years old and was growing weary of the student existence, and I had also accumulated huge debts and felt overdue for a full-time job. After passing my law exams, I got taken on as a rookie journalist at the *Rand Daily Mail*, which sent me off to Port Elizabeth for a training course, followed by six months on their sister paper, the *Eastern Province Herald*. Coincidentally, my old comrade, friend and lover Rosa was also transferred there to head a workers' literacy project for the trade unions. We decided to share a cottage and before moving in together we once again took to the Transkei, getting robbed in a cave along the way before completing our trail of the coast. On the way back we took a lift from a jovial uncle who let us drive his Mercedes and had – another coincidence – a connection with the world of fighting men. He was the son-in-law of one of the legends of the wartime white South African ring, Laurie Stephens, who had beaten Alf James in two out of their three classic battles in my father's childhood. The genial driver regaled us with tales of the era – from the rough-trade gay affairs of the former world light heavy-weight boxing champion Freddie Mills to the fighting spirit of old Laurie, and then drove us to see the old man himself. Age and too many punches had dulled Laurie's senses but not his beatific smile, which, I am told, he took with him to his grave a couple of years later.

We left punchy old Laurie to descend further into smiling senility, moved into a small cottage in Port Elizabeth together and got busy once again with politics. Our first encounter was with the local UDF publicity secretary, a seldom sober former Robben Islander whose preoccupation was to get his leg over Rosa or any other woman who entered his den, usually while disgorging the detritus of Marxian political theory he'd been gargling on in jail. We gave him a wide berth and concentrated on setting up a branch of the UDF in the conservative white suburbs of Port Elizabeth, drawing great satisfaction from this achievement. Between our day jobs we held public and private meetings and all manner of cultural activities to attract more converts, while sending out coded reports on political developments to the ANC in Zimbabwe. The security police were ignorant of the clandestine side but were outraged by our overt work and cracked down with an intensity they were unable to muster for the greater numbers of white activists in Johannesburg, Cape Town, Durban and Grahamstown.

There were constant attempts at infiltrating spies into our circles, the most persistent involving the farcical combination of two security policemen, Lieutenant Carl Edwards and Constable Billy Van Zyl. Edwards was a former Rhodes University spy who came out of the cold by betraying a friend and went on to become a junior officer in the Port Elizabeth security branch. He was a strange creature – lanky, a bit camp, melodramatic with a supercilious manner and an inclination towards curious behaviour. Once I bumped into him on the pavement in town. 'You better not shake my hand,' he said sniffily as he minced off, 'you don't know what I might be carrying.' His beat included the press and the white activist sector and I would often see him schmoozing all-too-willing political reporters on the *Herald*, which is perhaps why he paid me particular attention. One afternoon he marched into our cottage, saying that unless I agreed to cooperate he would make life impossible at the *Herald* and would ensure my arrest by the military police. 'Get out of my house, now,' I spat. I was surprised to see him skulking off, without even so much as a physical threat, but as he departed he said, 'Just you wait and see, Evans.' The *Herald* editors promptly took me off all political stories and three days later the military police came to get me at work, threatening to drag me off to report for the military service I'd been avoiding. I wriggled out of it by phoning the *Rand Daily Mail* editor, securing a letter stating I was on a registered training course (legitimate grounds for military deferment) while at the same time sending the army a letter saying I refused to serve under any conditions.*

Carl Edwards continued trying to get at me** but his pet plan involved Billy, his bespectacled 22-year-old protégé. The week before I arrived in Port Elizabeth Billy rented an outside room at the home of the parents of one of my closest friends and comrades, Brett, who was a conscientious objector preparing to leave the country and join the ANC's military wing. Brett visited his parents and instantly became suspicious. 'This Billy got motherless at a *braai* at our house the other day and kept asking me odd questions about my activities and making strangely ambiguous political statements,' he said. 'Watch him carefully. I'm sure he's a *spoek*.' We learned Billy came from a conservative Afrikaans farming family, and had talked of 'kaffirs' when he arrived at the *Herald*. Then, rather suddenly, he turned militant. He tried to befriend me, and was soon asking for help in avoiding military service. When

*The military wanted to avoid a high-profile conscientious objector trial involving a journalist and therefore agreed to give me study deferment, while I continued to oblige them by registering for various courses, eventually accumulating five university degrees, none of which I ever used.

**For instance, he tried to spread rumours about me, saying I was an informer, but his efforts lacked resonance and fell on deaf ears, partly because of my father's pro-liberation reputation.

I told him no more than the law permitted, he asked to see me privately. He spent a few minutes showing off his new 600cc scrambler and his killer crossbow and then beckoned me to come closer. 'I want you to help me to leave the country to avoid the army and join the ANC in Botswana. I feel I'm ready,' he said. 'So you must tell me who I should contact when I get there.' I shrugged. 'Sorry, Billy, but I really don't know anyone in the ANC. I only work within the law.' He pressed and pressed but I continued to stonewall.

Edwards gave us the proof we needed. He detained Lloyd, a young coloured journalist, and interrogated him, threatening him with trouble unless he agreed to cooperate. Lloyd refused, and immediately rushed around to find me. 'It was incredible,' he said. 'Edwards repeated things to me, word for word, that I'd said about the ANC to only two people.' One was a well-trusted female journalist, the other, Billy Van Zyl. 'It can't be Billy,' he said. 'He's a real radical.' Two days later Van Zyl drove off to Botswana on his scrambler. We had previously warned the ANC in Harare that he was a spy and they passed the message on to the structures in Gabarone, but the words didn't reach the right ears. A week later I received a call from a friend who'd settled in Botswana, on our bugged home phone. 'The ANC wants to know, can they trust Billy Van Zyl?' she said. 'He told us he wanted to join but complained that you wouldn't help.' I muttered: 'Don't touch him with a bargepole,' before cutting her off. We expected Billy to be detained immediately but it took over a year of prevarication for the ANC to come to the same conclusion. He was eventually seized and sent to the ANC's Quatro detention camp in Angola for four years. He was released in 1990 and returned home

131

to Port Elizabeth, after which the police acknowledged that Constable Billy was indeed one of their own.

The infiltration and blackmail attempts were backed up by more overt forms of intimidation and worse. My motorbike brake cables were cut while Rosa's tyres were overinflated with the aim of causing a blow-out. We were placed under constant surveillance and regularly harassed, and this kind of attention was extended to those associated with us. For instance, a left-leaning journalist friend of ours was dragged from her flat by a group of masked men – later identified as Military Intelligence operatives – and lacerated with *sjamboks*.

On Sharpeville day in March 1984, Rosa and I went to a political meeting in New Brighton township. As we were about to leave, our friend Mkhuseli Jack called us over, pointing to a white Ford Granada car. 'You see that dark-haired guy,' he whispered. 'That's Captain Niewoudt. He's a bad one and I'm sure he'll follow you because you're the only whites here. Watch out.' We were duly overtaken by the Granada, which stopped, turned around and drove at high speed towards us. As it was about to pass, another officer leant out of the passenger window and tossed a large rock at our windscreen. It landed on the join between the wind-screen and the roof, shattering the glass. Rosa narrowly escaped decapitation but had to be rushed to the Port Elizabeth General Hospital to have the glass removed from her eye.*

This lot may have been mild compared with the

*Many years later the other officer applied to the Truth and Reconciliation Commission for indemnity for this incident, admitting it was a murder attempt.

constant beatings and torture meted out to the black activists like Mkhuseli, but it felt too intense to bear for much longer, and the fraught state of my home life was hardly helping. I needed some release from this hamster-cage existence. At an amateur boxing gym in a poor white area of central Port Elizabeth I met up with my old Liesbeek Park gymmate Jan, and resumed training. 'You're standing too skew, *jong*, like one of those limey boxers,' the trainer told me. 'You need to stand squarer, so you can use your right more, and get your fucking chin down,' and I obeyed. On my next visit there I noticed a black welterweight – a novice professional called Brown Bongo – sparring with a white light heavyweight, and for a moment saw it as a sign of change in the segregated world of South African amateur boxing. But the trainer was quick to disabuse me. 'Some fucking do-good *kaffir-boetie* businessman is sponsoring him and asked me to let him train here, but I told them straight: "Listen, pal, I appreciate the money but I'm not having any fucking kaffirs joining my gym. He can spar, but that's all." ' Being exposed to white, working-class racists was no longer such an intriguing sociological experience, and after another week I made my excuses.

A month later, my journalism internship over, I was relieved to abandon Port Elizabeth. Rosa remained and would suffer from the security police's unabated attention – a year in detention, followed by four months in solitary confinement and a plot to frame her falsely on criminal charges. I admired her courage in sticking it out but was relieved that my option was different, less austere and apparently less dangerous. I headed back to a metropolis offering the relative safety of numbers, and moved into yet another activist house

– this one in what was then the white, working-class
suburb of Mayfair.

My new life was compartmentalized between my job
and my political work. I worked as a reporter for the
Rand Daily Mail, then in its last year of existence,
moving from crime to television previews to court
coverage, producing an irregular flow of passable
stories while regularly smoking dagga with the male
photographers and, very occasionally, getting laid by
one of the female reporters. I regarded journalism as a
fun way to make ends meet, flexible enough to allow
space for my true vocation, and that was the way
it remained. My ANC underground work took self-
conscious pride of place, although in retrospect it
was less significant than the work carried out within
relatively open anti-apartheid groups, which operated
in the shrinking legal space allowed under this racially
exclusive faux-democracy. Like most ANC recruits
I doubled as a member of several internal political
organizations and my main underground role at that
time was to keep the ANC informed of developments of
strategic significance while also disseminating ANC
'lines' on various issues and priming trusted comrades
for recruitment.

Most nights were taken up in organizational work
in Johannesburg. My favourite involved a rolling
crusade that reflected a rare vein of collective political
creativity. The End Conscription Campaign was
launched as a national movement to mobilize 'the
conscripted community' (whites) against compulsory
military service and over the next five years this
took up thousands of hours of my time. It was formed
at the suggestion of the ANC out of a loose alliance
between pacifist Christians and leftist students but

rapidly outgrew these confines, becoming a remarkably successful force with branches all over the country. ECC soon developed an enviable reputation as a sexy movement – a freewheeling style, a loose and open composition, and more shagging, more fun and probably more drugs than any other group I worked in. Within its first two years it drew thousands of young white people into the realm of resistance politics – many from within the army, but also the lovers, mothers and friends of conscripts, a fair sprinkling of out-of-the-closet gays, Protestant peaceniks, Catholic liberationists, anarchic Afrikaners, parliamentary liberals, environmentalists, actors and musicians and goodtime *jollers*. Most were attracted by the perpetual harvest of cultural activity – cabarets, art exhibitions, pop concerts and records, vigils, fasts, comics, agit-prop theatre and some of the most striking posters and stickers I've ever seen – all in the service of hard-edged campaigns to get the troops out of Namibia, Angola or the townships and do away with compulsory military service, but usually softened by a gentler peace and justice message.

The military and security police were incensed by the idea of dissent within their ranks. Over a hundred ECC members were detained for periods ranging from a day to a year. The police often succeeded in infiltrating spies into the branches. They also beat up members, sabotaged cars, petrol-bombed houses, burgled offices, broke up and banned meetings, threatened and black-mailed the vulnerable and launched smear campaigns against leaders. But apartheid was a power system that prided itself on its legal system and its adherence to its own rule of law, and this created many openings not available to revolutionaries in, say, Chile or Uganda or

Albania. On one occasion we received information from a soldier involved in a concerted harassment campaign against ECC. The leading barrister, Sidney Kentridge QC, represented us in interdicting the military against further illegal acts and they were forced to make several admissions – things like dropping pamphlets in the name of the 'Anti-Liberal Alliance' from a helicopter on an ECC fair – claiming this was justified because the country was in a state of war. The only activity they were too embarrassed to admit was burgling the ECC's Cape Town office and then instructing a private to take a dump in the middle of the carpet, leaving behind a steaming pile. Eventually they banned ECC's activities under the Emergency Regulations, but we then decamped to new areas, cultivating a parallel conscientious-objector movement which led to mass 'objections' by conscripts around the country, some of them from the officer ranks, with the figure eventually passing the thousand mark.*

Soon after returning to Johannesburg I was also elected to the executive of a rather more austere UDF organization called the Johannesburg Democratic Action Committee, whose main brief was to make an impact within the white areas. There were competing strategies: some wanted a conduit for supporting the activities of black community groups; others, like me, wanted to penetrate more deeply into the white heartlands by developing a wider base of sympathy for the struggle. Jodac did a bit of both – regular gestures of 'solidarity' and bits and bobs of assistance for the

---

*This demonstrated that you could get away with refusing a call-up by being brazen about it because the military could not afford the negative publicity of too many high-profile conscription trials.

'oppressed', and plenty of concerts, public meetings, conferences, poster blitzes, fun-runs, discussion forums and trips to the black townships to sell the cause to sympathetic whites. Fresh from working in conservative white Port Elizabeth I developed an evangelical zeal for 'working behind enemy lines' and urged my bemused comrades to try 'loving' their communities rather than despising them and to use just about any strategy and tactic for this end, even if it seemed a little out of step with the central thrust of ANC–UDF policy.*

But there were some who seemed well beyond the pale, even for me, and one of them was Diamond Wayne, although this did not stop me talking to him because we still had one common interest. In no time I became a co-conspirator within his fantasy world. 'I'm thinking of turning professional any day now,' he told me, explaining that he was a former provincial amateur welterweight champion. 'I've been sparring at Harold Volbrecht's gym and he says I'm ready. I guarantee you I could beat Greg Clark right now,' he said of the country's national light middleweight champion. 'I'll bet you.' Now and then I saw hints of what passed as prowess. A month after I met him he was forced to pay damages to a television cameraman he assaulted and once, when I questioned his martial boasts, he unleashed a combination at my head, the punches stopping just short of my nose. 'Now what do you think? Think you could beat me, hey?' he challenged. There was too much hubris in his demeanour for him to give off any scent of genuine menace, but I realized

*We later created forums not directly tied to the UDF, which attracted larger numbers of whites wanting to ally themselves with anti-apartheid causes without feeling tied to ANC coattails.

he was capable of violence when aroused. Volbrecht, however, had a different spin on Wayne's prowess and potential. 'Listen, Gav, don't believe everything he tells you,' Harold said. 'I mean, I first met him when I was his sergeant in the army and he was one of my *troepies*, and every time he got into trouble with the other *ouks* – which was quite often because he used to piss everyone off – he would hide behind me because he knew none of them would dare mess with me.'

Still, I was prepared to indulge Wayne with the benefit of my creeping doubt. He was my sole boxing buddy and my passport to the fights. Whenever I requested a ringside seat Wayne would deliver and so it was that a kind of friendship was formed around the sport. The other dimensions of my life were strictly out of bounds; never even hinted at. I wasn't too keen to get any deeper into his existence either. 'I've got a satellite set up, so you can come over and watch any American fight you like,' he'd offer. 'And I've also got hundreds of boxing videos – any boxer you want to see.' I was tempted, but felt this was a relationship best confined to the office, the road and the ring.

1984 was high renaissance time for South African heavyweight boxing: great white hopes were being pumped out, two by two, frequently falling over their own moustaches. The procession started with a solid rugby prop, Jimmy Richards, and a roly-poly puncher, Mike Schutte. Mike was trained by Alan Toweel, part of a Lebanese–South African dynasty from Mayfair, Johannesburg, whose younger members my mother had once taught in nursery school. One brother, Vickie, was South Africa's first ever world boxing champion; another, Willie, came close, but the shots were called by Maurice, the cantankerous, polio-crippled promoter brother, and chip-on-the-shoulder Alan, their asthmatic boxer-turned-manager brother. Anyone who crossed this plump pair was taught to regret it. One respected sports writer told me he discovered a Schutte fight was fixed – that a foreign boxer had been paid to take a dive. When Maurice heard the reporter was on to his scam, he threatened to have him killed, and the writer quietly killed the story. Their finest hour came in South Africa's first 'multiracial' bout of the apartheid era when they persuaded the government to allow the black American world light heavyweight champion Bob Foster to defend his title against their boxer Pierre Fourie in 1973. Fourie lost that one and three other world-title bouts, and was eventually replaced by Schutte as their most saleable piece of meat.

In his fourth fight with Richards, Mike lifted Jimmy off his feet with a massive hook and from then on this abattoir assistant made big waves at home and tiny ripples abroad. His proportions (a rotund 5 foot 10, 260 pounds), his robust style and his Neanderthal ugliness made him an institution in white South African life. The Tank, as they dubbed him, picked up a clutch of wins over recycled world-title challengers and the Toweels began their attempts to persuade Muhammad Ali to break the sporting boycott and defend in South Africa. Maurice swore to me that Ali was willing to sign, but instead Schutte was squeezed out by two younger, sprightlier white hopes; just as the Toweels were to be replaced by sharper suits. Mike, however, managed well enough without boxing. He was an engaging character who developed a neat line in self-deprecatory humour – the Mike Schutte joke (an adaptation of the Van der Merwe joke, in turn derived from the Paddy joke – all about congenital idiocy). He moved from a brief career as a professional wrestler to a down-market cabaret act, playing guitar, singing ballads and telling Schutte jokes.

Kallie Knoetze, who curtailed Schutte's career with a mighty right cross, had a more rapid arrival and departure. As a riot cop he achieved notoriety for crippling a schoolboy with a bullet during the Soweto uprising, and when he made a solitary visit to fight in the United States Jesse Jackson terrified him by leading a tiny picket to protest against his presence. The impression he made at home, both with his mouth and with his fists, was more flattering. He flattened the former American amateur star Duane Bobick, but he was limited by laziness and a brittle chin, and was stopped by John Tate in a world-title eliminator in 1979, after which losing became a habit. But Kallie succeeded in reinventing himself. After a spell as an 'enlightened' National Party supporter, this B-movie filmstar, farmer and professional character became an enthusiast for the 'new' South Africa, joining the ANC in 1999.

Which brings me to his main rival Gerhardus Christaan Coetzee, the finest heavyweight the country has yet produced and one of the strangest creatures I've ever encountered. I came to know him as a man of astonishing character shifts: kind, cruel, clever, dumb, gentle, vicious, considerate, gullible, sophisticated, simple, manipulating. He could do a convincing impression of the village idiot and yet was as wily as anyone I've come across in this dirty game. He was deft at the double cross but could look as vulnerable as a kicked basset hound. He was capable of outwitting teams of attorneys but once managed to convince a judge that he needn't honour a contract with a doctor who treated him for venereal disease because he was too thick to understand its terms. He was the first white South African boxer to speak out against apartheid and he seemed to adore his black boxers and servants, yet he could turn on them, threaten them and punish them like children when things went wrong. There was even a physical ambiguity. His hairless torso never approached ripped definition, he had a full-cheeked face with an obligatory *snor* framing soft, fat, wet lips, and his voice came in a high monotone, while his customary body language was phlegmatic. Yet he could switch into a bully of frightening proportions, issuing threats of violence and using his strength to get his own way.

Gerrie emerged from a large family whose male members – or several over the generations – established a reputation in their hometown of Boksburg for laziness and thuggery. Gerrie, the biggest and brightest of the clan, carried some of this within his soul, but there was more to him. His fellow white boxers tended to moon-light as cops or army boys. Gerrie became a dental mechanic, and it was from this base that he launched himself on the professional road in 1974.

He chose as his trainer a moon-faced man whose lackadaisical manner and establishment connections fitted the uneven relation between his ambitions and his insouciant work ethic. Willie Lock enjoyed a repu-tation for letting boxers go their own way. If you worked hard, wonderful. If you didn't – like several of his big white Afrikaners – so be it. However, his tight connections within the hierarchy of the game gave him an advantage over other trainers. Some white boxers spoke of being steered in his direction when they inquired at the Boxing Board offices about turning professional, and when fights were close, his white boys tended to get the decision. But Willie had another dimension to his reputation. In 1980 his flyweight Peter Mathebula became the first black South African to win a version of the world title, and even though he forgot to train and was blown away in his maiden defence, his achievement provided Lock with an image as a champion of the black man, which did not always match the reality. I was used to glib racism from white boxing people, but I did not anticipate it from a trainer of black champions. When the Boxing Board's offices moved from central Johannesburg to a site near Soweto, I chatted to Willie and one of his white boxers at a pre-fight function. 'Isn't it amazing, hey?' Willie said, turning to me. 'In Jo'burg these things were packed with kaffirs, but here we're round the corner from Soweto and there's hardly a kaffir around. Much nicer.'

Lock's partnership with Coetzee did wonders for the ambitions of both men. Gerrie arrived from the amateur ranks with sufficient resources of skill, speed, rhythm, reflex and right-handed power to dominate the local professional scene. Lock's connections, combined with the manoeuvrings of Coetzee's manager, Hal Tucker, allowed Coetzee to move quickly into world-title contention. He lifted the white South African title from Mike Schutte in one of the dirtiest fights ever seen in South Africa. Punches were incidental to the main menu of head butts, low blows, eye gouges, rabbit punches, and elbows, feet and knees to the groin. Eventually, after six rounds, Schutte was disqualified. Coetzee then outpointed Knoetze and battered Schutte for twelve rounds in the return fight, shattering both his hands. After months of reconstructive surgery he returned as the Boksburg Bomber with a 'bionic right hand'. Tucker manoeuvred him through the world rankings and by 1977 Gerrie, like Schutte the year before, was seriously mooted as the next challenger for Muhammad Ali. 'I can beat Ali – I'm faster,' Gerrie said. 'Do you know how old Ali is? He's 35. My father is 40. He's almost as old as my father.'

Gerrie's hopes were raised by the sanctions-busting relations between the South African boxing establishment and the WBA – ties cemented in the dark days of apartheid at a time when the rival World Boxing Council implemented the sporting boycott. The money that flowed from South Africa into the WBA's coffers, and into the pockets of its power brokers, did the job. The South African Boxing Board president, Judge H.W.O. Kloppers, became WBA president while two other white South Africans took up strategic executive positions, which meant that South African boxers had no trouble getting WBA world-title fights. The real world heavyweight champion was Larry Holmes, but the WBA set up an eliminator series to find its own, post-Ali champion. Tate beat Knoetze in one leg, while Gerrie travelled to Monte Carlo to knock out Leon Spinks in one round in the other. Then in October 1979, 78,000 people squeezed into the Loftus Versveld rugby stadium in Pretoria to watch Gerrie run out of puff and lose on points over fifteen rounds to Tate. A year later he secured a shot against Tate's conqueror Mike Weaver, but this time Gerrie's condition was even less impressive. He pounded Weaver, but could not sustain the effort and, utterly exhausted, was knocked out in the thirteenth.

He relocated to the United States where he was taken over by former Capetonian Cedric Kushner, until Gerrie spotted another gap in the market, dropping Cedric to sign up with Don King. Kushner was enraged. 'I've met a lot of devious shits in boxing, but none of them can match Gerrie,' he once told me. Coetzee quickly worked out how to play King's game – making anti-apartheid noises, deriding his white fans and then announcing he was voting a liberal 'no' in the government's 1983 constitutional referendum – and his presence went unprotested.

After several respectable results against world-class opponents he was rewarded with a third WBA world-title shot, this time against Weaver's conqueror Michael Dokes – a cokehead, who snorted and smoked a size-able chunk of his earnings. Gerrie furthered his cause by employing the American trainer Jackie McCoy to take over his preparations, with Willie Lock relegated to a supporting role. He was fitter and sharper than for any fight before or after. In the finest performance of his long career he survived a bad cut to outbox Dokes, stopping him in the tenth round to take the WBA world title. It was a big moment for white South Africa and a huge moment for South African boxing. The next plan was to take on Larry Holmes for the undisputed title, but the financial backing evaporated and the fight was cancelled. He would never have beaten Larry – he knew that: 'To be honest, Gav, I don't think I could've pulled it off,' Gerrie admitted to me years later. But he was dispirited about the cancellation because he lost a potential fortune, and returned home disillusioned to get on with the trucking business he'd recently acquired.

King eventually put Gerrie in with another of his fighters, Greg Page, in Sun City in December 1984 – with the Don taking a handsome cut from the boycott-busting venture. Page came from a generation of fat American heavies who thrived in the 1980s before weight machines, creatine, steroids and growth hormone produced the harder, bigger breed of today. Hailing from Louisville, Kentucky he drew comparisons with that town's previous big man, Muhammad Ali, partly because of this shared heritage but also because of a superficial stylistic resemblance. Ali announced that the talented Page was set to become the 'next great heavyweight' but his successor was a stranger to the rigours of training and lost both fights in the year prior to challenging Coetzee. Gerrie was in even worse shape. The fight came more than fourteen months after his title-winning effort, and a bout of venereal disease and renewed pain in his hands added to his state of depression. Shortly before the fight he took aspirin as a painkiller, without realizing it might slow him down and that it would encourage bleeding if he was cut. He was also not helped by the absence of Jackie McCoy. Nothing worked out. 'I had a sense that I wasn't going to beat Page,' Gerrie later told me. 'Everything went wrong and I wasn't in my best shape. On the way to Sun City I had a stiff brandy and Coke to settle me because I sensed this was the end of my reign. I was *gatvol* with boxing after so many disappointments.'

It was my first ever visit to Sun City and not one I advertised widely. In lefty circles Sun City was viewed as the belly of the beast – a glittering grand apartheid magnet designed for weakening the international sporting and cultural boycott. Built in a rural corner of the nominally independent 'homeland' of Bophuthats-wana, it was the premier tourist and gambling attraction in the Sun International galaxy, and was at the peak of its powers, with Frank Sinatra, Queen, Elton John, Chick Corea, Rod Stewart and Linda Ronstadt* all doing service along with some of the world's best golfers and boxers. Sun International was headed by Sol Kerzner, a stumpy, thick-set former boxer with a pugnacious manner. Sol loved fighting and was not averse to using his fists to get his way, but he was also a brilliant business visionary. The government's Calvinist roots prevented gambling from taking official root in the rest of South Africa but, under the guise of independence, they gave the nod and the wink to this lucrative homeland pastime. The details of Sun City's relation with the corrupt 'Bop' president Lucas Mangope remain obscure, but Mangope's government certainly benefited handsomely from its revenues. The South African government also scored and Kerzner made sure they were perpetually on side, wooing them and being wooed in return. Cabinet ministers were frequent beneficiaries of his hospitality – often taking up ringside seats at the big fights. Kerzner knew how to play them** and his role went beyond personal hospitality. By playing host to international stars, as well as to South African-funded 'fact finding' missions by the likes of Tory Monday Club MPs and American cold warriors, he was fulfilling a vital role in oiling the government's international public relations drive.

*Soon after I arrived at the *Rand Daily Mail* the newsroom experienced a wave of collective excitement when one of the photographers 'got off' with a major Californian popstar at Sun City, and returned with tales of coke-fuelled shags with her.

**Kerzner would later repeat the trick, with even more panache, by successfully wooing the ANC's Thabo Mbeki with parties, hospitality and who knows what else.

Sun City is a huge complex of hotels, motel clusters, casinos, golf courses and leisure complexes, set on hundreds of acres of rolling hills in the middle of the veld. I later became intrigued by the leering looks on the faces of the high rollers and the soft-porn punters as they scurried excitedly through the massive displays of Rider Haggard-ish high kitsch, with its pretend game lodges and rock art murals. I also came to appreciate its side-show attractions, like its overstocked crocodile farm which housed an 18-foot monster. But I was rather less cavalier on this maiden visit. The prospect of watching Gerrie lose his title was too enticing to miss but if I mentioned it at all it was along truth-bending lines – 'I'm helping with *Rand Daily Mail* coverage'. This fell within the margins of acceptability – a status I still regarded as worthy of cultivation.

We were hardly out of the Sun City parking lot when Wayne started working the crowd. I was introduced to Willie Toweel, standing outside the foyer with his gauche young charge Brian Mitchell. 'I'm betting on Aladin Stevens to beat you,' Wayne said, adding that he held no hope for Willie's other pretender Piet Crous who was challenging for the WBA world cruiserweight title. Willie smiled politely, Brian shifted his weight and said nothing and we wandered over to the swimming pool where Wayne ordered cocktails before bumping into Willie Lock. 'I'm betting on Gerrie to get knocked out,' he announced. Willie stormed off. An hour later, as we made our way to the arena, we came across a muscular Mediterranean man who looked vaguely familiar. 'Gavin, meet my *chommie*, Stelios,' Wayne said, and then it clicked: Stelios Orfano, leader of a gang called the Bouncers, out on bail, accused of murdering a man in a gay club by shooting him at point blank range. When we walked on Wayne explained: 'That guy he shot got what was coming. I'll give Stelios and them all the help they need. They're my closest pals.'*

Wayne was indignant when we entered the auditorium. We'd been placed a few rows from ringside, but he soon remedied the situation – finding us two plum press seats, one for him and the other shared by Harold Volbrecht and me. We watched Brian Mitchell out-pointing Aladin Stevens, Piet Crous winning the WBA world title, and finally it was Gerrie's turn, by which stage I was in a state of heightened excitement, enhanced by the jousting between Volbrecht, squeezed next to me, and Wayne on the other side. 'Gerrie's got no chance,' Wayne announced during the interminable renditions of three 'national' anthems. 'I phoned Angelo Dundee and he confirmed it.' Harold feigned indignation. 'How can you say that? Gerrie's a South African, and anyway, Page's got tits like a lady.' And so it went, with Wayne saying, 'What did I tell you, what did I tell you?' whenever Page registered, and Harold saying, 'Watch his tits.'

Coetzee moved slowly, throwing hopeful right-hand leads, but his problems really set in immediately after the bell to begin the second round. Lock was so absorbed that he failed to register the start of the new round, and continued to wipe away in the manner of an overindulgent parent giving a final spit-wash to a five-year-old when the school bell has already rung. Greg Page seized the moment by sprinting across the ring to deliver a heavy left and right to the head. Gerrie, still trying to rise from his stool, roared back, but

---

*Stelios jumped bail and headed for Cyprus. Wayne later told me he made it possible.

he'd clearly been hurt. He was the victim of a second error at the end of the sixth, this time with the referee at fault. When the bell tolled Gerrie turned and Page continued punching, dropping Coetzee. A more inspired trainer would have leapt into the ring, demanding disqualification, but Lock floundered and Page returned to his corner and proceeded to drop Coetzee again at the start of the seventh.

Gerrie was bouncing around purposefully in the eighth, and things were improving until he was confronted with the negligence of yet another player, the chief timekeeper Blackie Swart. The three-minute mark to end the round came and went with Blackie so absorbed in the action that he forgot what he was there for. 'Shit, this is a long round,' Harold said to us as Coetzee took charge. Page's trainer leapt up and screamed at Swart to ring the bell, at which point Greg sprang to life and registered with the biggest punches of his career. A heavy right to the head and pair of crisp combinations shook Gerrie, and then came a mighty left hook to the jaw, which landed flush and dropped the now-exhausted Gerrie for the count. Greg leapt into the air, his breasts following him down.* The time was 3 minutes 50 seconds – 50 seconds too long. 'We're feeling sick about everything concerning this fight,' said Lock. 'We've got a lot of thinking to do.'

The next time I saw Gerrie I had taken a job as Supreme Court correspondent for *Business Day* while

---

*Page was a dismal champion, losing his title in his first defence to another fatty, Tony Tubbs, who lost his first defence against flabby Tim Witherspoon – a boxer previously beaten by Larry Holmes. Page continued boxing for seventeen more years, until, aged 41, he was battered into a coma for a $1,500 purse.

moonlighting for a European news agency and for a new paper, the *Weekly Mail*. One of my first *Weekly Mail* assignments involved Gerrie's return to the ring in 1985. The opponent chosen to jump-start his title-regaining mission was the black Texan James 'Quick' Tillis – a former world-title challenger talented enough to hold Mike Tyson to a close decision, but not quite enough to beat the best. Coetzee was just another meal ticket, and Tillis didn't give a damn about where his meals were served.

Now and then boycott-breaking entertainers muttered dark thoughts about the system they were helping to support, but most kept their mouths shut. A wide range of singing stars, from Percy Sledge to Ray Charles and George Benson to Janis Ian, happily broke the boycott without a peep of protest, but a few, like Eartha Kitt and Jimmy Cliff, made their resentment known. So it was with the boxers. A month before Tillis's arrival, I watched Muhammad Qawi knock out Piet Crous for the WBA cruiserweight title. When it was done he sneered at his Sun City hosts, telling them he only came because the WBA gave him an ultimatum and would never return until apartheid was abolished: 'The conditions which blacks live in and the type of work they do makes me feel ashamed and depressed,' he said. 'I'm disgusted. I'm convinced that blacks in this country are repressed and not given the same treatment as whites.' Tillis had no such qualms and would return twice more, forever grateful. From the vantage point of his Johannesburg hotel he said he 'didn't notice any discrimination' and instead declared South African boxing 'free of apartheid'. It was the stuff the white establishment loved to hear but black boxing fans viewed it from a different angle. They saw the white-controlled power structure in South African boxing as a reflection of their position in society more generally. They held white boxers to be representatives of apartheid and saw their black opponents, even boycott-busters, in a gilded light. So when Tillis visited Soweto to watch a football game, he was introduced as 'the guy who's going to beat the white man's hero'. The crowd duly gave him a hero's welcome. Gerrie might have been different from the ex-riot cop Kallie Knoetze but that was not the point. He was the white man's hero and therefore the enemy.

My own passion for the sport took on similar colours. The struggle itself was different. The scale of injustice and cruelty was so vast that I had to separate it from the realm of perpetual outrage. I was also too deeply involved, too caught up in factional fights, organizational wranglings and intricacies of planning to feel a constant gushing flow of emotion. Now and then I would get riled on learning of an atrocity committed by the state, or I'd feel a wave of hatred for a particular cabinet minister or cop, or I'd glean some satisfaction from a meeting well organized or a spy uncovered or some successful plotting or a well-bombed military target, but this was always tempered by responsibility and calculation. How will this idea contribute to that tactic, and this strategy? Boxing allowed an outlet that was more contained and less restrained. Racist decisions, which blocked the progress of black boxers, hardly matched torture, assassination and community massacres on the scale of injustice, but they brought the bile to my mouth unmitigated by intellectual analysis. I was outraged by the behaviour of the board and its state-appointed officials and felt an intensity of emotion I stifled when it came to the struggle, with heroes and enemies slotted into political categories. I was for the black boxers and against the whites: a bit of a racist, in fact.

Only 3,000 of the 20,000 who arrived to watch the Coetzee–Tillis fight at Ellis Park were black, but they made their presence felt. When the inter-round women arrived carrying the orange, white and blue white South African flag, none cheered, and when *Die Stem* was played, they stayed silent, but when Tillis arrived, they roared. The whites cheered and sang heartily for Gerrie. They whistled for the white inter-round lady and remained silent for the black one and some made their feelings known when the action started in the ring. 'Drop your arm, you kaffir,' a man behind me with a face of hate screamed. Later, from another section, I heard: 'Hey, ref, the fucking Af-boy is holding.' They went home well satisfied. Gerrie picked up an easy points win.

This victory, and the Boxing Board's international connections, were enough to return Gerrie to the WBA's number-one slot. All he had to do was win a final eliminator against Britain's Frank Bruno in London. As a Thatcher supporter, who would later threaten to leave Britain if Labour came to power, Frank had no issue with fighting white South Africans. Apartheid was not his problem. Gerrie, however, made it clear from the start that it was a significant part of his problem. He drew incredulous giggles when announcing, 'I call a spade a spade,' and sympathetic sighs when he added that this particular spade was the 'ugly' political system he lived under. Gerrie's equanimity made the task of the ANC-aligned South African Non-Racial Olympic Committee that much harder when they campaigned to get the fight stopped, and they had to stress that it wasn't personal. 'We have nothing against Coetzee and are not doing this because he is white,' their secretary Chris De Brioglio told me. 'It's just that we're totally against sporting ties with South Africa until the situation is politically normal.' International sport gave whites the impression of normality. Blocking it meant a cost had to be paid for the system they were supporting. Conversely, readmitting South Africa to the world sporting community would be a vital carrot for change. I realized boycotts had to be unilateral to be effective, but I felt sorry for individual boxers – black boxers and self-proclaimed liberals like Gerrie – who were being punished for crimes they did not commit, and anyway I just wanted to see the fight.

Talk of Coetzee's hand troubles, of lethargy in training, and then his weight – 233 pounds (18 more than his best) – hardly inspired hope, but the method of his decline was astonishing. Usually elusive, he seemed to invite the ponderous Frank's right cross. 'He'd have to be a baboon to stand up to that right,' Bruno said afterwards, but then a baboon would have seen it coming. Gerrie hauled himself up and obligingly backed into a corner where Bruno whacked away, ending the fight with a hook that sent Gerrie halfway out of the ring where he lay suspended, neck hanging dramatically over the lower rope. Bruno kissed him. 'They love you, Frank,' said Harry Carpenter. 'I'm not that way inclined, but I 'ope they love me in a different way,' he replied. 'There'd 'ave to be six baboons in there to beat me tonight.' He paused to reassess: 'I'm sorry. I'm sounding a bit aggressive. I think I'll go for a run. I need to sweat a bit.' He jogged over to Gerrie's changing room. 'I'm sorry to have disgraced you in front of your wife and children, but that's cricket, old sport,' said Frank. Gerrie did not seem too upset. In fact, he was smiling.

He retired and for the next few years was largely forgotten while the search for the next great white hope resumed with a series of false starts* until, finally, something approaching the real thing materialized. Police sergeant Pierre Coetzer broke through after twice climbing off the canvas to knock out security police- man Bennie Knoetze for the national title. He then signed up with the loser's trainer, Alan Toweel. 'Pierre could beat all of them if only it wasn't for his skin,' Alan said. 'It's so sad because I just breathe on him and he bleeds.' Pierre was utterly dedicated, with immense courage, but his tissue-paper skin and his lack of innate flair limited his potential. He was an innocent, inside and outside the ring, compared with the sly Gerrie. He was polite to everyone although in the exclusive com- pany of white people he was not beyond making little jokes about 'coolies', and he was not averse to the occasional bout of temper. In one incident he was alleged to have assaulted a man with 'blunt objects' after his Porsche was accidentally damaged. He was good at following instructions – sometimes too good. When fighting in Britain he was instructed to under- play his police connections if the subject arose, and took his public relations lesson so much to heart that when asked to comment on his victory salvo, he told

---

*The enormously powerful Jimmy Abbott blew away Kallie Knoetze and then ate his way past 320 pounds, after which he ventured into wrestling and debt collecting and became a stalwart for the neo-Nazi AWB, before becoming a born-again Christian. He was out-speeded by the tenacious Robbie Williams, who, after proving to be too small, gassed himself and his children to death. Next came Kallie's brother, the security police sergeant Bennie Knoetze, who lacked the power and chin for the big time.

his British television audience: 'I just wanna say I'm not really a policeman, but just a police gym instructor, which is different actually.' In 1987 I watched Pierre avenge an earlier defeat against an American, Bernard Benton. A few seconds after Pierre's final hook, we heard an explosion outside. When we reached the carpark, the cops told us that a limpet mine had exploded under a BMW. My girlfriend's car was a few metres away and she was told she couldn't remove it. 'There might be one under your car too.' There were no more bombs, but soon after the ANC claimed responsibility. It was the closest I came to being wiped out by my own side.

Pierre's rival was the new star of the Willie Lock stable, Johnny du Plooy – promoted by Rodney Berman as the premier attraction of South African boxing, with his own theme song (a variation of *Johnny B. Goode*) and exuberant predictions of glory. A street fighter with a fearsome reputation, he came from a background where self-discipline was completely alien. His father, Dup, wanted to relive his youth through his lad, and Johnny liked to hang out with AWB stalwarts, but as one of his friends put it to me: 'He only really gets drunk with them. He's too lazy to get active.' For Berman this was a perpetual nightmare. To mention one example he offered me: 'When we were in America, Johnny, his father and Willie were in a car, and I asked them to give a lift to two black boxers, but no, they told me, "We've got no room for kaffirs." They were impossible.' Du Plooy smoked a pack a day, was regularly drunk and frequently in court – for offences ranging from driving at 230km/h to assault and attempted murder. Promoter Cedric Kushner decided the only solution was to place him under the control of one of

America's leading trainers, Lou Duva, but Lou couldn't handle him. 'When Cedric first showed him to me, I said, Ced, this guy's going to take it all – he has more natural ability than Holyfield,' he told me. 'But when you have outside interference on the home front it can never do a fighter any good. What a nightmare.' Eventually Berman agreed to put Johnny in with Pierre, who climbed off the floor to knock him out in the second round. Pierre became the IBF's number one contender, only to be low-blowed out of a final eliminator to Riddick Bowe, then rabbit-punched and bludgeoned out of another eliminator against Frank Bruno, and finally beaten to a pulp by George Foreman, after which he returned to police service, and re-emerged as one of Nelson Mandela's elite bodyguards.

While all this was happening Gerrie Coetzee was slipping from view, occasionally popping up in the courts and newspaper headlines. For instance, one of his trucking-business clients won a court interdict against Coetzee after it was found he'd sent one of his 'boys' to threaten the man that his wife would be raped unless he paid up immediately. Now and then I'd chat to Gerrie at ringside or hear about his movements. In 1988, for example, I was detained at police head-quarters, John Vorster Square. Two younger security cops entered. 'I hear you like boxing,' said one. 'D'you know Gerrie? *Ja*, well, he's family, sort of. I'm the son-in-law of his manager, Hal Tucker. I'll send Gerrie your regards. He'll be interested you're here. I'll tell him *all* about you.'

But I only really came to know him when he decided on a new venture as a boxing manager and promoter. Gerrie was impressed with my *Sunday Times* portrayal of one of his young protégés, Johnson Tshuma, as a champion of the future. He began to court me, phoning regularly to tell me how much he was doing for his black boxers. 'You know, Gav, I've just bought Johnson a brand new car out of my own money because of his progress,' he said. I admired his apparent humility and was flattered by his overtures to me, which bordered on the obsequious. I grew to like him, and we developed an easy repartee along the lines of: 'Gerrie, you're looking sharp – been working out?'

'Gav, if I didn't know better, I would think you was making a pass at me.'

There was one occasion in particular when he impressed me. Gerrie decided to put the novice Tshuma in with the country's big-hitting national middleweight champion Gerhard Botes. He invited me to join him in the corner and kept asking for advice. In the early rounds it was all Tshuma, but Botes came back and hurt Tshuma. 'Gav, man, tell me, should I throw in the towel?' Gerrie asked. I was flattered. 'No, give him another round or two' – which Gerrie did, until Botes battered his man to defeat.

By stressing his role in developing black boxers Gerrie secured a meeting with Nelson Mandela. He was told beforehand that the ANC leader liked to be called by his clan name, Madiba, and tried to remember this. 'Thank you so much, *Madina*,' Gerrie said after Mandela had complimented him. 'You know, Madina, if you wasn't in prison all that time, you could have been the first South African world heavyweight champion. You're a great man and a great leader, Madina, and I'm glad I never had to fight you.' Despite the naked opportunism behind this gauche gesture, I was touched. Here was a strong man from Boksburg, whose white community rated as among the most racist in South Africa, sucking up to the ANC leader. I liked the symbolism and thought better of Gerrie for it.

Soon after, Gerrie phoned me to announce his comeback. 'I know guys like George Foreman and Larry Holmes were all-time greats and let's be straight, hey, I wasn't,' he said. 'But there's lots of money to be made, especially if I could get a fight with them. I'm not going out to kick young arses but I'm 37 and these old guys are six or seven years older than me so I'd have a chance – and with me being a former world champion I'll be a big drawcard and that's what South African boxing really needs.'

A week later he phoned me again: 'I hear your car just got stolen and wasn't insured,' he said. 'How would you like a brand new car?'

'I'm not thinking of buying one right now,' I stalled, wondering how he knew this.

'No-no, Gav. I'm proposing *I* buy *you* a new one in return for some favours. I want you to agree to write a story about me or my boxers every week in the *Sunday Times*. Don't mention it to anyone – it will just be a deal between me and you, OK?'

I fell silent for a few seconds. Bribery wasn't new to me – I once refused a security police offer to release me from detention in exchange for information – but never from a putative friend or colleague. I was a bit shocked.

'So are we on, hey, Gav?'

'Gerrie, I don't take bribes. I don't want to discuss it further.'

'Gav, that wasn't the answer I was looking for. What would you do if, say, a new car arrived at your front door as a present to your wife, hey?'

'Then, Gerrie, I would have to return it to you. I don't want to discuss this further.'

'Gav, you're making a big mistake. A new car. You drove a Toyota, no?'

Another possibility occurred to me: that the bribe was a prelude to blackmail. I had several enemies in boxing – managers I'd accused of racism, referees I'd accused of bias, Boxing Board officials whose dealings I'd questioned. I'd received tip-offs that a trainer close to Gerrie 'absolutely hates you and is out to get you'. At one boxing event I'd seen him pointing me out to two of his henchmen, who attempted to follow me as I left. I also recalled that this was not the first time the Coetzee camp had been involved in this kind of thing. Several years earlier, Gerrie's manager, Hal Tucker, bribed one of my predecessors at the *Sunday Times*, and exposed this when the reporter was unwilling to continue delivering. The reporter was fired and frozen out of journalism. 'Gerrie,' I said, 'I don't want to discuss this further. Goodbye.' I immediately informed my editor and left it at that but a week later I received another phone call, this time at my *Weekly Mail* desk. 'Gav, it's Gerrie. When do we start with that offer I made you? You know, the new car?'

'Gerrie, I thought I made it clear, I don't take bribes,' I said, slamming down the phone. But Gerrie continued to phone me regularly as if nothing had happened, even though I became curt with him and was reluctant to take up his story ideas or to believe his claims.

In October 1992 I spent a fortnight in London covering the Coetzer–Bruno fight. When I interviewed Bruno he asked me if I ever saw Gerrie Coetzee. I assured him this was a regular pleasure. 'Huh, huh, huh,' he said. 'Send him my regards, won't you. Me and Gerrie got on very well. He was good to me. Huh, huh, huh.' Later he reminded me: 'Send my best to Gerrie, remember. Huh, huh, huh.' Back in Johannesburg I relayed the message: 'Bruno seemed very keen that I should send you his best wishes. He really seemed to like you.' Gerrie smiled enigmatically and responded in his high monotone: '*Ja* man, Gav, I mean you could say he had reason to. You know, all my losses, except that one, I felt inside me were going to happen, but Bruno was different. I knew I could beat him. I still say Bruno got lucky against me, in a way.' At this point another reporter joined us, and Gerrie clammed up. 'So how did Bruno get lucky?' I asked. 'Ag, Gav, let's just say something came up that meant I couldn't win.' And then a little quiet aside, 'I'll tell you about it some other time, hey.'

We never did get around to discussing it, but some time later a highly respected London-based journalist gave me a sense of what Gerrie had been referring to. 'Gerrie told me he'd taken a dive. He gave me all the details – the money involved and everything. He was very specific and I believed him,' he said. A few years later Gerrie's heavyweight protégé, Frans Botha, told me a similar tale. 'He was very proud of it,' said Botha. 'He told me he hurt his hand, so he decided to take a dive. He got a brother to bet on him losing in the first round – a huge amount he said. He told me he was laughing in the changing room afterwards. He thought it was a big joke.'

Despite all this I retained a grudging respect for Gerrie's treatment of his black boxers until I discovered that here too reality and appearance parted company. Gerrie's welterweight Luvuya Kakaza told of being locked up by Gerrie in a concrete room for several hours after a minor financial dispute. Three of his black boxers complained of being threatened or assaulted, while even his prize catch Johnson Tshuma said Gerrie was too volatile to endure. 'Eventually I said, Gerrie, I can no longer work with you. You could never tell what kind of a person you were dealing with because he'd suddenly change his mood and he kept breaking his promises. I was supposed to get sponsorship money direct, but I found he was taking half for himself. He told the press about buying me that new car, but what he really offered was secondhand and had just been crashed.'* Jan Bergman, his world-rated light welterweight, told me: 'He took me and Bokkie' – Bergman's trainer – 'and Frans Botha to America, but he never did what he said. We struggled to find food so we complained to his accountant, who complained to Gerrie, who then punched the accountant in the stomach and threatened us. Bokkie pulled a knife and we were jumping about screaming at him, so he backed off. He once threatened Frans, who said to him: "You hit me, I'll hit you," so he left Frans alone.'** Botha told me he once saw Gerrie hitting his wife, and that Gerrie later attacked him 'and we had a helluva fight', which left him lying there, covered in blood'.

Gerrie had a couple of comeback wins, retired again but returned to action in 1997 and had his final fight at the age of 42 against the 37-year-old former world middleweight champion Iran Barkley in Hollywood. Weighing a bulbous 253 pounds he stumbled around

*Tshuma fulfilled his potential after leaving Gerrie, winning the national and Commonwealth middleweight titles. He was training for a world-title fight in the year 2000 when he heard that he was one of a batch of twenty-seven boxers to test HIV positive, and lost his licence.
**Bergman left Gerrie, joined Rodney Berman and twice fought for versions of the world light welterweight title, getting stopped both times before winning the low-rent WBU welterweight title.

the ring, frequently hugging his equally grotesque opponent, prompting the television commentator Al Bernstein to quip: 'I would say something about what's going on in the ring, if I could think of something to say.' A reporter from a local paper found the words, describing the encounter as one between a boxer with the 'grace of a log' and another with the 'reflexes of a tomato'. Coetzee absorbed a ponderous hook in the tenth round and collapsed into the ropes. The referee stopped the fight but once more Gerrie left laughing – having secured a generous pension from the WBA in exchange for his retirement. Soon after he shot a man in Johannesburg, following an 'altercation'. The police said the man pointed a gun at Gerrie, who then pulled his own heat and blasted him one in the leg. The man was rushed to hospital. Gerrie returned to America.

The vain search for a Great White Hope continued in the guise of Gerrie's protégé Frans Botha* but it is

*Botha joined Gerrie in America after a sloppy professional start (he remained unbeaten only by virtue of two dubious decisions and one horrendous one – Wally Snowball doing duty once again). He then abandoned Gerrie and defected to Don King, who promoted him as the White Buffalo. When I asked King why he was punting Botha, he explained, 'You gotta give the white man a chance.' King paid the IBF boss to secure him a shot at their vacant world title, which Frans won on another dubious decision, but he was stripped of his title because of steroid abuse, then battered to defeat by Michael Moorer and flattened by Mike Tyson. He still became the first South African ever to fight for the undisputed world heavyweight title when he challenged Lennox Lewis in London in April 2000. Frans, who'd been trained, managed and promoted by black men for most of his career, confided in me about his mission: 'I hope I can persuade more white heavyweights into coming out. I would like to have more friends out there – white friends – and I hope I can be a role model for the white heavyweights.' Lewis, entering the ring to Bob Marley's 'We're gonna chase those crazy baldheads out of town', crushed him in two rounds.

probably more fitting to close with a story of black South African hope. Not the Great Black Hope – he has yet to arrive – but rather the tenuous thread of hope boxing can provide for poor men who can fight, like Jacob Mofokeng.

I'll pick up his story in 1984, the year Gerrie lost his world title and the year Jacob decided he'd taken enough beatings from a huge and brutal Free State farmer on a remote cattle farm a few miles from the little town of Bethlehem. 'That Boer was so bad,' he said with a lugubrious smile and a shake of his head. 'Shew! He was punching us farm workers or whipping us with the *sjambok*, including my dad and me. Often. He wouldn't let me go to school 'cause I had to work from morning to night from when I was a little child, milking cows and working in the garden. We were paid five Rand a month and he didn't give us food, so with me and two brothers and a sister and my parents to feed, we were often hungry.' Jacob existed in a state of indentured labour not far removed from slavery, and he knew that if he ran his parents might suffer, but shortly before his nineteenth birthday he finally decided he could take it no more. 'I didn't even tell my father. I just ran away for Johannesburg where I thought nobody could hurt me.' After several years of odd jobs he met Elias Tshabalala, a former Free State boxer, and realized that taking punches for pay was a soft substitute for the *sjambok*. 'I thought, I've got no education, no skills, no prospects, but I'm big and strong, so why not have a go at this boxing business?' Elias soon had him working with his own light heavyweight brothers, Ginger and Joseph, and was impressed. 'He was so raw but I thought he had the body and natural talent to make a go of it, so I started teaching him from scratch.' Ginger was later murdered in a robbery in Johannesburg's city centre while journeyman Joseph was killed in an industrial accident, but Elias remained with Jacob throughout his career.

And what a career it turned out to be. He lost five of his first ten fights on knockouts until it occurred to his trainers that a broad-shouldered 6 foot 2 body should not be squeezed into the light heavyweight limit. He won seventeen of his next eighteen, lifting the South African cruiserweight title, travelling to America to win the WBU 'world' title, and then in 1999 winning the South African heavyweight title. He was stripped of this title because of a positive stimulants test, but was offered a second chance in the year 2000. Jacob was up against a man who resembled that Free State farmer of old, the 245-pound Anton Nel. He knocked him cold in the second round – making him not only the first-ever black South African heavyweight champion, but also the first to win it from a white man.

All thought of Bethlehem evaporated. 'I don't want to return there because I've done well for myself, so I have no need for revenge,' he said. 'You see, I suffered a lot in the past but I must look to the future now.' When I last spoke to him he was still working full-time as a delivery man and renting a small flat in the slum zone of Joubert Park. 'It's very dangerous, with lots of Nigerian drugs gangs,' he said. 'I'd like to move to a nice area but I don't have the money. I'd love to improve my own education, but I've got my three sons and my parents to support and my brothers and sisters to help at school. I didn't want to become a boxer to make a lot of money – just enough to put a little away – and I want people to remember that Jacob Mofokeng was around.' He was hoping for one last shot at the big

time but it was a hope too far. After a long illness he
was rushed to hospital in 2001, suffering from severe
broncho-pneumonia in his left lung and a swollen
heart. He never boxed again.

For the sake of symmetry, here's a postscript about the
man who introduced me to Gerrie and secured my
return to the world of boxing: Diamond Wayne. The
last time I'd seen him was May 1986, a few days after I
returned from a six-week United Nations-sponsored
fund-raising trip to the United States, at a time I was
living incognito with my friend Maxine. One afternoon
he turned up at our flat. I had no idea how he managed
to find my address, and he skipped over the question
when asked. He made cursory conversation with me
before homing in on Maxine, asking pointed questions
about who slept where. Maxine, whose antenna was
always well tuned, said after he left: 'Don't trust him.
He has some other agenda. Are you sure he's not an
informer?'

After that I dropped him, but now and then news
filtered through – like when he hit the South African
headlines for 'seducing' the wife of a prominent
businessman and 'abducting' her to the Middle East
before 'abandoning' her. Then one afternoon in 1994,
in London, my wife Pat handed me the phone. 'It's
that old boxing friend of yours,' she said whispering
his name, and I whispered, 'Oh fuck,' but in truth I
was pleased because I knew Wayne would offer the
unexpected, and besides I wanted some answers.

I met him at a hotel in Bloomsbury where he
bounced up with his new, blonde, submissive wife, his
appearance still puckish despite a receding hairline
and paunch. 'How do you like this, hey, Gav?' he

began, sweeping the hotel lobby with his outstretched hand as a way of showing me he had arrived. And before I could answer, he added: '*Ja*, we flew first class. I only fly first class. How about you?' I informed him I always turned right on boarding, and he shook his head with mock pity. I asked him how he could afford first class and a new house in Hampshire. 'Gems, man. Diamonds. I smuggle them in and out, and take a cut.' In no time he was on to the story of how he 'abducted' the businessman's wife. 'I'd been smuggling gems out of the country for him but when I went to get my money he didn't want to pay, so I warned him not to mess with me. I only seduced his wife because he hadn't paid me my cut, and then I took her out of the country until he agreed to pay, and he paid OK, and then I dumped her.' He looked at his wife, who gave an obligatory smile. 'He had it coming, man, and I had a really great time.'

He took me to a nearby pizzeria where he boasted of his friendships with some of South Africa's most notorious thugs, but I was after something else. 'Tell me: did the security police ever ask you to spy on me?' I expected indignation but instead he beamed. '*Ja*, they asked me to go to your flat and find out all I could, so of course I did it, but I didn't really give them much that was hugely important. I mean, you weren't up to much, were you? There wasn't anything important to give, hey, Gav?' I deflected the question and diverted talk into a trainspotter's dispute about Sonny Liston's opponents in the 1960s. 'Let's bet on it. Fifty pounds,' Wayne said and dragged me off to a local sports bookshop, where Liston's record was found. He effected astonishment on discovering I was right. 'Ag, Gav, I just don't have it on me in cash,' he said. 'I'll phone and you can tell me where to send the cheque.' I wasn't about to tell him to drop it – not after he had confirmed my suspicions about spying on me (and I later learnt that Wayne's report had been passed on to a military hit squad, who attempted to assassinate me in 1989) – so I agreed.

Wayne phoned three days later. 'Gav, about that bet, give me your bank account number and I'll deposit it.' Instead I gave him the address of some friends, suggesting he post a cheque. Wayne pressed me over and over again for my banking details, trying several more times over the next few days, but eventually he gave up and disappeared from my life. The only mention I had of him came when I bumped into one of his former boxing friends and told him the story. '*Juss*, if I was in your boots, I wouldn't give him nothing, 'specially not my bank details,' he said. 'That guy has dangerous *chommies*, and he's mad. Once when I walked into his flat I found him trying to throw his chick over the balcony. She'd be dead today if I hadn't walked in.'

We moved to a new flat with an unlisted phone number, but a few years on he found me again, and his calls became a regular intrusion. When not suggesting new bets, he boasted of his fighting prowess inside and outside the ring. Late one night after a boxing match in Brighton, in England, I mentioned this to his former pal Harold Volbrecht, who burst out laughing. 'He was always telling me what a star he was, but then he came to my gym and he was useless,' Harold retorted. 'I couldn't do a thing with him. He was too scared.'

The next time Wayne phoned, he reminded me of his days as an amateur star. 'Harold told me you were useless,' I said, hoping this would end his calls. But Wayne's huge ego proved more fragile than anticipated. 'What did he say? What did he say?' he asked when he had calmed a little. When I repeated it, he announced: 'I'm gonna send my friend Nolan to deal with him because Harold's a coward and he'll shit off for Nolan.' Nolan was another of his Johannesburg connections, but I thought it was childish bluster, and forgot it. Wayne tried reaching me eighteen times over the next week, until Pat finally handed over the phone. 'Gav, it's me. Nolan went to see Harold, and Harold shat himself,' he began. 'Nolan told him that if he ever says any shit about me again, he's a dead man, because no-one says shit about me and lives. Harold was on his knees. He swore to Nolan he said nothing bad about me. He told Nolan that it was *you* who said I was useless. That's what Nolan said, pal. Was it you?' I assured Wayne on this point and then phoned Harold, feeling guilty that I hadn't warned him. 'No apologies are in order, my friend,' said Harold. 'He *was* fuckin' useless, but let me tell you, nobody came to threaten me, and anyway, you know me, the street's my home when it comes to fighting. So don't worry, pal, I can take care of myself, and if anyone wants to make a point of it, I carry a 9mm gat and I'll stick that between his eyes and see what he thinks.'

Diamond Wayne, smuggler and spy, phoned once more. I asked him for *his* number and address – 'just for my records' – and he became evasive, saying he had to rush off. It was the last I heard of him.

4

THREE MEN DOWN

Doornfontein, Johannesburg, July 1985. 'Ever been to Sun City?' the security police warrant officer asks as he whips the Ford Granada up to 170km/h. His question comes in response to my own nervous query: 'Excuse me, but, um, where are you taking me?' His snarling sidekick offers no more than, 'You'll find out soon enough, pal, soon enough,' but the warrant officer is in a good mood. He looks at me while the needle settles on the 180km/h mark, wanting a response to his Sun City query. I nod and give up a weak half smile for a half joke. Three days earlier I'd driven to Sun City to watch the 'golden boy' of South African boxing, Brian Baronet, climb off the canvas to knock out a Puerto Rican contender, and I'd interviewed him afterwards, pressing him on when he was going to fight the hero of Soweto, Arthur 'the Fighting Prince' Mayisela, so Sun City was fresh in my consciousness. But this is another Sun City – their name for Johannesburg Prison.

It's mid-winter, the last day of July, and I've just been detained at the Doornfontein Catholic cathedral. There were forty people present at our meeting but the only other detainee was Joy Harnden, a young woman we know is a security police spy. So they must have wanted me in particular, but what for? Are they on to my ANC trail? Sun City provides some reassurance. This is probably just an Emergency Regulations prison detention – one to keep me out of circulation for a while. I'm relieved. It's better than the security police headquarters, John Vorster Square, where the prime purpose of detention is the extraction of information.

Sidekick sergeant jams a tape into the Granada's player. He sings along in a raucous monotone about a homeboy being sent to a foreign land to kill the yellow man – 'Born in the USA!' he yells. Irritation begins to mix with apprehension. This is my man Springsteen, the bloke who donated £100,000 to the British mineworkers' strike, condemned the Cold War and damned Ronald Reagan, singing his anti-war anthem. The sergeant is belting it out now – Khe San, Vietcong, the defeat of the homeboys. Does he understand what he's singing? He certainly knows the words anyway: he leers at me when it's the turn of the 'shadowed *penitentiary*!' and then, with a look that combines malice, satisfaction and utter disdain, he spits out his take on the song's denouement, repeating it for emphasis. 'Nowhere to rrrun, pal, ain't got fuckin' nowhere to hide. Penitentiary here we come. Sun City!'

The Granada screeches into the prison parking garage, my handcuffs are removed, and I ask to go to the toilet. While they hover outside I flush and then force my keys down the sewage pipe – don't want to make their break-in job any easier. I am despatched for finger printing, photographing and some casual questioning by a security police major. With that, they march me to my cell and lock me in for the night. It's 10 p.m. and the lights have been off for a couple of hours, but I finally have time to think and plan.

There are a few things I can be sure of. First, like most elements of South African life, whites have a rather easier ride when it comes to detention without trial. Black detainees are routinely brutalized, often before any questions are asked. For instance, I know that my friend, the Eastern Cape consumer-boycott leader Mkhuseli Jack, has been viciously tortured and assaulted during each of his lengthy spells in security police detention, leaving him with scars all over his body. For whites torture is reserved for those suspected of underground activity – but that is precisely what worries me. I can hold out against a light slapping or throttling but I know torture is something else. I have this theory – this bullshit rationalization really – that Xhosa and Sotho men are better prepared for torture because they have to go through the agony of circumcision in their early twenties, which involves stoically withstanding several weeks of excruciating pain, and I know from my Xhosa friends that nothing compares to it. But me? Not so good on pain, actually. Even a hard body punch takes all the fight out of me. I'm not sure how I'll respond to questions about my comrades when faced with electric shocks to my testicles, or a plastic bag over my head, or being drowned in a bucket of water, or suspended with my hands behind my back and then spun around ('the helicopter', it's called). Or rather I know only too well I'll break quickly, and I know I won't cope with the remorse if that happens.

But I needn't fret. As detentions go, it soon emerges I'm in for an easy time. I'm held in a six-foot-by-eight cell, containing a narrow bed, a basin, a seatless toilet and a metal cupboard. There is no running water and my toilet floods the cell each time I flush. I have no Bible, which is supposed to be one of my rights, and no spare clothes – another right – and like all detainees I'm allowed no books and no visitors. Meals are served in the cell – breakfast at 7.30 (lumpy porridge and bread), lunch at 11 and supper at 3 p.m. (maize rice, bread, a chunk of dubious meat and a vegetable). I'm in solitary confinement, but the next morning I discover I'm allowed out to exercise in a small prison yard for an hour a day with seven other detainees, and for our regulation prison job of cleaning the floors for fifteen minutes a day. We set up a communications system with the common-law prisoners in the cells below ours, sending them cigarettes in exchange for paperback books, which we then hide in our mattresses. If we shout loud enough, when the warders aren't patrolling, we can get in snatches of conversation. They're mainly thieves and robbers and they all say their pre-trial confessions were extracted under torture. After a week a prison warder visits me. 'Listen, my name's Steve and I'm just here doing my national service so as to get out of the army. I don't know what you've done to be here and I don't really care, but I *skeem* you guys are OK. So when lights are out I'll make your lives more tuneful by piping Radio Five into your cells. Sweet. All the best, hey.'

I don't really mind being alone for twenty-three hours – time to think, sleep, daydream, fantasize and do hundreds of push-ups and sit-ups. I spend many hours thinking about Arthur Mayisela and Brian

Baronet and a few hours thinking about politics. I get quite passionate about Tony Sanderson, a Radio Five DJ with a barrow-boy London accent, who praises Sun City, denounces the sporting boycott and supports military conscription. But mostly I fret and fantasize and dream about the women in my life, and the woman I want in my life. I am recovering from the sudden end to an on–off relationship with a beautiful, disturbed activist, who, I have just learnt, shared her favours with several others. She's pregnant – not by me – and has just left to go into exile. I give it some thought and decide I'm relieved this one is over. Then I start to feel the residues of retrospective guilt and lust about a fling I've just enjoyed with the girlfriend of one of my friends – a good man, who forgave me.

Other past relationships – the ones I can't quite let go of – distract me further and then I allow myself to fret about the future, which makes a change. I'm particularly worried about the implications of my absence on my pursuit of my main love interest. I have started making friends with a fellow journalist and activist, Pat. I'd first seen her at a political meeting eight months earlier and couldn't stop staring at her face with its large mouth and big blue eyes, and her long brown hair. After a few months of staring I finally found some excuses to talk to her. I was fascinated by a background quite unlike that of the rest of the lefties I associated with – she hadn't seen her Irish father since she was one, she was raised mainly in an orphanage, then a foster family, had a child at 15, dropped out of school, worked in a bank until she completed a university degree, and then worked her way into journalism. Her activism was prompted partly by the mysterious death of her brother in the army. He had

173

been a boxer and she'd had boyfriends who'd boxed, so she knew the territory and had watched a few fights, which made her that much more interesting. And now she's an anti-conscription activist, a voluntary teacher of literacy, a cultural comrade. During those long hours in my cell I decide she's the one. She seems tough and determined and funny and I can't stop thinking about her. I train myself to dream about her too – if I think hard enough in the day, she'll emerge at night. My detention comes at a moment I think I might be making some progress and I begin to worry I will lose her. These concerns push my fears about interrogation out of focus.

My stories – my 'legends' as we call them – are honed down and polished to the last intricate detail. Why all those trips to Zimbabwe? To work for an American public radio journalist, and to see old friends and lovers. Why was I in Botswana in 1982? To help a former girlfriend who went for an abortion. Do you support the ANC? Its general aims, yes. You were spotted with this ANC member and that one! I may have met them socially, yes, but I am not and never have been a member. That's my story and I'm sticking to it.

I am questioned five times by four security police-men for about an hour a spell but I soon realize there is nothing serious to worry about. They don't ask about my trips to Zimbabwe, nor about any other movements requiring legends. By my second interrogation session I sense the security police are going through the motions, constrained in the ambit of what they are permitted to ask, although they still can't stop themselves playing a few games and trying a few tricks. I later learn that on day one of my detention the Reverend Paul Verryn, a friend of my parents, delivered spare clothes to the prison, but the security police claimed none arrived. 'Where are your friends now that you need them, hey, Evans,' Lieutenant Cole asks. 'They won't even send you clothes. You see no-one cares for you. No-one except us.' When that trick fails they start questioning me about Pat. 'We hear you've got eyes for her, Evans – got the hots for her, hey?' When that fails to draw a response they return to the standard questions about meetings and organizations, and I give them the standard pre-arranged answers. Then they try another trick. 'Look, Evans, we've got a deal for you. Provide us with the names of the ECC executive members, and we'll release you today. We can get them for ourselves anyway, so you may as well give them now.' I know their game – one small deal demands more, bigger ones. 'You can keep me as long as you want, but I'm not naming names,' I say. The next day they release me anyway – perhaps to give the impression I co-operated.

When I arrive home, I buy a Mars Bar and a hamburger, and then debrief my comrades and write a story in the *Weekly Mail* on time at Sun City. I soon realize I am being watched and followed, presumably in the hope I might lead them to someone more important. I assume that's why they restricted their questioning to the semi-legal realm – to make me complacent. So, after my quiet fortnight, I have much to worry about – more vigilance about covering my tracks while setting up a new safe address for the ANC to send me messages, and continuing business as normal with the semi-legal political groups: posters, pamphlets, committees, meetings and conferences, investigating suspected spies. It's a tense time, but it all feels so packed with meaning that the stress is seldom recognized for what it is. Every dimension, including my work and my fraught love life, takes its place behind my political imperatives. Strategy, tactics, intrigue – these are the things that fill my exhilarated brain.

In this politicized climate, boxing might have struggled to find a place were it not for one man: Arthur Mayisela. Arthur, and Brian Baronet, drew me closer, making the tenuous connections between my main purpose in life and my premier recreational diversion.

Boxing is a game taken rather more seriously in South Africa than most other countries. It's the second most popular sport (after soccer) among black South Africans and one of the biggest among whites. Its cross-over appeal is therefore enormous but in 1985, when white South Africa was still pretending that a whitewashed normality prevailed, those in control had not yet absorbed this reality. Black boxers were invisible to the money men and would remain so until Nelson Mandela was released from prison five years later.

I viewed Baronet's formative promoter, Rodney Berman, as very much the white man's champion, although I later discovered he was politically liberal, extremely generous and completely lacking in the undertone of malice that comes with the blood and sweat of this game. In his line of work, however, he understood the rules – how to play by them, bend them, bypass them, make them work for his cause – and one of those rules was that boxers are products or they are nothing. At that stage the only products to pull in the sponsorship Rands were boxers like Baronet – 'who just happens to be white' – and so it was that Berman's syndicate, Golden Gloves, focused on the pale side of the market.

Baronet was promoted as the country's hottest piece of boxing property. The white nation had been taught to love him and they did so on a scale that titillated the money men. For Sun City – the casino hotel complex, not the prison – Brian was *it*, the *boytjie*. He was the one to pull the better-heeled punter – the Johannesburg businessman who comes for an evening of boxing and a 'blue' movie, and then blows his Rands on the tables, or the rich farmer with a sideline in black prostitutes, or his wife with that habit of pumping coins into the slot machines, or the girl-friend guiding her overoiled *ouk* around the roulette wheel. For white South Africa, Brian was the money. Black South Africa felt very differently, but no-one was listening.

Berman's other idea was that even if your product was defective you could sell it as long as you dressed it up in pretty packaging, had the right people working for it, turned a blind eye when the occasion required, and made the right friends. 'Look, we knew Brian's limitations, and we had to work within them,' he later told me. 'Boxing's a business, right? And you have to look at boxers as the central component of that business. Obviously you make mistakes – you can't fix fights – but I never accept a fight I think is 50–50 or worse, not unless I get an offer to make it worth-while. With Brian we had a campaign to get him a world-title fight without exposing him to unacceptable risk. We did this by putting him in with respectable foreigners we knew were on the slide. It was easy to build his reputation because most of the South African journalists were too lazy to do their homework.'

Three days before I was detained, I drove to the other Sun City to watch Brian getting into serious trouble against one of these name fighters on the slide, a Puerto Rican contender called Domingo Ayala. Brian was dropped heavily and roughed up badly. Between rounds I watched Stan Christodoulou, the referee and reigning don of South African boxing, going to Brian's corner and giving him what looked like a piece of considered advice, although Stan subsequently insisted it wasn't quite as it appeared. 'No, no – I only told him that he mustn't retaliate if Ayala fouls again – that I would sort Ayala out.' Baronet gave the impression of a fragile boxer who required all the protection he could get. He duly found the punch to stop the Puerto Rican, after which the WBA world champion, Gene Hatcher, agreed to fight him. However, an Argentinian, Ubaldo Sacco, spoiled the plan by beating Hatcher. It was assumed that South Africa's cosy ties with the WBA would smooth the way, and the fight would happen on the scheduled date, 2 November 1985. But politics got in the way.

In 1985 the Sun City stakes were raised when Steve van Zandt launched his single, *I Ain't Gonna Play Sun City*, sharing the vocals with the likes of Springsteen, and the connection between white power, the 'homeland' of Bophuthatswana and its sole attraction became harder to ignore. If you wanted foreign stars to swallow the political implications of their presence, you had to pay increasingly hefty surcharges at a time when the value of the Rand was tumbling. This had a direct impact on Baronet's fortunes because the WBA and Sacco's people were becoming edgy. Sun City, however, had a date booked and their salvage plans would change the lives of three men and their families for ever.

The opponent the public wanted was Arthur Mayisela, the hard man from Soweto who had been baying for Baronet for two years. The attraction was that his background, constituency and persona were the antithesis of the Golden Boy's gilded rise. Mayisela was born in the 'black spot' of Sophiatown, on the western edge of Johannesburg, in 1953. When he was a young boy the Nationalist government forcibly removed all the black families, bulldozed their houses and moved in its own, white, supporters, renaming the new suburb Triomf – triumph. The Mayiselas were deposited in a tiny two-roomed shack in a corner of Soweto euphemistically called Meadowlands, where Arthur grew up rough and tough, developed a reputation as one of the most feared battlers in the area and was soon in trouble with the law, learning to hate the police as well as the white establishment. A prison stint reduced his job-seeking potential, so he decided to turn to professional boxing at the late age of 26. It was here he found meaning in life. He became known as *lpantsula* – a term of township endearment derived from the loose trousers worn by streetwise young men from the townships – and was later rewarded with the sobriquet the Fighting Prince, because, as one admirer explained it to me, 'He was royalty to us – a prince among men.' From the start he was a drawcard, an incipient hero who represented far more than just his fighting skills.

Despite a pair of points defeats on his way up he was thrown in with Baronet's cousin, the unbeaten former amateur star, Brett Taylor, in 1982. To the astonishment of the white fraternity, Mayisela's superior strength, jolting right cross and draining body attack seemed to make him a clear winner, but the white judges declared the fight a draw. Five months on Arthur won the national title and then travelled to the Cape border town of East London to defend it against one of the gods of black boxing, Nkosana Mgxaji. Happyboy, as he was known, was well past his best and could do no more than survive. However, such was his standing in the area that the crowd would accept nothing less than victory, and the local judges obliged. The Fighting Prince left the ring as an ex-champion. His contempt for the state-appointed boxing establishment grew more intense and he began to play by his own rules. In the return, Mayisela was unrelenting, putting Happyboy in hospital after seven one-sided rounds. The East London crowd responded by pelting the invader with beer bottles.

Arthur returned to Soweto and to his day job as a storekeeper at AEC Graffic, fighting for paltry purses twice a year. Baronet rose to stardom, thriving off the proceeds of regular action and comparatively huge ring earnings as well as his own clothing business and a string of modelling jobs. The Soweto man resented everything his rival represented – privilege, favouritism, white rule – and he wanted to make Baronet pay. For a brief period, early in their careers, they had trained together, and had given the impression of amicable co-existence, although they had very different versions of what occurred when they sparred together. 'He's strong but slow. I can box rings around him,' Baronet would chide. 'In a twelve-round fight I'll break him, no problem,' said Mayisela. In any event, what counted more than their versions of the past was the assumed nature of their futures: Baronet's golden; Mayisela's bleak.

When the *Rand Daily Mail* closed in 1985, I began writing for its 'alternative' successor, the *Weekly Mail*, dividing my attentions between politics and, for the first time, boxing. From the start Mayisela and Baronet featured prominently. I can't pretend I approached this dispute with anything resembling journalistic neutrality. I was a Mayisela praise-singer and a Baronet detractor. In mitigation, my prejudices were probably influenced by my political experiences over the previous three years. For one thing I received regular hints of the enemy's designs – ranging from threatening midnight phone calls to having my motorbike brake cables cut or the petrol tank spiked. I'd also had three spells of detention and interrogation, including my spell in Sun City. More significantly I had seen what the 'regime' was doing to others.

In early July that year I drove my aged Honda 550:4 down to the small Eastern Cape town of Cradock to join a 50,000-strong crowd of mourners at the funeral of a school teacher, Matthew Goniwe, and three other murdered Eastern Cape community leaders. It later turned out they'd been hacked to death by a team of military intelligence and security police goons, on the direct orders of a key cabinet committee called the State Security Council. After 'eliminating' these irritants, P.W. Botha's government used the presence of Communist Party flags at their funeral as an excuse to declare a State of Emergency in half of the country in a vain bid to reverse the climate of 'ungovernability' engulfing the townships and to break the consumer boycotts that were crippling white businesses. The

official final straw was a huge colour picture on the
front page of the *Sunday Times** featuring the mourners
walking in front of a Communist Party flag (with my
father in full bishop's regalia in the foreground of the
picture). Matthew was a man I'd met and admired
and I was moved by his funeral and enraged by the
government's cynical attempt to blame his murder on a
rival opposition group and then use it as an excuse for
further atrocities.

A few days after I returned from the funeral I interviewed Baronet for the first time, and, perhaps
inevitably, we didn't take to each other. He seemed
irritated with the direction of my inquiries and I was
exasperated with his curt answers. 'When are you going
to fight Mayisela?' I asked. From his reply I could see
the taunts were getting to him. 'I'm near the top of the
world ratings. I'm rated fourth in the WBA and soon I'll
be number one. Who's he beaten? No-one, that's who.
The only fight that interests me now is one for the
world title.'

'But don't you think you should beat him first – he's
South African champion after all?'

'He's nothing, man. He doesn't belong in the ring
with me.' He walked away, annoyed.

For a man with thirty professional fights Brian was
still astonishingly handsome, the scar tissue around his
fragile brows adding a bit of rough to his boyish charm
but nothing to frighten the aunties. He wore neither the
droopy moustache nor the long at the back, short at the
sides 'mullet' hairstyle that were *de rigueur* among

---

*The *Sunday Times* was then edited by the suave Tertius Myburgh, who was
at the beck and call of the National Intelligence Service and boasted of being
an 'emissary' for the apartheid-backed Unita movement.

white boxers, and had a more defined sense of style than the rest. Boxing people loved to describe him as a 'male model' (not a female one, to be sure) and he seemed to relish this. The way he walked, talked, carried himself, gave the impression of a young man well pleased with himself. We didn't click.

Arthur, on the other hand, knew I was on his side and would put his arm around my shoulder, joking with an air of amused resignation when discussing the nepotism of the Boxing Board. He would turn up in his shorts or his loose, khaki chinos, sometimes with his two children in tow – and that was another thing I liked about him: despite the estrangement of divorce from his wife, Mpho, he gave the impression of being a devoted father, warm and relaxed with his children. He was an intelligent man, not just 'for a boxer' – Zulu- and Sotho-speaking but fluent in six languages, quick-witted and capable of pontificating on topics way beyond the scope of his profession. He was also a proud man with a strong sense of himself and plenty of attitude without much hint of swagger. Whenever we spoke he was engaging and charming, but when the subject of Baronet came up, he would spit out his feelings. He had once liked the lad, but now he hated him, or at least despised what he represented.

I was so inspired by Arthur's defiant demeanour that I came to view his cause as symbolic of the wider conflict and soon the connections between boxing and politics became irresistible. The two worlds employed a common lexicography – struggle, fighters, bombs, explosive – sometimes borrowing clichés from each other. 'Comrade, we've got the government on the ropes,' or 'Hey, *bra*, this youngster's ungovernable – he won't train.' The black versus white rivalries, judged by a majority of white officials appointed by a white board, watched by a racially divided crowd, completed the picture. After Goniwe's assassination and my own detention, the compelling conceit that boxing was not only a metaphor for the struggle but an integral part of it was swallowed without the requisite scepticism, and so, not for the first time in my life, this game wormed its way back into the forefront of my obsessions, albeit under a conveniently political umbrella.

On my release from detention I began using my journalistic pulpit to push for a 'showdown' between the Fighting Prince and the Golden Boy. Two years before, Mayisela's Soweto manager, Marcus Nkosi, had approached the garrulous, open-minded young promoter Mike Segal, asking him to sponsor his charge. Until then, Segal, like his better-connected rival Berman, had been concentrating on the white end of the market, but he took a chance on a tentative venture with Mayisela – first as his sponsor, then as his business manager and finally as his promoter. When it came to marketing, black boxers were still invisible in the first half of the 1980s. 'But I was lucky with Arthur,' Segal recalled. 'I've been in boxing over twenty years and I've promoted extremely popular world champions, but none of them matched Mayisela when it came to grassroots black support. Even before he fought Baronet, he was really big in Soweto. When he was in my shop, people would crowd around. They wanted to be with him and he responded as one of them. There were no airs and graces – never – even after he'd made it big, he would still travel third class on the train, and the people loved him.'

Rodney Berman, however, was reluctant to allow this

popular rival to get in the way of his little earner. As he explained it: 'I've never taken seriously challenges that this guy is better than our guy, because to me boxing's never been a sport – it's purely business – and I didn't think Arthur was good for business.' But there were other pressures to be taken into account – bottom-line obligations to fulfil. Berman ceded control to Sun City, which had a date to fill and was prepared to take a risk, but Baronet and his manager-trainer Doug Dolan required persuasion. 'I approached Brian myself,' said Segal. 'He'd always told me he knew from their sparring sessions that he had the beating of Arthur, so I said to him, look, take it. The money's good, Sacco's not happening and Sun City have this vacancy, and so, eventually, he agreed, and Dolan came over too.'

Sun City's idea was to make the best of the world title disappointment by attracting large numbers of black boxing fans to the gambling resort for the first time. They built the moment to a local crescendo, making sure they filled the bill with three other black–white rivalries. Ringside seats were sold at a cut-rate price of R60 (instead of the usual R200) and the punters received R36-worth of free gambling vouchers. Despite all this, no more than 1,500 blacks turned up, with most of the seats taken by 4,000 white Baronet fans.

In the days before their encounter Mayisela told me over and over that Baronet's world ranking, his favoured-son status with the Boxing Board and his marketing contracts were all a product of his white skin. The rivalry became infected with racial trappings, which he would mix with personal barbs. 'Baronet's a chicken,' he would taunt. 'He's scared, *bra*. He's been avoiding me.' Standard boxing fare – ever since the early Ali days – but in South Africa it was a novelty from the black boxing fraternity, whose expected role was to drop eyes to the white man's shoes and mumble platitudes of gratitude with soft deference. Arthur's contempt for such conventions riled the establishment, and his rivalry with Baronet took on overtly political overtones of a kind seldom heard in South Africa. As Segal recalls it: 'You have to remember that those were still apartheid days, and Arthur viewed Baronet in that light. Here was a guy he knew he could beat, who was getting all this glory, whereas he was struggling. He carried a lot of anger on his sleeve, and much of it was directed at Baronet.' This anger spilled over to his supporters, who viewed his campaign as a national vendetta. The mission to defeat Baronet became a political cause.

I made the trip with my social worker-cum-activist friend and flatmate Maxine (her first ever boxing event), and my new girlfriend Pat (we'd finally got it together a week earlier, after three months of doe-eyed persistence on my part). We each remarked on the highly charged atmosphere. You could taste the tension, the sense of scores to be settled. '*Skop die bobbejaan*' – kick the baboon – I heard one white drunk shouting during a preliminary fight, followed by, 'Hit him in the guts, Sakkie – there's no point hitting a *houtkop*' – woodhead – 'in the head,' which drew the instant retort from the cheap seats: '*Shaya umlungu*' – beat the white man. As I returned to my seat after a toilet break, a white ringsider remarked to me: 'Jesus, it feels just like Dingaan and Piet Retief'* – only this time

---

*A reference to the nineteenth-century Zulu leader who, according to Afrikaner legend, tricked the Boer leader into an ambush and then slaughtered him and his followers.

the bystanders were vicariously involved. The inherent logic of the game kicked in: their war was to be fought by their champions. It was David and Goliath with the Israelites and the Philistines on standby.

Everyone was attentive by the third fight, featuring the national super featherweight champion Brian Mitchell against his old rival Jacob Morake. Mitchell, a tough kid from a deprived white Johannesburg background, was one of the rising talents of South African boxing. The son of a South African champion who had fallen to alcohol, he was a man who had reacted to his deprived childhood with great drive and a fierce determination. He always learnt from his mistakes and therefore showed consistent improvement until he became a double 'world' champion and one of the finest boxers ever produced in South Africa. Entering his third year as national champion at the age of 24 he was then still three years from his peak but already a formidable fighter who deserved his world ranking with the WBA. Unlike most white South African boxers, he had never shied away from fighting in the black townships, and it was there that he developed his early reputation as a hard man to beat. In fact, throughout Mitchell's 49-fight career, there was only one man who managed it: Jacob 'Dancing Shoes' Morake, but that was three and a half years before this fateful November Sun City night, and in the intervening years Mitchell had twice avenged that early points loss.

Morake was a thin man whose body looked even more vulnerable because it was terribly disfigured through the kind of childhood burning accident so common in houses reliant on open stoves and without constant childcare. 'He was 11 years old and making

187

the fire on the stove was one of his chores,' his sister Mercy told me. 'It exploded and he got horribly burnt and scarred.' Boxing was his way of winning respect, and he was good at it – a sharp, quick-footed boxer good enough to turn professional, good enough to win a provincial title, but not quite good enough for the very best. By the time of this, his fourth fight with Mitchell, he was on the slide, but his father was dead and his mother ill, which made him the family's sole breadwinner. The money he earned in his day job as a junior clerk with the Legal and General insurance company just wasn't enough to go around, so he said yes to the Sun City gig. 'You see, his boxing was helping to see us through,' said Mercy.

He took the fight at short notice, knowing he probably couldn't win – that Mitchell had his number – but hoping he would give a good enough account to be asked back sometime. And he certainly did his best, but this time his best was too much to ask. Jacob's courage, his trainer's desperate hope and the callous inaction of a police colonel who doubled as a referee secured his brutal demise. Fifteen years later, when I e-mailed Maxine in her home in Mexico City to ask what she remembered about that evening, she said she could still 'feel' the fraught atmosphere after Morake's demise. 'It had a profound emotional effect on me, especially being my first boxing match. I remember wanting that fight to be stopped because Dancing Shoes seemed badly injured, even in the round before he was knocked out, and I remember white men in the audience standing very still as his unconscious body was carried out of the ring. It was obvious to everyone that he wouldn't make it.'

Tragedies usually defy categories of taste, and boxing

is a sport where notions of taste seldom apply, but
the Sun City response showed a crassness that enraged
me. It was horribly apparent that Morake was in a
deep coma and that what remained of his life was
precarious. What the crowd needed, what I wanted,
was some acknowledgement – a sign of grace, of compassion, of contrition even: a delay in proceedings,
a moment's silence, a prayer. But no, instead we got
ring announcer Naidoo and his 'big hand for Charles
the Challenger', his 'be upstanding' for the boycott-
busting Aussie cricket 'rebels', his big welcome for the
'galaxy of stars', and finally the Sun City competition to
win the Isuzu *bakkie*. This did the job for most of the
whites. 'Oh well, I'm sure he'll be OK,' they seemed to
say and got caught up with the real reason for their
attendance. What Naidoo knew only too well was that
Morake and Mitchell were not what this event was all
about. They were just so much garnish before the main
course. The point was Brian Baronet, the Golden Boy of
South African boxing, the milk cow for Sun City, the
man to pull in the gambling crowd. Brian Baronet and,
yes, OK, his opponent Arthur Mayisela, but mainly
Baronet.

I had staked a small dose of professional credibility
on a Mayisela win – being the only white boxing writer
to incline that way. I reasoned that Baronet was open to
a right cross, that Mayisela had a thumping right, and
that Arthur was stronger with a more reliable chin, and
I knew he'd trained harder than ever before, building
his stamina by running up and down the mine dumps
while living in Segal's home under the supervision of a
dietician. But the real reason for my prediction was
simply that I wished it so. The formbook indicated a
different conclusion. Mayisela's sparse record showed

eighteen wins, a draw and three losses, and even if that was deceptive, it hardly indicated a world-beater, especially considering he was 32 years old. Baronet, at 25, had racked up twenty-nine wins out of thirty. He possessed quick hands, nifty footwork, impressive power in his right uppercut and left hook, a snappy jab, superb conditioning and loads of courage. And you just knew who'd get the decision if it were anywhere near to close.

But after the Morake tragedy, I *needed* Arthur to pull it off and I certainly wasn't alone. My friend Maxine still recalls the atmosphere. 'The blacks were very charged after that. Some were chanting, *Slaan die baas; moer die Boer*' – hit the boss; fuck up the Boer – 'It felt like Mayisela had the destiny of South Africa in his hands, and if he lost after Dancing Shoes was killed, the future of South Africa could never be won.' There was a measure of desperation in this hope because from what I'd seen the white establishment always found a way of securing its will, and no doubt about it, Brian Baronet was the establishment man.

Baronet's dancing entrance, to the inevitable sounds of Queen's 'We will, we will rock you', drew sustained white applause while Mayisela's more muted entrance drew a guttural roar of defiant hope from the bleachers. Then, as if to reassure themselves, the whites sung their national anthem with more than the mandatory gusto: *'Ons sal lewe, ons sal sterwe, ons vir jou, Suid Afrika'* – We shall live, we shall die, we're for you, South Africa. The blacks were more than usually silent. They had come in the hope of vindication through their champion, Arthur Mayisela, and the callous disregard for the fate of Dancing Shoes had sharpened that hope and added to it their urge for revenge. I was caught up with the emotion of the occasion and had abandoned all semblance of fairness and decency, let alone journalistic objectivity. 'Fuck him up, Arthur, *fuck* him up,' I muttered as he entered the ring.

I can still picture the contrast in their fighting styles revealed in those early moments. The stalking Mayisela, tautly muscled, round shouldered, shaven headed, smooth brown skin, moving forward with languid purposefulness, picking his punches carefully, his guard high, his unblinking eyes on his quarry; the elegant, athletic Baronet, square shoulders, neat build, white skin, hairy chest, straight brown hair, big brown eyes, moving quickly around the ring, firing off cocky combinations. For two minutes it looked an even contest and then Mayisela registered his first right cross and drove Baronet back, and it suddenly became starkly apparent that the Golden Boy had no defence against this kind of pressure and accuracy. He must have found it equally unnerving to discover that his own showy flurries had no effect on his opponent. Mayisela was a boxer who never knew what it was like to be dropped.

Arthur added to the pressure, driving Baronet back with his greater strength, hooking to the body and then slamming home his right over Brian's jab. Arthur was a heavy puncher, but not usually devastating, and the damage was accumulative. Every so often he would jolt the white man's head back, and the gaps between these moments shrank as the rounds progressed. In the seventh round, with Brian severely cut over the eye, the hope of the 1,500 finally began to turn to faith. They rose and began singing the inspirational mining song *Tshotshaloza* but this time like a battle hymn.

Many were crying at the sight of their hope being vindicated.

The body punches took away Baronet's legs, the head blows dulled his senses, and he was reduced to a hesitant haze. Mayisela picked him off at will, buckling him with every right, but referee Stan Christodoulou seemed reluctant to intervene. I wondered whether he was hoping against hope that Baronet would find the punch to reverse the tide, as he had done before. Whatever the reason, the final rites in the ninth round were brutal and unnecessary and Baronet collapsed to the canvas, unconscious for well over a minute. 'Oh shit, here we go again,' I said to Pat. I feared we were about to see a second tragedy, and in a sense we did.

Finally, Baronet, bleeding heavily and still thoroughly dazed and confused, was helped to his feet, his dreams, and those of his family and thousands of followers, obliterated. Many years later, when I spoke to his mother, Phyllis, about the fight, she still could not quite believe what happened that night. 'He should never have lost,' she said. 'I don't know how it happened. He saw the Morake fight, and that definitely affected him, because he wasn't himself in the ring, and then he was severely cut, but he should never have lost.'

The crowd at the back couldn't quite believe it either, and there was a momentary pause before they released a long-suppressed roar. I too felt a surge of unrestrained, undignified, unkind relief. But then I remembered Dancing Shoes and the three of us rushed off to the press conference for information on Morake's condition. After the drinks and snacks were dispensed, a Sun City jobsworth rose, thanked the boxers for a 'truly enjoyable evening', announced the date of the next show, and, oh, 'Just in case you wondered, Morake is recovering in hospital. He's doing very well and we expect a full recovery.' I turned to my friends. 'He's lying. He just made that up,' I spat. We drove through the night, elated with Mayisela, fearful for Morake, talking incessantly, trying to make sense of it all, knowing that the morning would confirm our fears. Five hours later Dancing Shoes was dead.

It was the Fighting Prince who led the phalanx of fighters fronting the procession at his funeral, running at an angry pace alongside the hearse from Rockville, from one side of Soweto to Avalon cemetery on the other. Brian Mitchell wanted to offer his support but was advised by officialdom to stay at home for his own safety – the township was too 'explosive' and politically 'volatile', he was told, and his presence might 'inflame passions'. Instead he sent a message of condolence, a wreath and a picture of himself posing with Jacob after an earlier encounter which had been adjudged the 'fight of the year' for 1982. He blamed the death on a combination of misfortune and Snowball's failure to stop the fight, but once the funeral was over he did his best to push it out of his mind. 'A lot of people are bugging me about how I feel about that fight,' he said when I discussed it with him two months later. 'But look, Gavin, *ja* I felt really bad, OK, but that's finished now. I have to get on with my career.'

The Morakes, however, had no careers to get on with. Jacob left behind his mother and siblings, his girlfriend and their two-year-old son, Ramoleta – all reliant on his income. 'It started to hit us hard in so many ways straight after the funeral,' Jacob's sister, Mercy, recalled when I spoke to her years later. 'The Boxing Board only helped my mother with the burial and they gave nothing else – only broken promises. I had to give up school to help the family, and then my mother became semi-blind so I had to look after her. For two years I couldn't find a job, and except for a tiny pension from my father's death we had no income, which meant no proper meals. There was never enough food and we just got used to not eating much. My other brother started helping out when he could, but he was stabbed to death in July 1987 and we were absolutely desperate, but the next month I finally got a job, and after that there was some food on the table. At least we weren't starving any more.'*

Arthur was voted South Africa's Boxer of the Year for 1985, but he had few illusions about where it would lead. He told me of his goal to make enough, as quickly as possible, for his family to be comfortable for life. 'I was hungry when I turned professional seven years ago and I am still hungry,' he complained. The WBA grudgingly rated him seventh in the world but he realized his chances of securing a world-title shot were remote and so, instead, he took whatever he was offered. Three months later Pat and I watched Arthur defending his national title against his old rival Brett Taylor. We all figured it would be an easy fight – he'd

*When I spoke to her, fifteen years after Jacob's death, Mercy was working as a bank manager, still living in Soweto and still struggling. 'I'm the breadwinner for the whole family, including my mother and Ramoleta, even though I have my own house and child and no husband to support me, and I have to pay for both houses, so it's still very hard. We still don't even have enough to afford a tombstone for my other brother.'

'beaten' the former amateur star last time, unofficially anyway.

I took an immediate liking to Brett. He was unassuming in a wide-eyed way, and treated black boxers pretty much the same way as he treated whites – with respect and sometimes with generosity too. When he learnt that Arthur trained in a gym without a ring or even a floor covering, he offered him R25 to buy new equipment – not much, but sincerely meant. The Boxing Board, however, seemed to view Taylor in a different light – as the man to settle *their* scores – and so it happened that nice-enough Brett would come to succeed pretty boy Brian in a role he never aspired to: a representative of white rule.

The board had banned all professional tournaments in Soweto and other black townships on the grounds that it was 'too dangerous', by which they meant that they didn't want to travel beyond their own suburban borders. Hall number 10 at the Crown Mines showgrounds, however, was a 15-minute bus ride from Soweto, so this time over 5,000 blacks packed in to see their hero while only a few hundred whites bothered to make the trip. Every plastic chair went for R10 so there was no chance of buying your way to the front. You either made it there early or you stood at the back. By 4 p.m. the February heat was becoming unbearable and the panels were lifted, letting the afternoon sun stream in. The fans cooled off with Coke, and the men used the parking wall as a urinal. The children played in the open spaces as the boxing progressed – an afternoon's fighting was a family event. The atmosphere was jolly, devoid of racial hostility, with disco music blaring out through cheap loudspeakers and a plump, beaming township mama in crimplene shorts and sandals doing the inter-round cardgirl duties. 'Our women . . . oooh, aaah,' the *pantsula* sitting next to me remarked as she went through her hip-swivelling routine. When Mayisela entered the ring, the wildly cheering and ululating crowd danced along with him, carrying banners bearing good tidings to Prince Arthur. The inter-round woman could not contain herself and shouted her support for him. There was much banter between the black and white fans, but it was taken in good humour, even when overtly racist. 'Go for his lips, Brett, you can't miss,' said one white, and everyone laughed. Then came the retort: 'Hey, Arthur, I saw Brett in a hippo' – riot police vehicle – 'in Soweto – so you better get the *umlungu*.' But it was only a joke.

No-one outside Mayisela's camp realized that Arthur's trainer Richard Letsatsi had relied on dodgy bathroom scales. Arthur came in four pounds over the limit and had to make three long trips to the sauna and do a spell of running and skipping in Segal's basement to get down to 140 pounds on the morning of the fight. It took him three hours, and he looked lethargic in the sweltering mid-afternoon heat. He moved more slowly than normal and his punches lacked conviction, although he still dominated the first half with his superior power and in the seventh round dropped Taylor with a stiff right cross. But the effort drained him and from the eighth onwards Taylor's hooks and jabs began to get through, and Mayisela lost the last five rounds. It was a close encounter but my no-doubt-biased perception was that Arthur's early efforts were sufficient to retain his title. However, when I saw Stan Christodoulou clench his fist and whoop with unrestrained delight after checking the scores, I feared the worst. Predictably the two white judges – one of them Colonel Snowball – gave it to Taylor, while the sole black judge made Mayisela the winner. Arthur was disgusted, partly with himself for failing to make the weight, but also with the judges and the white boxing establishment. 'That decision was racist,' he complained. 'But from now on I won't be leaving it up to the judges.' I drove home with Pat, feeling disgusted and angry, but it was not something I had time to dwell on.

The following day the wheels of my motorbike collided with another vehicle at 90km/h. I was wearing shorts, T-shirt and flip-flops, and as I skidded across the tarmac the skin on my arms, hands and legs, as well as five toenails, got left behind. I also suffered a broken foot. I was therefore wrapped in plaster of Paris and bandages when Arthur next fought, again at Sun City, three weeks later. Pat – by now my official photographer – drove me there for an evening oddly free from the political tension that was about to swallow the country. All the opponents were foreign and so everyone supported the locals. 'Kom, Arthur, kom, Suid Afrika,' one white drunk started as the Soweto man shuffled out of his corner. I was delighted to see him back on form, knocking out a Panamanian called Pedro Avila in the sixth round before celebrating with a backwards somersault. He looked happy afterwards, teasing me about my careless driving and my bandages. He then told me of his plans to avenge the Taylor setback and work his way through the world rankings.

We drove home and I packed my things to fly to New York to represent the End Conscription Campaign at the United Nations. As I passed through customs, however, the airport security police nabbed me and confiscated all the copies of a hundred-page report on military conscription I'd compiled for the UN Committee Against Apartheid. British Airways officials arrived on the scene, telling the customs men they were delaying the flight, and while they argued I managed to lift three copies of the report from the customs desk and slip them into my jeans. While the argument progressed, I sneaked off towards the gangway and five minutes later was in the air and on my way for a six-week American tour to raise funds from the likes of Joan Baez and Pete Seeger, meet with white American peace groups and black American divestment campaigners, and make speeches and media appearances to rally support for South African conscientious objectors. It was a happy time, spent with people for whom politics was all about principle and symbolism, untouched by the realism prompted by real power, real risk and a real prospect of victory or death. My return was rather different.

A few weeks later Maxine and I were swapping *skinder* – gossip – at midnight when the phone rang. Maxine answered, and after a few seconds I heard her saying, 'Who is it? Who's there?' A minute on she slammed the phone down, telling me she'd just been given the deep breathing treatment, followed by a rough Afrikaner voice saying: 'Hey, Maxine, Maxine, we's coming for you tonight. We's coming to *chew* you. Does you like being chewed, hey, Maxie baby?' and so on. We discussed whether to take this seriously and decided it was probably just a pack of bored security policemen treating themselves to some laddish laughs. I whipped up a banana milkshake and we resumed our *skinder*. Ten minutes later the phone rang again: a Cape Town friend telling me my brother, Michael, had just been detained again (his second of three spells – this one for six weeks in jail) and in two minutes we were gone. The security police rounded up tens of thousands of activists for what turned out to be the start of a new, national State of Emergency – far more all-embracing than the partial one of the year before. Maxine took a chance by going to work the next day and once again found herself in detention. I began an itinerant existence that had me staying in twenty-seven flats and houses over the next four years, eighteen of them over the next six months.

I returned to our flat three days later to collect some belongings. Once that was done I lingered, phoning my American connections to rustle up some publicity for the cause, and then I thought, *What the hell, why not have a quick bath?* Happily soaking away 72 hours of rush-around grime, I was disturbed by an insistent thumping on our heavy, triple-lock front door, accompanied by angry voices demanding I open up.* I leapt out of the bath, pulled my shirt and jeans onto my dripping body and waited. They then pumped teargas through the letterbox, and I sneaked barefoot to the back window, trying not to cough. I had been too scared to jump from the window a week earlier (when I'd been locked in and couldn't find my keys) and had struggled to climb down with a rope. This time there was no hesitation. I jumped, landing safely on the grass 18 feet below. I sprinted down a back street to a friend's flat and phoned Pat, who came to get me, but she was followed by two security policemen and ran

*I later learnt there were six shotgun-wielding plainclothes cops.

inside, shouting, 'Run, Whitecross is behind me!' and so, still shoeless, I vaulted the wall, then the walls of two neighbours and escaped. The next day, I had my hair curled and dyed and put on a suit and sunglasses. Later I shaved off my hair, grew a scrawny beard and wore a heavy biker jacket, and for the next half year I moved in disguise from house to house to avoid detention.

A week after the declaration of the State of Emergency I made another decision – that, whatever the risks, I would continue attending fights and writing about them, even if I couldn't go to the office to file my reports. I calculated that while South African boxing was packed with cops, most weren't drawn from the security branch and they would not be on the lookout for activists, and I assumed the security police and military intelligence were too overstretched to think of tracking activists at boxing matches. They had tunnel vision and tended to focus their surveillance on tip-offs about political meetings they received from informers. The difficulty, however, was in dealing with the usual suspects while in disguise. What would the boxing community make of my new hair colour, for instance? To get around that one I wore a cap. No-one asked any questions and I had no trouble at all.

The immediate imperative was a Sun City fight between Arthur Mayisela and the WBA's top welter-weight contender, Harold Volbrecht. Happy-go-lucky Harold the Hammer was a laugh-a-minute ladies' man. I enjoyed his company from the first time we met when we shared a seat at the Coetzee–Page fight. Unlike so many white South African sports stars, there was nothing sullen about him, and he had no need for alpha-male displays of machismo. He knew he could flatten any man in any house if the need arose, and when it occasionally did he would carry out the job with admirable nonchalance – like the time in California when a behemoth blocked the path of a boxer he was helping, and he removed the fellow with a single right hook and kept right on walking. I also liked the way he related to black boxing people, including some of the protégés he was training. I never detected any sign of the barking martinet behaviour of some white trainers of black boxers – 'Listen! Do this! Do that!' – nor the speak-slowly-and-loudly-in-single-clause-sentences patronage that was the forte of others. He hung loose, enjoying life's fruits, joking away in his high-pitched voice, and yet he was always in impeccable shape – his thing was women, not drink, drugs or gluttony.

By the time of the Mayisela fight, he was at his peak – widely regarded as the country's number-one professional boxer – a tricky, elusive veteran southpaw with a huge hook when he needed it. Harold was a short man with long arms and broad shoulders who came from a rough street-fighting background and started out his professional career as a brawler. But in 1978, when winning the 'supreme' South African welterweight title (in the days when there was still a white champion and a black champion), his opponent, Morris Mohlai, remained unconscious for over ten minutes. After that Harold seemed to fear his own power and held back. He became even more reticent after being stopped in five by Pipino Cuevas in a bid for the WBA world title – boxing off the back foot and seldom taking chances. But over time he managed to mould the two styles into one to become an extremely elusive power puncher. Now 29, Volbrecht was set for a second world-title shot, and viewed Mayisela as a useful vehicle for a tune-up. I feared that his power, the weight difference and the gap in experience – a mere four losses in forty-four fights, many of them at world-class level, for Harold the Hammer – would be too much for Arthur, but there was simply no way I could miss it.

Once again the mood was set in a full-to-capacity Sun City by an undercard fight. Brett Taylor retained his national title with another controversial draw against a black opponent. The black section of the crowd were angry, booing for several minutes, and even before Arthur's entry there were shouts of *Amandla* – power – along with the freedom song *Senzeni na*. For three rounds, however, there was nothing to excite this bubbling passion. Volbrecht confused Mayisela without seriously inconveniencing him. Only in the fourth did it begin to crackle, beginning with a 'clash of heads'. Arthur, the streetfighter, the man who had vowed never again to leave matters to the judges, dipped his skull onto Volbrecht's left brow, and the champion emerged with a serious gash. But the referee, Alfred Buqwana, missed the trick and allowed the fight to progress. Arthur assumed control, bashing Volbrecht around the ring, catching him frequently with his right until it looked like he might stop him. As the bell rang to start the sixth, Harold was still in his corner, and his Argentinian trainer, Carlos Jacomo, was trying to stop the blood. But it was no use: Harold decided he could not continue. Carlos hugged him, consoling him in defeat, while Arthur performed a jubilant somersault.

The Boxing Board, however, needed Volbrecht to win. He was due to fight for the WBA world title, at a time when the WBA was considering banning South Africa. A victorious Volbrecht would be a bridgehead. Whatever the reason, the result followed this logic. Despite the fact that the referee and the doctor had not objected to the fight continuing, and that it was Volbrecht himself who opted to retire, Stan Christodoulou took it upon himself to overrule Buqwana, deciding that the fight had been officially stopped at the end of the fifth round because of an accidental head-clash. Five minutes after the round ended it was announced that Volbrecht had retained his national title for the sixteenth time on a technical draw. The black part of the crowd erupted, kicking over chairs and throwing punches. 'The AWB were here tonight,' said a Mayisela second, in reference to the neo-Nazi paramilitary organization. 'We're never coming back,' Richard Letsatsi screamed at a Sun City official. 'We're gonna boycott your tournaments, do you hear? We're gonna boycott Sun City.'

Arthur returned to a Soweto under police siege, bitter and angry – his prize stolen from him. Three months on he was given an outing against a top Venezuelan welterweight contender at the Crown Mines show-grounds near Soweto. Two days before his fight, I watched him sitting with his arms around his children, Adelaide, 14, and Stephen, 12, chatting lovingly to them. He looked up and began telling me what he would do to Volbrecht next time – break him, just like Baronet, beat him up – but had to curtail the conversation because he remembered he was required for family business. 'See you next week. We can talk properly then,' he said.

He had been reunited with Mpho a month earlier and for the first time in nine years the family was living together in Arthur's Soweto home. Today, Stephen remembers it as the happiest time of his life: 'My parents divorced when I was three. I don't know why but my father must have done something horrible to my mum because she didn't want him to see us, although he tried. We went to live in Benoni before the Baronet fight and then she let us see him again, and to me he was a brilliant father. In the little time we had together he was very warm, very loving, definitely very good to us. I loved him. I watched his fights on TV, and for sure he was a hero figure to me. And then after the Volbrecht fight he and my mum were reunited and we moved in with him and I think it was fate – that it was meant to happen then, because he didn't have much time left, but it was a good time for us.'

I watched his fight incognito, standing a few rows from ringside with my friend Steve, a one-time Willie Toweel protégé who had recently emerged from a spell in detention. Sharing top billing, a black prospect called Siza Makhathini lost a disputed decision to the white security policeman Bennie Knoetze for the Transvaal heavyweight title. When we arrived, in the third round of the Knoetze fight, Steve stared at Bennie, turned to me and remarked: 'Jeez, that's the same *boer* who was at John Vorster Square when I was assaulted. He just stood there watching and laughing while they hit me.' He was about to elaborate when a white man behind me screamed: '*Kom, Bennie, jy moet daai kaffir moer*' – come on, Bennie, you must fuck up that kaffir, to which his chum added: '*Vang die bobbejaan*, Bennie' – catch the baboon, while the man next to us yelled: 'Don't let the side down, Bennie – kill him.' That shut us up but a few minutes later, when a blonde lady did her card-carrying thing between rounds, the baboon man nudged me, leered at her crotch and flickered his tongue purposefully, punching his right fist into his left palm while chanting rhythmically: 'Some *ouks* are only going to *naai*' – fuck – 'their wives tonight, hey.' With that he left for a drink, missing the final fight which saw Arthur finishing his six-foot opponent with a series of sharp hooks to the head and body in the third round. 'We want Volbrecht, we want Technical Draw,' the blacks in the crowd chanted. Arthur smiled and left happy, beginning to feel the good times were returning.

Three days later, on 17 September 1986 – the day before our scheduled interview and three days before his thirty-third birthday – Arthur collected his children from their school in Benoni, and stopped off at the Boxing Board office to sign his contract for a return fight with Volbrecht. He then drove home along the M2 highway to Meadowlands, Soweto in his new BMW. He was happy – the purse of R50,000 was the biggest of his career, and he loved driving with his children, spending time with them after the years apart. But along the way he had a blow-out and pulled over to the yellow line on a narrow section of the highway's hard shoulder. With Stephen still inside the car, and Adelaide on the roadside, he went to work removing the spare wheel from the boot. At that moment a van driver who was not concentrating slammed into Arthur from behind, crushing him against his car. Arthur died in Hillbrow Hospital later that night. The distraught van driver was later convicted of reckless driving. Stephen climbed out with only a bump on his head. 'But the whole experience was devastating for me,' he said, many years later. 'I'd just got to know him and then this – seeing him die that way. It was horrible. It haunted me for ten years and in a way I'm still trying to get over the trauma of it.'

The way I looked at it, in the fourth month of the national State of Emergency, was that if the Boxing Board hadn't 'robbed' him of victory against Volbrecht, then he wouldn't have been in their office that day, and he wouldn't have been on the road at that time, and he would still be alive. So they were to blame and my rage against the board became more intense. That's the kind of mad logic that comes from living in eighteen houses in six months. Today it just seems like another South African road tragedy. A few years before Arthur, two other heroes of the white South African ring, Arnold Taylor and Pierre Fourie, were killed on the road. Several of my close friends died the same way, and I had survived four potentially fatal accidents – one of them a head-on collision with an 18-wheeler truck, which was overtaking on a blind rise. Around 25,000 people a year die on South African roads. Wrong place, wrong time.

Still, it felt so unjust that it must have been political, and that's the way it was received in Soweto. Under the State of Emergency all political activities, including 'political' funerals, were banned, and so it was that Arthur's ostensibly secular funeral acquired an added significance. At the time I was working for the UDF publicity secretary, Murphy Morobe, in the move-ment's then-clandestine national secretariat, and I persuaded the structure that we needed to make a presence. We therefore wrote an obituary that was read at his funeral, praising him for being 'a great fighter, a great human being and a hero of the op-pressed people of the country'. It went on to eulogize:

'Whether squaring up against his opponents in the ring or against the racist white South African boxing authorities, Mayisela was a fighter to the end. *Lpantsula* was an example to the people of Soweto and to all who knew him or watched him fight. We will miss him but his memory will be an inspiration to all of us.'

It was certainly an impressive send-off. Sixty thousand people lined the streets as the procession began. A guard of honour, consisting of a hundred boxers in their fighting gear, all punching the air, jogged the six miles from the small church in his home zone of Meadowlands to the Avalon cemetery, while police and soldiers watched nervously from their Casspir armoured cars as hundreds of Young Lion activists in political T-shirts sang freedom songs and chanted ANC slogans. The presiding minister, the Revd Vilikazi, who was the brother of a treason trialist, began by saying: 'Arthur was a hero who lived like an ordinary man. He identified with the ordinary people and would be seen boarding third-class trains to be with the people.' One of Soweto's leading boxing trainers, Solly Selebi, called him a 'true son of Africa who had been the conqueror of white hopefuls and the torchbearer of black hope in the boxing world'. He added that Mayisela was 'victim of biased decisions by the boxing authorities' and led a rallying cry for a new, non-racial boxing board. Only one white boxer, Brett Taylor, was present and only one Boxing Board official – their ringside doctor – bothered to turn up. No doubt he reported back to his superiors, who heard everything and learnt nothing.

And that was the end of the Fighting Prince. It could be said that his life had left behind a large stain, in

Samuel Beckett's sense, although sadly I would have to add that the stain quickly faded in the heavy-duty wash of 1980s South Africa.*

But the story doesn't end with Arthur. In the final South African WBA title challenge for the next six years, Harold Volbrecht fought the elegant New Yorker Mark Breland for the vacant welterweight title in New Jersey in February 1987. Breland, an Olympic gold medallist and part-time actor, fought with a broken hand, but still managed to stop a strangely lethargic Volbrecht in the seventh round. 'I had a terrible dose of flu I'd picked up from running in the snow, and my temperature was 103 when I got into the ring, so I knew I'd lose even though I could have beaten him if I'd been right,' Harold told me afterwards. 'You see, I really needed the money and was told that if I pulled out, there'd be no second chances because of the politics.' Volbrecht fought on, finally retiring two years later, still a South African champion. He became a highly successful manager–trainer but his happy-go-lucky life was also touched by sadness. A few years later, his estranged, depressive wife put a cushion and a pistol to

---

*The tragedy reverberated for his family, however. 'After his death came the hard times,' Stephen recalled. His mother's attempt to run a fish and chip shop failed and she had to return to her factory job and withdraw her children from their private school, sending them to what Stephen called 'a lower-class state school', but in the end they pulled through. Adelaide left school, got married, had children, and then trained to become a teacher. Stephen tried his hand at boxing, but eventually accepted his mother's advice to 'use your brains, don't lose them'. He worked in Mike Segal's store, which helped him pay for college, and when I last spoke to him, fifteen years after his father died, he was a manager in a merchant bank, had bought his own house, and his mother was living with him. 'I'm cool now,' he said. 'I think of myself as a man.'

her head and pulled the trigger, with Harold and their daughter in the house.

The most avoidable of all the tragedies involved erstwhile Golden Boy Brian Baronet. The brutal beating he received at the purposeful hands of Arthur Mayisela should have ended his career, there and then. The picture of him lying unconscious on the Sun City ring canvas should have embedded itself in the minds of those around him, but they couldn't let it go and neither could Brian. They shared a dream and they couldn't drop it.

It is said that the only way to keep your senses together in the ring is to learn to avoid flying leather. And if you can't manage that you'd better be able to absorb it. For all his flash, Brian wasn't very good at either the avoiding or the absorbing, which meant he was putting his health on the line every time he answered the bell. After the Mayisela beating he was even more vulnerable, and yet he continued doing what he thought he knew best. He resumed his career in the United States, picked up three wins and a WBA rating, and once again was lined up for a shot at a world title. All he needed to do was win an American title, and his chosen opponent was one he'd already beaten three years earlier. But the 26-year-old Baronet had deteriorated alarmingly. This time, in October 1986, Harold Brazier dished out a severe beating, carving him up and finally stopping him in the tenth round.

Like so many fighting men Brian simply could not keep away. The son of a South African bantamweight and featherweight champion, the nephew of another double champion, the cousin of a South African light welterweight champion, he was too deeply immersed in boxing to drop it. He had started at five and no-one could stop him. The memory of all that adulation, and the hope of a fortune, but most of all the addiction to its motions, drew him back. 'You know, he just loved boxing so much,' his mother, Phyllis, said. 'He never drank, never smoked, never went out much, but he ate, slept and drank boxing. It wasn't like he needed the money because he had a beautiful clothing agency that was going well, but he thought he could make a successful comeback, and none of us discouraged him because we were behind him whatever he did. My husband, Ernie, had a beautiful gym, so he started coaching him again, but it's never a good thing for a father to train his son, so Doug Dolan came back, because he'd been with Brian since he was five.'

Dolan asked Berman to pick up where he'd left off, but this time the Johannesburg promoter refused. 'We knew there was still money to be made, but we also knew what had happened against Brazier. Brian was badly hammered, to the point where he was refused a licence in New Jersey, and I said no.' Dolan and Baronet then went to a rival promotional group, co-headed by Mayisela's old promoter, Mike Segal, who was delighted to have him, and the Boxing Board allowed him to renew his licence. 'Brian has the talent and matinee-idol good looks to pull the crowds, and he's a natural with the fans,' their fight publicist and former Springbok rugby centre Dr Wilf Rosenberg purred. Today, Rosenberg's former employer, Mike Segal, sees it differently. 'All I can say is thank God it's been the only tragedy of this kind of my promotional career. But in a way, I can also say we were deceived. His people told me his loss to Brazier was no big deal, just cuts, so I said OK, and although he didn't look so great in his first couple of fights, he was winning, and he was pulling the crowds like never before, and you know, it's hard to turn your back on something like that.'

He looked awful in his first fight, but the awkward moments were blamed on his 15-month layoff, and sweetened by 15,000 fans. Soon they were talking of securing another world ranking. 'Just as long as he bowls them over we will provide the backing,' Wilf chanted. He won again, but only after another struggle. His third opponent, a feather-fisted American lightweight called Kenny Vice, who had lost his previous bout and two more before that, was supposed to clinch the deal on Brian's home turf in Durban in June 1988.

Ten days before the fight Brian was shaken up in a car crash. A few days later he suffered a severe cold but the fight was put back by only a day. 'I remember him saying he didn't want to box,' Phyllis recalled, 'but, you know, he was addicted to boxing and wouldn't refuse.' For nine rounds Vice boxed careful rings around him. 'Brian looked strangely lethargic,' a confused Dolan said afterwards. 'He took a lot of punishment, but seemed to think he was in command. I told him he was losing the fight but he thought he was winning.' Always with an eye on the upside, that was Brian Baronet. Shortly before the bell to end the penultimate round, Vice wobbled Baronet with what seemed like an inconsequential punch, and when Brian rose from his stool for the final round he still looked dazed and shaky. Vice charged in, raining punches on Brian's half-protected head and one on the back of his neck as he collapsed. I remember thinking, 'Oh no, not another.

He's not going to get up.' Brian was counted out, and the only sign of life was the spasmodic twitching in his legs.

He was rushed to St Augustine's Hospital, already in a deep coma. Phyllis, Ernie and their older son Robert sat it out at his hospital bedside until he died four days later. 'In a way, that helped me because I knew he was going, and I had time to say goodbye,' said Phyllis. 'It was a terrible tragedy for the family but today I can look back and say Brian died doing the thing he loved most.'* Thousands attended his funeral.

I never really knew Brian Baronet and had been prejudiced against him but I felt sadness for the dead man and his family, and for those like Doug Dolan who must have been full of remorse. But by then I was becoming numbed to death. It's just that it was all around me. Friends, comrades, colleagues, acquaintances getting killed in car crashes, or murdered, or assassinated, or committing suicide. And by mid-1988, the second anniversary of the national State of Emergency, the numbers were rapidly mounting. In boxing too the carnage continued, one way or another. The former South African heavyweight champion Robbie Williams used a hosepipe to gas himself and his

---

*Phyllis said the family members reacted in different ways. 'Even today Robert can't look at those scrapbooks. Brian was his little brother and it was totally devastating for him.' Ernie died six years later as a result of a heart bypass and a brain haemorrhage. 'I won't say Brian's death caused Ernie's but he had a lot bottled up, seeing his son dying like that,' she said. Her own reaction was different: talking about it helped her to come to terms with it and she began counselling other bereaved parents. 'I also found it hard to put the pieces together, but then I grew through it as well,' she said.

children to death. Then one of Harold's boxers, the former South African light heavyweight champion Sakkie Horn, killed his two children and then himself with his pistol and Harold's wife ended her life with a bullet too. Then Richard Smith, a top trainer and former Transvaal bantamweight champion, was murdered by carjackers. Then one of my favourite boxers, the brilliant light heavyweight Ginger Tshabalala, was doing a favour by dropping a friend in town, where he was gunned down by carjackers – his life cut short when he was on the verge of a world-title fight. Then, in one scoop, thirty-three South African professional boxers were banned after testing HIV positive, including several national and 'world' champions. Within a few years many were dead.

In any event, I was too preoccupied to dwell on it. When Brian died, I assumed I had more important things to worry about than just one more death in my favourite sport. Today I feel differently. I'm well aware of what my friend, the Irish trainer Brendan Ingle, calls the 'drip, drip, drip effect' of head punches that happens in sparring. For every boxer killed in the ring, thousands suffer brain damage, or eye damage, or kidney damage, or breathing problems, and I know that the sport I support has done this to them. Even though they have chosen this profession themselves, I can no longer defend it with conviction. It may help a few thousand lads out of the ghetto and keep them from a life of crime. It may preoccupy them enough to re-channel their violent instincts. But I'm sure there are gentler ways of achieving that.

I have received several lucrative job offers from boxing promoters in the years since these deaths, but whenever I feel tempted I arrive at the conclusion that

I don't want anything more on my conscience. I prefer to maintain the fiction of distance. Drugs, alcohol, tobacco, jogging, chocolate – I've never felt remotely addicted to any of them. I have even managed celibacy when required. But boxing is different. What it comes down to is an addiction, a drug I can never quite shake off. I need my regular fix. And so, while I can no longer honestly justify it, I'm not sure I'd like to be forced to do without it. Just like Dancing Shoes, and the Golden Boy. And, in a way, the Fighting Prince too. Except they paid the price.

5

SUGAR AND SPIES

Springs, November 1987. Sugarboy steps off the scales, baring his perfect teeth in a perfect smile. 'After I'm finished with you, Sakkie, it will be a long time before you write out another parking ticket,' he says. I catch his eye and grin. It's just the kind of thing I love to hear from Thulani 'Sugarboy' Malinga about Sarel 'Sakkie' Horn.

I am about to write another round of law exams, and planning another motorbike expedition to Zimbabwe for yet another spell of ANC training, debriefing and instructions, but there is never any prospect of missing a chance to see my favourite boxer. Especially not for his 'rubber' match – a third fight after a win apiece – with my pet-hate traffic cop. For this, I am joined by Mark, my close friend, fellow law student and ANC underground comrade, and we arrive early at the indoor arena in the southern Transvaal town of Springs to witness vengeance and vindication.

The initial signs are wonderfully positive. Sugar comes in eight pounds lighter than the last time, full of confident intent, and it is immediately apparent he is in for an easy night. Fighting out of his pronounced crouch with his legs wide apart and his left hand dangling by his thigh, he shifts his head this way and that as the bigger man's fluttering jabs fail to connect. Sugar pumps home his own treatment with more purpose than usual, all the time smiling at his adversary, and Sakkie simply has no answers, no legitimate ones anyway.

But the traffic policeman is a trickster who knows where to find help. He turns to referee Colonel Wally Snowball for assistance. Snowball – he of the Mitchell–Morake tragedy – is just so obliging and Sakkie has already made his job that much easier by pulling his trunks up to four inches below his nipples. Every body punch thrown by Sugarboy produces a display of ham-acted groin clutching. Snowball glares at Sugarboy with cold grey eyes, issues warnings and orders point deductions. Three points deducted. But it's not enough so Horn tries to make up a little more of the deficit with some affirmative action – a couple of low blows, some head butts and then a trio of hearty chomps on Malinga's shoulder, once in full view of Snowball, who misses it despite the angry red tooth-mark indentations. But Sugarboy refuses to be deterred. By the end of the eleventh round he's way ahead, battering Horn with controlled precision without taking anything in return. In the final round he goes for the kill, knocking Sakkie all over the ring. With a minute to go, he belts Horn fractionally below the navel, and the traffic cop collapses. Once again Sakkie's gloves find their way to his groin and he rolls around in an inept display of agony. Snowball seizes the moment and disqualifies Sugarboy Malinga.

For a few silent seconds there is disbelieving hush in

the crowd – the final minute of the final round, this referee must be joking – and then as the realization dawns, the black section erupts, throwing chairs and surrounding the colonel. I hear Sugarboy's wheelchair-bound manager Maurice Toweel yelling: 'You racist, Snowball, you racist, you bladdy racist, you're a bladdy racist, Wally.' The police form a cordon around their man, and as I watch them bustling him away, I feel a surge of hatred, deep and passionate, and with this hatred comes an extra dose of adoration for Sugarboy.

He has come to personify boxing's version, my version, of apartheid's righteous victim. I need heroes and I'm falling short of them. My struggle heroes – well, they are really heroes no more. They are all flawed. I know them too well, or know too much about them. They too are fighters and tacticians, brave and strong, and some are kind and caring, but they are also schemers, philanderers, power brokers, people of personal as well as collective ambition, single-minded altruists – perhaps a few – but also liars and back-stabbers. They are too much like me, and I know I can be a bit of a shit. But Sugarboy – ah, he's different. He exists in a more exalted realm – a boxer of wonderful creativity, a warm and witty fellow, a family man who loves his wife and children, a brave and defiant victim of injustice. But most of all he is taking his place as my new personal representative of the cause of the masses – the punching, smiling antidote to the 'system'. That's what matters most to me. He's my new main man.

Standard Bank Arena, Johannesburg, February 1988. 'And definitely the most beautiful man I've ever seen,' my former girlfriend Toni whispers in a tone of deep admiration, and I certainly have no option but to agree, nor any inclination to dispute her verdict. It is two months after the Snowball heist and we're watching Sugarboy go through the motions against his next opponent, the Irish light heavyweight champion Harry Cowap. It is Toni's first Sugarboy moment and she isn't quite done. 'No, I mean, he really is lovely. Just look at that face: it's perfect. Just perfect.' And on she goes, extolling the wonders of his seat-warming smile before progressing to the prominence of those cheekbones, the breadth of those shoulders, the narrowness of that waist, the firm elegance of those thighs and calves. 'If he fights half as well as you say, he should be huge,' she concludes, and sits back to watch.

I'm gratified when Toni extols his beauty – it justifies an aspect of the hyperbole I've been offering all my other friends on a periodic basis. I've told them he's a lovely man, not just handsome but caring and intelligent, and not given to using his looks to get his way with women. In fact he seems embarrassed when reminded of his physical appeal. And there is so much more to go on besides his beauty – a good man forever on the cusp between triumph and tragedy. I tell them how this victim of terrible injustice continually defies the system, and when I've caught their curiosity I tell of the wonders of his boxing brain – thoroughly unpredictable, here sizzler, there somnambulist, but always fascinating. And Sugar is up for this one, playing the angles, nullifying attacks with those odd twists of his shoulders, shifting his handsome head a centimetre so that the incoming traffic passes harmlessly by, and now and then whacking wide to the body and then grinning at his adversary. Toni, a producer at an American television network, comes away utterly convinced. 'This guy is brilliant. Really, if he was in America there'd be no limit.' Actually, I reply, I'm not quite sure about this. Sugarboy's skills may be too subtle and variable, too hard to define for the Americans, but her endorsement convinces me that he is indeed a prophet without honour in his own country.

Yeoville, Johannesburg, April 1988. 'So what you think-ing of?' Wendy asks, while I'm lying on the bed, waiting for her to join me. I think for a moment and then I answer truthfully – truthfully but too coldly: 'Sugarboy.' It's not what she wants. I can see that. I could see that before I answered, but I couldn't stop myself. '*Ja*, Sugarboy Malinga . . .'

Wendy – that's what I'll call her – is the third since Pat and I broke up a year earlier, and she's the one. This time I'm sure. Well, almost sure. For a while I cling to this hope. Intelligent and kind, tough and vulnerable, my kind of pretty. And, hey, our politics, music tastes and pathologies all gel so nicely. And then, for no clear reason, I'm no longer sure. There's a song that keeps playing in my head – first introduced to me by Toni a few months earlier and now coming back incessantly – a Springsteen ballad about a cautious man, with LOVE tattooed on his right hand and FEAR on his left. He's determined to build a loving relationship, remain steady, not to run, but one night he wakes in sweat and takes to the highway, except that when he gets there, he finds no relief, only road. The man goes back to his wife but the song's message has to do more with reluctant discovery than victorious redemption. He feels a coldness inside him that he knows, like those tattoos, is there for life. This song has just been playing in my head and I start to console myself by saying, *Actually, this isn't the one*, but I also begin to wonder if, like the cautious man, I'm cold to the core, damaged goods. I'm starting to blame politics for this, with its nefarious sets of competing identities, its lies, layers of truth and its many disguises, and I worry I've lost the capacity to commit or to feel emotions beyond the world of the movie house; other than hate and rage and fear.

I don't like to dwell too long on these thoughts. They're disturbing. They don't fit, and it's at times like these that my mind sneaks back to boxing. The one follows the other. I'm taking one of these little moments when that most dreaded of questions – the one about what's on my mind – floats my way and I feel the coldness rise inside me. I realize Wendy wants so much more, but more is not on offer. '*Ja*, I mean, Sugarboy was absolutely fucking brilliant the other night,' and off I go, watching her as she looks away. A few downhill months later she breaks it off, and, as always, I'm relieved. I can dream of happy, loving worlds over some other rainbow, unimpeded by the real. Boxing is so good in that way, and, today, Sugarboy certainly helps.

There are many ways of distinguishing boxers, but the most common is between the fighter–brawler (the come-forward, square-stance attacker who takes two to land one, works up close and relies on hooks) and the 'scientific' boxer (who typically boxes side-on, leading with the jab and throwing straight punches, with the idea of hitting without being hit). With the stylistic inventions of the last few decades these definitions have become blurred and no longer provide a rule-of-thumb division between the best fighting men. I prefer another distinction: between script interpreters and the improvisers, or to stretch the metaphor and put it to music, between the classicists who work from a score, and the bebop jammers who work from imagination and possess that rare capacity to break stylistic rules and invent. There were some early probes in this direction but it was really Muhammad Ali – boxing's Charlie Parker if you like – who shattered the mould, and from then on they flourished, breaking rule after rule in their bid for an edge.

Sugarboy was one of them: a creator of moves, a boxer whose motions were unpredictable, who seldom moved in straight lines, who made it up as he went along and did things no other boxer had done before. Like many innovators he relied on an inconsistent supply of inspiration. He always looked unusual, fighting from a low, wide-footed, dangly-handed crouch, but when the mood was wrong, nothing would flow. His motions would become jerky, his punches slaps, and he would retreat into a defensive shell. But there were moments when his ability to invent was remarkable. He would find angles, exploit gaps and avoid fists in a way that was unique. And on the rare occasions when he put it all together he had the capacity to astonish. This set him apart.

He first made his name by beating up white men, and white South African men don't play the free jazz of dissonance. Everyone in the game knows it: they brawl or box to formulas, now and then so well that they can beat the best in the world, but they don't go in for open-ended jamming. Black South African boxing, on the other hand, consistently throws up the unorthodox, the unexpected and the undisciplined. This, of course, is not a genetic thing, although it is so often perceived that way. My friend Maxine, who is Jewish, tells me Jews don't have it in them to fight, and she has no ears for my old-time religious stories of the divine Benny Leonard or the magnificent Ted 'Kid' Lewis or any of the other great Jewish battlers. Rodney Berman goes further, insisting that 'white boys can't fight', and every example I give him to the contrary is explained as the 'exception that proves the rule'. Actually, exceptions disprove rules – and there really are no DNA-related formulas linking ethnicity to fighting prowess. The word 'cultural' is also too glib because it relates to a million collective impulses, which have to do with notions of God, family, community and the individual, of time and place, and we're only talking boxing after all. But it might just have something to do with the backbeat boxers grow up to – its rhythms and melodies – or, conversely, with the absence of music. When I watched white South African fighters going about their business I couldn't help thinking that a bit of the regimentation of their schools, families and armed services found its way into their arms and legs, and I was also tempted to suspect that the unpredictable volatility of township life was reflected in the black boxers' motions, producing men who lived and died by their wits. The better trainers from both ends bent the stick in the other direction, revealing the limits to this ethnic generalization. So let's not push this stereo-typing too far except to say that it's unlikely that white South Africa could have produced a boxer like Thulani Malinga.

When Thulani was born in 1955 South Africa was entering its most brutal phase of National Party rule. They were preparing to make the shift from old-fashioned *baaskap* racial domination to what they regarded as a scientific theory of segregation, apartheid. The plan was to relocate the country's African population (70 per cent of the total) to ten 'homelands' – comprising 13 per cent of the land – which were given a kind of nominal sovereignty over their own affairs, eventually leading to putative 'independence'. Thulani grew up on a farm near to the conservative farming town of Ladysmith, on the edge of Chief Mangosuthu Buthelezi's KwaZulu homeland, where the mainly Zulu inhabitants provided labour among the cane rats and black mambas of the Natal sugar fields and other farms. Thulani's father, who died when he was five, worked the cattle; his mother, who died when he was twelve, worked in the kitchen.

An intelligent boy who excelled in school, his early ambition was to become a doctor, but the death of both parents put an end to this. John, the oldest of seven brothers and three sisters, struggled to keep the family going, so Thulani had to work on the farm after school, increasing his workload when his twins – a boy and a girl – were born soon after his nineteenth birthday. 'Each day when I finished classes I had to milk the cows and things like that, just to help us survive,' he explained to me, 'so I couldn't really be thinking of training to become a doctor or going to university because the family needed money. I had to keep on working on the farm while at school, and then after I finished school, when I was twenty, I went to work in a furniture shop, and stayed there for nearly twelve years.'

He was an extremely frustrated young man who watched his ambitions fade into the drudgery of labour, and these frustrations were sometimes expressed through his fists and his feet. 'I had a very quick temper in those days so I used to fight a lot in the streets, and I was very rough and would always win,' he said. He tried out karate for a couple of years, until John took him aside for a chat. 'He said to me: "I think you'd better do boxing." I said: "You think it's going to help me?" And he said: "Yes, it will teach you to fight properly," so I went to the gym to learn and right from the start I was sparring with much bigger men and I enjoyed it because I didn't like getting beaten by other men, no matter how big they were, and I found I could handle the big ones. I was boxing nearly every day in the gym and so I stopped fighting in the streets.'

Thulani had found his new vocation – the business of hurting overcoming the urge for a career in curing. The prime influence was his older cousin, Maxwell Malinga, an elusive, clowning, slapping welterweight who hovered on the fringes of the world ratings in the early 1970s. Teenage Thulani began sparring with Maxwell while also winning South African amateur titles in three weight divisions. Along the way he adopted the name 'Sugarboy' without any thought of the implications of being called 'boy' in apartheid South Africa. 'You see I came from sugarcane country, but also it was because my style was sweet-as-sugar.' He won his first professional fight in the first round in 1981, at the age of 25 (while claiming to be 21). He and his partner, Nomso, already had three children and he viewed boxing as a way of supplementing the income from the furniture shop.

Maxwell taught his cousin many of his good old tricks and some of his bad old habits. He knew very little about the rigours of modern boxing training and had never been the greatest advertisement for dedication but in Thulani's world, family came first, and in any event there were no other options in Lady-smith. Maxwell started him out as a light heavyweight, next boiled him down 21 pounds to light middleweight and then after only eight fights threw him in with the South African middleweight champion Samson Mohloai. Thulani's immense natural talent prevailed and to the astonishment of the punters he won easily on points despite damaging a knuckle on his right hand. Today it seems bizarre that the promotional powers of the day failed to pounce on this display of potential – a handsome 23-year-old (supposedly) lifting a national title while still in the early novice stage – but this was an epoch when promoters and sponsors believed that commercial pull required a white skin, so for several years his potential was ignored.

But some of the problems were of Thulani's own making. He languished in obscurity until Sun City offered him a minor slot on a world-title bill in July 1985, when he was to face a hardy white middleweight, Pieter de Bruin. It was the kind of occasion he could have used as a staging post to launch himself. Instead he blew it. He had just married Nomso after the birth of his fourth child and was not fully focused, so he clutched and clowned his way to a boring victory. Six months later, without Sun City to impress, he fought de Bruin again and knocked him cold. He went on to wipe out the rest of the division, with everything flowing beautifully. The tongue poking, mimicry and gentle mockery may have been derivative – borrowed from Maxwell who lifted the idea from Ali – but there was nothing tired about it. It was more a case of drawing notice to the vast gulf between the depth of his own imaginative skills and the shallow predictability of the opposition. None could touch him and he seemed to be having a great deal of fun driving this message home. Soon he had run out of men his size left to beat, and so he decided to step up two divisions to challenge the national light heavyweight champion, Sakkie Horn.

A word on black–white rivalries in the 1980s: part of the problem was that the texture of the country's political life made its imprint on the sport. The amateur game was run on apartheid lines under the say-so of an army brigadier who did not believe in racial integration – or at least not until a sudden conversion in 1992, shortly before the Barcelona Olympics. He insisted on separate white, coloured and black championships, the only concession being that permission was granted for a supreme champion in each division, with the catch that the bulk of the officials came from the white body.

The professional game prided itself on being apartheid-free since 1979, but this was not the full truth. For one thing, full integration was legally impossible. In the mid-1980s black boxers could still not spend time in white 'group' areas without special permission. But it was more than inconvenience. The Boxing Board of Control was an all-white, government-appointed structure. Later, when its international position was under threat, the government appointed a black board member for the first time, although he was replaced by a white military general as soon as his presence was no longer expedient. Dissenters, including 'rebellious' black managers, were frozen out and the majority of officials were white. In title fights featuring black and white boxers the usual practice was to appoint two white judges and one black. If it was close it went to the white lad. The result was a perception within the black boxing fraternity that 'you have to score a knockout to get a draw with these Boers' – as one black manager put it to me. The Malinga–Horn rivalry solidified this perception, with the feeling made more intense by the fact that we were four months into a national State of Emergency – or at least that was the way I saw it from the skewed vantage point of an activist in hiding from the police.

So let me divert even further from Sugar and Sakkie to say a bit more about how it felt. Before the national State of Emergency my life seemed predictable enough. Sure, there was always the possibility of detention or assault and for a few months the 1985 partial Emergency offered an ominous sense of what was to come, but there was a discernible pattern to existence. I would do my day job as a journalist while my evenings were taken up with political meetings, and once every fortnight or so I would send out a coded report to the ANC on political developments. Now and then I would travel to conferences around the country, and at the end of each year I would ride my motorbike through the night to Harare for a week of ANC training and debriefing under the guise of doing research work for an American public radio journalist. I loved these trips – not just because they made me feel important, but because they were relaxing. I had to be careful of surveillance, but at the same time I was temporarily out of reach of the regime – a guest within a 'liberated' zone that, unlike Johannesburg and Cape Town, felt African.

The national Emergency changed all this. First there was the excitement of jumping out of windows to avoid the security police, and then going into disguise, and moving around from house to house to avoid detection – always on the run, with no sense of personal obligation and a loosening sense of personal morality. There was a kind of freedom in it – plenty of clandestine meetings and tasks, but most of the time I could move at my own rhythm. For instance, a few weeks into the Emergency I rode my bike to and from Cape Town on some supposedly urgent mission, and on the way back the chain broke. I pushed the bike three miles to the nearest *dorp* – village – arriving at 9 p.m. I was short of money so I went to the local police station, asked them to put me up for the night, and ended up sharing a locked cell with a harmless drunk – the safest place in the middle of a State of Emergency, I thought. The next morning I bought a spare link, repaired the chain and rode home, with none of my comrades any the wiser.

Before the Emergency I dreamt of inertia: I had something vital to complete – a law exam, an organizational task – and I could never get it together; something would always get in the way, I couldn't move my feet or get off the mark, and the moment would draw closer without progress. In other dreams I was fighting but without power or strength. I would try a head butt up close and my head would flop. I was ineffective. But with the Emergency I had a new, recurring dream. Often it would start with detention and escape, and would always progress to a chase. I would run and run effortlessly, without feeling tired – always in Cape Town, the place of dreams, usually through forest and mountain – and every night I would leave them behind and wake up with a smile on my face.

But once the thrill wore off, the running dreams were over and I was left with a feeling of perpetual insecurity. All the political groups I was involved with were banned or restricted. Some individuals – like Pat – were slapped with restriction orders banning them from attending political gatherings, while thousands of others were detained without trial. Having avoided detention I had to step up my political role, with early morning meetings of the publicity directorate of the UDF held in distant suburbs, as well as a fresh range of ANC activities including heading a new underground unit.

The security police lacked the resources to watch every activist, and therefore relied even more heavily than before on their spies and informers, and this was the issue that was haunting me at the time of the first Malinga–Horn fight. It was the backdrop to every meeting and relationship I had – can I trust you? Will you betray me?

Spies and rumours of spying had always been part of the currency of the activist milieu. These rumours often turned out to be false – a personal grudge, a mistaken assumption, a dirty-trick whisper emanating from the state, some idle speculation burning out of control – with horrible consequences for those wrongly fingered. The state sometimes turned this climate to its advantage, either by exacerbating existing suspicion or alleviating it. Their usual trick was to detain their informers – give the spies a rest, allow time for debriefing, strengthen their credentials. Sometimes they were more innovative. Once they printed pamphlets naming a suspected activist, announcing he was a spy. The effect was to allay suspicion – if the cops were defaming him he must be innocent. A year later, however, the suspect was spotted driving in the back seat of a car with two senior security policemen, and then ducking down on the back seat when he thought he'd been spotted.

The climate of suspicion was not restricted to Afrikaners. The ANC was even more paranoid about foreign journalists. One case I was directly concerned with involved a British journalist. I first met this debonair colonial when a pair of lefty South African reporters – I'll call them 'Intrigued' and 'Besotted' – asked me to join them for supper. They told me in gushing detail about this fresh catch – Oxbridge, southern African specialist, military past, but 'sympathetic' (even though he worked for a conservative paper), 'and he wants to meet comrades like you.' 'Dashing' was as described – ruddily handsome, public-school posh, stylishly dressed and, apparently, right-on politically. After supper we went to Besotted's flat, and when I was well stoned, Dashing began to test me out. 'I think the ANC should go further – really take its war to the heart of the white areas – give 'em something to think about.' I asked him what he was suggesting. 'Something like a nursery school,' he said. 'Yes, that would do it; go and bomb a nursery school – strike a bit of terror and realism into their hearts. Don't you agree? What do you think, Gavin?' I told him I strongly disagreed, but over the next few weeks he pestered me for meetings, asking me to put him in touch with comrades. I reported this to my ANC superiors, who warned me to keep away – he'd been expelled from an African country for possession of unlicensed firearms, his spell in the military was spent in the intelligence services, and he was on a list of British agents supplied by their Soviet sponsors. I warned Intrigued but a few months later she told me that one night, while sleeping over at a house shared by Besotted and Dashing, he entered her room, pinned her to the bed and raped her. 'He must have had some terrible experiences in the military,' she said, 'because there was a mad violence about him I'd never seen before.' I still can't be sure Dashing was a spy, but whatever his angle, he got away with it. Soon afterwards he was featured as an eligible bachelor by a local style magazine, then returned to England, still eating out on his African adventures.

I was also involved through the ANC underground in investigating the bona fides of several prominent black leaders, and the process revealed a snakepit of opportunism and betrayal. One case involved 'Comrade Mayibuye', an immature young man with a high-pitched voice whom I first got to know through a strike support committee in Cape Town, where his childish antics were tolerated by older hands because of their amusement value. A few years later, however, he pitched up in Johannesburg and emerged as a trade union official, where he worked with some of my closest underground comrades. During the middle of a particularly significant strike Mayibuye disappeared and a week later pitched up at the union offices in a state of high-pitched panic. 'I just stabbed a student in a fight in Cape Town,' he said, 'and he bled to death. The police are after me. What must I do?' My comrades told him to disappear because a murder committed by a unionist was the last thing they needed in the middle of a strike. Mayibuye vanished, but a month later reappeared, operating openly. 'You're mad,' my comrades told him, but he seemed unconcerned, telling them, 'The police have lost interest.' Soon after he re-emerged as the lieutenant of a youth leader who, the ANC leadership insisted, had been turned by the security police. A few years later Mayibuye and his youth mentor went on to become extremely wealthy ANC MPs, the slate of their past collusion wiped clean.

While these were big fish, at the time of the first three Malinga–Horn fights the two cases that caused me most anguish, time and energy involved a pair of lower-level white women spies who infiltrated white activist groups, before joining the ANC.

Joy Harnden was a baby-faced little woman with a boyish swagger who came from a broken family – growing up under a different name, thinking her mother was her sister – within a small town Afrikaner town. She apparently avoided politics while studying journalism in Grahamstown, yet as soon as she set foot in Johannesburg in 1984 she thrust herself to the forefront of a range of political groups. I was immediately suspicious and was later sent to Grahamstown to investigate, returning with hard evidence of her security police connections. I sent the ANC regular reports on her movements, and when she visited Maputo with her activist housemate in 1985 my underground unit made sure the ANC was tipped off before her arrival. However, bitter factional rivalries within the ANC prevented the message from reaching its destination and instead of being detained she was recruited into an internal ANC unit headed by an activist called Iggy Mathebula. Joy returned to Johannesburg and met with Iggy, who disappeared soon afterwards. The ANC pleaded with us not to expose her because they were worried that this might further compromise Iggy's position, and instead asked us to encourage her to visit Harare, where they could seize her. But by this stage Joy knew she was under suspicion. The security police detained her a couple of times and she made her excuses not to travel. We blocked her from leadership positions but when the Emergency was declared her presence became impossible to deal with and so eventually, despite ANC opposition, we expelled her, creating a furore among members who trusted her. A few months later she emerged publicly as a security police lieutenant. Iggy was never seen again.*

The other case was more disturbing than tragic. Olivia Forsyth was a large, gregarious woman who joined the UDF-aligned student movement in Grahamstown as a postgraduate student in 1981. She was soon under suspicion – her radicalism too shrill, bits of her background unaccounted for and she seemed overly keen to sleep with every male activist who crossed her path – but the search was put off by internecine struggles within student circles. In 1985 a student leader came to talk to me about the problem. He was close to the group backing her but felt she was, indeed, a spy. I had never respected Olivia but wasn't convinced. I reminded him that members of the other faction had previously 'branded' three young men who turned out to be innocent, but he persuaded me to take it seriously, warning me she would soon be moving to Johannesburg. When Olivia arrived my flatmate, Maxine, who had never met her before, said there was something about her she didn't trust. 'No-one who eats seaweed rings true, and she certainly doesn't,' said Max. 'She was drunk and puking on the carpet. She's under strain and she's not who she says she is, and I don't think you should trust her.' I blocked Olivia's access to various local political groups she tried

*Joy changed her name again and returned to low-profile trade journalism.

to join. Frustrated by their protégée's lack of progress the security police launched Operation Olivetti and Olivia suddenly announced she had found a post as a continent-trotting African researcher. The ANC recruited her, despite the warnings, but caught her making contact with her security police handlers. They accepted her plea that she'd been recruited as an impressionable 18-year-old at a time she could have gone either way, and went along with her offer to become a double agent, but it soon became clear she was stringing them along and she was despatched to the ANC's Quatro detention camp in Angola where she spilt the beans on several other spies (all caught and imprisoned). A year later Olivia escaped from house arrest after developing close relations with her guards, and took refuge in the British Embassy. The ANC was embarrassed but kept shtoom, although local activists took to wearing 'I never slept with Olivia' buttons. Lieutenant Forsyth then emerged in a blaze of publicity, falsely claiming she'd infiltrated the top levels of the UDF and ANC.*

These cases revealed an astonishing depth of incompetence within the exile-based ANC. I was beginning to realize there were serious weaknesses I had previously been blinded to by loyalty. Messages weren't reaching their intended destination. Spies were infiltrating their ranks or slipping through their fingers. The lives of good comrades were being compromised or lost through bungling. Far from a unified movement, the exile-based ANC was beset with power struggles. For the first time in my six years of ANC underground

---

*She later married a cop, had two children, left the cop and emigrated to Britain.

membership it began to dawn on me that the machine I was serving was faulty, and liable to break down without warning. I was becoming concerned about these problems, and the constant moves from house to house, the shortage of money and the prospect of detention exacerbated my unease. It was an extremely unsettled existence, driving me into a kind of outlaw mode of operating. I had long played loose with the law in all sorts of areas, but with the Emergency this reached new levels.

To take one example: late in 1986 I drove off on my motorbike for a meeting with an habitually tardy trade union official at Mike's Kitchen restaurant in Johannesburg. On the way I was stopped at a roadblock and gave my name as Richard Johnson – one of several I used for such purposes. The officer radioed headquarters where it emerged that a Richard Johnson, driving the same vehicle, had failed to stop at a stop sign nine months earlier, and had also failed to pay his fine. The bike was impounded, I was finger-printed and had to sign several forms in the name Richard Johnson – fortunately producing something resembling my original signature – and then I was taken to John Vorster Square, where I kept my head down in the hope that I wouldn't be spotted by a security policeman. I had R197 on me – a fortuitous withdrawal that morning, which depleted my bank account – and after a charm offensive I managed to 'borrow' R3 from a kind-hearted cop and was released on R200 bail. However, to get my bike back I needed to appear in court the next day in the name of Richard Johnson. The case was to be heard by an extremely fierce-looking martinet of a magistrate but I managed to persuade the policeman on duty that I was a real basket case and should be switched to the woman magistrate in the adjacent court.

'How do you plead, Mr Johnson?' she asked.

'Guilty, definitely very guilty, your honour.'

'Do you have anything to say for yourself in mitigation?'

'There are no excuses for failing to pay fines, your honour. I know this.'

'So why didn't you pay?'

'Your honour, I'm fully to blame. I went to my parents' home in East London two weeks before the fine was due and gave the money to my girlfriend, Gloria, and asked her to pay, but she didn't get round to it, which I know is no excuse because I should have checked.'

'Well, Mr Johnson, I presume you had a few words with, um, Gloria, yesterday.'

'No, your honour, actually she left me last week.'

The magistrate let out a little giggle, at which point Richard Johnson's face fell and it was touch and go whether the tears would flow.

'I'm sorry,' said the contrite magistrate. 'I'm so sorry. I didn't mean to laugh.'

Her going rate for unpaid traffic fines that day was R300. She rather apologetically fined me R50, plus the R50 of the original traffic fine, which meant I was able to sign Richard Johnson's name for one last time, get back R100 of my bail money, and drive off on my bike. Two days later I met up with the tardy trade unionist.

'Why didn't you come for our meeting?' he inquired rather aggressively.

'I did. I was there,' I insisted. 'Where were you?'

'I didn't see you.'

'Well, you must have been late again.'

'No more than ten minutes, at the most.'

'Yes, comrade, but you know we have a five-minute rule, so after exactly five minutes I left. We can't take unnecessary risks.'

'*Ja*, OK, sorry then, but I actually had trouble getting there. There was a roadblock.'

'Sure, comrade, sure.'

My biggest Emergency problem was money. I was unable to risk working from an office and therefore earned almost nothing. I had no other source of income and was too proud to ask the ANC for help. Eventually I decided to take matters into my own hands. I had done my share of gratuitous nicking in my early student years, but this felt different – there was an element of noble necessity. I stripped my broken motorbike, sold the parts, dumped the shell and claimed the insurance. When that was paid I bought a bigger bike and then insured the contents of a slum-zone flat where I lived for a couple of months, removed them, smashed the window and made another claim. The assessor, an ex-cop, was dubious, regularly arriving early in the morning to interrogate me. 'Where did you say the hi-fi was?' or 'What colour was the lining of the leather jacket?' and I would respond in a tone of gratitude, which exasperated him because he wanted me to feel I was against the wall. Eventually they coughed up the full R8,000, allowing me to continue avoiding the office, fund my legal studies and deliver 20 per cent to the ANC. My final act of dispossession came when I moved into my eighteenth flat in a year and decided I needed a security gate as a precaution against early morning door-kicking raids. I walked into a department store, put a huge metal grid under my arm, and strolled out. No-one in their right mind lifts security gates but perhaps I wasn't quite in my right mind. Certainly, in none of this did I have the slightest tinge of conscience. I rationalized that it was all necessary for me to operate effectively in the struggle.

There was, however, one exception to this pretence of Robin Hood altruism: boxing. It had become the one constant in my life, my sole sustained detour from the outlaw lifestyle, and at the same time a diversion that seemed to mirror aspects of conflict in society. And this often had a greater clarity than the world it reflected. On the one side there was the struggle with its intrigue and uncertainty, its spies and its rumours of spies, its cabals and factions, and on the other was boxing: beautiful and simple, featuring hand-to-hand combat between the champions of the masses, like Sugarboy Malinga, and the champions of the system, like Sergeant Sakkie Horn.

I should mention that this was not quite how Thulani saw his own role. His family made a point of avoiding public allegiances in 'struggle' politics because, for life and death reasons, they did not want to be positioned on one or the other side of the war between the ANC and Inkatha in Natal. He spoke out against racism and apartheid and showed great admiration for Nelson Mandela, later wearing the logo 'Madiba Magic!' on his trunks, but that's as far as he'd go in public. His own life was a struggle of a different kind: against poverty, against injustice in his career, against fortuitous tragedy and against the natural elements. But that wasn't my angle on the man. I was on the hunt for a new hero, following the death of Arthur Mayisela. So let me backtrack to a warm spring afternoon in 1986 when Sugarboy began to assume this role – for me, certainly, and I suspect for thousands of others who turned up at the Portuguese Hall that Saturday.

Sakkie Horn was always polite when I spoke to him, but for me it was contempt at first sight. He had a soft-chinned face, decorated with a thin moustache and a pudding bowl haircut – a combination that spoke of, say, Pretoria Department of Home Affairs clerk, although he was in fact a traffic cop from the Johannesburg dormitory suburb of Brakpan. There was something conceited about his thick-lipped mouth, child-like nose and hooded brown eyes. Those eyes in particular revealed arrogance, fear and cruelty and that was certainly how he fought – tricky, opportunistic and scared. Despite always being in impeccable condition Sakkie could never manage anything approaching definition in his big-hipped, hairless trunk, even when he went into weight training, but he had good, strong legs. He moved well and was schooled to a point of considerable competence – poking out his jab, running, occasionally taking a chance with a right cross. There was nothing attractive about it, but it could be effective. He was only 24 but already in his fifth year as a professional, long enough to learn his way around the rules. But my biggest gripe related to what his rise said about the state of the game. His family was closely connected to the white establishment that still controlled the game in those days. Sakkie, the older boxing brother from a large boxing family, was consistently given generous favours when it came to close fights. They ignored his younger brother, Jan, because he lacked the talent to cut it, but Sakkie was different: he was treated as something special. The Boxing Board made sure that whenever he fought he was under the protection of tame white referees and judges – men who bent over backwards for him, particularly when it came to black opposition – and I hated that.

Thulani was therefore taking on rather more than just another predictable white boy when they began their four-year rivalry, but he relished the opportunity. Horn, with his upright, darting, jab-and-move style had no clue how to handle this smaller, smiling, stalking man in front of him. Sugarboy would slide in, bang him to the body, snap in an uppercut and then evaporate, while Horn's frightened punches would pass harmlessly. In the fourth round he dropped Sakkie then cut him under the eye and Horn's only answer was to grab his own groin in hope of rescue. This time it didn't work. The fight was so one-sided that in the last round Sugarboy decided to have some fun. He dropped his guard, stuck out his chin, and finally Horn got to him with the biggest right of his life. Malinga went down and down again, but regained his composure sufficiently to survive. I went home relieved and delighted with his victory.

I had no meetings that day and went off to work on some law and smoke some dagga with a friend, before traipsing off to another friend's flat in Berea, Johannesburg. I left at midnight, still thinking about Sugarboy, shadow-boxing as I trotted down the empty road, when I was grabbed from behind by two *tsotsies* – township thugs. They looked about 18 years old and presumably were new to the mugging business because they turned out to be less than competent. I wriggled around and kicked one in the groin. He dropped to the pavement with a little groan and I forgot about him. I was busy wrestling with the other – trying to recall my rusty judo moves of old – when the fallen one rose, clutching a carving knife in his hand. I managed to catch his wrist as he drew his arm back but I suddenly felt the sense of calm reason that sometimes comes with sheer terror. *What if number two gets the knife – he'll cut my throat from behind?* And so, still gripping extremely tight, I negotiated my way to surrender: 'OK, I'm going to let go – you can have what you want – my leather jacket, anything – but don't stab me,' and I released my grip. They made me lie down, said nothing, and cut me lightly around the throat – just a skin cut because they wanted no more than to scare me – but I felt the blood and then the sting and feared the worst. They then divested me of my jacket and wallet and ran, still not saying a word. Feeling angry and stupid for not screaming and most of all ashamed that I had given in – that I had snatched yellow defeat from the jaws of red-blooded victory; that once again I had been a coward – I too ran, reached the flat, grabbed my motorbike and tried to find them, but I was relieved that they had vanished. I then rode to Pat's Yeoville flat – we were still part-time lovers then – for comfort and reassurance, and so ignored the risk of a police raid, feeling more than ever that things were not quite in control.

Two weeks later I drove my rather ancient Honda 750:4 up to Harare for a fortnight of ANC tuition, debriefing and training. I trusted my ANC controllers. They seemed like good men and women – all rather intense, and without much indication of any non-political hinterland to their lives (though they might have suspected the same about me), but they were reliable, friendly and dedicated. I needed reassurance, although I didn't say as much, and they provided it.

The fuck-ups over the spies, well, those mistakes were made by comrades in Lusaka and Luanda, I was told, but they won't happen again – comrades have been disciplined. They soon had me writing detailed reports on political developments and recommending military targets I had tentatively surveyed before departing, while providing further training in the theory of 'military combat work' and counter-surveillance. When all this was completed to their satisfaction, Comrade Roger and Comrade Harris (as they were then called – names kept changing) put a question to me: 'Comrade Rory, we would like to invite you to join the party.'

Once again, there was no hesitation. 'Yes, I would feel honoured.'

'Usually you are required to fulfil a six-month probation but the party feels you have served with distinction in the underground for long enough so that we can waive this.'

'Yes, six years now.'

'Well, yes, this should have happened earlier,' said Comrade Roger. 'But there was some concern in the party a while ago when you expressed, um, reservations, about the Soviet Union's role in Poland and Afghanistan, but we assured them that you've come around to a mature understanding of these questions.'

'We all enjoyed your contribution on Left Wing Communism: an Infantile Disorder,' Comrade Harris added, in reference to my marshalling of Lenin in an internal strategy and tactics debate.

They told me of the rules and regulations and I was happy to abide by all of them, nodding in agreement when they mentioned the theoretical possibility of the 'ultimate sanction' – the death penalty – for those who betrayed the party. This, of course, was something I would never do. I rather liked the idea of the ultimate sanction.

In any other mid-1980s context, membership of a pro-Soviet South African Communist Party would be a dubious distinction, but the SACP had a special symbolic place within the ANC at that time. The party, which was banned in 1950 – a decade before the ANC – regarded itself as the intellectual, strategic and military vanguard. It played the central role in setting up the underground and the ANC's army, Umkhonto we Sizwe, and recruited most of the leading comrades from that era. I later learnt from a trusted party leader (who was also a key member of the ANC National Executive Committee and who'd been an underground comrade of Nelson Mandela's in the early 1960s) that Madiba himself joined the party after the ANC was banned – partly because it was seen as useful in winning the trust of the Soviets and their clients.*

The party saw itself as a political home for the best and the bravest within the ANC. However, it had no independence from the rest of the movement – it was not a case of the tail wagging the dog – and its exalted status owed much to its role as a channel of funds, arms and favours from the Soviet bloc, which meant that even non-communists accepted its legitimacy. After all, Britain and America denigrated the ANC and under Reagan and Thatcher provided active backing to

*In the Rivonia treason trial the state produced a document in Mandela's handwriting in which he told why he was a communist, but it was excused as his attempt to explain to a young communist probationary the way he should phrase such a declaration – a deceit that suited the ANC, the party, the CIA and even the apartheid state. In fact, the politburo member insisted, Mandela did indeed become a member.

the government and Inkatha – Thatcher called Mandela a 'terrorist' and some Young Conservatives called for his hanging. The idea of taking money, arms, bursaries and training from the other side seemed logical. There was no debate here. Even those who preferred Western ways, like Thabo Mbeki, were prepared to serve on the party's leadership structures as long as it fitted in with the ANC's programme and their own ambitions. And while some of us may have had closet misgivings about Soviet socialism, this shouldn't be overstated. For instance, I never heard a whisper of criticism about Cuba, which at the time was generously assisting the ANC and fighting the apartheid-backed (and American-backed) Unita terror campaign in Angola.* In fact we all adored Cuba and at least grudgingly respected the Soviets.**

I was still a true believer in the mid-1980s. When not kicking against authority, I was very much the party man: a line-taker and line-dispenser, a castigator of political deviants and vacillators, an advocate of doctrinal certainties. I had this vision of a post-insurrection victory march behind the red flag, through the centre of Johannesburg, like that scene out of *Reds*, with hundreds of thousands of us lustily singing the *Internationale*. More immediately, I was seduced by the veil of silence and recognition bestowed by party membership, and Comrades Harris and Roger were

---

*Soon after, Cuba inflicted a strategic defeat on the South African military in Cuito Cuinivale in Angola, which accelerated decolonization of Namibia, and ultimately the settlement at home.

**I later discovered that several comrades I was close to, including some extremely senior cadres who later served in government, had been recruited to the KGB.

quick to press this point home. 'We're going to take you to meet a very senior leader of our party and our movement,' Harris said, and I was made to lie face down on the back seat in their car, so that I could not see where we were going, and could not be seen.

When I was ushered into the meeting room and saw the face I was immensely gratified: Chris Hani, an ANC military leader whose courage, wiles and exploits had grown into legend. There were others in the ANC who were technically his superior but none could approach his status among members of the military and underground, nor his popularity among the masses at home, and I felt honoured that he had wanted to see me. We spent ninety minutes together in a stuffy little room on a summer's afternoon, somewhere in the outskirts of Harare, discussing military targets and political factions. We were soon laughing and joking, the best of friends, and as we left I patted his tummy and told him how wonderful it was to see him, 'but you're a bit bigger in the flesh than I expected'. He roared with laughter, and I went home a confirmed Hani fan.

I rode back to Johannesburg the next night with a reinvigorated faith. A hawk rose from the road to brush my helmet and I had to stop for a giraffe that had wandered onto the road. I arrived home ready for the unexpected. The Emergency had prompted new ways of working and new strategies and my ANC underground unit was particularly full of vigour and enthusiasm – making regular reports on political issues, recommending fresh recruits, and carrying out various tasks assigned to us.

On one occasion a Wits lecturer tipped me off that Major Craig Williamson, a notorious security policeman, former spy and assassin,* was living in a large house outside Johannesburg. She provided me with all the required details, including the restaurant he visited for lunch. He was certainly a suitably 'hard' target, albeit one with a grotesquely soft body, and I was delighted with the chance to have him killed. We hired a vehicle, changed the number plates, surveyed the house, took photographs, worked out positions of attack and delivered the details to the ANC, who assured us they would mortar him. But nothing happened and the Wits lecturer must have given up on me and turned instead to some of her students, because six months later we read a little report in the *Star* newspaper that the outer walls of the house we reconnoitred had been graffitied with slogans like 'Fascist scum' and 'Pig'. The owner, another Craig Williamson, pleaded with those responsible to stop because he was not Craig the cop, but Craig the liberal businessman. We sent an urgent message to Harare telling them the news, and received a reply that it was just in time – they were about to move. *Yeah sure*, we thought, *pull the other one*. It was at times like this that the ANC's incompetence was a blessing.

The day after that *Star* report, my sister Karen arrived to join me in Johannesburg. She had been coaxed by a journalist friend from her school days to assist a radical news agency called Port Elizabeth News, and was sent on a training course run by the *Weekly Mail*. Michael and I had always viewed Karen as our baby sister – five years younger than me, seven younger than Michael –

---

*Williamson later admitted responsibility for several letter and parcel-bomb murders, with the victims including the wife of one ANC leader he hated and the wife and daughter of another.

and therefore she operated in a different realm, seldom included in the political discourse. But now we were near-neighbours who also worked closely together and helped each other, and the experience pulled us closer. Three months later, however, Karen's fairweather friend abandoned PEN to seek her fortune in Johannes-burg, after which the security police burgled the office, forcing Karen to drop her course and rush back to sort out the mess. The next day her house was raided by the security police, who dragged her off to the office, photographed the equipment and cleared it out the next day – once again under the pretence of robbery. The experience turned Karen into a seasoned activist, determined to revive the agency, and somehow she pulled it off. Seven years later the security police admitted responsibility for the burglaries and offered to return the equipment (but never kept their word).

While all this was happening, Sugarboy Malinga received a world ranking with the WBA after defending his national title in brilliant style against a huge-hitting bruiser called Freddie Rafferty, but it took six months before his next fight, once again featuring Sakkie Horn, this time in the white section of the rightwing-controlled Northern Transvaal town of Pietersburg. Maxwell figured it would be easier second time around, and Thulani's training was lackadaisical. He came in well over his peak weight but was doing just enough to win, despite the chants of a hostile crowd. Horn resorted to holding and head-butting, but Sugarboy decked him in the eleventh and knocked him around the ring in the twelfth and everyone at ringside, includ-ing the white commentators on state television, felt he had won. Except that this was the hostile deep north and the two white judges outvoted the one black judge to give it to Horn. 'There in Pietersburg it felt like I was fighting under the rules of the AWB, not the WBA,' Sugarboy sneered.

He decided he needed a change of direction and gave up his job in the furniture store, said goodbye to Maxwell and moved to Benoni, ten miles east of Johannesburg. In the 1970s Maurice Toweel's Springbok Promotions had dominated South African boxing but collapsed after the demise of Mike Schutte. The wheelchair-bound Maurice had an acrimonious fall-out with his brother Alan, and instead went into alliance with another brother, Willie, and together they started to assemble a stable of professionals. Willie was a capable trainer, but his best prospects became frustrated with his lack of vision and left him when he was suspended by the Boxing Board after a minor fall-out.* Thulani, however, knew none of this. Maurice was the big name in boxing promotion from his youth, and he assumed the largesse that had accrued to the likes of Fourie and Schutte would come his way, and in a way he was right.

Willie immediately noticed obvious flaws and instructed him to stop slapping, and Sugarboy learnt his lessons. Maurice implored him to stop mimicking his opponents. 'I said to him, Pal, you either want to be a filmstar or a fighter, and the clowning and tongue-pulling stopped immediately.' When Maurice secured him a rubber match with Horn seven months after the Pietersburg calamity, he was delighted, assuming that with Willie's methods, his own dedication and

---

*Piet Crous abandoned him soon after being guided to a WBA world title – later admitting it was the worst decision he ever made – while Brian Mitchell did the same soon after gaining a world rating.

Maurice's connections, a second defeat was an impossibility. What they did not count on was the selective vision of Colonel Wally, with his final minute of the final round disqualification. It was a blow that made the Toweel brothers feel they too were victims of apartheid injustice. This feeling was enhanced when Snowball laid charges against Maurice, saying that his chants of 'Snowball, you racist' might have got him killed, but Maurice denied he'd said anything of the sort and of course Snowball couldn't produce a single witness to back him up, with the result that Maurice was acquitted. He wheeled himself away from the court with a rare smile and the feeling that he had struck a blow against the racist system.

But the elements seemed set against his favourite boxer. A few weeks later a flash flood in Natal wiped out Thulani's savings and damaged his little house in Ladysmith, leaving him with nothing. 'It is such a tough and sad blow to take,' he told me. 'Those waters just came and they took everything. Our furniture, our clothing, the lot – all washed away or ruined. I am left without possessions.' His entire purse for his next fight went into paying off his R15,000 debts and he was now completely reliant on boxing. When he returned to Benoni, he became a highly focused professional and the Toweel brothers, whose past had been restricted to white boxers, were so enthused by what they witnessed that they made him their special project. That made them my allies. I'd always liked Willie, a brilliant boxer in his time, and a rather kind but naive gentleman since. Maurice had once been the power player in South African boxing, a thin-skinned, tribal creature who was not beyond playing outside the rules and the law, but now, stripped of his power, he was a figure of pathos, given to outbursts of rage but also to a kind of whiny self-pity. Still, I liked the fact that his remaining energies were being channelled in Sugarboy's direction and once again their man did not disappoint, boxing at his best by swarming all over the big-hitting, world-rated American Jim McDonald.

Thulani was back in the world rankings and Maurice turned to his sometime benefactor, Rodney Berman, who agreed to help for no other reason than he pitied Maurice. Berman contacted Cedric Kushner, who used his ties with the International Boxing Federation boss Bobby Lee (which Kushner later admitted were oiled through bribery), and secured Malinga his first world-title shot, against a tall, rough and unbeaten Italian–German southpaw, Graciano Rocchigiani, in West Berlin in January 1989. Berman was delighted with his new acquisition. 'I'm really sorry he wasn't with me before,' he said, 'because he's very talented, very handsome, has great charisma and is a helluva nice guy – one of the wasted talents.' Sugarboy assured me he would prevail but was overwhelmed by the experience of his first trip outside South Africa and retreated into a defensive shell, not landing enough to seize the title. Maurice felt his man deserved 'at least a draw' but Berman had to be persuaded to give Malinga a 'final' chance.

This time he went for broke, making Malinga the Sun City bill-header against a swarming American, Nicky Walker, who was a top contender and had already dished out a comprehensive beating to Sakkie Horn. Sugarboy came in sleek, light and focused and delivered the finest performance of his career, dancing on his toes, moving this way and that, throwing punches in snappy combinations of five and six, seldom missing, mixing up the blows and taking nothing in return. It was beautiful to watch – the master boxer at the peak of his game – and there was nothing a world-class operator like Walker could do about it. The American merely swiped at the ring lights as the South African picked him off, winning every round with grace and ease. The multiracial crowd rose to cheer him, knowing they had seen a performance of rare brilliance. One boozy editor decided Malinga was so astonishingly magnificent that there must be more to it and wrote an editorial claiming Sugarboy's performance was fuelled by performance-enhancing drugs. His only evidence was Thulani's form. But I knew that my man didn't need chemical assistance to get him through his job. He was an original at his inventive best. He had finally arrived.

A string of victories against foreign opponents led to a Colombian gig against America's John Jarvis for the IBF intercontinental title, but this time Sugarboy fought below par. He still dominated – the American television commentators gave Jarvis only one round out of twelve – but the American judges gave it to their man by majority decision, and it was only through Kushner's influence that the IBF agreed to retain Malinga's name among its top contenders.* Sakkie Horn, meanwhile, was showing marked improvement under the tutelage of his new trainer, Harold Volbrecht.

---

*After the fight Maurice pleaded with me to interview him on the scale of this injustice. I agreed because I too was outraged. Maurice sent the story to the IBF boss, Bobby Lee, who was incensed by Maurice's criticism and threatened to remove Malinga from the ratings. Maurice then pleaded with me to say I had misquoted him, but of course I refused. In the end, however, Kushner's money smoothed the way.

He was still receiving undue generosity from white officials* but it was clear that he was hitting harder and displaying more panache. He felt that a win over the world-rated Malinga would serve him well and so it was that they squared up for their fourth encounter at the Nasrec Arena near Soweto.

Sugarboy gave away nine pounds but he was at his best, moving forward, getting under Horn's jabs and slamming in a tattoo of his own punches. He kept them high, recalling Horn's groin-clutching displays, and instead teed off to the head and chest. Round after round the gap grew and Sugarboy's dominance became absolute. He dropped Horn in the tenth and although Sakkie survived, there was nothing the judges could do to save him. I sat with my close friend Mark on one side and the boxing judge, police warrant officer Abri Schutte, on the other, and not even Schutte could find the Horn punches to swing it. Willie Toweel paraded his man around the ring and then for five minutes wiggled his bum in a dance of celebration until exasperated Boxing Board officials chased him out of the ring, and I laughed and then began to choke up a bit. It was just lovely – the sight of beaming Sugarboy and dancing Willie relishing their vindication.

Sakkie knew he'd been lucky in their second and third fights, but in this, their fourth fight, he'd felt sharper than ever and yet the Sugarboy's dominance was even more absolute. He was 28 years old and at his peak, but he'd been so comprehensively outclassed that he decided there was nothing left for him in boxing. He

*In 1989, for instance, he was soundly whipped by a black challenger, Howard Mpepesi, but once again the two white judges gave it to Sakkie, while the lone black judge went the other way.

developed a deep admiration for the man who retired him and turned to his conqueror for help and advice. Sugarboy, in turn, felt he had nothing left to prove against his old adversary, and responded with gentle magnanimity, humouring Sakkie when he came to him for succour.

There was nothing surprising about this in the rapidly changing South Africa of that time. White men like Sakkie were beginning to sense that power was passing to black men like Thulani. Some resisted it, but most made their peace with reality. Thousands of deals were being made each month between old apartheid warhorses and their former enemies. Some 'comrades' went further, by drawing a line under the past even when they couldn't gain from it. A few years later, for instance, Karen's future husband, Mkhuseli, received regular requests from his former torturers for bursaries for their children, and, even more astonishing to me, he would help them out. 'Open-mindedness and a good heart is also a way of celebrating your victory,' he advised me. 'I celebrate my victory when I see the people who tortured me and the people I fought with working together with me. I don't believe I will benefit from seeking revenge.' That was part of the climate in the changing South Africa – along with thousands of acts of racial revenge and vindictiveness from both sides. So the idea of Sakkie turning to his conqueror and being met with grace is not so astonishing, particularly considering the nature of the man showing kindness.

Professional boxing and fundamentalist religion are habitual bed partners – probably because of the demands of a job where men put their bodies and souls on the line every time they go to work: it tends to concentrate the mind on matters of destiny. Six months after he finished off Sakkie Horn, Thulani became a born-again Christian of Pentecostal bent. As he explained it to me: 'I was doing things by myself and failing and so I prayed: God, take me to where I want to be, and it was then that I gave my life to God and things started happening. My whole life was changed a lot when I accepted Jesus into my life. Everything I had was through the love of God.' He was soon preaching to his local congregation and conducting prison visits twice a week to spread the word to those who had fallen, and I noticed a change in the way he presented himself. He was no longer the brash showman of old, and had adopted a more forgiving public persona. So when Sakkie came knocking, Thulani was there for him. 'I was quite surprised,' he said. 'He wanted to be my friend, and kept telling me he admired me because I was the one to retire him, so he would visit me quite often to talk about his troubles.'

Lacking the will to return to boxing, Sakkie soon ran short of cash but found his job as a traffic cop wasn't paying the bills. Like so many of his colleagues he began to accept bribes but Sakkie was one of the few to get caught and after being found guilty at an internal tribunal he was fired from the police force. His marriage broke down, he left home and became depressed. One moment he was South African champion, always getting the benefit of the doubt, with a day job to fall back on and a family to come home to in a country still ruled by his people, and the next all these pillars had been swept away and he was left with nothing – no job, no prospects, no family, no home, no money, no security. He began to talk of killing himself, and like so many other suicidal white Afrikaner men, the idea of leaving his family behind was intolerable. He thought it would be better to take them with him. Either that or he decided on the ultimate form of self-centred vengeance against his estranged wife, because what Sakkie did next was to blow the brains out of his two pleading children before turning the gun on himself. His wife was left childless. 'Class act from a class guy,' I sneered. But Sugarboy shook his head and said, 'Yes, you can say that, but it was still very, very sad.'

Thulani said that the day after this tragedy Sakkie's brother Jan phoned him. 'He told me that Sakkie collected his children from school, took them to where he was staying and locked them in a room with him,' he said. 'Sakkie then phoned Jan, crying and saying he was going to shoot himself and his children. Jan told me he could hear the children down the phone line saying, "Please don't shoot us, Pappie, please don't shoot us," and Jan pleaded with Sakkie to wait and he would come. And then he heard a shot, and one of the children screaming, "Please don't shoot me," and then another shot, and then a third, and then silence. That's what Jan told me and I felt very very sad for him and for all of them.'

Malinga travelled to Rome and lost a second world-title fight – a close decision to the American Lindell Holmes – and at the age of 35 it looked like the end. Instead, a new stage was about to start. Willie Toweel's boxers had been training in a plush Johannesburg gymnasium owned by a pushy, British-born businessman, Nick Durandt. For a while the 27-year-old Nick and the 55-year-old Willie worked closely but the young man felt he could take the boxers and himself further. 'I called all the boxers together and I said, You can stay here with me, or if you want to go with Willie, there's the door,' Durandt told me. 'What would you do? I had the gym, the equipment, the financial backing, everything. Willie had nothing.' Nick also had his assistant Elias Tshabalala, a former fighter who enjoyed the respect and loyalty of the black boxers. Willie went off alone and never again trained a boxer with any potential.

Nick's own boxing history was limited to a handful of amateur fights and he hardly looked the part. He had the most obscene mullet I had yet encountered – short at the front with peroxide-blond tresses past his shoulders – and with his bulky muscles, his paunch and his occasional cigarette he carried the bearing of, say, an aspirant biker rather than a trainer of champions. He was prickly when it came to criticism, which made him enemies within the game, including most of his fellow trainers who regarded him as an impostor. His manner was perpetually churlish and he was given to barking in a staccato monotone, pitched deeper than seemed natural in a way mastered by white South African lads en route to puberty. My New York-based friend Tony once watched a television broadcast of a Malinga fight, and phoned to ask: 'Who was that arsehole in Malinga's corner snapping at him in Fanigalo [an African esperanto, used on the mines]? And why does Malinga put up with it?' Part of the answer was that this tone was not reserved for black boxers. Nick once boasted to me about what he'd told a promoter's one-legged driver. 'I said, Listen, pal, next time you're late I'll break off your other leg.' And yet he proved himself an outstanding trainer – a quick learner who was open to the new techniques and training methods. He would get up at 5 a.m. to take his boxers on runs, supervise their weight training, study the styles of their opponents and work out intricate tactics. And behind his barking manner he had a deep respect for his men, and proved it over and over again. When Ginger Tshabalala was murdered, Nick went out of his way to help his family, and there were many other instances that saw him doing that little bit extra for his men. I gradually got to know him, and despite all my reservations, came to like him too.

Under Durandt's guidance, Sugarboy returned to Mike Segal's promotional fold. Segal in turn used his partnership with the Essex promoter Barry Hearn to secure Malinga a shot at Chris Eubank's WBO super middleweight title in Birmingham, England in February 1992. I liked Segal, but was less sure about Hearn* and his tight relationship with the apartheid-cosy WBO** – especially given what seemed to me to be the favouritism shown by the WBO towards Eubank. The strutting, lisping, preening, high-camp Brighton man was, however, the real thing. Like Malinga he

---

*Hearn was fined £2,000 by the British Boxing Board after it was found that the scales for a 1990 title fight had been deliberately miscalibrated on the instructions of his Matchroom organization – to allow one of his weight-drained boxers to make the limit. He later lost a £2-million lawsuit against one of his boxers, Steve Collins, after the judge declared he had 'fundamentally breached his managerial responsibilities'. His case came unstuck when the referee from Collins's first fight against Eubank told the court that Matchroom men tried to persuade him to swing the fight in Eubank's favour.

**The WBO was established as a breakaway from the WBA, partly because of the WBA's ban on South Africans. It fostered close ties with the SA Boxing Board of Control. Its representative for Europe, for example, was George Christodoulou, brother of Stan – a man with no previous dealings with boxing from a country – Cyprus – with no professional boxers. South African promoters began doing regular business with the WBO, which frequently meant paying bribes to its Puerto Rican boss, Pepe Cordero.

could fall asleep mid-fight and had a tendency to coast, but even at his worst he was a heavy puncher with a great chin and he was hard to tag. He was unbeaten in twenty-nine fights, the last of them a return against Michael Watson, which secured him the WBO super middleweight title and left Watson in a coma and later a wheelchair. He was expected to roll Malinga over, but Sugarboy rose from an early knockdown to outbox him, his confidence growing with each round. Eubank was the heavier puncher, but Thulani was throwing and landing more, shaking the Brighton man in the sixth round and enjoying himself down the final straight. Once again, however, it was not quite enough for victory. One of the judges went his way; the other two went with Eubank. Never again, however, would he suffer a crisis of confidence at the top level.

Whatever Eubank could do, Nigel Benn felt he could do better, which is why he agreed to meet Malinga in Birmingham three months later, once again under Barry Hearn's auspices. There was something of the obsessive about Benn, a former army squaddie whose reputation in the street was even more fearsome than in the ring. He could not get over the humiliation of his 1990 loss against Eubank, at least not until he fought Eubank to a draw three years later, and the way he hoped to show it was by walking through Malinga in quick time. But Malinga had acquired the confidence to feel he could beat the best in the world, and under Durandt's guidance and with God on his side he trained harder than ever before. For two months, he worked with weights two hours a day and then chopped wood for another half hour, in addition to his usual diet of running, sparring, bag and pad work, skipping and ground exercises. He looked harder and stronger than ever before and in sparring his power had visibly increased.

The fight was a non-title affair, which meant the British referee would be the sole judge – a bizarre system, certainly, but perhaps no worse than relying on the appointees of the WBO. The British, I felt, could be relied on to be fair and they tended to favour boxers like Malinga over fighters like Benn. Over the next decade I would be reminded over and over just how wrong I had been. Some of the officiating by British referee-judges involving foreign boxers is among the worst I have seen anywhere in the world, and Paul Thomas's bad day in Birmingham on 15 May 1992 was one of them.*

Benn was nearing his peak but he had the misfortune of catching Sugarboy at his best and the wild Englishman simply couldn't compete. Malinga moved gracefully, jamming his low left into Benn's face from a distance and then working him over with hooks to the body and uppercuts on the inside. He won as he pleased and by the tenth round Benn was wobbling. Most ringside observers gave the Englishman no more than three rounds, and yet referee Thomas didn't hesitate in raising Benn's hand. It felt like Wally Snowball all over again but this time there was no politics to give it shape. It was just sad and ugly – the fifth time I'd seen my favourite boxer denied his due. Malinga was shocked. 'It's a disgrace,' he said. 'Benn was nothing. I completely outboxed him. I even outpunched him. I had him wobbling all over the ring in the last round,

---

*It was not his last either. Several years later Wiseman Jim of Cape Town outclassed Dean Pithie of Coventry, throwing double the number of punches, yet Thomas made his countryman a three-round winner – a verdict prompting ripples of shock in British boxing.

and if it had been a twelve-rounder I would have knocked him out. This was not even a close fight and I just didn't expect that kind of treatment from a British referee – an out-and-out robbery, the worst experience of my boxing career. Those Sakkie Horn decisions were a joke, but then those were apartheid officials. The Jarvis fight happened in Colombia so what do you expect? All right, the Eubank fight may have been close, but I beat Benn easily, fair and square.'

Their careers moved in opposite directions* but Sugarboy eventually returned to Berman's promotional fold, put together a series of knockouts and moved up the rankings once again. Assisting him along the way was Berman's new partnership with the British promoter Frank Warren, who at the time was also a junior partner to Don King, who in turn was effectively the senior partner in the World Boxing Council, which moved Malinga into the mandatory contender's position. The Warren connection made my relationship with Berman more difficult,** but it meant I saw more

---

*Benn won the WBC world title and made millions defending it ten times. Malinga was finally offered another big fight, this one against the finest boxer in the world, Roy Jones, in St Louis Bay, Mississippi. He had to take it at short notice, only to find Jones insisting on a weight below the super middleweight limit and in two weeks he had to boil down from 185 pounds to 165. Jones's speed, power, reflexes and skill were unequalled in his and perhaps any other era and Malinga was stopped in six rounds.

**Warren, who resembled a mid-career Kingsley Amis with a blond rinse, was not one of my favourites. Among other objections, he was extremely thin-skinned about even the mildest criticism. I interviewed him for my biography of Naseem Hamed, but on publication he demanded its pulping, saying he would also claim substantial damages. Following legal advice, my publishers ignored it, after which no more was heard from Warren on the subject. I never spoke to him again. Berman, however, was happy to sing his praises – at least until the pair fell out a few years later.

of Malinga, as he made several visits to London, fighting on Warren's bills.

Once again his life was going through turmoil. One of his sons, then aged 17, began to experience severe headaches and was diagnosed as suffering from a brain tumour. The specialist's prognosis left the family with little hope. 'The doctor took us aside and said he might die and there was also a strong chance he will be a vegetable,' Thulani said, 'but we prayed and prayed while they were busy operating and God was wonderful because he became very strong and remained healthy.' Thulani owned a butchery, run by his wife, but the medical bills left the family penniless, so when Berman told him he'd secured a return with Benn, they were delighted. Berman recalls: 'He came to my office and said he wanted to speak to me. He said this prayer and I waited for a few seconds while he closed his eyes and said Jesus this and Jesus that, and then he looked up and said to me: "Rodney, I had a dream last night and God came to speak to me in this dream." I said, Oh, and what was your dream about? He said: "God said, You must tell Rodney he is not paying you enough." Well, with that kind of authority what can you say? So I said: OK, Sugarboy, you can have another R50,000 if you win, and he didn't forget.'

He sparred six hundred rounds, chopped wood and lifted weights to build his strength, while praying every day. Still, the odds against him were prohibitive. A year earlier Benn had shocked the boxing world by stopping the highly fancied American world champion Gerald McClellan in ten rounds. It was a brutal fight, from which both men required hospital treatment, but while Benn recovered, McClellan fell into a coma, and emerged blind, partially deaf, wheelchair-bound and brain-damaged. I watched Benn's next two title defences and he seemed to have lost some of his intensity but Malinga also seemed to be in decline even though his self-belief had solidified into divine certainty. A few days before the fight he told me he'd had another dream. 'I saw myself knocking out Benn in the sixth round,' he said. And to top it all, on the day of the fight he received a telegram from Nelson Mandela wishing him luck and he couldn't stop smiling.

To the astonishment of the British crowd Malinga once again outboxed Benn, knocking his head back with his long jabs and then working his body on the inside. It was a carefully calculated performance, which seemed to go precisely according to plan. In round six Malinga heeded the call of his dreams and went for a knockout, but instead found himself on his back from a Benn right cross. He rose, smiled at the realization of the mix-up in his dream, and went back to business. Benn's face was a bruised, lumpy mess by the final round and he was starting to stagger. Malinga dropped him with a right cross and although Benn made it to the final bell, Thulani was world champion at the age of 40. He had trounced one of the big names in world boxing for the most prestigious title in his division – perhaps the finest achievement in the history of South African boxing.

Before he left the ring he grabbed a mobile phone to tell his wife that God's will had been done (and she needn't worry about the overdraft or those outstanding medical bills). When I saw him again in his hotel the next morning, he said: 'I kept asking God to make me a world champion and then he gave it to me with the whole world watching. I tell you, Gavin, I'm so, so happy because this is the thing I've always wanted.' I don't think I have ever been more delighted with the result of a boxing match. When I hugged Thulani afterwards I felt great warmth for him, and a joy in his achievement. He returned home to a hero's welcome – Mandela's guest of honour, a flow of invitations to celebrity events, the target of advertisers – but there were no airs and graces from his side. He continued with his preaching and prison visits while dreaming of a long and lucrative reign.

His first defence was against a tricky and volatile Italian, Vincenzo Nardiello, in Newcastle. This time Sugarboy came in too light and struggled to get his punches off but in the eighth he sank a heavy hook to the midriff and Nardiello collapsed, hesitating before pointing to his groin. From ringside it was clear the punch was well above the belt and this was confirmed through the television replays, but the referee, Mickey Vann, was conned by Nardiello's act and deducted a point from Malinga's score.* Vann's mistake had a direct bearing on the result. Malinga stopped punching to the body at a time when a few more body punches would have ended the fight. The deducted point made the difference between retaining his title and losing it on a controversial split decision.

Thulani looked sad but said he was accustomed to this sort of thing. 'I used to take the disappointments

*Three years later I watched a British boxer land a massive uppercut flush on the testicles of an Italian boxer, who collapsed. Vann ignored the infringement and began counting. But the verdict that marked his name in boxing history was delivered in 1993 when he saved Julio Cesar Chavez's unbeaten record by awarding him an outrageous draw against Pernell Whitaker – one of the worst decisions in boxing history.

hard but then I realized there was a reason for everything and that there was something I could learn from them, so I came to accept them and I always believe that one day, when God wants it, things will come right.' Berman did his best to put things right, complaining to the WBC, pointing out that Vann's error changed the result, and his appeal was upheld, meaning that Malinga was returned to his status as leading contender. But Berman's partnership with Warren made this more difficult. One of Warren's unbeaten young stars, Robin Reid, was offered first shot at Nardiello's title, and after stopping the Italian, Reid was in no hurry to meet Malinga, with the result that Sugarboy had to sit around while Reid racked up a trio of title defences.

He was 42 years old by the time his number came up again and he hadn't fought in seventeen months. The 26-year-old Reid was quick, strong, powerful and unbeaten. Yet Thulani seemed unnaturally calm, informing me it would be an easy fight, and I dutifully reported his words, but without much conviction. This time I travelled to Newcastle more out of nostalgia than hope and I wondered if the end for my man was going to be short and brutal or prolonged and painful. But from the first bell Thulani's jab rocked Reid's head back, keeping him off balance and discouraging his efforts. Soon Reid was running, looking thoroughly confused, his handsome face becoming battered. Now and then he would charge but Sugarboy would effortlessly duck under his telegraphed right and then bang him in the face or body with one of his own. It was a remarkable achievement, making Malinga the second oldest man in boxing history to lift a world title. 'This victory means so much to me,' he told me when I talked to him in his changing room after the fight. 'What belonged to me, I got back.'

Durandt was hugely relieved. 'I really needed this one,' he whispered as we walked to the changing room. Members of a rival boxing camp – old-style racists, accustomed to privilege and inclined towards thuggery – had been out to get Nick after one of their best boxers defected to his camp. They were also incensed about his relationship with Rodney Berman, claiming Berman was pushing them out of business. When a Durandt boxer was about to compete in America, they succeeded in getting the fight cancelled by using a Boxing Board letterhead and a forged signature in a fax to the American state board claiming Durandt's boxer was unfit to fight. They also used threats of death and violence against both Durandt and Berman, stole one of Berman's cheques and sent it to a newspaper with a false story about its purpose, and threatened his employees. These men bugged their enemies' phones and eventually scored a direct hit with Durandt, recording him speaking to his wife. The doctored version of the tape included derogatory remarks about 'kaffirs', Indians and Jews. Following the example of a similar 'hit' in the rugby world,* the tape was sent the South African Broadcasting Corporation, which played it on television.

A public outcry followed and Berman announced he would cease working with Durandt: 'The people who leaked it are racist scum – complete thugs who waged a vicious dirty-tricks campaign against me and mine, but

---

*Springbok rugby coach Andre Markgraaff lost his post in 1997 after a neo-Nazi player, who had it in for him, taped him talking about 'fucking kaffirs' in a telephone conversation, which he leaked to the media.

still, I can't let this one pass,' he said. 'I can live with the anti-Semitism – I've learnt to expect it – but I can't live with employees or partners of mine talking of kaffirs. What was said was morally reprehensible and indefensible and I can't align myself with someone making racist and ethnic remarks, whatever the circumstances.' Durandt refused to apologize, insisting the tape was illegally recorded and selectively edited, and the sound quality was unclear. When I asked Nick about it, he was extremely defensive: 'It's a fucking load of crap. I don't want to discuss it,' he said. He was more forthcoming to other white South Africans, however, saying that his wife had just been robbed by a black man and that he was feeling upset about this at the time and that the way it was spliced meant that his words were taken out of context. Later he said the offensive words didn't come from his mouth.

Thulani and most of the other boxers wanted to stay with him. 'I think he made a terrible mistake but that kind of racist language is out of character for the man I know, because I have been with Nick for a long time and he's no racist,' Malinga said. But eventually, under intense community pressure, the black boxers confronted him in the gym. His then-assistant Elias Tshabalala recalled: 'We told him, "Look, Nick, we can hear it's your voice. There's no use denying it, but we want you to stay on. What you need to do is publicly apologize and we'll forgive you and so will the public." But he was too proud, he wouldn't do it, so most of the boxers asked me to train and manage them.' Nick Durandt was cast out into the wilderness, just as had happened to Willie Toweel six years earlier. His marriage, his family life, his livelihood, his reputation were shattered, but he gradually clawed his way back to the top,* still insisting on his innocence. His alleged sins were not quite forgotten or forgiven, but in a typically South African way, kind of pushed to one side.

Malinga's next outing was against yet another Warren fighter, Telford's Richie Woodhall. He was a tall, upright, highly experienced boxer** in the old British tradition, moving on his toes, leading with his jab, snapping in his right cross, and at the age of 29 had reached his peak. An earlier version of Malinga would have closed him down, but now, well into his forty-third year, with his training disrupted by the Durandt upheaval, he lacked speed, balance and timing. Woodhall landed a right cross in the third round, and Thulani went down, and although he fought his way back, he couldn't close the gap.

Sugarboy seemed more resigned than devastated in his changing room. When I asked whether this was the end, he looked at Nomso, smiled sadly, and said: 'We'll have to talk about it at home.' Nomso nodded in a way that suggested she would be delighted if he retired. Rodney looked at her, then put an arm around Sugarboy's shoulders. 'We had an agreement that if you lost tonight that would be it. There always comes a time when enough is enough.' The boxer offered an ambiguous grin and I knew then he couldn't let it go. He failed a brain scan at home and lost his licence but

*He began to work with Berman again, rebuilding a top-flight stable and regaining his status as one of South Africa's top trainers and managers, eventually ending up in the corner of Hassim Rahman when he knocked out Lennox Lewis to win the world heavyweight title.

**Woodhall won an Olympic bronze medal and then, as a professional, the Commonwealth and European titles before a final-hour elbow operation contributed to his sole loss, in a world-title fight.

was re-tested in Denmark, where his scan was clear. Berman, however, refused to promote him, so Thulani went back to Segal, who despatched him to Copenhagen where he stopped a pair of promising prospects to lift and then defend a paper 'world' title. He then fought a 'unification' bout against the holder of yet another low-rent title but suffered a serious break to his right hand and retired in his corner at the end of the tenth round. He went a year without a fight until in March 2000 Segal offered him a short-notice shot for another dubious honour at a higher weight. His opponent, Ole Klementsen, was fifteen years younger and a genuinely world-class light heavy. Malinga dominated early, dropping Klementsen in the third, but he was unfit, ran out of steam and was stopped in the eighth.

He was still reluctant to retire. As Segal recalled: 'He liked the money – that was his only complaint against me – and he kept asking me to get him a return because it was true that he only lost because he ran out of gas after taking the fight at the last moment after that layoff, but I said no. I remembered what happened to Brian Baronet and I didn't want to take any risks. I felt sad for him because he's a really wonderful human being – a genuinely good man who was a real pleasure to work with, but I thought it best for him. Everyone has his time, and Sugarboy's was over.' Thulani was reluctant to accept it. 'But after a while I said to myself, What's the point of going to the gym every day for nothing, and so I decided that was it. I thought, Well, I've had a good career, which I'm very proud of. I think I've done a good job because God was helping me. I know if I was by myself I wouldn't have achieved so much but with the Lord's help I succeeded.'

*   *   *

The Lord's help and mysterious will has been central to the life of my favourite boxer for over a decade. In my own life, the most I can say is that this dimension may lurk somewhere in the hidden subtext. I have long recognized the value of religious faith in binding communities, but I still tend to roll my eyes at the deluge of irrationality it demands. Every now and then, however, I think about how much I have missed through losing belief and faith – in God, in revolution, in salvation. Disaster, tragedy, death – these things are easier to accept when you see them as the will of the almighty whose wisdom is too great to understand. Sometimes I feel that without this faith in God (or a materialist dialectic in history) I am on my own, creating meaning on the hop while looking into the void with one eye, with the other focused fearfully on my children's futures, hoping that tragedy can be staved off indefinitely. In a way Sugarboy's story brought home to me the cost of living without it. It has not taken me closer to belief, but from his experience I have to admit it's an opiate that is sometimes worth the fix.

Three months after the Klementsen fight I was travelling home on the tube and picked up a copy of the *SA Times*. I read a story that made my eyes well up. The headline stated: 'Sugarboy's grandson dies in fire.' Thulani had been more like a father than a grandparent to his only grandchild, Sabelo Simleane, who was six years old. When he talked about Sabelo he radiated love. He cared for him in his lakeside home in Benoni, and adored him. One day on his way back from a business trip to Pretoria Thulani received a phone call on his mobile phone to say his house was on fire. He rushed in with the firemen and eventually they found

Sabelo in a wardrobe in his bedroom. He was already dead. I immediately wrote to Thulani and then phoned him. 'It was a very terrible experience for me and for my daughter,' he said. 'He used to go with me when I went to the gym, and when I stopped going, he would always say, "Let's go to the gym." He wanted to be with me all the time and that day he wanted to go with me to Pretoria, but I told him that if he didn't wash he would have to stay behind, and in the morning, when I had to leave, he didn't wash, so I left him, and he said, "OK, but can you just get me some chicken nuggets," because he liked those, and so on the way back from Pretoria I went to get the chicken nuggets, and then I got the call to say my house was on fire and it was just terrible to arrive and find he wasn't there. He had climbed into the cupboard to get away from the smoke and fire and that's where he died.'

The fire was caused by an electrical short-circuit in the roof of the house, and while the insurance went some way to helping Thulani to rebuild it, its contents were not covered and all their savings went to re-furnishing it at a time he was in deep mourning. Mike Segal is convinced that Thulani's faith helped to sustain him through the trauma. 'He was very close to that little boy. He treated him like a son and they spent a lot of time together, so it was tremendously sad for him. He was devastated. But he had a way of coming to terms with it. He said to me, "It's God's way," and I think that helped him.'

When I asked Thulani about it over a year after the tragedy, he acknowledged Segal's perspective and inadvertently reminded me of the potential price of a life without faith. 'I lost everything when Sabelo died, but God helped me a lot,' he said. 'It was my faith which allowed me to accept all these terrible things that happened to me.' Nomso continued to run their butchery and clothing boutiques, while Thulani set up two businesses – one manufacturing cleaning chemicals for machinery and the other in transport – and they thrived beyond his expectations. He was also appointed to the national Boxing Control Commission, which had once denied him his due. 'The life I'm living now is because of God's help,' he reminded me again, smiling once more. 'I'm living a nice life. God has been good to us.'

6

NAMING THE ROSE

Ellis Park, Johannesburg, January 1989. 'Jou *poes*' – cunt – 'jou fokkin' *poes!*' The words land directly in my ear, spit and all, launched from pointy-nosed distance, so there's no mistaking that it is my existence, and not that of any of the other ringsiders present, being mistaken for a vagina. My first response is one of genuine bemusement.

The spitter – I'll call him Attie – is a rotund writer from one of the Afrikaans newspapers, and his spluttering invective has been prompted by my response to his prior question: 'Evans! Who do you think won?' The options are Daniel Londas, the super featherweight champion of Europe, or Dingaan Thobela, the Rose of Soweto. I plump for neither. On this hot evening Dingaan has been overanxious and has come in four pounds too light. He's had the first of many off-nights and has not looked the part of a genuine rival to Attie's chum, the WBA world champion, Brian Mitchell. However, in the view of everyone else at ringside – everyone other than Attie and me – Dingaan has done enough to win, and that is also the unanimous verdict of the judges. Unfortunately my answer – 'I scored it a draw' – is not good enough for my passionately anti-Dingaan, pro-Brian interrogator.

Cowardice plays a strong part in my first-blush responses to physical challenge, and so I look down at my notepad and ignore the fact that a fellow reporter has just likened me to a woman's genitalia. This non-response does not have the desired effect. Attie hovers for a few stewing seconds, then moves directly behind me and spits again: '*Kaffir boetie*, jou fokkin' *kaffir boetie*.' For a moment, as I absorb this compliment, my bemused state over his motives turns to confusion over his logic. Yes, Dingaan is black, but Daniel is blacker and, anyway, what's the problem? I scored it a draw. But there's no time to discern the purpose behind Attie's bile because by now he has boiled over. He places his meaty hands around my neck and starts throttling me from behind.

My response falls into the category of desperation. I wriggle loose, swing, connect. Attie steps back and the trajectory of his elephantine legs is blocked by a chair, sending him crashing into the laps of the next row of ringsiders. I turn around to seek out my trade-unionist friend Alan, whom I've inveigled into the photographers' ringside seats. My disorientated search lasts about a second before the next surprise catches me between the eyes – or a few inches above them. The sound of bare fist on the hard bone is a kind of crack-thud without resonance. It's a shocking sound and it causes all eyes, and camera lenses, to leave the ring and turn in my direction. There is no immediate pain and barely a second of further disorientation. Just rage, which requires an object. As I look up I see Attie's assistant – a surly, thick-set, bearded man I'll call

Bokkie – standing in front of me, holding a still-clenched fist. I assume he's the one. There's no one else in sight.

Just like Attie's reaction, mine has its own history. But at this moment it is blind, pure and, for once, living only in the context-less present. Bokkie, who, apparently, thought he'd just get a quick one in while my eyes were turned, is taken by surprise. I rush in, closing the distance, and start throwing short hooks, and for the first time in several years feel the thrill of fist on face. No strategy, no tactics, no organization, just the jarring shock of knuckle after knuckle connecting. He grabs, pulls my head down while at the same time fastening his teeth on my shoulder. It's a sharp pain, despite my leather jacket, and my rage is arrested. Time treads water. There's enough of it now to think, and I think, *Testicles, testicles, testicles.* Knee is good, underhand uppercut better, but I'm after a fistful, like Gene Hackman got from the meanest-looking redneck in the bar in *Mississippi Burning.* But that thug was seated, while Bokkie is standing in his tight polyester chinos. I grope for a firm grip, but it doesn't quite take. I grab again and after what seems like several seconds of exploration I finally dig a thumb and middle finger in what feels like the top of his scrotum and his body shudders into limpness.

With my right hand still on his balls two uniformed policemen pull me off and start dragging me away. But Alan and the rest of the ringsiders have seen all. 'He was just defending himself,' they shout, and with Attie by now back on his feet – I don't yet understand why he didn't join the fray (though I later discover Alan managed to get in a good long punch of his own), my fellow reporters turn on him, telling the constables *he* was the one who started all the trouble, and so the officers cart Attie and Bokkie off, and then lose interest. A police boxer is about to fight, and they allow Attie to sneak back to his seat, while Bokkie goes to the toilet to wash the blood from his face. Just to be sure, I move beside Alan in the photographers' seats. 'Just wait 'til afterwards when I fucking catch you, you cunt,' says Attie. 'Fuck you too,' I respond weakly, avoiding his eye. I notice two other pals have joined him, and I'm starting to sweat.

My fear, however, is eased by Alan's presence. Of all my friends, I can't think of anyone whose physical proximity would be more appropriate. So let me say a few words about Alan: trade union leader, underground activist, nice guy. He grew up as one of eight children of a coloured community matriarch in the Northern Transvaal border town of Mafeking and first made his name as a streetfighter, for which he received regular kickings from the police. His attitude to whites at that stage was simple – 'racist bastards' – and it was this nascent black consciousness which inspired him to lead a strike after a white foreman beat up an old black worker in 1975. The police dragged Alan in and worked him over. 'They beat me to pulp and wanted me to own up to ANC things which completely bamboozled me,' he once told me, laughing about it. 'I'd never heard of the ANC and didn't know about politics. I didn't have a single political idea other than racial militancy. Anti-white sentiments.' He was blacklisted by employers and so skipped the border to Botswana, joined this ANC organization the police had interrogated him about, and was instructed in the politics of socialist non-racialism. Over the next decade he moved from organizing community groups in Cape Town to food workers in Johannesburg. Two years before the Thobela fight I moved into a slum flat opposite Ellis Park rugby ground with an old friend and comrade, Derek, who had just emerged from four years in jail for ANC activities and would one day become a member of Nelson Mandela's cabinet. A week later Alan moved into the upstairs flat, and the three of us shared hot water, meals and tips about security. He was also called on to help other tenants, like Philemon and his son Themba, who ran a *shebeen* in the basement quarters. Alan once heard Themba screaming and ran down to find two *tsotsies* trying to stab him. He tossed Themba a motorbike chain and the two of them drove off the knifemen. A while later he kicked down a neighbour's door after hearing a woman screaming and saw she was about to have her head bashed in with a spanner. Alan put the beater in hospital but a week later he re-emerged at our front door with his knife drawn. 'You can stick it here, here, or here,' Alan said, pointing at his neck, heart and stomach while walking forward purposefully. The man turned and ran. On another occasion he was attacked by a thug who doubled as a karate champion. After absorbing a few kicks Alan caught hold of him, dropped him and head-butted him into unconsciousness. So you get the picture: a good comrade, a loyal friend, and an extremely useful ally in a spot of bother.

As we are about to leave Ellis Park I notice Attie, Bokkie and two of their chums waiting for us with mean intent. Alan calmly issues instructions: 'Stick your keys between your fingers like this to make a *lekker* knuckleduster,' he says, demonstrating. 'Now pick up a big stone and throw it at that one's head when you get very close. We'll take two that way and *donder*' – fuck up – 'the others.' But it's not necessary. As we walk out I notice a tall black welterweight who has just beaten a white prospect and ask him to join us. Attie and friends evaporate and I feign nonchalance as I join Alan for coffee at his flat.

The next morning I look in the mirror and discover a lump just under my hairline – testimony to Bokkie's knuckles – and I'm relieved that my external damage has been unseen. When I arrive at work I open the country's biggest-circulation daily, the *Sowetan*, and come across a picture and a story on our little scrap (although the reporter did me a favour by omitting my name, and the picture doesn't show my face). A few minutes later my editor requests an explanation and then phones Attie's editor to complain. Attie tells his editor: 'I only called him a *kaffir boetie* after he called me a fucking *boer*.' It's a lie and I want to make him pay for it. I'm torn up with hatred and indignity. My newly acquired sense of peace and harmony with the world is gone.

A month earlier I had experienced a kind of epiphany as I was loading up my old motorbike to drive down to Cape Town. A journalist friend came to visit. 'A little tripping present,' she said. 'You look like you need it.' She handed me some blotting paper with Mickey Mouse imprints. 'Share this with someone special. Good stuff.' The 1,500-kilometre ride to Cape Town always put me in the best of moods, particularly with my first sunsetting glimpse of the mountains, soon followed by the first sniff of the sea. I decided then that the acid required a trip to the beach and that I would share it with an old friend and comrade, with whom I had enjoyed a brief affair.

A week later we dropped the acid caps at Cape Town

station and boarded the all-stations train. After eighteen stops the narrow-gauge line reached the seaside and ran along the rocky coves, bringing back the luscious memories of a hundred childhood bucket-and-spade adventures. The Indian Ocean looked more vividly blue and the sky dazzled brighter as the train clickety-clicked along. By the time we were disgorged at the last stop, the naval village of Simonstown, time, colour and perspective were well into the process of transformation. We stopped for Coke floats at an al fresco café, only to watch with alarm as a family of Neanderthals emerged from the waves and walked menacingly towards us. I gripped hold of the sun umbrella and informed my friend that I might be required to drive the spike through them. But she smiled as the Neanderthals grunted benignly and went on their way, and suddenly the world was a place of glorious harmony.

We walked a mile in the morning sun in the direction of Boulders, a hamlet of self-contained flat-sea beaches where I'd first learnt to dive with snorkel, goggles and flippers, where I'd first been stung by jellyfish and where I'd seen my first mole snake and sand shark. It's an unfolding series of coves, with each set of rocks providing an obstacle for clambering over before unveiling a fresh delight – rock pools, penguins, caves – then more boulders. Now, it was a place of adventure. The rocks, mountains; the little caves, mazes; the colours of the sea, sky and sand, magically luminous. The salt water tingled and was lovely. The sense of physical limitation and caution evaporated.

But it was the people who had the most lasting impact. Until then, my relation with old people had been patronizing. They belonged to a different generation – one that didn't understand, that lacked a sense of irony and was incapable of change. But on this December morning, I acquired a new perspective. The experience of losing self-awareness – where a single word sets off a meandering stream of consciousness for an indiscernible period of time – made me reluctant to attempt normal conversation with anyone other than my friend and the older 'seniors' I took to greeting. They seemed to understand my rambling thought-train and for the first time I felt I could appreciate theirs. I'd also not given much thought to children, but when we reached the main beach, we came across a little girl and boy playing in a rock pool, and I found myself drawn into their world. They showed us how the 'sea enemies' would suck on fingers if gently prodded, and we shared in their wonder. Together, the four of us explored for what may have been ten minutes or an hour, dipping in and out of reality.

As we walked back to the station in the late afternoon, I began to make sense of these experiences. I decided I loved people, and wanted to relate to them in a way that was simple, direct and honest. I wanted a community of peace and sharing. I longed to be good at heart. I wanted to be surrounded by children. I would have children of my own. I would adore them and never hit or threaten them, and I would offer them all the freedom they could cope with. I could not see the point of working hard or striving for ambitions. I was struggling to remember the point of irony. I was repelled by the idea of fighting. We returned to Cape Town and as the trip wore off, I smoked a spliff and then went to Tony's house to watch a televised version of Johnny du Plooy knocking out an American patsy. The picture of these men bashing each other seemed, for the first time, comically unreal. The idea that I should enjoy watching this seemed absurd.

A few months earlier I was recruited into a leadership position within the newly established ANC and Communist Party national underground network known as Operation Vula. I was told that on my return from Zimbabwe I would be contacted within three days by one of the leaders of the structure, the former Robben Island prisoner Billy Nair, and in an exception to the usual rules I was instructed to carry the materials for the new secret communication system. I had previously transported money for underground networks, but not anything else because of my high political profile, but this time I was told my package was too sensitive to entrust to anyone outside of the structure. A man I knew as Comrade May handed over several souvenir artworks, one of which, he said, contained the Soviet-produced codes. As soon as I returned I was told to steam the back off, retrieve the code sheet and hand it over to Nair, who would visit me at a safe house. They strapped the curios under my motorbike seat and I drove through the night in order to arrive at the border post first thing in the morning, when the police were still sleepy. I reached my destination, and steamed off the back of the picture, but the paper disintegrated. A week later, when Nair still hadn't arrived, I became paranoid and destroyed the remains of the souvenirs. But the next day Nair finally arrived, and I had to explain what happened, and once again I learnt that the broken telephone had been in operation: the contents were not the codes but the Soviet-produced encoding pads, which were moulded inside the picture. Nair chuckled, washed my pile of dirty dishes and hinted I may have inadvertently done him a favour. I later learnt that this little disaster persuaded the High Command to abandon the old communications system, and transfer to computer codes, sent via modem, which proved to be far safer and more efficient.

The next day I was sent to meet Mac Maharaj, another former Robben Islander. He was the only member of the Lusaka-based ANC executive and the Communist Party politburo who had been smuggled into South Africa (pretending to exiled comrades not in the know, after feigning illness for several months, that he was off to Moscow for a kidney transplant). He explained that the idea was to create a national network of internally coordinated ANC and Communist Party cells, with the leader of each unit reporting to a higher structure. I was seconded to the Communist Party's Transvaal command, serving as education officer and treasurer.

My activism moved at a more frenetic pace – 5 a.m. meetings in factory premises, political reports, education sessions for probationary members, setting up secret offices and bank accounts, pamphlet production, underground network building and spy investigations. I hated those meetings and the demands they produced but at least the structure operated efficiently and pulled off a few triumphs. For instance, shortly before my acid train trip, we planned the escape of three key UDF leaders who had been detained without trial for over a year. They managed to persuade their jailers they had severe medical problems requiring weekly check-ups at the Johannesburg hospital. A perennially sleepy guard gave them the opening they needed and the plan worked to perfection (although my own role was a minor one – finding false number plates for the getaway cars). We spirited them away to the American Embassy where they remained for several months, creating an international incident that severely embarrassed the government and in this way contributed to the relaxing of Emergency detention.*

Soon after, I was detained again by the security police and held for several hours of interrogation in John Vorster Square. Assuming they knew nothing of my clandestine work and that my journalistic profile gave me protection, I decided to stonewall – refusing to answer questions or to give them my address. 'Why not? Do you think we can't find out where you live for ourselves?' asked an exasperated young security police-man. 'I'm living with my girlfriend,' I replied, 'she's not politically involved and it would be an act of dishonour to say where she lives.' He seemed to appreciate this, and wasn't quite sure how to proceed, but at that moment a fat, short-tempered warrant officer, Paul Erasmus, stormed in. Erasmus hated me because of an incident three years earlier, when I stupidly threatened to citizen-arrest him after he threatened to beat up a photographer at an anti-military protest. 'Remember me,' he snarled and slapped me hard. He began scream-ing at me when he was called to the phone. I couldn't hear the conversation but he was saying, 'Ja, ja,' in a hangdog way, before handing the phone to the young officer, who seemed equally obsequious. An hour later I was released, but as I was leaving Erasmus pushed his face up to mine, telling me I could expect 'a

*Each of them went on to play a significant part in the country's transition. Zwelakhe Sisulu headed the South African Broadcasting Corporation, Murphy Morobe currently heads the government's Fiscal and Financial Commission and its National Parks Board, and Valli Moosa is in his ninth year in the cabinet, currently as tourism minister.

letterbomb or a bullet in the back'. Many years later he admitted to the country's Truth and Reconciliation Commission that when working for the State Security Council he had drawn up a list of people to be 'permanently removed from society': 'As a result of a personal grudge I included Gavin Evans.' I wasn't aware of this at the time, but I noticed there were more concerted attempts to keep me under surveillance and I became worried that they had something more than detention in mind.

So, with detainees to 'spring', assassins to avoid and slaps to absorb, my vision was tightly confined and existential questions could safely be shelved for another day. Then, rather suddenly, came that beach-side epiphany. It was not as if my startlingly unoriginal insight on friendship, love and violence had never previously occurred. It was no doubt a throwback to my brief bohemian gap year between Christianity and Marxism a decade earlier, but its thrust had largely been forgotten, not being an integral part of South African revolutionary thought in the middle of a prolonged State of Emergency. This time, however, it lingered. When I rode back to the fumes and flames of Johannesburg, I realized I wanted a different kind of existence and needed a way out. For the first time I doubted what I was sure of. I decided I could no longer accept the intellectual baggage I'd inherited, like the linear nineteenth-century logic of Marxism, or its political baggage, like the violent compulsion of Soviet-style socialism.

The only meetings I had in the week after returning came with the gentler spirit of the Five Freedoms Forum (one of the organizations formed to help nudge liberal whites into supporting majority rule), and the creative energy of the End Conscription Campaign, rather than the more severe demands of my underground task masters. And my opening post-holiday work assignment was to cover the inspired campaign of the young Rose of Soweto in his first major international fight. So I was still at peace with the world when I arrived at Ellis Park indoor stadium, and it took Attie's grip and Bokkie's punch to shake me out of it. Afterwards, when we returned to Alan's flat, I was surprised by my reaction. Temper had never been part of my emotional range, not even in childhood, and yet I had evidently lost it for a while. It was enough to shortcircuit my harmonious phase and bring me back to the world I knew – the world of struggle and intrigue – and for the next year or so I remained a dutiful comrade.

Regular reminders of my ringside encounter helped to set this mentality – the gap between perception and reality widening as the story grew out of control. The promoter, who'd seen Bokkie washing the blood from his face in the toilets afterwards and who hated Attie, sent the word around that I'd given both men a severe hiding. This was untrue, but it didn't stop there. Years later I was still getting boxing people and reporters saying they'd heard I flattened them, and the like. And the more I denied it, the more it was taken as fact. But still the question always arose: why did they pick on you?

A month or so earlier, when arriving at the Sun City ringside to cover a tournament, I found my seat occupied by a reporter from another Afrikaans daily. When I politely asked him to move, he told me to fuck off. I refused and started pushing the impostor away, and a scuffle ensued – this time quickly broken up by security, which restored the preordained order. When I put these two incidents together, I began to wonder: perhaps Attie's outburst reflected a general resentment about this *kaffir boetie* pontificating on their sport? Or perhaps it was more specific – tip-offs from the security police that I was trouble. Over the previous two years my motorbike had been tampered with or vandalized five times – brake cables cut, tyres and seat slashed, petrol tank punctured – and I felt wary about what Attie and his friends might try next. I started parking it a few blocks away from the venues. I watched him carefully at boxing events, while at the same time avoiding him, and I realized I was becoming paranoid.

Eventually it dawned on me that the reason for his rage related not to struggle politics but to the minutiae of boxing politics. Attie was Berman's batman, doing press jobs for the promoter in exchange for a retainer. Brian Mitchell was also in the process of joining Berman's promotional stable. His prime local rival was Dingaan Thobela. I noticed that Attie became enraged when anyone criticized Berman's boxers and eventually I decided that this was the reason for his outburst: the sight of a white reporter writing up a black rival at the expense of a national hero promoted by his boss was just too much for him. But as it turned out, this was this same boss who inadvertently prompted Attie in the direction of peace.

Berman used to quip that I was the enemy because I supported the cause of boxers in rival camps and criticized his own stars, and there was some truth in this. Shortly after the Attie fight I asked Berman for an interview, with the idea of sticking the knife in. I anticipated a Machiavellian, hard-hearted streak, and perhaps a hint of racism. Instead I found a self-deprecating *mensch* – open to criticism, up for a joke, far more liberal than I assumed and devoid of any semblance of macho egotism. Berman, a senior partner in a thriving law firm, came into boxing by default by accepting the big-hitting, fragile-chinned light middle-weight Charlie Weir as payment from Maurice Toweel for a legal debt. Friends said he was nuts, but he so enjoyed the thrill of it that he persuaded his partners to join him in creating the Golden Gloves promotional team, which became the biggest in the country. At first he focused his attention on the lucrative white market, but in the mid-1980s he realized the future lay elsewhere and established a relationship with the leading East London-based manager–trainer, Mzi Mnguni, with the idea of developing a stable of black stars. He was interested in my connections with the black side of the game, and we talked in depth about this. I continued to criticize some of his boxers and promotions, but after this we gradually developed a kind of professional friendship.

Now and then he would hand out little mementoes to all the boxing writers. A few months after my scrap with Attie I was put on Berman's little list for the first time, and so, in obeisance to his boss, Attie approached me, offering his hand to shake while saying, 'Bygones, OK?' He handed me a Golden Gloves trinket. I felt uneasy about accepting but under the circumstances I felt it was the lesser evil. Over the next year, relations with Attie settled into arm's-length caution rather than spitting hate.

But more of that later, because it's finally time for another tale of passion – between the odd couple of South African boxing, Dingaan Thobela and Brian Mitchell. And this too had its origins in history: Dingaan's, Brian's and in a sense South Africa's.

*　　*　　*

My own take on the Thobela portion began in the southern Transvaal town of Springs in 1987. Two undefeated featherweights, one white, one black, squared off for a fight that would chart their destinies. In the far corner was Shorne Moorcroft, a heavy-handed brawler who was a little more experienced than the sleek 21-year-old stylist opposite him. It was supposed to be an even fight but Moorcroft was obliterated in five one-sided rounds, and was never the same again.* The other fellow took off and remains one of the most recognizable faces in South African public life. That small but seminal fight provided me with my first glimpse of the Rose of Soweto and I came away enticed. The balance and grace, speed of hand and foot, rhythm and reflexes, the bursts of power, blurring combinations and sudden killer uppercuts marked him as something extraordinary. Never before had I seen such innate potential in a local boxing ring.

Dingaan was named after a nineteenth-century Zulu king.** It was a fighting name chosen by a fighting father, but this Dingaan was nothing like the archetype of the warrior king. The man-child I first met in the late 1980s was a lean, broad-shouldered, beautifully pro-portioned 5 foot 7¾, with a soft voice and a smile that was dazzling and infectious and at the same time slightly reticent and suspicious. This Dingaan was a pretty boy, whose understated machismo was certainly not of the swaggering variety.

---

*Moorcroft retired and switched to knocking out karate men in kickboxing contests.

**According to oral history, Dingaan murdered his uncle, Shaka, and massacred Piet Retief's Voortrekkers, only to fall to their guns in the Battle of Blood River.

His arrival was impeccably timed. He turned professional three months before the death of the country's previous black boxing hero, Arthur Mayisela, but Dingaan represented something very different. Arthur was an ex-con, a hard man, a *pantsula* who made his name by pulverizing the golden boy of white South African boxing and then by sticking it to the racist white establishment. He was defiantly working class – kept his day job, jived to township *kwela* music, travelled third class on the trains and said what he thought. Dingaan came from another generation and milieu. He emerged as a symbol of black success rather than defiance, as the toast of the Soweto socialites, the escort of beauty queens, the foil of the highrollers. He was a full-time professional who hummed along to Luther Vandross, played squash at the health club and avoided public transport.

Not that his upbringing was easy. This was, after all, apartheid South Africa, where a black skin was unlikely to survive without a few scars. Dingaan was one of seven children – four girls, three boys – of a panel-beater and former boxer whose wife died when Dingaan was a child. Godfrey Thobela was a good enough provider, but money had to be stretched. Living in a four-roomed shack in Chiawelo, Soweto, it was a bit of a squeeze and so Dingaan was sent to live with his aunt. 'It was always a struggle for my family,' he told me the first time I interviewed him. 'There was no room to move because we were such a large family in such a small house, and that's why he sent me to live with my aunty, but my father made sure there was food on the table.'

Much of the hardship came from outside the home. Before he turned ten the students of Soweto marched against the forced imposition of Afrikaans as language of instruction. The state's murderous response left nearly eight hundred dead. Over the next decade Dingaan's school career was interrupted by school boycotts and state violence, and there was also plenty of criminal violence to avoid. Godfrey Thobela was concerned about his son's survival and taught his sons to box as a form of self-defence. 'His idea was for me to be able to defend myself against other kids without a *panga* or a knife,' Dingaan recalled.

It helped that the teenager seemed to be good at everything: a capable student who matriculated and then moved on to teacher-training college; an outstanding sportsman, who excelled as a middle-distance runner, played squash, tennis and table tennis with aplomb, and by the time he finished school was playing right wing for the Soweto football club Guinea Fowls. But boxing was his thing, and he transferred his dreams of a place with Orlando Pirates Club to emulating Muhammad Ali and Sugar Ray Leonard. 'It was like a call to me. I became very anxious to be a real boxer,' he said. His father had a boxing trainer friend, Norman Hlabane, and so he walked his 16-year-old to the gym. Dingaan racked up eighty-three amateur fights, winning eighty and lifting the national featherweight title before turning professional at the age of 19, with Hlabane as manager–trainer and the white mayor of Barberton, Thinus Strydom, as his promoter.

He moved quickly through the ranks, winning the South African title in his thirteenth fight, after which the talk moved on to the what-would-happen-if? subject of Brian Mitchell. This rivalry, stoked by Strydom, smothered by Berman, was founded not just on the presence of two stars in the same division, one white, the other black, but also on the contrast in personality and lifestyle.

In some respects, the order was reversed from the usual white-privilege, black-deprivation thing. Take poverty: in the way it is experienced it's a relative concept – relative to what we see of the lives around us and therefore to expectations. Dingaan grew up in a tiny shack in a working-class zone. He had to leave home early because there was not enough room, was not allowed in white areas without a permit, had to negotiate his way through criminal and political violence, saw his mother dying young, and saw some of his friends and classmates dying even younger. And yet he did not have a sense of himself as one who emerged from deprivation. In a relative sense his family was not poor because there were hundreds of thousands in Soweto, and millions nationally, who were worse off. His experience was typical of young men of his age, but his gifts of brains, looks and physical skill made it easier to negotiate. He thought himself blessed.

Brian's background was more troubled in many ways. His father, the first Brian Mitchell, was a professional boxer in the early 1960s – a chilling puncher who won the South African flyweight title but squandered his gifts. His mother, Cecilia, divorced Brian senior when Brian was a young boy, but his early childhood was blighted by the brawling father's descent into alcoholism, and it certainly left its scars. 'Jesus, I mean we were poor – like really poor,' he once told me. 'We didn't have much furniture and my mother struggled to put the food on the table.' His abiding memory is of deprivation – being worse off than his cousins or his friends in white, working-class Malvern. He lived on the edge of the feeder zone for a top state school – Jeppe Boys – but the predominance of middle-class pupils exacerbated his sense of being the underdog. He felt he didn't fit, kept to himself, hung out with his own and left when he turned 16. 'I wasn't unintelligent or anything and I was doing OK,' he recalled, 'but I just wasn't a guy who liked school. It wasn't for me, so I said to my mother I wanted to go out and work, but I had to push her into it.' He completed an apprenticeship as a tool- and die-maker, completed his two years military service and worked as an artisan.

Given his father's past, the brawling direction of his drift was inevitable. Usually it was fists, knees, heads and elbows, but a couple of times he was attacked with knives too, and once slashed. It became part of life, something he expected and even relished. 'I had that background, and I enjoyed the street fighting when I was younger,' he told me a couple of years after winning the world title. His amateur boxing career was unexceptional – unlike Thobela's. He was a rough fighter, who lacked his father's natural power. Nevertheless, he turned professional shortly before his twentieth birthday, mainly as a way of topping up his tradesman's wages. At 5 foot 6, with his sloping shoulders, big head, hooded eyes and large, well-spread nose, he would never enjoy pretty-boy appeal. He made his way as an underdog, forging his reputation as a white boxer who was prepared to box in the black townships. Trained by Willie Toweel he made gradual progress, winning six then dropping a decision to Jacob 'Dancing Shoes' Morake in Kwa Thema township; winning a couple more then getting a draw against Frank Khonkhobe in Sebokeng township; and then there were no more blemishes.

He remembered his father's troubles, stopped drinking and married Kathy, his 17-year-old sweetheart. Kathy was a pleasure to behold. 'Stop holding, you coward – just throw him, my doll, break his arms off,' she would shriek from ringside. 'Shake his bloody eyeballs out, Brianie,' or 'Kill him in the solars, Brianie, go for his bod,' or just plain, 'Careful, lovey, go careful.' With Kathy behind him Brian developed a reputation as the most dedicated boxer in the country. 'I went through a stage when I was hanging around clubs and drinking with friends, and I knew that I was a professional boxer so I could do a lot more than I used to do, and I had lots of street fights,' he said. 'That was when I was still looking for fights, but you grow out of it. I knew if I was hanging out at the Belgravia Hotel, guys would coming looking for me, but after I married Kathy I became a family guy and stopped going to those bad little places where guys look for fights.'

He beat Morake and Khonkhobe a couple of times each, and won the South African title, before making his Sun City debut on the undercard of the Gerrie Coetzee–Greg Page bill in 1984. This was the big time for little Brian, and it was the first time I saw him. My response was one of mild pity. Standing with Willie Toweel, looking boyishly shy, anxious but extremely eager and determined, he was shifting from foot to foot, waiting for the hours to pass until he got into the ring with the formidable national lightweight champion Aladin Stevens. As I wished him good luck I thought: *You're not going to make it tonight*, and felt sad that honest little battlers like Brian had to work so hard for so little, when pretty boys like Baronet got world-title chances on a plate. But Mitchell wasn't going down. His brow burst open but his fitness and tenacity won him a close decision, and I can still see his fist-pumping look of ecstatic triumph and relief.

Our next meeting came after he killed Jacob Morake eleven months later and there was something different about his face. It was more than the new moustache and the added scar tissue. The naiveté was gone, replaced by a single-minded sense of purpose. I felt he was trying to cut the death from his consciousness or place it within an amoral context. When he talked about it – which he did with obvious reluctance – he would turn it around to the question of whether it would affect him in the ring, and made it quite clear that he would emerge an even better boxer.

Brian was a practical man, not given to introspection. Like so many boxers he had a spell as a born-again Pentecostal Christian, but he wore his faith lightly and allowed it to slip without much sign of remorse. His attitude to the risks of his sport was that they were part of the package. He was sad about Morake, yes, but he never regretted turning professional, and never questioned continuing after Jacob's death; it would not stop him punching as hard as he could and it wouldn't make him more scared of taking punches either. 'No-one comes out of life alive, hey,' he once said to me. 'I could get knocked down while crossing the street, or blown up by a bomb watching a rugby match at Ellis Park. You can drive out your driveway and it doesn't have to be your fault. Somebody drives into you and that's it. Lots of rugby players are getting broken necks and paralysed and those guys aren't even getting paid for it, hey. I don't view the risks involved in boxing as anything out of the ordinary.' He was talking about himself but in a sense I think Jacob Morake was also there. 'If a boxer makes a mistake in conversation then everybody says he's had too many fights, whereas a normal person's mistake would be ignored. OK, there's always the possibility you take too many punches and overstay your welcome, but I believe if God gives you an ability you must make the most of it. If you're born a great sportsman, like me, you must use it.'

Willie Toweel had also killed an opponent, but unlike Brian he suffered from intense remorse and was never able to punch with his full weight again. Brian dropped him as his trainer and signed up with Carlos Jacamo, an Argentinian closely connected with the WBA, and he began to move through their super featherweight world rankings. Along the way he transformed himself from a much-hit, often-cut brawler into a highly skilled, hit-without-being-hit boxer – still aggressive, but never wild. Finally, in his thirty-first bout, after more than five professional years, Jacamo secured him a shot at the weight-weakened, under-trained, altitude-drained Alfredo Layne for the WBA super featherweight title.

I still was feeling the effects of Arthur Mayisela's funeral, one or two too many teargassings and a nomadic life in hiding when I arrived at Sun City in the fourth month of the National State of Emergency. It is perhaps for this reason that my memory of the most exhilarating night in Brian's life is jaundiced. As much as I admired his tenacity, I hardly felt delirious when he entered the ring to the *Rocky* theme song, with his orange, white and blue South African flag on his trunks, cheered on by rugby royal Naas Botha, Sol Kerzner and his temporarily unestranged ex-wife, the former Miss South Africa Annaline Kriel, all introduced by right-wing radio announcer David Blood – a quartet of my pet hates in South African public life.

I remained seated for the anthems before being ordered to my feet on the instructions of a Bophuthatswana cabinet minister.

This time the man of the moment was announced as Brian 'Raging Bull' Mitchell, having previously been Brian 'Mean Machine' Mitchell, but neither of these borrowed monikers stuck – he wasn't the sort for nicknames or mass affection. In this spirit I felt neither here nor there when Layne built up a lead and cut his left eyelid, and then his right brow. But Alfredo's inclination to do what was required to hold on to his title was abandoned somewhere between the wild parties of Panama and the high altitude of Bop. He had struggled to lose four extra kilos in two weeks, and when his early efforts failed to draw a conclusion he lost his way. Despite what they claim, no boxer ever gets stronger as a fight progresses – it just feels that way because the other fellow is getting weaker faster. As Layne's strength drained, Mitchell appeared ever stronger. He turned the fight around with his body punches, with the crowd chanting, 'Bria-nie, Bria-nie, Bria-nie.' Layne had nothing left for the riposte, and by the tenth round his long legs could no longer hold him. With each head shot his world would stop for a second as he shuddered, and after three knockdowns it was over. Brian Mitchell, WBA champion of the world, was running around the ring with his fist in the air, while Stan Christodoulou, WBA official, was leaping up and down and whooping with delight.

One of the many things I admired about Brian was his willingness to box in the black townships. It meant he wasn't riding on the privilege of his white skin and was prepared to take his chances in a world he'd been taught to fear. I was a little disappointed when, in the course of a chat while showing me his trophy collection, he referred to a boxer whose name he couldn't recall as 'this darky'. I soon realized, however, that nothing pejorative was intended. He was not using it with a Willie Lock, 'those kaffirs' sneer, nor in the Lenny Bruce-ish 'I'm so liberated I can play with words like darky' sense, which some in the 'whitey' left liked to indulge in. With Brian it was just a word used because no-one told him otherwise, and as I got to know him better I noticed that the way he talked to and about black boxers bore no hint of prejudice. His sparring partners, black and white, absorbed the same jokes, same teasing, same demands, same beatings. Still, for reasons beyond his control he was viewed as a white man's champion.

It all related to South Africa's pariah status abroad. Shortly after Brian's title victory the WBA succumbed to international pressure and banned its world champions from fighting in South Africa, followed by a ban on South Africans fighting for its laurels (with Mitchell exempted for as long as he remained champion). It meant all Brian's title defences had to take place abroad, with occasional non-title bouts at home thrown in for his local fans, and this had a deleterious effect on his pulling power. For his white followers the lack of local action meant Brian did not become an instant celebrity, and his public persona hardly helped his cause. In private he could be considerate, funny and articulate – as well as enraged and moody – but in public he tended to come across as aggressive or defensive, and he'd get drawn into prolonged harangues with critics. He was too honest, too straightforward and too combative for the PR game.

This defiance did not help his cause with the black

public because it spilled over in his resentment about the boycott. It was all politics, which he didn't understand, and so he went along with little patriotic gestures like wearing the flag on his trunks. Government heavyweights like General Magnus Malan and Pik Botha were ringside guests at his fights, giving the impression of Mitchell as an ambassador for the regime, whereas, in reality, his political views were more liberal than most. He frequently expressed opposition to government policy – 'I have openly come out against apartheid but I'm not here to represent South Africa – I'm a sportsman not a politician,' he would say when fighting abroad – and publicly supported the 'yes' vote in the 1990 white referendum on constitutional negotiations with the ANC. Yet whenever the flag was waved, or *Die Stem* sung, or when he shook the hand of a cabinet minister, it enhanced his status a representative of the white establishment – the white man's champion. When Dingaan Thobela arrived on the scene it was inevitable the rivalry would take on a politicized hue.

For Brian, the issues had nothing to do with colour. He resented posturing and thought the youngster was eating off his own hard-earned success. In a reversal of the usual coordinates, Brian, the white South African, felt that Dingaan, the black South African, hadn't paid his dues, and he despised his easy ride. Everything flowed so naturally for this upstart who always landed on his feet. While Brian had battled away in the townships, coped with cuts, lumps, bruises and dodgy decisions, with the death of an opponent and with obscurity and the life of a road warrior, Dingaan had none of this. He never cut or bruised, his early fights took place mainly in white or coloured Johannesburg and he was never obscure. In contrast to the former tradesman Brian, education student Dingaan was charming and pretty and his rise was seamless. It all came so easy. His celebrity status expanded from Chiawelo, to Soweto, to black South Africa and finally to the country as a whole. He took to it with what looked like effortless grace, and they took to him.

Brian had no comparable sense of community or fan base. He was delighted to leave Malvern as soon as he could afford it and moved into the upmarket Johannesburg suburb of Bedfordview, 'the place of my childhood dreams', where he kept to himself and his own. His public rapport took several more years to percolate. 'In a way I was lucky,' he told me when I visited him at home in 1989. 'I had so many fights and I wasn't getting recognized, and I thought, Jeez, I'm fighting so well and nothing's happening. I started being on TV more, but it was a gradual build-up. Most top fighters don't know what to do with the big money when it suddenly arrives because they've never had it before, so they start partying and that's the end of them – it affects their training and they go over the hill. But I've kept my temperament because it was a slow process to become famous.'

He acquired some of the insignia of instant wealth – the house, the bar, the gold chains, the restaurant, the left-hand-drive Corvette convertible with customized number plate – and seemed to relish what they said about him, but when recognition finally arrived his relationship with his public was more ambiguous. 'It's great for people to recognize you but it's not so easy to live with,' he said. 'It's not always nice. I mean, look at Mike Tyson. If you're famous like him, no matter what you do they want to publicize it. If a normal guy in his house chucks a bit of furniture around in an argument, so what? Nothing gets said. But when Tyson throws the furniture out of the window when he's having an argument with his wife, it's on the front page of every paper what a terrible person he is. He's as human as the rest of us, so he also gets into moods and has fights. So you see, there's a lot of disadvantages. It affects your privacy. I walk into the bank and everyone says, Look who's there, and when I look at them they look away. It's not so nice. You feel like you're on show the whole time, like an ornament in a showcase. But I'm not complaining because I'd rather be famous than not famous.'

The rivalry between Brian and Dingaan was formally consummated by a sparring session in 1988. Brian was in his third year as world champion and it was just another couple of rounds in preparation for another fight – no big deal. A year later he remembered he'd 'handled Thobela, no problem' but the details were vague. For the novice Dingaan it was everything. 'It was like a war in there,' he told me, still excited, three years on. 'I definitely got the better of him and he knows it. I was quicker than Brian, I beat him at long distance and I was even better than him on the inside. And it wouldn't be any different in the ring. In a real fight I would stop him.'

This kind of talk got to Brian more than he cared to admit. When I would ask him about Thobela he was dismissive: 'They're bringing this kid along too quickly, rating him too highly too fast.' 'The gap between me and him is too big – what has Thobela won?' 'He hasn't fought the calibre of opponents I faced.' 'The fight means nothing to me.' Strydom tried a new tactic – putting Dingaan in with Brian's former opponents, with

Thobela usually doing a better job than his rival.
Dingaan, rather than Brian, was voted Boxer of the Year
for 1989. This too got under Brian's hide. 'It means
nothing putting him in with guys I've already softened
up,' he'd sneer. Despite his protestations I sensed he
was tempted but Berman wouldn't have it, saying it
wasn't in Brian's 'financial interests'. Years later, however, Berman admitted to me: 'I made lots of excuses,
but it would have been a huge money spinner at home.
The real reason was because Brian was my boxer
and, frankly, I wasn't convinced he could pull it off.
Dingaan was just so quick, and I was worried he'd cut
Brian to ribbons with those combinations.'

Instead Berman paraded Brian's talents with the
best foreign opponents he could find, while attracting
sponsors and advertisers to the cause. He found a
world-class trainer, the black American Murphy
Griffiths, to work with Harold Volbrecht in preparing
Brian for the bigger things to come in the last lap of
his career. 'I only realized how professional I could
be when I joined Murphy,' Brian told me soon after
joining Griffiths. 'At such a late stage in my career
he started teaching me the basics of jabbing again.
When you get to San Diego and the guy puts your
one hand behind your back and works on your jab
for two weeks, just the jab, you think, *Jeez, I'm a
world champion with seven title defences*, but then
you realize how unprofessional your previous trainers
have been because they didn't pick up on those
mistakes. They just thought I had everything because I
just kept on winning, but you never stop learning in
this game.'

The fighter that emerged from this re-education
camp was on the brink of brilliance. He still looked

the same – fighting out of a crouch with a look of intense concentration on his features – but there were fresh touches to his work: a more solid and persistent jab, an added talent for slipping and ducking, a greater precision in his punching. Everything flowed beautifully, and there were seldom any mistakes. His fellow professionals would marvel at the appearance of perfection, and still do. Thirteen years later, for example, a young Cape-based Zimbabwean flyweight called Sipho 'Spider' Mantyi cited the Mitchell of this era as his prime inspiration. 'The way he fought was out of this world. His prowess wasn't typical of an *umlungu*. His agility was like a streetwise black township boy – without being offensive to whites.'

It was May Day, two days after my twenty-ninth birthday, three months after my scrap with Attie, and I was sitting in a café in Rocky Street, in Yeoville, sipping a banana milkshake and discussing with a couple of comrades the logistics of a conference to be held in Lusaka between the ANC and 120 white notables, when my bleeper bleeped. 'Phone Mike Olivier, urgent' it read. A minute later I was on the phone speaking to Mike, the president of the Five Freedoms Forum. 'I'm afraid I have some terrible news for you, Gavin,' he said. 'David Webster has just been murdered outside his house.' I fell silent for about ten seconds, and finally I found my voice to say, 'I'll be there in five minutes.'

I was numbed by this news, unable to think about it until I arrived at David's house in Troyeville, three miles away, and noticed the blood congealing on the pavement. I went inside and saw his partner, Maggie, sitting on the sofa, in a state of shock but trying to be brave. I put my arm around her and muttered, 'I'm so sorry.' Somebody whispered that a car drove by, a man leant out of the window and fired at David's chest at point blank range, and that he staggered and then died a few seconds later. As I heard this story I started to feel a surge of intense anger and hatred and I could no longer stay seated. I jumped on my motorbike and raced off, not knowing where to go or what to do.

By then I knew of several comrades who'd been assassinated, some of them people I'd met and liked, but Dr David Webster was my first *friend* to die this way, and aside from that, he was such a genuinely *good* man. Not like the rest of us, not like me anyway – a far better, kinder person; one without burning personal ambition or malice or guile or intrigue. A prominent anthropologist, a pragmatic socialist, an ANC member, an eloquent debater, an activist of phenomenal energy working simultaneously in five semi-legal organizations, but more than all this, a humanist – a man whose motivation was his love of people and his intense hatred of their suffering. His most important work was to support detainees and their families, and he went about this with tireless patience and dedication. When Joy Harnden was detained for the first time he'd already been tipped off that she was a spy, but this did not stop him driving 300 miles to the Northern Transvaal to console her family. He was like that – never losing sight of the individual. I had stayed over in his house and shared hotel rooms with him over the years, and when we were alone together I would talk about debates and campaigns while he would steer the conversation back to people with problems who needed help. He was someone who made me feel unworthy, although that is the last thing he would have wanted.

About 10,000 people attended his funeral, where I was instructed by the Operation Vula command to deposit thousands of Communist Party pamphlets in the toilets for spontaneous distribution. The pamphlets, which I helped write, told of learning lessons, but the only lesson I could draw was a sour mix of rage and despair. The rage sustained my activism for a while, and I threw myself into campaign mode – the Lusaka ANC conference with the white elite; a mass objection to military service by 771 conscripts who publicly refused to obey their call-ups, risking up to six years in jail; the recruitment of new ANC and party members – but as the months passed the despair added a bitter and cynical edge to my rage. I became far more excited by vengeance than liberation.

Shortly after David's murder, I was tipped off that I was next on the death list. It emerged soon afterwards that I'd been saved by chance. This is what happened: five members of the Civil Co-operation Bureau – a military hit-squad network – had one of their get-togethers in a Johannesburg hotel in March 1989. Their regional boss, Colonel Daniel 'Staal' (Steel) Burger – a senior military intelligence officer and former head of the Brixton murder and robbery squad – had just received a 'priority' death list from his national boss, the army special forces officer, Colonel Joe Verster.* Staal consulted this list and issued an order: 'Slang,

---

*Verster, in turn, would later claim the names were approved by his commanding officer, the special forces head General Eddie Webb, who doubled as CCB chairman. Webb denied this.

you do Gavin Evans. Ferdi and Chappie, you *ouks* do the research.'

So Lieutenants Ferdinand Barnard and Leon 'Chappie' Maree went to work on their £3,000 research tasks and supplied my work address, five possible home addresses and my pager number, and the information that I drove a 1600cc Ford Sierra. Lieutenant Abram 'Slang' (Snake) van Zyl contacted his Cape gangster connection, Edward 'Peaches' Gordon, with a £2,000 commission: 'Follow Evans, stab him to death outside the *Weekly Mail* offices, steal his watch and wallet; make it look like a robbery.'

I was probably helped by the chaotic nature of my lifestyle. Surveillance is assisted if the watchers can establish a consistent pattern of behaviour – regular times for leaving home, arriving at work, returning home and familiar travel routes – but with me there was no pattern to work, home life, sleep and leisure. Also, motorbikes are trickier than cars to follow, and my chaotic driving habits must have made it even harder. I would regularly lose the way when not concentrating, pull over, turn around, and then shoot down one-way roads and jump traffic lights. I was also aided by the fact that Ferdi and Chappie's homework was only so-so – Peaches couldn't track me at the out-of-date addresses he'd been supplied; I did not go to the office on the days he lurked around the garage; I did not possess a Ford Sierra; and I did not respond to Peaches' pager message to meet him because my ANC trainers had warned me about this kind of thing.

Peaches reported failure, but before a second attempt could be initiated the assassins were hit by their own crisis. Fresh from murdering David Webster, Barnard and his Transvaal rugby lock chum Lieutenant

Calla Botha* were arrested while trying to set up the assassination of another friend of mine in the garage of a building rented by a business group called the Urban Foundation. This came at a time when sections of the regular police were asserting their independence from the security police. Botha and Barnard were photographed and released but soon afterwards another CCB hitman, Donald Ascherson (an Irishman who was being interrogated by the regular police for his role in the murder of a leading Swapo official in Namibia), was shown pictures of suspects in the Webster murder while being tortured. Eager to avoid another dose of electrodes, he immediately identified Botha – hard to miss with his 23-inch neck. Botha and Barnard were then detained without trial and spilled a few beans of their own, after which Peaches broke ranks and confessed all.

My initial reaction to the combination of David's murder and the news that I'd 'survived' an assassination attempt included an uneasy mix of relief and guilt. Why David? I kept on asking, and the corollary of that question was, Why not me? But I also held a ghoulish curiosity to meet the men at the business end of the plot.

I never got to exchange pleasantries with Peaches because, after 'singing' in exchange for immunity, the life of this 27-year-old gangster** was ended courtesy of a .22 bullet in the back of his head while he was

---

*It emerged that Barnard was the man who pulled the trigger. This brutal, coke-sniffing ex-cop who'd already done time for murder was eventually convicted and jailed for life. Years later he named his driver on the Webster 'job' as Calla Botha.

**He was a member of the Cape coloured gang, the Americans.

sitting in a stolen car. Two young lovers who were chance witnesses to his execution were also bumped off.

But I accepted an invitation to meet his handler, the soft-faced, snake-eyed Slang van Zyl. At the end of a surreal two-hour tea at his beachside house, this former police torturer turned military assassin informed me I was 'chosen' because of spy reports, 'and you must remember we have the best intelligence network in Africa'. I meekly protested that my activities were purely of a peacenik brand. 'You *know* what you were involved with,' he replied enigmatically before insisting he was only doing his job and had no regrets. 'I am very proud to have been a member of the CCB,' he volunteered while smiling at his wife. 'I think they did good work. I am not sorry I was a member and I will never apologize for anything that I've done whilst I was a member of the CCB.'*

I later doorstepped Staal Burger at the brothel he was covertly running for military intelligence, catching him by surprise. I was on crutches after an accident in the mountains, and although this behemoth said little else of interest, as I left he casually remarked: 'I'd be careful if I was you, Evans. People on crutches can easily meet with accidents.'

While all this was happening, Brian Mitchell was beginning to tire of his profession. His marriage was under strain, he had two young sons and a daughter on the way, and he wanted a break from the life of constant travel, pain and weight-making. He was

---

*A decade later, while pleading for indemnity before the Truth and Reconciliation Commission, Slang claimed he had 'sincerely apologized' to me.

finding it harder to squeeze his chunky body down to 130 pounds and the self-denying routines were more difficult to sustain. And yet he was at the peak of his powers – perhaps one of the top ten boxers of any weight in the world – and was finally being offered one of the big, career-defining fights he craved. Azumah Nelson, the great Ghanaian who held the WBC world title, remained out of reach because the WBC still maintained the anti-apartheid sports boycott, but in March 1991 Mitchell travelled to Sacramento, California to fight the IBF world champion, Tony Lopez, in a title unification bout. He seemed a clear winner, only to hear the judges score it a draw. He returned home bitterly disappointed, feeling he had been a victim of hometown shenanigans and inter-national power politics.

When I learnt I was to spend two weeks with the Mitchell camp in Sacramento for their return fight, I was both excited and apprehensive. It was five years since my previous American trip and I was delighted to get the chance to see the conclusion of Brian's career. I was also relieved to get time off from covering the 'low-intensity war' in the country. For instance, I had just returned from the Northern Transvaal town of Ventersdorp, listening to threats from the buffoonish neo-Nazi leader Eugene Terreblanche while covering a confrontation between his troops and the local black community, who were boycotting white stores. 'If they dare to come here I'll knock the hell out of them,' a tipsy Terreblanche told me when I visited his offices. 'Did you get that down? You must write that if they come I'll knock the hell out of them.' He roared off with his gun-toting henchmen to 'patrol' the black township. It was good to take a break from perpetual confrontation by travelling to a fight 16,000 km away.

But I was less than delighted by the idea of spending a fortnight with my old connection Attie. The publicity my name had been attracting over the previous year made me particularly apprehensive. There had been a spate of newspaper and television reports on the exposure of the plot by the CCB hit squad to assassinate me and these stories prompted boxing people to treat me differently. There was a mixed response. Berman, along with many of the black managers and boxers, regarded the fact that the state wanted to kill me as a badge of honour. However, some white managers and writers seemed to regard it as confirmation of my enemy status. I was sure Attie would be in this camp, and the idea of spending two weeks with him in Sacramento was hardly inviting.

Minutes after putting my bags down, I learnt that Attie, who was in the adjoining motel room, was in the midst of a low-intensity war with a rival reporter, and soon both were offering me their side of the conflict. My first assumption was that Attie's welcome was all about finding allies for his latest dispute, but after another day it was clear it was more profound. He began to share intimacies with me – he talked of his weight troubles, of his inclination to rage, of his passion for women and how he controlled it, and of how much he loved his new wife. He requested nothing in return, but one afternoon in the hotel pub, he asked if he could pose a question. I knew what was coming. 'Tell me, hey, Gavin – you don't have to say, it's up to you – but why was the CCB trying to kill you? D'you mind me asking: what were you actually involved with?' Honesty was not the best policy, I decided. 'Aah, nothing really,' I said. 'I was a member of a group opposing compulsory conscription and the CCB thought I was more involved than I actually was. They must have got their wires crossed.' He shrugged and invited me to join him on a trip to San Francisco. The subject was never mentioned again, but Attie's little generosities continued. The day before the fight he invited me to join him in Brian's bedroom suite as he wound down before the fight. All other journalists were barred.

Never before had I witnessed such single-minded intensity in preparation for one 45-minute, life-defining moment. Brian always trained harder than his opponents, but this time, for what he thought was his last fight, at the age of 30, he gave it more. His two young sparring partners, Philip Holiday, who went on to become an IBF world champion, and Lucky Lushaba, who went on to become an American student, were both talented young lightweights but Brian pushed them to the limit and they struggled to hold him off. They could not quite keep up with him in his roadwork either, and he went about his work on the pads and bags with ferocious intensity. When we met in his hotel bedroom the work was over, and he had to 'sniff lettuce leaves instead of eating', as he put it, and concentrate his entire will on the man he would be facing; he seemed to appreciate the time spent sitting on his bed, talking of past battles and future relief. By this stage I had also come to know and like his opponent Lopez, a gregarious, easy-going, womanizing joker who was happy to welcome South African reporters into his home. So there was no enemy, but I was all for Mitchell this time. I was willing him to triumph. I felt he had earned his dues and paid a higher price than Tony.

Lopez's weight troubles were even more severe than Mitchell's and he failed to make the limit. Two hours later, in his final attempt, he was still half a pound over. The Mitchell camp agreed to look the other way rather than risk a cancellation and an official weight of 130 pounds was recorded, but it gave Mitchell a crucial edge. He had timed things to perfection; Lopez hadn't, and Brian, the former brawler, produced the most elegant display of his ten-year career, outjabbing Lopez, defusing his rushes, countering his lunges, moving in and out and around to his right, always within range, but seldom in one spot for long enough to take any punishment. He was boxing from an intricately conceived score, but such was his mastery of the mechanics that he felt able to innovate at the edges by adding inspired flourishes. After twelve rounds he had stilled the Sacramento crowd and persuaded all three judges that he was the new world champion.

It occurred to me that this was the first time since the days of Arnie Taylor in the early 1970s that I was throwing my full emotional support behind a white South African boxer. It also dawned on me that my previous routine support for black boxers over their white opponents had more than a hint of inverse racism about it, and that perhaps the irritation of the Atties had some justification. I felt contrite as I went to the post-fight celebratory dinner, but as I sat down I found myself alongside a table dominated by a large, avuncular, jug-eared slaphead who was trying to envelop the world champion into his own largesse, and I felt sick. The Mitchell embracer was the minister of defence, former chief of the South African military, the big boss behind the CCB military hit-squad network which murdered David Webster and tried to murder me, a man I held responsible for numerous massacres all over Southern Africa: General Magnus Malan, boxing fan and Brian Mitchell aficionado. I had written several scathing stories on Malan, and had seen him at fights and military functions, but sitting three metres away in the Californian capital made me feel tainted. I wondered for a moment what a member of the Resistance would have done finding himself dining with Göring and I thought that if I had any guts I should follow Magnus to his hotel and put my steak knife in his spine, or at least introduce myself: 'Gavin Evans, ANC, SACP, intended victim of your CCB.' But I just kept quiet, staring and hating and feeling sullied by the presence of an apartheid killer.

On the way home from Sacramento we stopped off at Heathrow, where I was met by my sister Karen and my brother-in-law Mkhuseli, then completing an economics degree at Sussex University. As a British citizen I had rushed through ahead of the rest of the party who required their passports to be checked. 'Where's Brian, where's Mitchell?' said Mkhuseli. 'I want to congratulate him on his historic achievement.' The sports boycott against South Africa was on the verge of being lifted, and for Mkhuseli, a former political and community leader, who had survived four years of detention without trial, whippings, burnings, cattle prodding, electric shocks to his tongue and testicles, water bags, suffocations and a couple of assassination attempts from Magnus's minions, this was enough to embrace Brian. They were both South Africans, and Brian's achievement was an achievement worthy of celebration. It made me feel a little less tainted.

Attie shook my hand warmly when we arrived at

Johannesburg airport. 'Gavin, I think you'll agree I've done my bit to put things right between us, hey?' I gave an embarrassed smile and nodded. 'Any time you want you can come and join my wife and I for *potjiekos*. I'd like that.' I agreed that was a fine idea and even though the invitation for *boer* stew never arrived and we went our separate ways, relations remained amicable.

Brian announced his retirement while Dingaan travelled to Texas, moved up to lightweight and survived heat stroke to win the WBO lightweight title. He remained in America for his brilliant first defence but then went off the boil. The Soweto celebrity life-style as well as a broken right hand, which eventually required surgical reconstruction, left its mark. He was fighting once every six months against moderate opposition, and no longer looked as sharp as before. He insisted his commitment was unchanged but the physical evidence suggested otherwise.

We were seeing each other regularly through various media and business projects and as I came to know him better, the image of Dingaan as the cat that always lands on its feet began to slip. I no longer viewed him as one quite so at ease with his world as I had once assumed. He was a cautious man who revealed less than you wanted but sometimes more than he intended if you could read between the frown lines on his brow. The first time I interviewed him I noticed merely vulnerability in those wide eyes. They would display sadness, disappointment, caution and fear to a degree that was unusual in a top-flight boxer. He was more reticent with words but occasionally this would spill over, like when he failed his first-year exams at the Soweto teachers' training college. 'Gavin, I am so very disappointed because when I wrote those papers I was so confident. I was doing so well, but I just didn't get through. I don't know why.' He shook his head lugubriously, paused for a moment and came up with an answer and a solution. 'I'll be back next year and I don't envisage any more problems because I still want to be a teacher. Boxing affected my performance.' At the time I considered his response as a positive sign of his inclination to overcome adversity, even though he never returned to college. But another way of looking at it was that he was too ready to blame outside forces for failure. Like so many boxers, there was a strong element of self-righteousness in his makeup, creating a gap between self-perception and reality. He was never at fault. Whatever he did could be either justified or denied, if it didn't fit with his own view of himself and his motives.

This emerged more clearly after he won the WBO title – a heightened sense of his own importance, combined with a deep suspicion about those who did not treat him accordingly. He was struggling to handle the pressures of fame, displaying confusion about how to conduct himself. On one occasion, when we were enjoying a long, late breakfast together, he became extremely upset with a waitress who politely asked us if we wouldn't mind finishing up because they had to set the tables for lunch. I nodded, thinking it a reasonable request, but for Dingaan it was an insult. 'I didn't want to make a scene, but that was no way to treat us, or anyone,' he muttered to me half an hour later, and marched off to give the girl a quiet roasting. Obeying decorum. Being treated just so. Not making a scene. These things were important to Dingaan. He had strong political beliefs, but in contrast to Mayisela he wouldn't make a scene about them. 'I am very concerned about politics,' he said, 'but I've opted to leave politics to the politicians.'

Dingaan's image-projection sometimes seemed bizarre, not least when it came to his moniker, the Rose of Soweto. The name was not one that emerged organically from the heart of the township, but rather an inspired invention by one of his professional sponsors who went beyond the usual habit of recycling American ring names in the knowledge that the local fans were ignorant of their boxing history. The Rose of Soweto was a grand and rather effete title which seemed to fit much of what Dingaan represented, and it stuck to the point where it unshackled itself from its adman's origins and became his own. He protected it fiercely, once phoning me in a state of distress. 'You've got to help me,' he pleaded, and went on to explain that a Soweto business was using the name 'rose' in its advertising. 'I'm the *only* Rose. I *am* the Rose of Soweto. They've no *right* to do this,' he said. I told him the word 'rose' was not his for the keeping, although I assured him that no other smelled as sweet. He seemed to feel I had let him down in his hour of need.

His identity as a Sowetan was particularly important to him. From the start he made it clear to me that he was a gift to his community and that the community shared this view. 'I find that many people like me to be near them,' he said. 'They come up to me on the street all the time and want to talk to me and be with me, and I'm actually very happy about it because it makes the people of Chiawelo and the rest of Soweto happy.' This, however, carried obligations: the loyalty needed to be reciprocal. One of his sponsors, the brewers King Korn, placed his picture on billboards all over the city under the slogan: 'I may be champion but I haven't forgotten my roots'. Dingaan took it seriously. 'I love Soweto so much,' he said during lunch one day. 'I grew up here. I know each and every corner. I was groomed as a fighter and a human being here – it's made me what I am. I'm one of them.' When I asked him about what he planned to do with his wealth, he made a point of insisting he would never leave the township, 'no matter how much money I make.' Soon after, however, I heard he'd quietly abandoned Soweto for the leafy 'white' Johannesburg suburb of Kelvin. He asked me not to write about this 'because I'm *still* the Rose of Soweto'. The disjuncture between perception and reality was clear to Dingaan, but there was no hint of embarrassment – merely an assertion of his need to maintain a lifestyle that contradicted the public image.

His overdeveloped sense of his own image, status and destiny began to rub up against the rather limited range of his promoter. Dingaan felt Strydom was not treating him right and that he should have been an international celebrity. With Mitchell out of the way he abandoned plans to drop back down to super feather-weight and instead started talking up his chances against one of the finest boxers ever, the American Pernell Whitaker, for the world lightweight title. When Strydom couldn't deliver, he felt victimized, and signed up with Rodney Berman, then left Berman and returned to Strydom, then returned to Berman again, a pattern that would lead to ten promotional switches, a feature of his career. Berman eventually secured him a shot at the WBA lightweight title – held by Mitchell's old connection, Tony Lopez.

So once again I was back in Sacramento, this time without Attie, or Magnus. I was happy to be there, to spend time with Dingaan, to renew my acquaintance with Tony Lopez's friendly family, visit the comedy clubs and go running along the river. But all was far from well with the Thobela camp. Cedric Kushner employed Jesse Reid, a Houston-based trainer, to assist Norman Hlabane. 'It must be a great help working with someone of Reid's experience,' I said to Hlabane when I arrived in Houston, two weeks before the fight. 'Actually, it's been me alone,' he replied, 'because Jesse's been ignoring Dingaan and focusing only on his own boxer, Todd Foster.' Hlabane, a quiet, courteous Sowetan, did not know how to handle this self-promoting Texan and the situation deteriorated. Reid's group took off for Los Angeles in the Thobela camp's van, leaving the others stranded. The irritation levels rose. When the Texans returned Reid only had eyes for Foster. 'Todd, break Dingaan's body,' 'Todd, throw the hook when he comes in,' 'Todd, watch his uppercut,' Reid would shout. Dingaan was being treated as the hired help. Five days before the fight Reid told Foster not to spar with Thobela because Dingaan was giving him a rough time, and took to barking instructions at Hlabane. 'Norman, get Todd gloved up for the next round!' he shouted in the tone he might use for a bucket boy. Dingaan was sullenly resentful at this 'white *baas*' treatment and the local newspapers picked up on it, noting the effect on his preparations. Reid was incensed by the reports and I overheard him plotting with Foster whether to use his fists or his elbows in beating up one of the Californian reporters: 'I feel like flattening you, you piece of shit, you sick sonofabitch,' he said when the young man arrived at the gym. Meanwhile, Hlabane, who was trying to keep the peace, went down with a severe dose of flu.

By the time of the weigh-in Dingaan was morose, but worse was to come: Brian Mitchell arrived. Their animosity had been revived a few months earlier when Brian announced he would return to the ring. Berman accommodated his desires by telling Dingaan that Brian would take his place in challenging for Lopez's IBF lightweight title, although the situation was later reversed for financial reasons – with Berman offering Brian a third fight with Lopez if the American won. When Mitchell arrived at the weigh-in, he ignored Thobela and embraced Lopez, wishing him good luck before announcing that Thobela was a 'boring' fighter who would lose on a knockout. Dingaan snapped back, 'Lopez has fought men like Mitchell but never anyone of my calibre.'

Dingaan climbed into the ring, wearing an odd, S&M-type leather halter in place of the traditional gown, and throwing roses to the crowd, but he looked a forlorn figure. He was prone to bouts of sullen introspection, and this was not the best state of being when up against a rampant opponent who appeared far sharper than the weight-drained figure who succumbed to Mitchell seventeen months earlier. But Dingaan is a volatile and unpredictable man. He can shine in the face of adversity, and stink the place out when expected to shine. With Nelson Mandela's wishes in his ear, and the knowledge that millions of South Africans were watching him, he delivered an inspired performance, moving around the ring gracefully, threading his jab into Tony's reddening face and then sliding away again, just out of reach. Now and then he would plant an uppercut under the chin, and whenever Lopez mounted an attack Thobela would meet him with a rapid-fire combination, periodically shaking him. By the seventh round Lopez was starting to leak blood from his puffed right eye and was getting caught frequently. Coming into the final round there was unanimity in the press rows that Dingaan was ahead, and he finished in style, battering the bloody-faced Lopez until he was reeling.

Over the next two minutes the status of South Africa's two premier boxers would shift irrevocably. Coming into the fight Brian Mitchell had established himself as a former world champion with a lucrative line in motivational speaking at business functions. He was a white sporting celebrity whose victory over Lopez had won him a grudging respect among black boxing followers. Dingaan Thobela was a former champion with a high profile among black South Africans, but there was a sense he had failed to fulfil his immense early promise. Their reaction to the judges' verdict – 'The winner, by unanimous decision, and still champion, Tony "The Tiger" Lopez' – changed all this.

In South Africa, where the television images gave the impression of an even more overwhelming victory than the flesh and blood version at ringside, a collective horror prevailed. Nelson Mandela was on the phone, expressing his outrage to the WBA, and this view was certainly not confined to black viewers. This was a blatant robbery against a South African, and for whites, who had grown up with the assumption that the term 'South African' applied only to their kind, Thobela's plight shocked them into a realization of a wider national identity: an injury to one is an injury to all.

Then Dingaan hugged Tony and wished him well – so not only a victim, but a gracious one too, even when he sadly spoke to the television microphone: 'I congratulate Tony but deep down he knows Dingaan Thobela is world champion. It was a hometown decision but I hope he'll fight me again – I'd really appreciate a rematch.' In this moment the Rose of Soweto became the Rose of South Africa – the country's first ever cross-over sports star. He had arrived at a moment when South Africa desperately needed figures of unity, and his victim status at the hands of the American judges, and his magnanimity, did the trick. He had transformed himself from a black hero to a truly national hero.

A beaming Brian leapt into the ring, oblivious to the impact of the pictures and words absorbed by his fellow South Africans. He was thinking of the imminent Mitchell–Lopez 3 – a couple million more against a man he knew he could beat, another world title, then retire again. He was happy about this and was delighted to see the ambitions of his local rival quashed. He hugged Tony and then bounced over to the television microphones to say he thought Lopez deserved it. 'Thobela always said he could beat me, but you saw tonight he bit off more than he could chew. I don't think he could beat me on any day of the week.' With those words the prospect evaporated of Mitchell returning to the ring. He was now a villain, castigated in newspaper columns and letter pages and radio station phone-ins. A couple of months later I saw him being introduced at a boxing match in Johannesburg, and noticed his eyes welling up when the crowd booed him. It must have been hard for him to understand: he had just been speaking his mind, as he always did, giving as good as he got, and now this. I went up to say hello afterwards, feeling embarrassed and sad for him. He had proved dispensable – booed, cast off, vilified.

Thobela's change in status was apparent well before his return to South Africa. On the plane home I tried my best to console him, saying that I was sure he would get another shot and that the result would make him more popular than ever at home. As I was speaking, a steady trickle of white South African men got up from their seats and walked over to congratulate him, telling him they had heard about the 'robbery' and that they were behind him all the way. When we landed the ground crew provided a guard of honour, clapping as he passed, while several hundred fans gathered to greet him. Over the next month he was inundated with appearance requests from local and foreign television and radio programmes and was guest of honour at numerous public events.

Berman staged an elaborate press junket (featuring Thobela sparring with a tiger cub) to announce the return fight for Sun City, following a verbal agreement with the Lopez camp. What he had not counted on was the wiles of Gerrie Coetzee, in his new incarnation as a boxing manager and agent. After Lopez agreed to Berman's $600,000 offer, Gerrie travelled to Sacramento and offered Lopez $700,000 to sign a one-fight deal. Lopez signed. Gerrie presented this fact to Hlabane, and Thobela signed. Later that day Gerrie phoned me, elated. 'Guess what, Gav.' Having previously turned down a bribe from Coetzee I curtly said I couldn't possibly imagine what. 'I've signed Dingaan.' He said he'd 'stolen' him to get at Berman. 'Go ask Dingaan yourself, Gav.'

Thobela flatly denied he had signed with Coetzee. I asked him again, and once more he denied it. 'Hey, Gavin, you mustn't believe everything you hear,' he said. I asked a third time and his reply was emphatic:

'Gavin, I promise, I've signed no contract. I know nothing about this.' But Gerrie produced the proof. Perhaps I had no right to expect the truth from someone who, when it came down to it, was more expedient acquaintance than friend, but I still felt let down. Berman, who'd been abandoned at the altar by Dingaan once before, was incensed. 'I don't mind being outbid by another promoter but I do resent being stabbed in the back by my own troops. I could have made millions from putting on Mitchell–Lopez 3 but I stuck with Dingaan. He has disappointed me with his lack of loyalty.' When I asked him about it eight years later, his perspective had mellowed. 'What I came to realize with Dingaan, as with so many young boxers, is that they have an unrealistic view of their own financial worth and what it takes to get them to the top – you know, the strings you need to pull with promoters and control bodies to get the title fights. So they walk as soon as someone offers them a slightly higher purse, and then they come back again, and gradually they realize how it all works. That's what happened with Dingaan and I don't hold it against him.'

At the time, however, recriminations sprayed back and forth, tarnishing Thobela's image, but the fight went ahead under Gerrie's banner. The Sun City sequel did not live up to the Sacramento premier, but the outcome was more satisfying. Dingaan dominated the early rounds with his jab, hurting Lopez with occasional right crosses, but in the second half he began to tire and dropped several rounds through his lower workrate. Still he emerged with a unanimous decision. At the age of 26, Dingaan Thobela was finally WBA world lightweight champion and 100,000 people from Soweto and other townships poured onto the streets for a night of non-stop revelry. Tony Lopez was gracious in defeat: 'I was beaten by the better man and good luck to Dingaan. I hope he holds the title for a long time.' To which Thobela responded: 'This title is for the people of South Africa.'

However, his gift turned out to be a miserly offering. Four months and four hundred parties on, Dingaan made his first world-title defence against his mandatory challenger, the unbeaten Russian Orzubek Nazarov. He struggled to sweat down from 155 pounds to the lightweight limit of 135 and was distracted on learning the promotion was in trouble – eventually cutting his losses and approaching Berman again. The show was rescued but the jilted Coetzee was enraged. He made his move shortly after the weigh-in when the drained Dingaan was about to leave for his first proper meal in several weeks. 'He waited until I was alone and then stormed in with this blank piece of A-4 paper which he said I must sign,' Dingaan told me. 'I said I wasn't prepared to sign a piece of paper. I told him I don't sign blank contracts, so he threatened to beat me up, and when I still said no, he grabbed me by the clothes and started pulling me and shaking me, until some people came in and intervened.' Dingaan, a man given to obsessing over details while missing the big picture, was even more upset by Coetzee's failure to keep a promise to deliver his WBA title belt. 'I really wanted to wear it into the ring, but he never brought it, and I've still never got it. This and his assault on me and my weight troubles took away my concentration and affected me badly so that I was weak and unfocused.'

A listless Thobela dropped Nazarov with an upper-cut before running out of gas and losing his title on points. For the return Kushner sent him to

Massachusetts to work with Goody Petronelli, trainer of Marvelous Marvin Hagler, 'but it was so cold that I couldn't sweat off the kilos,' said Dingaan, 'and I had to squeeze myself beyond what my body could take. Unless you've done it you won't understand how much weight-making can take out of you. I had nothing left.' He was again outpointed and his days as a world-class boxer ended – for a while. He changed promoters again, travelled to England, lost again, returned home and began a stop-start process of building and bashing down.

With Dingaan out of the picture Brian Mitchell began to think about that comeback once again. His marriage was finally coming to its own stop-start end and he was 'overdoing it on the beer front' as he put it. Memories of his father's predicament swirled around in his head and his weight rose to 170 pounds, some of it muscle from bodybuilding with a fair amount of lard thrown in. Most of all he was missing the adulation of the ring and growing bored with speech-making, and anyway the invitations were becoming sparse. He started at light welterweight with the aim of eventually getting down to lightweight to take on Thobela's conqueror, and looked good in his two fights, and then suddenly he gave it up again. A few years later, when we were having a pint together, I asked him why. 'It came to me all of a sudden when I was lying down in the changing room after that second fight. I'd won but every part of me felt sore, my body, my face, my arms, and I said to Kathy: That's it. I don't need this any more. I just didn't want to put my body through hell ever again. I just knew it was over. I had gone out on a win, I'd had a brilliant career, I was nearly 34, I mean, I couldn't complain.'

And the Brian who emerged was very different from the fighting version. When he was boxing he had always told me that the thing he would never do after he retired was become a trainer. 'I just don't have the right temperament, you know, the patience,' he'd say. But that's exactly the course he opted for – training and managing boxers at his own gym – and he proved to be an extremely patient teacher and a master tactician, instructing feather-fisted dancers to punch, and brawlers to box. But the biggest change was that the intensity of desire had dissipated, replaced by an easy-going bonhomie. His marriage finally ended and whenever I saw him he had a pretty young woman on his arm, smiling and joking and not taking things too seriously, even when his luck was down. I spent a few hours at a hotel pub one night after a fight, when he had lost a small fortune in a bet. He laughed about it and then asked how I was doing. When I told him Caitlin, my second daughter, had recently been born, he said it was time to teach Pat how to have sons. 'You just lend her to me for an hour and I'll take her into the blue room, and I promise, nine months later she'll have a son,' and he roared with laughter. He no longer saw any point defending his hard-won reputation, and when he talked about his fights he would say how lucky he was, and how close his opponents had come to beating him.

Brian's status as a trainer grew rapidly, but no-one, least of all Brian himself, could quite believe his next acquisition: Dingaan. The old animosity had evaporated and after Dingaan dropped Norman Hlabane the pair worked together without conflict. Dingaan seldom held grudges for long, which is why he found it so easy to return to promoters he felt had let him down, and he was intrigued by Brian's success. Once the bitterness of rivalry was over, it was something he felt he could draw on. For Brian, it was a business relationship first, but I also sensed he felt honoured by Dingaan's request, and the pair of them hit it off without any hint of past acrimony. 'Actually, it worked out better than I expected, and you may be surprised but we actually got on pretty well,' Brian told me when they were still together. It also made him reassess his views on his old rival's talents. 'I sparred with him a couple of times, and had him sparring with my top guys, and it made me realize how good he was. Sure, he has trouble staying focused and problems with weight and he stays away from the gym between fights, but you can't believe the natural ability. I mean, I have to admit that even at my peak I might have had big trouble with him. I never realized how good he was until I had him myself.'

After a string of victories Dingaan lost concentration and was stopped for the first and only time in his career against an inferior opponent. He then left Mitchell – nothing lasts long with Dingaan – eventually ending up with Sugarboy Malinga's trainer, Elias Tshabalala. But he seemed to be fading fast. In 1998 he fought for the WBC international welterweight title and embarrassed the Boxing Board by hitting the scales 20 pounds overweight. He was now a figure of ridicule in boxing circles at home, and when I met him in Manchester the following month I realized why. He looked older than his 31 years. His nose bone was skewed and the cartilage had spread. His whole countenance had lost its boyish sheen, replaced by a look of frustration and worry. He said he was on the verge of big things and would show the world, but I took it as the sad illusion of a man surviving on memory. I refrained from pushing him too hard, but as I looked at his chubby body I couldn't help asking him how he, as a one-time featherweight, could possibly survive seven weight divisions up. 'I can't take the strain of starving myself any longer,' he said. It sounded like an admission of defeat and I expected Dingaan to descend further into pugilistic ignominy.

Now and then we'd speak – he'd phone me in London about a problem, or I'd phone him in Johannesburg to find out how he was doing – and I was relieved to hear he was putting more energy into television commentary and various business ventures, rather than fighting. But then I heard things were going wrong again – the businesses were floundering and creditors were baying for that mansion and the fleet of cars, and soon he was knocking on Rodney Berman's door once more. Once again, Berman agreed to help, offering him a charity shot at the well-seasoned South African super middleweight champion Soon Botes. Despite the roll of fat around his waist, Dingaan dropped the bigger man twice and took the title.

Berman was also the promoter of the WBC world super middleweight champion Glenn Catley, who agreed to defend against Thobela in Carnival City near Johannesburg because he assumed it would be an easy ride for good money. Catley's shaven head, broad shoulders and collection of tattoos spoke of English male with attitude aplenty and yet he had gentle eyes which told a different story: kind, considerate and polite and never a bad word about anyone – not even his opponents. But he was a rough, dirty fighter, as adept at using his head, elbows and shoulders as his fists, and I was worried about Dingaan's health and what remained of his dignity.

When I spoke to him before the fight I realized he was viewing it in terms of vindication. He knew this was his last chance at financial security, but more than that viewed his mission in grandiose terms. 'I'm doing it not only for myself but for my country. My people have been through hard times and I feel they need me right now,' he told me after one hard session in the gym, where he worked over his five sparring partners. I got the impression he really meant it. 'He's training like a dog,' his trainer Elias Tshabalala informed me, and when I wondered whether that was a good or bad thing, he elaborated: 'I promise, Gavin, Dingaan knocks him out.' Dingaan seemed to draw on his trainer's faith. 'He's no more Elias. I've renamed him Ezekial because he's like a prophet to me. What he says will happen, will happen.' He elaborated on this contention: 'In a boxer's life he sometimes has to go through a descending slide, and then he can either quit or re-focus and set a new destination for himself. I know I've had my off-days and Catley thinks I'm lazy and it will be an easy win. What he forgets is that hungry boxers go back to the drawing board and work for what they want, and I am a hungry boxer once more.'

I knew by then that for all his charm Dingaan was frequently self-deluding, dishonest, self-centred and callous about the concerns of others, and he lacked the capacity to laugh at himself. Catley was direct, warm, gentle and self-deprecating. But our interlocking South African histories meant I had eyes for one boxer only: I wanted success for the Rose of Soweto, even if success meant no more than survival. When that moment finally arrived, Brian Mitchell wished Dingaan well and left the ring. Dingaan entered, his brow furrowed, his eyes, as always, wide. He waved solemnly to the crowd, removed his gown to reveal trunks in the colours of the national flag, and mouthed the words of the national anthem. I thought, *Jesus, Dingaan, I just hope you don't get hurt tonight*.

The early rounds suggested Dingaan's tight defence might protect him from serious injury, but not much more. Now and then he'd slam home a stiff jab or snappy combination but Catley was busier and his punches hurt. 'I'd never been hit so hard,' Dingaan said afterwards. 'It took me a few rounds to get used to his power so I concentrated on defence without running, and bided my time, trying to make my punches tell.' Thobela gradually narrowed the gap, forcing the champion into retreat, periodically rocking him. Catley resorted to using his head, elbows and shoulders but in the final round he connected with his payload punch – a hefty right cross to the jaw. Dingaan wobbled and it looked like his brave challenge was coming to an end. Catley rushed in, and Dingaan met him with a shattering uppercut under the chin. As the champion's eyes rolled Thobela landed another right to drop him heavily. Catley wobbled up but he looked in no condition to continue and Thobela just picked him off with huge punches. The final blow was a massive right hook to the chin which sent Catley sprawling across the ring and onto his back. He staggered up at nine, but the American referee had finally seen enough, and seven seconds from the end Dingaan Thobela was world champion once more.

Catley then produced a photograph showing a protruding edge under the tape and bandages covering the knuckles on Dingaan's raised left hand. 'Every shot he hit me with was a sickening blow,' he said after claiming that Thobela reinforced his bandages with a foreign object. 'I've never been hurt like that before. I am not a bad loser but I was getting scared of being hit in the end.' The pictures also indicated that there was no signature on the bandages, suggesting the hand was rewrapped in the hour before the ring entrance. Thobela dismissed the claim with contempt, calling his opponent 'yet another whingeing Englishman'. The Catley camp witnessed the bandaging, he said, 'and why would I pose with evidence? If I had anything to hide I would have cut the bandages off the moment they removed my gloves.' Brian Mitchell agreed. 'Dingaan won that title fair and square. You put something hard under your bandages and try punching for twelve rounds, and you'll do huge damage to your hands.' But Catley persuaded the WBC to give them a hearing, and the tribunal found that something was amiss with Dingaan's bandaging and reinstated Catley as mandatory contender. In effect, Dingaan Thobela, the man who said he was doing it for his people and his country, had been officially branded a cheat.

Berman decided to squeeze in the easiest possible voluntary defence – against a 37-year-old Canadian brawler called Davey Hilton, who had made his little mark as a welterweight, retired, returned to action as a middleweight, and lost his last fight. A member of a notorious Montreal fighting family, Hilton was scheduled to stand trial on charges of prolonged sexual assault against two girls. One of his bail conditions was to live in a home for recovering alcoholics. He did his best although it did not seem to be enough. Most ringsiders, including Catley, agreed Thobela deserved to win, but when the scores were announced it emerged he was a split-decision loser. Hilton broke bail to avoid the compulsory drug test. Soon after he was sentenced to seven years' imprisonment and stripped of his world title. Dingaan left Canada a bitter 34-year-old ex-champion. 'What am I supposed to do?' he asked. 'Kill my opponent every time I get into the ring?'

He returned home to face his own trial – for aggravated domestic assault. It was not the first time the dark side of his private life had appeared in the public arena. In 1995 he denied reports that he had assaulted his then lover, the former Miss South Africa, but the allegations on this occasion were backed by the force of law. Dingaan's sister-in-law, Paula Viera, said he attacked her after accusing her of 'taking Sandra [his wife] to meet other men'. He grabbed her by the hair, pulled her off a chair, pushed her, tripped her, kicked her, sat on her while she was on the ground and grabbed her by the throat, she said. When she wriggled away he grabbed her by the blouse, pulled it off and punched her several times, after which she ran half naked to the neighbours, she added. Viera refused various offers to settle out of court.

Dingaan said there were 'differences' between them after she accused him of having an affair, and that he did no more than 'help' her out of the house. 'She had no bruises, no cuts, no doctors' report, nothing,' he told me (although two independent doctors' reports noted scratch marks on Viera's neck and reported her complaint of 'side pain'). Some of those around Dingaan said he had no chance of beating this rap but early in 2001 he was acquitted when the magistrate found there was insufficient evidence. Viera's lawyer later made a formal complaint to the director of public prosecutions, saying the case was mishandled by a prosecutor who failed to call two key witnesses.

For the record, Dingaan insists he's no woman beater: 'I love them too much to beat them up. I only use my fighting skills in the ring. I will continue with my love life and with my boxing career.' And so he pressed on, searching for that final shot at vindication.* For me, however, the moment had passed. Perhaps he was as innocent as he claimed. Perhaps not. But I couldn't forget a remark he made the first time we spoke, thirteen years earlier. 'I'm deeply concerned about violence,' he said. 'I grew up with violence in Soweto. In a sense it was a part of me, and still is.'

The last time I spotted the Rose of Soweto, at a boxing match in South Africa, I avoided his eye and kept on walking. I thought it was time to move on, for both of us.

---

*Soon after, he parted ways with Berman once again, signing up with Don King after securing another world title shot. At the end of 2001 he struggled to make the super middleweight limit and was stopped in eight by the new WBC world champion Eric Lucas. He then dumped trainer Elias Tshabalala, citing 'irreconcilable differences' and went back to his original trainer, Norman Hlabane. At the time of writing, in June 2002, he was planning an assault on the South African light heavyweight title and even talking of a heavyweight title fight. He said he would box on until he was 40.

7

PIGS, SLAVES, PRISONERS

Barberton Prison, December 1990. Farmer Hennie has a question: 'Tell me something, what *are* you?' The bar falls silent, every ear strained. His query is directed at my colleague Justin, and it arrives about three minutes after we stagger out of our newspaper's Toyota in a jolly but slightly dazed state to join the Barberton Prison reception *braai*, an essential prelude to the Barberton Prison boxing show. After being herded into the prison warders' watering hole it doesn't take us long to gather where the inquisition is heading, especially after Hennie offers his chums a full-sized conspiratorial wink.

'A photographer,' Justin answers, playing it straight. Hennie rises to his full 6 foot 7 of Dutch genes, prime beef proteins, rugby and riches, wraps an arm the girth of an African rock python around little Justin's hunched shoulders, yanks him in, rough buddy style, and barks: '*Ja*, but I mean what *are* you?' My strangulated effort to forestall a total descent into buzzing giggles escapes public notice because all eyes are on Hennie, and Justin is still playing him along with

nonchalance no doubt drawn from previous experience. 'Oh, yes,' he stalls, 'I'm also an assistant director
for feature movies.'

'*Ja, ja, ja, ja*,' Hennie mumbles, and an edge of
impatience creeps into his voice. 'But I mean, *what* are
you?' The *what* is barked, with a guttural, resonating
final consonant and it comes out more as a command
than a question. But Justin isn't ready to allow him his
ounce of flesh. He won't roll over quite yet. The big
man will have to wait. Justin offers a cupboard love
beam at his interrogator. 'I'm a South African!'

Hennie is taken aback by the appearance of
enthusiasm, and feels that perhaps more explanation is
needed. For a second he softens a little, forgetting his
audience. 'OK, OK, sure, you're a South African, I'm
sure you are, but, I mean, what *are* you, man?'

'Oh, I see, I'm a *Capetonian*,' Justin says with a
look suggesting he's just so pleased to be giving the
big man what he's after. By now Hennie is beginning
to show his exasperation with the rules of his own
little game. 'But what *else* are you?' he snaps. And
finally, feeling peckish and seeing no other end to this
charade, Justin decides to give it up for the farming
man: 'Oh, *now* I understand. You mean, like, am I . . .
Jewish?'

'*Jaaahh*,' says Hennie, beaming back triumphantly.
Justin offers him a little child's smile, pauses for a
second, and then a trusting nod, and finally, with the
bar all ears, the smallest 'yes'.

Hennie can't contain himself. He delivers the
heartiest of rock-python-strike shoulder slaps, rubs
Justin's balding pate, fingers Justin's pony tail, raises
his bunch-of-bananas hand in commanding triumph
and tells his assembled entourage, 'I told you, didn't I

tell you, hey?' There's a look of quiet admiration all
around and many nods. 'What did I tell you? What did
I tell you? You tell them, Pieter.' Pieter, a slightly
smaller specimen, nods his head in obsequious
acquiescence and then informs the pair of us: 'He says
he can spot a Jew at fifty metres – and he never gets it
wrong – *never*.' Hennie, sponsor of the prison *braai*,
past purchaser of prison labour, and current bene-
ficiary of prison contract business, grins triumphantly.
'You tell them, Pieter, you tell them.'

With this we are plied with Lion Lagers and Hennie
draws both of us in, an arm around each of his dimin-
utive guests, and begins to tell us about the previous
week's hailstorm which cost their small town on the
country's north-east border R40 million (£13 million at
the time). 'Those fucking hailstones was as big as
tennis balls – small tennis balls – and they were so hard
they bounced when they hit the concrete,' he begins,
before another farmer cuts in, pointing me towards the
holes in the roof and the damaged bar furniture below.
'They went straight through the fuckin' roof and you
should have seen the cars.' This fellow is becoming
excited by his turn at entertaining the aliens, but
Hennie is growing edgy again – this is his prison party,
he paid for it – and if he wants the exclusive attention
of the soft city-boy journalist and the strange-looking
Jewboy photographer without any competition from his
cohorts, then by God he'll get it.

Hennie raises his hand for silence and the room
obeys. 'Hell's teeth, you *ouks* look like you need to
chow. 'Specially you, Justin – it's a pork *braai* tonight,
hey? Pork. *Pig*. You wanna try some pork, hey, Justin?
Huh huh. You like pork, Justin? Yustin? Just-in-time?'
He's guffawing now; has the group's attention again.

He's hovering on the edge of open malice, but no, no, no, he pulls back, this is going to be clean fun, and so the big wait-for-it wink again while he anticipates Justin's response.

'Sure. *Ja*. I love pork. It's like my favourite meat, actually,' says Justin, growing weary of the charade or perhaps just hungry. 'Thanks very much, hey.'

Not the response Hennie is expecting. He's sure *Joden* don't eat pigs; he read that somewhere – and so, reluctantly, he changes tack, at last losing interest in his little game. He introduces himself – Hennie, a local *boer*, a friend of the prison, a former employer of black prison labour for the hard, hot work on his farm, a man highly disappointed that this ancient practice is on its way out for the farmers. Like so many things. But then again, some things are coming back.

Take slavery as a little example. Officially not seen in South Africa since the British abolished it in the Cape 175 years before, but actually never entirely eliminated. And now it has been making a perky little comeback, just down the road. This is, indeed, the main reason why we are in this part of the far north-east of the country.

A month earlier the *Weekly Mail* uncovered a large-scale lucrative slave-trading ring on the Mozambique border. In essence it involved enticing desperately trusting Mozambicans to South Africa with the promise of jobs, and then selling these people to farmers for R200 to R300 each, or in the Johannesburg area for R350. The 'owners' paid them no wages, and refused to allow them off their farms. The men would be put to work, the women made workers or concubines or, usually, a bit of both. If they demanded pay or disobeyed, the farmers would call the police to arrest them and deposit them back across the border where they would face starvation or murder by Renamo terrorists. The women were frequently raped, the men forced into backbreaking work for long hours, and both were regularly beaten. Some disappeared, never to be seen again – possibly murdered, worked to death, whipped to death or perhaps sold for witch doctor's *muti*, it was said. The traders referred to them simply as 'stock' but by any normal definition they were slaves. In order to prove its case, one of the paper's journalists purchased two Mozambicans for R200 each before securing them temporary accommodation at a refugee centre in a nearby town. Justin's initial tasks were to collect some previously stolen cameras from a nearby police station, and also to collect one of these freed slaves from a refuge centre and then drive him to Johannesburg where he could start a new life.

During a previous photographic sortie to the area, Justin had noticed a small advertisement in a Barberton newspaper about a 'first-ever' boxing event featuring prisoners. 'Just up your avenue, I thought,' he said, handing it to me; 'why don't you give them a call and we can do it together on the way to collecting the slave.' The *Weekly Mail* was much hated by the government and periodically censored and banned, but these details seemed to have escaped the notice of the Barberton Prison colonel organizing the show. He was delighted by my interest, sensing his fifteen minutes was about to arrive, and without the whiff of scandal too, and so he invited us to their show and the preceding *braai* on the understanding that I would give their efforts my full attention.

It was the summer of 1990, hot and dry, and we'd

had an unintended extra hundred miles to drive after our shortcut was short-circuited because I hadn't bothered to check whether my passport was still valid, and was informed at the Swaziland border that it had expired two days earlier. I was used to working with highly strung, coke-sniffing, heroin-smoking, white-mischief photographers – young men packed with physical courage and attitude and always ready to stand their ground or snap into rage at the slightest provocation. Justin had a different approach. A genial smile, a shrug, a sense that the world was bigger than this or that incident, a way of keeping his cool and his distance. And he always got results. Like when we were working together on a story called 'Johannesburg's ten worst landlords', and an enormous flat-owner started waving around a large axe. I was terrified, but Justin just smiled his trusting smile and without the raving axeman noticing he shot the front-page picture. He smiled again when we had to do a U-turn at the Swazi border, shrugged his shoulders and said, 'Pity, but hey, no problem. Still a *lekker* drive.' And so we drove – on and on in the midday sun.

Even on the hottest days I have always loved the dreamy feel of the road with its flashcards passing, unhinging time, space and context as you move from one image to another. The background road music – for me, all earnest women at the time: Sinead O'Connor on emperors with new clothes, Natalie Merchant on fallen beatnik howlers, Bonnie Raitt on dead prostitutes and dying relationships – was serious stuff, but Justin had a way of creating a calm, languid mood, made more so by the grade-one Swazi ganja we used to pass the time and the miles. We talked Cape Town and movies and dogs, and laughed a lot, and finally arrived at the prison garden, still full of smiles, a bit wobbly from the sun, an hour late, and ready for anything that could possibly come our way.

Having baited his Jew, and filled us with his pork chops, pork stew, pork sausages and Lion Lagers, Big Hennie paraded us as a pair of visiting journalistic dignitaries to the local assembly of farmers and business leaders who had grown fat on prison labour. For instance, there was professional boxing promoter-cum-Barberton mayor Thinus Strydom, who was chatting to Corrie Sanders, the South African heavyweight boxing champion, who had just arrived in a minibus full of policemen. Sanders appeared a bit embarrassed to see me there, especially after Hennie announced, 'Corrie is here in his *official* police-sergeant capacity, but will be doubling up as a boxing judge.' Corrie looked around and then muttered, sotto voce: 'Actually, uh, Gary, I'm only doing a compulsory police camp as part of my national service, but I'm really a full-time professional these days, not really an actual policeman.' It was ten months after Mandela's release and even the whitest boxers, or the smarter white boxers at least, were getting a bit edgy on the subject of police and army connections, once a source of so much unchallenged pride. They sensed that the things that had won them respectability in the past weren't doing the trick any more – in fact, they were becoming a bit of a problem.

Such specific sensitivities were a long way from the consciousness of the prison colonel who strolled over to introduce himself. 'Glad you guys could make it because what you've got here is a real scoop – a *real* scoop, hey, Gav,' he began with the kind of familiarity that a certain kind of public official learns to affect. 'It's the first time in the history of this country – ever –

that something like this has taken place,' he added, explaining that the novelty lay in holding the event outside the prison and opening it to the general public, for the profit of the prison. The white governors of Barberton's black prison were still smarting under the institution's reputation for brutality, acquired from many years' practice and consolidated a few years earlier when three prisoners died from dehydration as a result of forced labour without water in the searing mid-summer heat.

This boxing event was therefore partly an exercise in public relations and, since we were the only reporters to gobble their bucket of bait, the prison establishment laid it on for us thick and greasy. 'My aim is to improve the lives of the prisoners, give them an incentive, an opportunity to show the town what they can do,' the colonel droned. A couple of local businessmen gushingly concurred, explaining that while prison farm labour was now officially frowned on, 'ordinary businesses' were permitted to use the inmates. I guessed that the gap between 'ordinary' and farming had been subjected to a little creative blurring. 'The way it is,' said one, 'is that this is a chance to give back something to the prisoners. I had a strike recently and was very grateful to the prisoners for helping out.' Helping out. It all sounded so wonderfully voluntary, the way he put it.

The colonel, who was tossing back the brandy and Cokes at an astonishing rate, was starting to take to us in a big way, sharing small intimacies. We were the Johannesburg *press*, the *English* press, and yet, this time at least, he had nothing to hide. We expected caution, but no, he was oh so proud of this little project of his, and oh so grateful that we had come all this way to report on it. By then, still stoned, and a bit drunk already, I was entering into the spirit of the occasion on something approaching its own terms, showing them all a wallet picture of my baby daughter, Tessa, and telling them about Ben, my oversized ten-month-old Staffordshire terrier, who had just won his first serious street fight against a Rottweiler, and Brinjal, his slightly smaller, female sparring partner. Dogs, it seems, can go a long way to break boundaries of experience, culture and perspective through their role in reflecting the aspirations of their owners, and in this part of South Africa the aspirations of the owners were assisting me to ease my way in.

It was a particularly strange time in my life: a time that felt uniquely light and ephemeral, unburdened by higher callings or even any sense of duty beyond my little daughter. This background, enhanced by the hours of road music, made a prison *braai* in Barberton seem suitably unhinged, appropriate even.

Let me explain again: I had been active in the South African struggle for twelve years and had watched and worked from the late 1970s through the 1980s and into 1990 as the international sanctions drive was sustained by the mass action within the country, which in turn drew inspiration from what passed as the armed struggle and the support from the underground networks. The financial sanctions in particular made it impossible for the government to move, so that by the end of the decade the pillars of white power were no longer viable. Those supporting them knew that their previous reliance on the excuse of being the antidote to the now-collapsing communist world no longer cut it, and in any event they were taking heavy hits from the

Cubans in Angola. They were in retreat on so many fronts – from the rest of southern Africa, from some of the fundamentals of apartheid legislation and from the incarceration of their enemies – while at the same time attempting to decimate this enemy by conducting a desperately vicious secret war of assassinations, massacres and dirty tricks. Yet still, under the new state president, F.W. de Klerk, it was becoming clear that with the start of the new decade we were entering the new era of the endgame.

There were good reasons (altruistic or otherwise) for remaining active – for harvesting the sticky fruits of my political labours, one way or another – but for well over a year I had been looking for exit signs from activism without much hope of a way out. I had grown impatient. I had lost the appetite. I couldn't stomach the next stage of the struggle and was desperate to leave the table. And I was starting to eat out.

For over a decade I held it all together as a dedicated, motivated, line-holding, faction-fighting, fist-clenching struggler, but then, quite quickly, the many inconsistencies of my position became pressing. I could no longer stomach the dishonesty inherent in my multi-personality political, professional and personal existence. As a journalist I was trying to march to different beats, combining my jobs as investigative political writer, gossip columnist and sports reporter, but the political fracturing was far more profound, involving several clashes of mutually exclusive identities: the above-ground, supposedly liberal campaigner working with concerned whites and business people; the conscientious objector who was encouraging other conscripts to object; the underground ANC and Communist Party committee man working with black trade unionists and student leaders. It had been tolerable when I still thought of myself as a true believer but over the previous year I had become jaded, sceptical. The lies of necessity had become lies of convenience, and these were no longer working for me.

It wasn't that I regretted the broad thrust of what I had done over the previous decade. I still felt pride in the tiny role I played in a movement that helped push the government to the point of negotiation. It was more that the core tenets of faith that once inspired me – Marxism, Leninism, the Party, the Movement, the Leadership – now struck me as absurd, a bit like the Christianity of thirteen years earlier. I smiled over the fall of the Berlin Wall and had to suppress a bout of 'told you so' gloating. I no longer had a core of cast-iron belief I could fall back on and the Marxist idea of a hierarchy of social causation – 'all history is a history of class struggle' – seemed quaintly nineteenth century in a world defined more by chaos, chance and disorder than linear progression. Yet this was a period when the demands on my time, commitment, concentration and political imagination were escalating out of control. By the beginning of 1990 this inner conflict between duty and personal freedom had reached its point of crisis.

One hot Saturday afternoon in particular stands out: two activist friends and I made our excuses from the meeting schedule and drove to Johannesburg's huge Emarentia Dam where we unpacked our picnic, unwrapped our caps of acid, swallowed them and began walking. We were two young men and a young woman, all ANC members who sensed each other's connections without mentioning them, each of us in similar positions from different angles, desperate to escape.

The space, the distance, the sun, the constant changes of scenery and the drugs made the trip seem like an epic journey. By the time we got around to the other side of the dam we were drifting in and out of reality. My take was to engage fellow travellers in deep rambling discussions about their dogs, feeling unexpected compatibility with their owners. They were happily relaxed sections of humanity and I felt a fresh desire for unaffected human connection. These snippets of spontaneous warmth would last until some new flicker of consciousness took over and the sequential thread was lost, the conversation forgotten, and the dog people, presumably, went their own way a little confused.

We moved to a wooded area where what seemed like black-clad commandos were leaping out of bushes and into canoes – some training mission, we guessed. They looked ominous and the trip became dark, until we re-emerged into the sunlight and I felt a great desire to dream-run without stopping. But the thought of leaving this sanctuary introduced an edge of paranoia, and when we left Emarentia in the late afternoon and made our way to crowded, crime-thick Hillbrow, my unease became intense. I feared we were about to enter a situation we couldn't control and that I was going to have to fight, and so I pleaded for retreat and we drove around the perimeter of the city, watching the lights, and then went home to watch a silly video, coming down slowly.

I felt a little depressed afterwards. The trip – my last ever – had ended a little off-colour, leaving the residue of a foul taste, and this unexpected after-shock carried persuasive weight. I emerged the next morning even further removed from the disciplined activism that had been dominating my life and despondent at the prospect of soldiering on. I so wanted to be free and no longer coupled this with freedom for all.

Then, rather suddenly, five days later – 2 February 1990 – freedom arrived. Sitting with my colleagues in the *Weekly Mail* office I watched F.W. de Klerk announcing on television that the ANC, PAC and Communist Party were, henceforth, unbanned. My response was one of manic elation – not only with the momentous political implications of the news itself and the prospect of imminent victory for my side, but also, selfishly, with the promise of personal liberation. Yet the paradox of my position kicked in an hour later when I remembered I had an arrangement to keep and had to rush off to a secret venue in the city centre to meet a new party recruit who had completed his six-month probationary period and was about to be seconded to assist me on the South African Communist Party's Transvaal underground education committee. He was a much-detained black youth and civic leader who went on to become one of the ANC's senior functionaries, while I was a closet cynic, and a young white one too, and yet by some uncomfortable quirk of circumstance I was supposed to be his organizational superior. I had to do my best to affect enthusiasm for things I no longer believed in, all the while feeling desperate to get out. I was embarrassed by my lack of commitment and ashamed about my pretence of dedication. I was just so eager to break away but, as yet, unable to find the appropriate gap or the courage to do so.

This personal dilemma took on political clothing, which soon started to pose as its underlying rationale. I no longer trusted in the integrity of the movement I had joined a decade earlier. There were so many areas of bitter distaste – the unchecked corruption of some senior officials, the naked careerism of once-austere activists, the cynical stripping of the veneer of non-racialism when it was expedient. I was particularly exasperated when the ANC refused to confront Winnie Mandela because of her position as the Wife, despite the fact that in the underground we were presented with ample evidence of her involvement in a series of crimes way beyond any feasible political remit. I was also incensed about the way the ANC allowed blatantly corrupt functionaries and, worse, unrehabilitated former spies and police informers to remain active when it suited their immediate purposes or when exposure would prove too politically costly. I could no longer restrain myself on these questions and began to draw flak for writing too critically about Winnie and others. This astounded some of my underground comrades who were shocked at my lack of discipline.

Three weeks after the ANC was unbanned I was in East London, covering a story, when I received an urgent message on my bleeper: 'Mandela to be released. Phone office,' and three hours later I was in Cape Town, waiting for our leader at the Grand Parade.

The day grew hotter and the crowds grew more agitated, with Jesse Jackson and so many others doing their best to calm the mood. Every so often I would sprint off to the office, a few hundred metres away, to catch a glimpse on the television of Mandela's departure from the Paarl prison gates and his somnambulist progress, delayed by his wife, the media and the crowds. Seeing him 'walking hand in hand with Winnie Mandela', as the song *Free Nelson Mandela* had pictured, deflated my sense of the occasion, and when I returned to the Grand Parade the crowd had grown resentful. When he showed no sign of arriving, criminals on the edge of the crowd, joined by youth militants, took to looting the local shops. There was a lot of shooting but the police, showing unusual restraint, killed only one of them – a child who took a chest full of birdshot. Another was killed by a shop-owner and we were told that three people died of suffocation. One older comrade commented dolefully: 'You see, Mandela may be out but these kids know that when they go home tonight they're still unemployed. They'll sell these things for a quick buck.' With the sun beginning to lose its sting, and still no sign of Madiba, a section of the crowd began to chant: 'We want Nelson!' to which one of the harassed organizers responded: 'Comrades! He has waited twenty-seven years for his freedom. We have only stood here for five or six hours. Where is our patience?'

And finally, at 6 p.m., five hours overdue, Nelson Mandela emerged, surrounded by minders who cleared his way. He climbed the steps to the podium, looking impassive, with his fist stiffly raised. I watched this tall, lean man who looked so different in body shape and countenance from the pictures of the bulky, hard-eyed heavyweight boxer of thirty years before, and said to myself: 'OK, there's my leader,' and then tried to catch the words of the unmemorable speech he delivered in his unusual, staccato, stentorian voice. The next day I flew home thinking, *Well, that's an era over, that's me done, this is my station, this is where I get off – as soon as someone opens the doors.*

Meanwhile my friend Maxine was organizing 'safe' houses for Mandela in Johannesburg where he could

meet his internal comrades, and I was getting breathless reports of his charm, dignity and presence. Three
days later I joined my colleague Shaun Johnson to
conduct the first long press interview with him at
his house in Soweto. I was re-inspired by Nelson
Mandela's immense gravitas, his brilliantly concise
grasp of the issues, by his wonderful magnanimity and
particularly by his twinkling sense of humour. Underground and exiled comrades who had known Mandela
before his 1962 arrest described him as a hard
patrician, a bit of a martinet, while some of those
who worked with him on Robben Island talked of his
imperious manner, moodiness, his ambiguous relationship with the 'collective' and his tendency to go his
own way. But with us, for an hour or so, he talked of
negotiation and compromise, of principle and strategy,
of his respect for his political enemies, and his
answerability to his comrades. He joked a lot, putting
us at ease. 'Why are you so serious? Why are you not
laughing?' our leader wondered. When it was over, I
couldn't resist asking him about his boxing days. He
laughed his ho ho ho laugh again. 'You know, young
man, I loved to box but I had to stop even before I went
to prison because there was no more opportunity and
time for that type of thing, but you will no doubt be
pleased to hear I still follow it very closely.' I was
delighted. Forget the politics, Nelson Mandela would
be reading me on boxing.

With that I went to the office to write up the story in
all its gushing detail, and then, the same afternoon,
remembered I had another to complete – on Winnie
Mandela. It chastised her and ridiculed her claims,
while hinting that it was high time the ANC distanced
itself from the former Mother of the Nation. Both

stories were run in the same edition. The next time I saw Nelson Mandela, at a press conference a week later, he glared at me, not acknowledging my greeting. I could hardly blame him, given the juxtaposition of the two pieces, but I felt despair in seeing him standing by his sociopath wife. It was something I could understand but not defend and I began to worry aloud that my leader's fatal flaw would be found in his uncertain ability to read people close to him – that he was a great judge of strategy and a poor judge of character. As I watched Winnie attracting scoundrels to his realm while making outcasts of honest men and women, I felt even more distanced, even more eager to cut my ties.

My initial strategy was to sue for a downgrade as a prelude to what I hoped would be a graceful dropping out. In April 1990 I spent two weeks in Lusaka, helping to organize a conference between a group of mainly white officers linked to the South African Defence Force and a delegation from Umkhonto we Sizwe (the ANC's military wing), led by Chris Hani. While I was there I had a private dinner at the Lusaka home of the Communist Party leader, Joe Slovo, who was also one of the leaders of the Operation Vula underground structure I was working in. As I was about to leave I requested a moment alone with him outside, and popped the question: 'How would you feel if I withdrew from the Transvaal leadership committee? I'm far from indispensable and I think that having two whites out of five is completely wrong.' Slovo saw my point, but said no. I was in charge of the region's finances and its underground library, and had too much information at my exclusive disposal to be downscaled. I returned home even more frustrated but shortly afterwards I was finally offered a way out. The

Communist Party decided to go public and I was able to turn down my nomination to the regional structure as well as to various ANC positions on the basis that as a political journalist it would not be fitting to have that kind of profile – I needed a semblance of objectivity. Their understanding was that I would remain a loyal supporter, who would assist them through my writing. My unstated understanding was that I would do nothing of the sort.

But just when I thought I was free, or at least limited to a few, manageable, low-level tasks, the three heads of our underground structure, Mac Maharaj, Siphiwe Nyanda and Billy Nair, were detained, along with the leadership of the Natal underground wing. As a result, I was briefly re-activated on party orders – having to rush around closing down offices, removing money and documents from safe deposit boxes without being detected by the security police, desperately worried that I was about to be detained for a past I was trying to leave behind. But whatever else I thought of them, my leaders were hard men, who, to my eternal gratitude, managed to withstand torture and not name names.*

There was still a risk of detention when Pat, newborn Tessa and I flew down to Port Elizabeth for the wedding of my sister, Karen, and my friend and comrade Mkhuseli Jack. It was a massive occasion, drawing tens of thousands of people from their houses and shacks, not just because it was one of Port Elizabeth's

*They were eventually released and Maharaj went on to spend five years in Mandela's cabinet while Nyanda became chief of the defence force and Nair served two terms as an MP.

first mixed marriages, but because it brought together the city's key community and political leader with the bishop's journalist daughter and was viewed by both the black and white communities as an occasion of symbolic significance – a kind of meeting of minds and bodies after the bitterness of the detentions, political murders and consumer boycotts of the previous decade.

The two days of rolling celebration started at a huge church in New Brighton township, followed by a conventional reception in a Greek community hall, where Mkhuseli – or Khusta as he was usually called – presented my father with a plastic cow in lieu of *labolla*, or dowry. The next day it was the turn of the traditional Xhosa festivities in Zwide township, where our family was adopted by the family of a local priest and taken to a house near to Khusta's. The 'negotiations' started when Khusta's family arrived at the house and said they wanted the bride. The request was refused. They asked again and again until Khusta's family could present us with a symbolic bottle of brandy, carried for the occasion by my friend and comrade Brett, who had recently returned from ANC exile. This sealed the deal and Karen was brought out to join Khusta, after which the whole group walked to Khusta's house to listen to the family elders dispensing advice to the newly-weds. 'Khusta, when you are angry, do not hit your wife, but take your coat and go for a walk until you feel better,' an elder cautioned. My father gave a talk on uniting two families and communities, and after a traditional ox-slaughtering meal, Karen was dressed by the women in her *makoti* – newly-wed – outfit (a German print skirt and top, towels around her waist and a headscarf). She was told to sit on a grass mat and her Xhosa name was announced: Nomelisizwe, which means 'representing the nation'.

When I asked her about it a decade later, she said she was still sometimes astonished at the public response. 'I only realized how big it would be when I walked out of our house in Walmer suburb before the wedding and the neighbours and a group of domestic workers greeted me with cheers and ululating. After that it was overwhelming, with the traffic cops directing the cars, and the huge crowds and the outside loudspeakers for those who couldn't squeeze into the church. Even today I still meet strangers in the supermarket who come up and say, "Aah, Nomelisizwe, I was at your wedding."'

We flew back two days later, flushed with happiness from the overwhelming goodwill we had experienced at my sister's wedding, and I felt another brief surge of hope for the country. Returning to Malvern – entirely white and working class until the late 1980s but now rapidly transforming its complexion – I felt safe again. Less than six weeks had passed since the detention of my leaders and they were still being held and tortured, but the wedding gave me the sense that the foul air was being cleared and the danger lifted.

Years later I discovered that at this moment, Colonel Joe Verster, the special forces officer who headed the CCB, was initiating a second attempt on my life, and it was only the exposure of the CCB's activities through the newspapers and then the courts that saved me. Far from suing for peace, the assassins and their political paymasters were regrouping for a last, desperate duck-shoot, picking off lower-profile activist leaders, arming anti-ANC migrant-worker hostel dwellers, training

Inkatha armies, planning and sponsoring massacres on commuter trains, bombing political offices and stoking rivalry between political organizations, leaving 16,000 dead over the next four years – more than double the number of fatalities in political violence over the previous six. But there were no more political detentions, my leaders were released a month later, and I was no longer active in the movement and therefore had nothing substantial to fear – nothing I knew about anyway. As a result I felt compelled to get on with life on its own terms, for its own sake: a frightening prospect after years of voluntary servitude of one kind or another.

The combination of journalism and bits and pieces of professional acting had kept me busy enough to take the sting out of withdrawing from activism in the early months of 1990. But still, in what felt like the last months of my old life, I was suffering from something approximating adrenaline withdrawal symptoms and I was also in need of physical stimulation. I tried parachuting, bungee jumping, stunt flying, combat shooting, getaway driving, unarmed combat classes, and of course there was more than enough cocaine and speed in the media circles I moved in to fuel these childish, dying-of-the-light little adventures.

And then there was boxing – the temptation to return to the physical side of the game for a final fighting fling. It began when my friend Anton, an airways pilot, former housemate and running partner, asked me to join him working out in the garage gym set up by Alf James, the son of the old South African champion with whom my father had once swapped punches. With two pairs of gloves, a heavy bag and a speedball dangling invitingly from ceiling hooks, I could hardly resist.

I began teaching Anton and soon other friends and comrades who joined us. It became a weekly affair, with each volunteer taking his turn to trade light punches with another within a little circle on the front lawn.

We were just getting into a regular weekly routine when the old man Alf arrived from England, where he had been in and out of jail for nicking and bilking and the like. I had heard bits and pieces about him from Pat, who was once his younger son's lover, and I was intrigued by him – not only because of the connection with my father, but because at the age of 71 he retained so much of his charm and vigour. Once a gang of street robbers assaulted him with an iron bar. He was severely beaten and bruised and yet within a couple of weeks had made a total recovery, which he claimed was the product of meditation. Whenever we arrived he would always make an appearance and soon took over the teaching – showing us how to put weight behind a jab, how to counter a jab with a right, how to maintain balance when throwing a cross. When I told my father about it he was delighted and repeated his story of his moment of glory thirty-four years earlier.

This impromptu boxing club flourished for a few months but inevitably we pushed things to the limit. We were all young men, most of us living on the edge of normality and out of the habit of behaving in a way that could be considered usual. There was, for instance, my boxing-watching friend Mark, a tall human rights lawyer who had worked with me with impressive courage, dedication and perspicacity for several years in an ANC underground cell, later taking on various risky tasks within the Operation Vula network. In one sparring session he tried to take my head

353

off with huge wild swings until I caught him with a lucky hook and he went down and out. Then there was Danie, an 18-year-old spectator, who used to watch from the fence and one day asked if he could have a turn, mentioning in passing that he was a Transvaal senior amateur lightweight champion. Fortunately, he was no puncher but I failed to land a single meaningful punch of my own on him after a three-minute round while he peppered my face with his jabs. And there was also Ronald, a muscular, ANC business type with a martial arts background, who refrained from holding back and started hurting the weaker volunteers. During one joint shadow-boxing session he lost control and, in a departure from the rules, deliberately whacked me in the face. I responded in kind, and then we kind of stepped back, nodded in acknowledgement and walked away.

It should have ended there but I thought I might try my hand at just one or two more rounds – this time by sparring with a decent professional, and surviving to write about it. Of course, it had been done before – Paul Gallico with Jack Dempsey, George Plimpton with Archie Moore, Ernest Hemingway pressing his luck with Gene Tunney – and although I had fallen seriously out of shape in the three-month gap since my last comradely session, I knew what it entailed, or so I thought. My first choice was Dingaan Thobela, but he was out of the country, so finally I settled on a world-rated super featherweight, November Ntshingila (who would later go on to win a minor version of a world title). I liked November, not only for his accomplished skills, but also his laconic sense of humour, his activist past and his defiance in wearing the shorts in the ANC's black, green and gold in the days the ANC was still banned. 'The main reason I wear these colours, Gavin, is that, you see, I am a comrade,' he had told me a year earlier, when it was still dangerous to say such things.

The day after arranging the prison visit, I arrived at the low-rent sweathole called the Champions Gym in Johannesburg city centre, with Justin in tow to take the pictures. It was 3.15 p.m., and by then November had already run five miles in the midday sun and completed four rounds of skipping. We shadow-boxed for a round and then his trainer, Victor Mphyakhe, gloved me up with sixteen-ounce mitts, strapped on my groin protector and handed me a gumshield. 'Take it a bit easy, hey,' he told November, and called time.

I decided to make an early impression by sailing in – jab, jab, right cross, left hook. November jabbed back and I blocked two and slipped the third while dancing away to my right. *I'm doing brilliantly*, I thought, though in truth the blows which felt like they were landing were being half-deflected by his gloves or softened by slight twists of his head and body. After assessing my work, I steamed in again, and this time November decided it was time to demand a small price for my impudence. Whack! Whack! Whack! A short jab to the nose, a right cross to the mouth and a left hook to my ribs. November was pulling his punches, but even with the pillow gloves I could feel their sting, and I suddenly realized that if this young man felt like it he could take me out with a single punch at any stage he liked. My arms grew heavy and my chest started heaving mightily. I moved into retreat, hoping the bell would toll, and then I heard three terrible words: 'Two to go,' and Victor wasn't talking seconds. I had been reduced to throwing tentative jabs one at a time, never daring to venture a right. Full survival mode, but

November was being kind – carrying me without doing any more serious damage. After what felt like half an hour, Victor called time. The end of round one.

I rested while November did another eight rounds with a bantamweight and he still wasn't breathing heavily. We then alternated six more on the heavy bag, after which I could no longer lift my arms, and November went on to work on the speed bag, the pads and then twenty-five minutes of ground exercises. When my ninety-minute session was over, I was breathing in desperate pants, raining sweat and feeling bile rise to the surface while the vomit was percolating in my stomach. My nose was sore, my elbow bruised, three knuckles were bleeding and my body felt like it was going into rigor mortis. November, still well in breath, grinned, shook my hand in comrade style and announced: 'You know, Gavin, I really want to be a journalist.' To which I replied: 'You know, November, I really don't want to be a boxer.' As we went our separate ways I felt relieved that I came from a background where I had a choice on these matters. I was free to walk away from a beating, from a struggle, from *the* struggle, never to return.

And so, finally, back to Barberton Prison. In early December 1990, three days after my little venture with November, still feeling stiff, I entered a world where no such choices existed. There I was, to observe and enjoy, a free man in jail, basking in my new-found state of grace, operating under what certainly felt like a convincing illusion of exhausted happiness, celebrating it by watching a bunch of prisoners experiencing a brief taste of the outside life, before being locked up again.

Tessa was three and a half months old then, and I was

finding that she was unleashing emotions in me that were utterly new, and perhaps others that had been dormant for a decade or so. I had never experienced anything really comparable to this intense sense of protective love that I discovered when she was born and I was determined to work hard on building my relationship with her. In this way my new role as a father was filling some of the void created by the absence of higher meaning, and it was certainly filling the struggle-shaped void in time. When not writing or acting I was changing nappies, making bottles and calming bouts of colic, or just dancing around the house with Tessa in her pouch. The prison trip was, I think, my first away day since she was born and I was determined to take advantage of this momentary freedom.

Inside the prison, the chosen few readied themselves to leave their place of incarceration for three precious, painstaking, painmaking hours on the town. These were the twenty Champions of Champions of the prison – the two best in each weight after a series of in-house preliminaries – along with two rival trainers, and a fellow called Humano, their chosen ring announcer, all of them prisoners. They ranged between 20 and 46 years old, 120 to 176 pounds, and were incarcerated for crimes ranging from housebreaking to rape and manslaughter – no first-degree murderers among them, we were assured. For the handful who had fought their way here from the maximum security prison it was the first smell of life beyond the bars in several years.

The venue was a large prefabricated hall on the outskirts of town with a single entrance. Aside from a scattering of uniformed policemen, several well-positioned hired heavies guarded it, each carrying a loaded double-barrelled shotgun. I decided that if these boys got trigger happy the result would include a fair sprinkling of 'collateral damage' from flying buckshot and so I made a mental note, planning the quickest bellydive underneath the seat in front me.

We were late for the event, but the already well-pissed colonel still managed to take the time out to organize us a constant flow of cider from Crossbow, one of the sponsors. The hall was filled to capacity with over four hundred townsfolk, mostly white and male, but with a few black and Indian business-men sitting nervously among the bearded, khaki-clad commandos, the farmers, and the farmers' wives in their floral dresses, big hairdos and white stiletto heels. There were no prisoners other than the boxers and their three aides, but the colonel made allowances by filming the event for the benefit of those inside who behaved themselves.

When we were finally permitted to focus on the fighting instead of the drinking, I noticed that one Sugar Ray was in the process of boxing crudely effec-tive rings around a Small Killer (one of three Killers of one brand or another on display). Sugar Ray belted the Small Killer with the kind of punches that would put even the average professional out of his misery, but this was evidently not an occasion for going down. Killer somehow remained on his feet, as did all the boxers in the event, despite some fearsome batterings. Do prisoners have harder heads, I wondered? I decided it was all down to habit. Go down in the ring and you can get up again; go down in the cells and your troubles begin. The final bell rang at the end of the fourth round, and Sugar Ray was declared the unanimous victor. The men hugged each other, smiled, waved and returned to their places under the watchful eyes of the shotgunners.

Two fights later, when lightweight Killer (plain and simple) lost to Man Groovy, the sponsors began pouring in the bucks. 'Barberton Liquor is offering fifty Rand for the winner of this bout,' Humano announced, and the other businessmen began rummaging in their pockets. During the eighth bout, when welterweight Mankiller received his deserts from Mfanzo Shah, the sponsors were starting to outdo each other under the influence of the cider, and the slurry colonel was entering a state of fuzzy ecstasy. 'Trugonnings Garage is offering ten Rand for each loser,' Humano told the crowd, who cheered raucously, while the colonel nudged me in uncontained enthusiasm. 'And there's a hundred Rand on line if anyone wins on a knockout.'

The final bout featured the tall, lean, ripped 176-pound 24-year-old Smodern and the short, squat 46-year-old 165-pound Victor Galindez – named after an Argentinian WBA light heavyweight champion who successfully defended his world title four times in South Africa in the 1970s. This prompted the punters into an extremely brisk trade, with Smodern being the overwhelming favourite. The colonel, however, knew his men. He was sure the aged Galindez would once again prevail, and not only that but win inside the distance. He was therefore a bit disappointed that his wily, defensively minded protégé merely jabbed, ducked and parried his way to victory, managing no better than a unanimous points triumph over his wild swinging rival.

'*Ag*, you know, Victor's getting a bit old now. In a year or so I'll have to retire him.' The colonel turned lugubrious at this point, wrapping his arm around my shoulder, his face and rancid breath too close to mine for comfort, and mumbled, '*Jurrah*, Gav, you know, me and Victor have been together for a long, long time, *jong* – over eight years now, so I know him very very well. We've been through a lot together, hey. He's a lifer, you know. I've been good to him and he's been good to me. You know, I was the one who secured Victor's transfer from maximum to medium security, so he's very very grateful.'

Victor and Smodern reluctantly left the ring and the announcer Humano, another lifer who everyone agreed had excelled at his night's work, made a little speech in terms the white overseers could understand. 'We are prisoners and we have fallen along the way, but you have shown us you can still accept us in the society. It has been a worthy cause for us to show you what we can do inside those four walls.' The prisoners were then presented with Crossbow Cider T-shirts for their labours and given a final pep talk by the slurrily sodden colonel, after which they were ferried back to their cells in a prison van, singing the African national anthem, *Nkosi Sikelel' iAfrika*, as they eyed us through the grid. The colonel was fighting back the tears as he joined the escort to their cells.

When he returned ten minutes later we were preparing to depart, but it became clear there would be no clean break. He was feeling mightily pleased with his achievement, with all the loyalty shown to him by his boxers, with the money made, and with the way this would advance his number in the prison system. Then a new, unsettling thought wormed its way into the haze of his alcohol-addled mind. Apparently it hadn't occurred to him before, but what if we were there to find fault, to pour scorn, to take the piss? 'You know, Gav, for me it doesn't really matter how this is reported by you,' he slurred. From the pleading look in his eyes I could see it meant the whole world. 'But for the prisoners it was something really really big big big. You could see it on their faces afterwards – what it meant to them. You know what they said to me before they went to their cells?'

'No, colonel, what did they say?'

'They said, *Siyabonga, vader* – thank you, father.' His voice was choking at this point and he wiped his eyes. 'And I *am* like a father to them, you know.'

I assured him we were mightily impressed and that there was no cause for piss-taking, and the colonel seemed relieved and forgot all about this concern. Still, the whole business demanded three more brandy and Cokes, pronto, and he swallowed them one after another, without pause. We were finally about to sneak off, unannounced, when the colonel caught us at it, and he was certainly having none of it. 'No, no, no, you are not leaving – you are our guests for tonight,' and the thought occurred that we might just be set to join the three Killers in their cells. 'You see, Gav, we treat our guests right. We have really lovely accommodation on the prison farm. It's a guest accommodation for visitors and you're our guests so you're staying there. It's all organized, and one of the prisoners will bring you your breakfast in the morning.'

There was no point arguing, and we followed the colonel whose prison *bakkie* weaved this way and that down the road, a minute on the right side, a minute on the left, with the occasional item of oncoming traffic magically anticipating the problem and taking serious evasive action just in time; no doubt well aware that at midnight on Friday, when the colonel is on the loose, it's time to take care. When we finally settled into the safety of the prison cottage, and the colonel's vehicle meandered its jolly way back to its owner's prison house, we rolled another spliff, reminisced a bit and slept the sleep of free men.

But there was to be no instant release after breakfast. As we were about to drive off our path was blocked for a third time and we were escorted to the office of the head of the prison. The brigadier was a tall man, well groomed in his prison uniform, with a perpetually curt turn of phrase and given to a staccato delivery, broken down into bite-sized little sentences. He required a little more than his fifteen minutes, thanks very much, and started us out with a tour – medium security only, mind; 'Can't let you see maximum, oh no, no, no.' Thirty men in each grey cell – treble the number it was designed for. I imagined it was rather different when backs were turned or when the lights were out, but then, and for us, not a fibre was out of place, the blankets folded and stacked in neat piles on the well-scrubbed concrete floors. The few prisoners not working in the fields were standing firmly to attention, waiting for the brigadier to pass.

'Discipline's good, but, you know, you still need a – what-you-call-it? Sanction. That's it. What is your opinion of physical sanction, Mr Evans? Corporal punishment?' He snapped the question out as we were being paraded through the rusty brown- and grey-painted corridors to meet the eyes-down, hands-together prisoner cooks, making their *pap* and leftover meat for the men's lunch.

'You mean for prisoners?' I asked, stalling.

'Not only, but also.'

I had recently completed a lengthy exposé on physical

punishment in the South African judicial system, schools and homes for *Cosmopolitan* magazine, and, as a new parent, held passionate opinions on the subject, all of them vehemently anti, but this wasn't the time or place. 'Um, I haven't given it any thought, to be honest. Does it still have a place, do you think, brigadier?'

'Oh yes, oh *yesss*. It has a place all right. I'm quite upset, actually, about these moves for its abolition. A little unhappy you might say. More than a little, actually. Sometimes a good whipping solves a problem, you know – *hwissshu, hwissshu, hwissshu, hwissshu, hwisshhu,*' he went, in what I presumed was a whipping sound. 'Nips it in the bud. It's worked for us – whipping has. Very very well, as a matter of fact.' And from here he moved on to another thing on his mind: how the 'ultimate sanction' – hanging – also solved so many problems for so many people and how he was so worried the noose too was on its way out. He was, indeed, a worried man.

'But not to worry,' he said with a nonchalant little hand-flick. 'I want to show you some of the good that we've achieved.' He took us around the farm and at this point I noticed him eyeing Justin carefully, then quizzically, as if he couldn't quite work this one out. Balding, beaming Justin, with his pony tail, leather thongs, flowing shirt and slow *shew-wah* alternative Capetonian speech patterns, was certainly not a specimen the brigadier had previously encountered. I worried for a moment that words like 'fokkin' hippie' and 'bladdy beatnik' were making connections in his cellular brain, but no. He smiled a little and relaxed and it became clear he finally had Justin all worked out. An Israelite! Something traditional. Someone from a book. Something from the Book. Not a problem.

A funny little Jewboy photograph-taking man in his native dress. *Shame.*

Then a fresh idea passed through the brain of the brigadier. 'Justin – uh, Mr Evans too – I want you to come and see our piggery. I have a little surprise for you.' He nodded at Justin, winked at me and led us to a shed where a large pig, called Amos I think, was rolling contentedly in the swill. His keeper snapped to attention and the brigadier motioned him aside and whispered, pointing in Justin's direction and smiling conspiratorially – and the brigadier was not a man who smiled easily. The keeper re-emerged ten seconds later with a kind of gun, which he proceeded to load. He held it to Amos's now rather resigned head, and fired. The bolt shot into Amos's brain, blood spurted from the hole, and the piggy squealed in what was either extreme pain or extreme shock or probably a bit of both. His squealing lasted for around three minutes and then, suddenly, he rolled over, dead, his life curtailed for our entertainment and ultimately for the culinary delight of the prison, or at least its officers. 'Now what did you think of that, hey, Justin?' the brigadier asked. 'You like pigs? All for your benefit, hey.' He was smiling again, but then so was Justin.

We were escorted to the brigadier's office for a final chat on the glories of the prison system and a lecture on how these glories were threatened by too much reform, and then, all of a sudden, it ended. He rose abruptly and extended his hand. 'You know, it's been a pleasure. I want you boys to come back some time. Promise me. Any time you want a holiday, you must come to the prison farm, with your wives and children. You have wives and children?' We both nodded. 'You too, Justin, hey. You are both more than welcome. Any time. You just give me a call and I'll arrange it. A lot of people do it, you know, and they have a wonderful holiday here. Wonderful.'

Off we drove, to collect our slave. But on the way back we made a quick stopover at a police station in another little Eastern Transvaal town where, in a rare miracle of South African policing, Justin's cameras, stolen on a previous slave-related visit, had been recovered. The sergeant on duty was ever so pleased with himself – with his honesty and the brilliance of his detection methods – and I sensed he too was after a little piece of fame. He pointed out the thief, who was sitting morosely with his head down in his tiny cell. 'We got a tip-off so we picked this *ouk* up and of course he denied it – they always do – but, uh, we treated him a bit,' the sergeant said, winking at us, touching his wrists and pointing again to the sad cell squatter. I noticed the thief's wrists were covered in deep, nasty circular welts and cuts, presumably from the standard detection tactic of the 'helicopter' – hanging prisoners up by their wrists and ankles and then twirling them around. 'And then it all comes out, along with their *kak*' – shit – 'It always does.'

The thief was on his way to Barberton Prison. We were on our way to a refugee centre to pick up Jorge, 'our' 17-year-old liberated slave. Jorge was Portuguese-speaking and said very little we could understand, but he was grinning the whole way, delighted to escape from Renamo terror and starvation in Mozambique, and then, perhaps worse, from slavery, beatings and hunger in the Eastern Transvaal where his previous owner was a tobacco farmer. For a couple of weeks after we dropped him off, Jorge, and another former slave, Immanuel, made themselves at home on the carpet of the newspaper office before being resettled at the paper's expense in a flat in central Johannesburg.

With the slaves feeling lucky, laughing and smoking in the office storeroom, I wrote my story – straight and kind enough to delight the colonel, who, presumably sober, phoned to thank me so very much, 'And of course, any time you wanna come for a holiday, you can be my guest – the brigadier said to remind you, hey.' I then received a letter from the announcer, Humano, also thanking me profusely for mentioning him in my story and requesting ten copies to distribute among the prisoners. Of course I obliged.

A few years on the colonel and the brigadier, and probably Humano too, found their world turned upside-down. The death penalty was abolished, racial segregation in the prisons reluctantly staggered to an end, and the white, rightwing-controlled prison service crossed paths with the astonishing notion of affirmative action for the first time. For the white prison warders – many of them open about their far-right racist political allegiances – this was too much to handle, but then again it was adapt-or-die time in South Africa. Some died of course – a fair number at their own hands and guns, together with the wives and children they felt compelled to take with them – but in time many adapted. The alternative too ghastly to contemplate became the alternative you could just about live with, with a few adaptations. Adaptation, in this case, meant self-help; free enterprise if you like, taking individual initiative. And so it was that the incipient corruption in the prison system, fed by practices like taking bribes to help out men like Hennie with his labour problems, burnt rapidly out of control, until richer criminals could simply buy their way out of prison, individually or in large numbers, and resume their criminal careers on a scale which threatened to overwhelm the new South Africa.

Those who couldn't afford the price of an escape started organizing themselves. Shortly after our Barberton Prison visit I met up with a rough former professional boxer and ex-con called Robbie Lombard, a white man in the process of a fundamentalist political conversion to the left. Lombard, who had been jailed for four years for robbery, told me his reputation as a boxer and a *breker* – brawler – saved him from the sexual assault which was virtually *de rigueur* for the young male prisoner. 'It helped that I had friends there, and so, after I had knocked two of the top guys' heads off in fights, and then won the prison's light heavyweight championships, they left me alone,' he explained. The warders, however, were a different story and he soon ran into conflict with them. 'There was a group of them who would give prisoners *dagga* and money, let them out to "steal" from their homes and then claim on the insurance and reclaim their belongings later. I reported this and was victimized in all sorts of ways. They even tried to get me declared a schizophrenic.' After his release he joined up with a black ex-con, Golden Miles Bhuddu, and started rallying the country's 120,000-plus prisoners into a group called the South African Prisoners' Organization for Human Rights.

In time the prisoners won new rights – including the right to vote. They also acquired a little more freedom of speech, which meant they could write to people like me, requesting assistance. As a result of these emerging rights, and more specifically because of my Barberton story in the *Weekly Mail*, I received a steady flow of letters from boxing-inclined convicts in prisons all over the country, with some of their pleadings even making it to my unlisted home address in London several years after we moved there. From one Zolile Phini, Correctional Institute, East London, RSA, for example:

> We would like to ask for donation because the problem is we need boxing equipment, together with socks, boots and shorties. We would like to develop our sports here in prison because we still have a chance to educate through this manner in our community. God bless you = Hebrew chapter 13 verse 3.

Or one from Vuyo Nyathela, a former boxer sentenced to five years for theft in St Albans Medium, Port Elizabeth:

> I am the above-mentioned black boxer from Uitenhage. I don't want to use my sentence unfruitfully. I plea to you sir to consider this if there is help you can assist me I promised I won't waste any money which comes from you. Please sir, make your own investigation to 'Wonderboy' Nene [a leading South African flyweight]. I was his stablemate and he knows me better. Sir if you have old boxing gloves please send them to me because I'm searching for young talented boxers black/whites. The promotion will come after the transformation of Correctional Services has take place in all S/African prisons. What does the confession of The Holy Scripture as the authoritative word of God mean in our time?
>
> Your faithfully prisoner, Vuyo 'Happyboy' Nyathela.

I dutifully replied to each of them, never forgetting to pass the buck by reminding them that Nelson Mandela once trained as a boxer and that he still adored the game, and that I was certain he would be only too delighted to assist if they wrote to him. My standard response went like this: 'I know Madiba loves his boxing – he told me so himself. I'm sure he will help you out if you ask. Good luck with your boxing. I hope it helps.' Perhaps it did.

8

ALI'S HERE (BUT HANI'S DEAD)

Central Johannesburg, April 1993. I swing into the *Sunday Times* sports department, drop my bag, and tell Colin, the sports editor, sorry I'm late, but I'm now ready to move. Colin looks up from his terminal. 'Uh, you've heard the news I suppose?'

They all know that I once lived precariously as an extremely political animal. They must have read occasional bits and pieces of this story in the papers. Not that they'd ever allude to it directly (and neither would I) – they're too polite – but at a time like this they can't mask the assumption that I'm in the loop. They're wrong though. I'm out of the loop and haven't even read the wires. 'What, is Ali's flight delayed or something?' I inquire, with genuine innocence, feeling quite hopeful at the prospect of missing the sight of a somnambulant former hero on his maiden pilgrimage to South Africa.

Colin pauses for a moment, his eyes registering surprise – confusion even – at my professed ignorance. He seems not quite sure how I will respond to the news he is now forced to break. 'No, actually, Gavin, um,

370

Chris Hani's just been killed – assassinated. Some right-wing maniac they say. Shot him. Happened this morning, outside his house.'

I miss a beat or two as the implications of this news ripple through my consciousness but the habit of keeping my sport, politics, journalism and relationships in separate compartments quickly reasserts itself. I resist any incipient urges to sit down with my hands on my head, or scream, 'Fuck them!', or walk out mumbling incoherently, and instead I just shut it out for the moment. I do not want to think about all of this right now. Later, yes, but not here, not now. After a few seconds of dazed silence I regroup, trying something inane. 'Tshew!' I say, to emphasize I'm not in the know. And then, desperately trying to show that it's nothing personal, *'Ja*, they were bound to get him sooner or later.' And finally, when I think my display of nonchalance has convinced them, I say to Colin: 'Um, we've only got about an hour before Ali's due to arrive. I think we'd better go.'

All contemporary boxing stories pause for Muhammad. Whatever our angle, if we're drawn to this game, we're sure to draw from him, or to claim him as our own. We still find inspiration from his triumphs. We borrow him for our analogies, recreate him, cleanse him, use him for our own devices, make his words our clichés, worship at his many-headed altar. Me too.

It seems somehow fitting that I eventually get to meet him on the day of the passing of another of my heroes – a sort of political hero. I'll return to that later. For now it's enough to say that I sometimes clocked my early life in terms of Muhammad Ali's existence, and then I sort of forgot about him and moved on, or more

371

accurately I suppose, moved around in circles. And then, one day in early autumn 1993, Muhammad Ali popped in to take me by surprise in a way only he can do.

I was in the business of closing down my South African existence when the call came. 'Sure,' I said, thinking no more of it. Covering Ali's week-long visit to South Africa felt like just another time-consuming job at the *Sunday Times* in the countdown towards our departure for the rainy place of my birth. I was preoccupied with a mixture of anticipation and foreboding about our plans to swap Johannesburg for London for six months and was becoming increasingly agitated about the whole business. I felt uncomfortably guilty about this move and yet the voices telling me to leave had reached a crescendo and could no longer be resisted.

To take one example: in 1992 Tessa and I had eight days alone in Cape Town while Pat returned to work in Johannesburg. As the holiday drew to a close my compulsion to climb Cape Town's mountains became irresistible and I phoned my friends Brett and Sarah, who suggested Kloof Nek as a quick alternative to Table Mountain. I left my toddler with my parents who were holidaying on the other side of town, saying I would be back in four hours. We scrambled to the top, absorbed the view, checked the time and started racing down – just a bit too quick. A slip on a loose rock and I was down – snapping the anterior tendon on my ankle with a loud crack, sending me rolling into a ball of excruciating agony. By the time I reached the bottom of the mountain, with Brett and Sarah propping me up, eight hours had passed and it took another hour to reach my anxious parents.

And there was Tessa, playing contentedly with her granny and grandad, happy in the knowledge that Daddy was coming back and that he loved her. I drove with her to my brother's house with my ankle going through spasms of shock every time I braked, but the tears in my eyes were not from the pain. I was overwhelmed by a feeling of gratitude for my daughter, and overcome with the sense of how much she trusted me and needed me – and from there to a little vow, that whatever happened in my domestic and working life, I would remain steady and take no more risks, and I would never abandon her or leave her. It was then that the idea of a safer life in England first occurred to me.

I returned home to Johannesburg, had an operation to replace the snapped tendon with a strip of silicone, and another operation, on the other leg, to repair a running injury, and was reduced to crutches for a month. I used this as an excuse for taking it easy, the habits of political discipline and application easily broken by an innate laziness, and I started taking long lunches at the Carlton Centre in Johannesburg's city centre, frequently fitting in an afternoon movie. I was crutching my way in to see the 1 p.m. showing of *Wings of Desire* when six young men grabbed me in the dark of the cinema, bundled me against the wall and snatched my wallet. I clutched on to one of them, wouldn't let him go, and eventually a doorman came to help, but by then the wallet had moved on. I watched the movie, loved it and took a minibus taxi home, where Pat had a better story. 'This man came charging down our street and dived under my car,' she said. He was followed a few seconds later by a trio of Inkatha fighters, each carrying 'traditional weapons' – in this case spears and *pangas*. 'Did you see a man running away, madam?' one of them asked. 'Which way did he go?' Pat asked them why. 'No, madam, we don't want to bother you – we just want to kill him.' She told them to keep running, and when they charged off, the man under the car wriggled out, said 'Thank you, madam, you save my life,' and went on his way.

Another month, and another pair of well-armed Inkatha hostel-dwellers chased me on my bicycle for 50 metres down Malvern's main drag, Jules Street, for no apparent reason: an attempted bicycle-jacking, I guess. Then the Indian owner of the general store on the corner of our little road was shot dead while handing over the money to the robbers. A week later the owner of the Portuguese corner store was hospitalized with a bashed-in head after a robbery. Then the owner of our local pizzeria was shot dead while trying to cooperate with the robbers and Pat was mugged at knifepoint in her office garage.

A month before the Ali call, Pat and I were married at the Johannesburg magistrate's court, but only after narrowly surviving a city centre carjacking attempt on our way to the wedding, after we were rammed from behind by another car, with Tessa in the back.* A week later my car was stolen from a park, with the help of the security guard in the parking lot, and the next morning the police came to arrest me, confusing the words 'complainant' and 'suspect' on the charge sheet – after which they lost the file. From all this I was finding

---

*After which we went into the court building to tie our knot and found that Pat had left her identity book behind, prompting Mark, my best man, to rush me home and run out of petrol on the way back, and finally when it was all done, a Pretoria government department lost our marriage certificate.

plenty of excuses for leaving – reasons for a six-month break in London. Too much violence, too much tension, too much confusion and too much fear for my daughter's future.

And then there was the politics. A couple of years earlier I had turned down nominations to stand for office within the ANC and Communist Party. I chose not to renew my party membership at the end of 1990 and declined to renew my ANC membership at the start of 1992, while my other political involvements were rapidly downscaled. But despite all these resignations and withdrawals I was finding it difficult to make a clean break from my typecast role as an activist. For one thing, elements in the now-decaying South African state still assumed I was involved – I later discovered that military intelligence continued keeping tabs on me until at least 1995. This official perception created problems when I was trying to interview them as a journalist – they naturally assumed I had a hidden agenda.

I had no fixed agendas but also no clear sense of where I fitted in. Having viewed myself as a lifelong politico, I now had to choose another calling, but I couldn't get my mind around that kind of commitment. I received a spate of job offers from various foreign media services, South African newspapers and local business groups, and the offer of legal articles at a large Johannesburg law firm, but I turned them all down. I simply had no ambition in any of these areas. I did not want to be told what to do, and I did not want to tell anyone what to do. My self-perception had shifted from 'revolutionary activist' to, perhaps, 'dedicated parent' and my evenings were spent caring for Tessa. I was still busy with academic studies* but if I harboured any ambition it was to become an actor, and with this in mind I took daily classes in mime, movement and improvisation at Johannesburg's Market Theatre, while also retaining private acting and singing teachers. After Tessa was asleep I would absorb myself studying Stanislavsky or memorizing monologues from Ibsen, Miller, Osborne, Pinter, Ionesco and the rest.

The demands from these unconnected passions meant that I needed an easy avenue for money-making. I was still writing on politics but sports writing was pressing to the fore, and my politicized image was also a hindrance here. More to the point, I despised it. I had recast myself as a cynic and resented being treated as a hack. It's not that I had exactly reversed my political beliefs – I still despised the logic of capitalism as much as ever (or more so perhaps, because I was no longer tied to the Marxian view that it was a progressive stage on the road to socialist nirvana) – but I could no longer chant the mantras of old. It was all rubbish, I thought, and I preferred not to spend time with anyone who couldn't match me, sneer for sneer. I would bristle when people expected the sentiments and behaviour of the comrade.

This perception, however, was not easily extinguished and it extended to colleagues and casual acquaintances. I would become enraged when accosted by people who expected me to slot into the straightman role of defending the ANC. Shortly before Ali's arrival I went to a party at a friend's flat, also attended by some

*At the time I was completing a masters thesis on business and politics in South Africa, which eventually grew into a doctorate on the politics of 'participative' management.

members of one of my favourite bands, the Cherry Faced Lurchers. One of their louche groupies spent several minutes goading me in these terms, aggressively taking the piss, and as he moved closer to my body space I felt myself losing control, wanting to tear his throat out. I spat out a 'Fuck you!' at which point the band leader, James Phillips, gently put his arm around my shoulders and led me off, saying, '*Ag*, just ignore him – he can be a real arsehole sometimes,' and then asked me all about my life. I felt a combination of embarrassment at my prior outburst and gratitude at his kindness.*

At the same time former comrades would either expect political favours and support or, more often, would express extreme disappointment and hurt about my lack of loyalty and my increasingly open criticism of their leaders. Once I received a surprise visit at home from a senior Communist Party functionary who asked me to lay off investigating or exposing an ANC leader whom we both knew to have been identified by the leadership as a police informer** – we had been

---

*A few years later James was killed in a car crash.

**In 1989 the underground leadership structure I was serving in was instructed to help investigate the firebrand Youth Congress leader Peter Mokaba. Its subsequent report referred to an activist who said Mokaba tried to recruit him to an apartheid intelligence structure and another who said Mokaba had instructed him he would be collected for an ANC mission – only to find that the people who arrived were the security police. It also stated Mokaba was involved in spreading spy rumours against one of his prominent ANC-aligned critics, who turned out to be innocent. The report was delivered to the ANC by a fellow member of this underground committee, Sydney Mufamadi, who reported back to us that the ANC's heads of security and intelligence, Joe Nhlanhla and Jacob Zuma, had informed him that Mokaba had confessed to being a security police agent – an account later reiterated to me by several other ANC leaders. Mufamadi returned to

377

informed by the heads of ANC security and intelligence, among others, that this leader had made a full confession, but it seemed the informer had been let off the hook because too many people were compromised or embarrassed by this revelation. 'We all

(cont. from page 377)
Lusaka and the following week reported back to us further details of Mokaba's alleged involvement in the security police, but said that the ANC president Oliver Tambo had decided this revelation would be damaging to the ANC and dispiriting for the youth, and that Mokaba would therefore be rehabilitated on the quiet. However, other ANC notables took it upon themselves to leak this information – first to trusted comrades and then more widely, including to prominent liberal sympathisers in politics and the press. When I was in Lusaka in 1990 I pressed an ANC grandee, John Nkadimeng, on why this information wasn't officially disclosed. He confirmed to me that Mokaba had indeed confessed, but claimed he had only agreed to become an informer while in security police detention, and that his sin was failing to inform the ANC voluntarily. Others, however, said his state involvement was more long-standing. In 1991 Philip van Niekerk of the *Weekly Mail* and David Beresford of the *Guardian* picked up on these rumblings and published the story. Mokaba threatened to sue but failed to do so. By this time some of Mokaba's ANC and SACP accusers had come to the conclusion that his public disrobing would boost the case of their internal enemies. The issue was fudged by the ANC, which merely stated he was a member 'in good standing'. He survived to become an ANC MP and deputy minister under Nelson Mandela, later being dropped by Thabo Mbeki. In 1994 I published a fuller account of the Mokaba spy story in the magazine *Leadership* and repeated this account on SABC radio. Again Mokaba threatened to sue, but failed to act. Instead, in 1997 he demanded the ANC clear his name. The party went through the motions and after a cursory investigation (in which Mufamadi, Zuma and Nhanhla – by then all cabinet ministers – denied any knowledge of the allegations against him), he was cleared. Soon afterwards a leading black Askari (a member of the police killer unit, consisting mainly of turned ANC guerillas) claimed to have been Mokaba's police handler. After contracting Aids (while denying that the disease existed and opposing the use of anti-retroviral drugs to treat it) Peter Mokaba died in June 2002, aged 43.

know his past,' my party visitor said, 'but he's not a real danger at the moment.' Instead he asked me to redirect my focus on another ANC leader, who was one of the party's pet hates. I ignored the request, but it made me feel more vulnerable to their criticism and left me with an uneasy sense that perhaps I still owed them a duty of loyalty.

Most of all I wanted some personal distance from my politicized past. I wanted a taste of something different, a more anonymous existence, removed from expectation and reputation, and separated from the constant sense of danger. I was relieved when Pat agreed to give London a try and yet I could not escape the feeling that I was running away from duty and obligation. Added to this my father had just been diagnosed with motor-neurone disease, after finding he could no longer button his shirts. From what we'd been told by his doctors he was unlikely to last more than another three or four years. Six months seemed a liberty in his context.

With only a few weeks to go, I was still finding it difficult to let go of my existing world. I was up for my final domestic acting role – three male parts in a play in Pretoria called *Shakespeare's Women* – while hurriedly completing the final chapter of my thesis, at the same time as demanding payment from freelance employers and buzzing around trying to get around document-losing, braindead jobsworths in order to get passports and marriage certificates organized, and I was still writing for two newspapers and a foreign news agency while doing voiceovers and scripts for a sports phone-in service.

I was barely holding it all together and sometimes found myself behaving extremely oddly. Events, or rather my reaction to them, constantly confounded me. For instance, three days before Ali's arrival, I lost my temper with the editor of the *Weekly Mail* after a minor dispute over a correction. I was normally polite, slow to take offence, keen to avoid personal conflict and inclined towards the appearance of deference with authority figures. I seldom swore in arguments and was certainly never one to issue gratuitous insults, yet I ended my diatribe saying, 'Go fuck yourself, arsehole.' I actually liked the editor and there was no real justification for my rage. My reaction astonished me. It just seemed so out of character.

I was feeling unfocused, edgy and hard to please when that Ali call came, and his imminent arrival only added to the sense of unease. The night before his plane took to the air from Miami, Chris Greyvenstein, one of the country's most esteemed sports writers, made one of his regular boxing-gossip phone calls to my home, but this time he seemed more agitated than chatty.

'Gavin, I'm a bit worried – I want your advice.'

'Why, Chris, what's up?'

'Well, it's Ali, you know. I'm just not sure I should meet him.'

'Why – you've been eulogizing him ever since I learnt to read.'

'*Ja*, Gavin, but that's the problem. I heard he's not all there, you know. That the stories he's *really* all there and just a bit slow are bullshit. Man, I heard he dribbles. What do you think I should do?' I convinced this huge, humble journalist to see for himself, but I was churning over doubts of a different kind.

It would be fitting to claim that I cast my mind back to the first time Ali and I made our acquaintance, but I'm afraid that would be stretching it. Closer to the truth is that over the next 24 hours I gave Muhammad several serious minutes. I had sort of forgotten him for fifteen years, pushed him aside for more contemporary pugilistic concerns, relegating him to the status of a distant icon. But in the day before he arrived it occurred to me that, as to so many boxing trainspotters, Ali's influence was pivotal to my view of this game, and even to my view of the world. Any yardstick can be dreamed up to measure a life, and Ali has certainly been one of mine. There have been times when I have chosen to mark the chronology of my existence in terms of my Ali moments, or Ali fights to be more precise. I retain a clear recollection of that first 1966 exposure, after the second Henry Cooper fight, to the man my father called Cassius Clay. It ended with the absurd conclusion, 'We need a Joe Louis or a Rocky Marciano to give him a hiding,' which, if you take away the racial dimension, now seems so reminiscent of the Jack London rallying call for Jim Jeffries to leave his alfalfa farm 'to wipe the golden smile off that nigger Jack Johnson's face'.

That moment sowed the seed of fascination that was in full bloom by the time of the first Joe Frazier fight in 1971. I got my prediction right on that grand occasion and stamped my emergence as my school's resident expert on all things pugilistic. It marked my own transition from engrossed fan to serious obsessive and it certainly reinforced my ambition to grow into the heavyweight champion of the world.

But over the next few years, as thoughts of God and dreams of girls got in the way, it began to dawn on me that the optimum size of the big boys was moving steadily, alarmingly, upwards while I was failing dismally in that department. Ali and Frazier were being eclipsed by a new generation represented by George Foreman, while my own body was showing a stubborn reluctance to fulfil its destiny of eventually delivering my sport's premier title. I remember watching on film the five minutes when George brutalized Joe in Kingston (the same day I received my maiden secondary-school caning), after which he became the embodiment of the title he held: sullen, silent, violent, with his Afro and Alsatian and his aura of menace. Foreman seemed unnaturally enormous* and utterly invincible.

Twenty months later, from my seat in the enchanting old Alhambra cinema in Cape Town's Foreshore, sitting next to my friend Kevin, I witnessed the vindication of a desperately hopeful prediction I'd been making: that George would fall to Muhammad, just like Sonny Liston did. I had written this in the letter column of the *Cape Argus*, winning the grand prize of twenty Rand, but I'd pronounced it more out of desire than faith and when the moment approached I doubted my own words. Yet somehow, in a jungle half a continent away, under the malevolent aegis of a CIA-sponsored mass murderer, Ali stumbled upon George's vulnerable chink and in his idiosyncratic way exploited it to a marvellously illogical conclusion. From then and for ever George would be stamped with the mark of Muhammad, just like the rest of us. But for me it ended there – for a while.

It was Ali again, nearly four years later, who helped inspire my reacquaintance with the world of boxing. I had been inching in that direction anyway, but the first Leon Spinks fight in March 1978 sealed the deal. I was

*Although at 217½ pounds when he beat Frazier he was quite small by today's standards.

living in San Marcos, Texas, in a house without a television, and so I trotted over the hill to the home of my intellectual friend, Shannon, and together with a dog who'd lost a leg to a rattler, we watched a slow, fat Muhammad getting outworked by a small, not overly talented seven-fight novice. If it had been Larry Holmes or Ken Norton I would have been satisfied, but the toothless Leon Spinks was unworthy. Ali's career could not possibly end on such a sour note. It demanded a more satisfying end, and I was relieved when Leon avoided Ken and then fell to pieces with too much cocaine, alcohol and fun, while agreeing to a return with Muhammad. It seemed the only way Ali could become champion for a third time, because by then it was apparent that he was no longer a genuine top-ten fighter.

For the return I secured the keys for the student television den, and, alone, whooped and punched the air with unrestrained delight as the aged Ali outboxed the confused Leon for the final victory of his glorious career, as for one last time, in the fifteenth round, Muhammad Ali danced on his toes on his way to glory. I was up on mine too, shadow-boxing in the comfort of my solitude, and with that I was hooked again – enough to desire an emotional goodbye to Ali. I hoped he would make good his promise to stay retired because, unlike Leon, the rival champion Larry Holmes was the real thing – perhaps even good enough to beat Ali at his best, but certainly far too strong, fast and talented for this fading imitation. Two years later, when Ali returned to face Larry, I had no desire to watch. I knew what would happen and it made me sad, but by then I had given up on Muhammad.

He had lasted longer than the rest for me, though. At

first it had been Joe Louis, the Brown Bomber. Then came Ali's predecessor, the first black heavyweight champion Jack Johnson, and then finally, under the weight of my second reading of my fourth Ali biography, I succumbed. I remember rushing into one of my father's prayer meetings with a piece of news that simply couldn't wait. 'I've drawn up a new top ten, Dad, and Ali's at the top this time. At his peak he would have beaten Joe Louis and even Jack Johnson, for sure. He's definitely the greatest. He *is*.' My father, a kind man, told me this was interesting but not quite the time or place, but I was hooked on Muhammad and from then on angrily refused to countenance any questioning of his absolute superiority in every department that mattered.

As a boxer Muhammad Ali was 'sublime'; as a political figure 'heroic'; as a thinker 'profound', and as a person, well, truly magnificent. Even his doggerel became poetry. I suppose it can be said there remains a case for the airbrushed version of his fighting prime – toned down by a few decibels. When prodded by the squad of friends I regularly enticed to boxing matches, I could still rattle on about Ali being boxing's greatest innovator. And from there to his astonishing speed, timing and unorthodox defensive brilliance in the ring, as well as his guts and ability to absorb punishment.

I was also happy to pay lip-service to the Great Man view of boxing history that asserted that Muhammad Ali changed his own sport for ever, single-handedly, and perhaps there's some truth here too. Certainly he had a major stylistic influence on boxing, and without him it would have taken far longer for boxers and other sports stars to find their own voice. He was also the first global sports star – for over a decade or so the world's most famous person – and through his use of this perch he opened the way for the likes of Michael Jordan and Tiger Woods. Far more significantly, he offered hope and direction to millions through his example in seizing control of his destiny and defying the white establishment before, equally remarkably, seducing that same establishment into an unquestioning, ahistorical adulation.

And yet if I look at it now, it is clear that in each of the zones he inhabited he was far from flawless. As a boxer Ali was an arm puncher and a head hunter who had trouble with unorthodox pressure fighters. He was knocked down twice on his way up by men we'd consider small cruiserweights today and, aside from the ageing, alcoholic Sonny Liston, who may well have taken a pair of 'dives' against Ali, he was never really tested in his prime, from 1964 to 1967 – at least not by a fellow elite heavyweight at or near the height of his game. He was in prime condition for only a handful of fights after his return in 1970 and his record was inflated by some stinker verdicts in his favour.

I'd also read enough to know that he was not always the best of human beings. He once slapped his first wife Sonja around, as well as his father and his cornerman Bundini Brown. He was extraordinarily sexually voracious and his attitude to women could most generously be described as antediluvian. He was cruel – way beyond the call of duty – to several of his opponents and seemed to take pleasure in hurting them inside the ring and humiliating them outside. As a religious figure, he gullibly fell under the spell of a nasty little fraudster, Elijah Mohammed, adopting Elijah's most outlandish beliefs on everything from racial purity to divine spaceships circling the earth, and when it was demanded of him, he callously snubbed his closest friend in the movement, Malcolm X. He followed the Malcolm route towards conventional Islam when the Nation split but at this point the extent of his political naiveté became apparent – backing right-wing Republicans because they seemed nice to him, for example.

A flawed hero then, like all the rest: cruel, kind, silly, wise, myopic, visionary, self-centred, altruistic. These conundrums do nothing to detract from his immense significance through his roles as rule-breaker and inspirer, but by the time he beat Foreman in Kinshasa in 1974, the Vietnam war was ending and mainstream America had followed the rest of the world by transforming its hate into love, and so Ali was transformed from a symbol of resistance to 'mere' iconic celebrity. And for fifteen years that was the way he remained for me – a figure from my past, and the past was something I wasn't too good at dealing with.

In the intervening years my teens and twenties were gobbled up, after which I covered myself with the protective armour of cynicism to allow me to rationalize my withdrawal from the struggle and to justify my retreat from altruism and my fear of personal commitment. In this frame of mind icons no longer interested me. Symbols were there to be deconstructed and laughed at, which was perhaps apposite at a time when symbolic gestures were thick in the air of pre-liberation South Africa.

The termination of the anti-apartheid sporting and cultural boycotts had seen scores of wannabe dignitaries of one kind or another pompously lining up to take their places at the turnstile for a look-see and, more important, a look-and-be-seen. A month earlier, for instance, the bloated world heavyweight champion

Riddick Bowe waddled in, preceded by his pugnacious manager Rock Newman – a shoulder-chip black man in an inconveniently white skin, of whom a Soweto-based reporter innocently asked me (accompanied by a roar of collegiate laughter), 'Hey, comrade, what's that whitey doing trying so hard to talk like a brother?' Big black Riddick and plump white–black Rock were busy avoiding a fight against my new, chess-playing 'British' hero Lennox Lewis, and instead were touring the world to pay homage to their African brother, Nelson Mandela, before scuttling on their way to see the Polish Pope. Soon-to-be-punch-drunk Bowe, punch-drunk Ali, what's the difference – another entrance, another exit.

My car had been stolen a month earlier and a week later my ancient 750 Honda exploded into flames outside the Hillbrow post office while I was riding it after someone had nicked the side covers and the petrol leaked into the wrong places. I ran for cover, dragging people using the phoneboxes with me, before it exploded, leaving behind a barbecue of burned rubber and melted metal (after which someone hung a sign on the handlebars saying, 'The New South Africa'). So this time I climbed on my bicycle and pedalled my way to the *Sunday Times* offices in central Johannesburg to meet Colin, my cricketing sports editor, who wanted to join me on the Ali junket – just for a glimpse of the great man. Colin was thrilled by the idea of putting flesh on the image; I wasn't so sure.

But when I arrived they were consumed by another piece of news – a piece that hadn't reached me yet. As I stood there, stirred but stoically unshaken, my fellow sports reporters started to fill me in on the bits and pieces they'd absorbed of how Chris Hani had been gunned down in his driveway, with his 14-year-old daughter watching.*

Chris was the movement's most popular leader after Mandela. He had recently beaten his sometime rival Thabo Mbeki into second place in the ANC's elections for its National Executive Committee and then had defied political logic by taking over the leadership of the South African Communist Party, which was still umbilically connected to the ANC. Some thought this move disqualified him from the race to succeed Mandela, but Hani was an extremely canny operator whose nose for reading the political wind was as sharp as they came. Certainly he was a shoo-in for a senior cabinet position and those who knew him felt he would go even further.

There were powerful elements in the state, and perhaps some in the ANC as well, who would have preferred him dead. My immediate assumption was that a military hit squad was responsible, although it turned out slightly differently. The man behind the plot was one Clive Derby-Lewis, an English-speaking Catholic ultra-conservative with a handlebar moustache who was a favoured guest of the Tory Monday Club whenever he visited London.** His hitman,

---

*In a sense Nomakhwezi Lerato Hani became a second victim of this tragedy. She never got over what happened to the father she adored, and a few years later her pain was compounded by another horrific violation when she was gang-raped at a party. She died in 2001 at the age of 23 – three months after Chris's mother and nearly eight years after her father – possibly from a drug overdose.
**Several years later, when I was writing a story on the Monday Club, the club's president Lord Sudely spoke warmly to me of his meetings with Derby-Lewis, while another Monday Club leader, Denis Walker, raised the subject unsolicited. 'What do you think of Derby-Lewis?' he asked. 'A murderer,' I replied. 'But he didn't pull the trigger,' Walker countered. 'Personally, when I first heard it, I didn't believe it and some of the people I spoke to didn't believe it either. People do stupid things.'

Janusz Walus, was a Polish neo-Nazi, and his address was supplied by a humourless, cowardly little conservative called Arthur Kemp, who had once served with me on the University of Cape Town Student Representative Council (before joining the police).*

Chris Hani was a sort of friend – not really intimate, but I'd been taken by the bluff familiarity of a man who made everyone feel like a chum. When I wasn't giving him earnest reports on potential military targets or factional disputes, we'd banter and tease each other. It was six and a half years before, on the day I was recruited to the ranks of the South African Communist Party, when I first met him and like thousands of other ANC members I liked and admired him more than anyone else within the movement.

Oliver Tambo was the wise old leader; Nelson Mandela, the imprisoned symbol of resistance; Thabo Mbeki, the suave, hard-drinking diplomat who lacked the common touch; Joe Slovo, the military strategist and party ideologue. But for the activists, Hani was the man: the integrity, the brain, the physical courage, the military genius, the political wisdom – they, we, worshipped him. Everyone had a pet story to whisper: his guts in fighting the Rhodesians in the ANC's 1967 Wankie campaign; his nerve in taking on the jaded ANC conservative leadership in Morogoro, Tanzania a year later, goading them into a more militant approach; his miraculous escape from the South African army raiders in Lesotho, and many more. Technically he was then second-in-command to the ANC's military commander Joe Modise, but Modise was widely

---

*Derby-Lewis and Walus are currently serving life sentences for Hani's murder. Kemp was a state witness in their trial.

despised, treated with deep suspicion and blamed for
the manifold failures of the ANC's military campaign.
Even Modise's staffers seemed to share this view on the
quiet*. Hani, the thinker, the fighter, the man of action,
was the one they wanted to follow.

Over the next few years Chris became one of the
key leaders behind the Operation Vula underground
structure I served in but I didn't see him for a while.
Soon after the ANC was unbanned we spent a week
together in Lusaka at a conference which brought
together an ANC military delegation headed by Hani
with a delegation of South African Defence Force
officers – the official idea being to develop a common
understanding on each other's positions. The moment

---

*There were persistent rumours with the ANC that Modise's relationship
with the apartheid state was compromised. In 1994 I talked to a well-
respected London-based journalist who gave some meat to the skeleton of
these allegations. He had interviewed MI5 and former KGB operatives for a
book he was writing on Soviet-era espionage. In separate discussions, both
told him that Modise was known to their agencies as a South African
Military Intelligence agent. Soon after, a South African newspaper was
contacted by two former senior officials from South Africa's apartheid-era
Military Intelligence, who claimed Modise (and an ANC deputy minister)
were both former MI agents. Modise got wind of this and tried to prevent
publication (the story eventually appeared, without mentioning either of
their names). At about the same time the British *Sunday Times* ran a report
stating: 'Generals in the old SADF used to boast they knew "what the ANC
was doing before they even did it." It is widely believed that, still serving in
the new SANDF, these generals have such a hold over Joe Modise that the
"truth" of those times will never see the light of day.' In 1996 several reports
appeared in South African papers stating that 'Comrade September', a
notorious former ANC cadre who gave state evidence in several ANC trials,
was in fact Glory Sedibe, the late brother-in-law of Joe Modise. Sedibe's
links to the apartheid state went back to the early 1980s. When Modise died
in 2002 he was facing allegations of accepting kickbacks for arms sales – not,
by a long shot, the first time his name was linked to corruption.

he set eyes on me, a few hours after arriving in Lusaka, he displayed his phenomenal memory for personal detail. 'Comrade Rory,' he whispered, using my underground codename while taking my hand and patting it on his muscled stomach. 'You see, it's gone – hard now,' reminding me that I'd teased him about his waistline three years earlier. 'I'm running every day. Why don't you join me?' I left this task to the army officers, who were bowled over by his charm, athleticism and wit.

I said goodbye to Chris feeling enormous warmth, gratitude and admiration, even though my own life was moving along a different trajectory. But in the two and half years that followed I came to realize there was another side to him I'd never encountered. I gradually learnt more of his military ruthlessness in settling exile problems, and I became disillusioned by his soft-glove treatment of Winnie Mandela, where expediency seemed to get in the way of principle. But perhaps more than all this, my own politics had shifted in an anarchic bent, very different from Hani's. The idea of a communist party reliant on and beholden to the ANC and lacking any real independence seemed pointless, and I felt that for all his tactical suss, he'd somehow taken a wrong turn in agreeing to lead it when he could have hung on for so much more. So no longer a close comrade and not a real friend either, but still a man I deeply admired.

On the drive to the airport I tried to push Chris Hani out of my head – stuff to think about when I returned home. Colin certainly made no attempt to raise the subject. Instead we made conversation about Ali Bacher, Kepler Wessels, Dingaan Thobela and

Muhammad Ali. I didn't want silences so I talked incessantly and inanely on any aspect of these topics that came to mind, which seemed the only option in the circumstances. When we arrived at what was then Jan Smuts airport there were already a couple of hundred Ali watchers on hand, almost all black, and they too were trying to reconcile their shock at the morning's news with the thrilling anticipation of seeing the Greatest. At first, from those who knew me, black boxers and reporters, it was lots of 'Hey, *bra*, terrible news,' and I would concur.

But then a curious thing happened. We were there to see Ali and were not about to have a Polish Nazi gunman and his Colonel Blimp puppeteer pissing on our parade, and so we allowed Muhammad to take over, and we all began to chatter about him. Everyone had a personal take on why he meant so much and, gradually, I let myself become excited. The numbers swelled past the five-hundred mark and the shuffle and hum grew more frantic. As the airport terminus was taken over by the crowd I lost Colin for a while and was swept along, and finally I spotted that famous face – fatter, less animated than I remembered, but still handsome.

The crowd pressed in, reaching, touching, while Ali moved slowly, his body heavier than I had expected, actually quite chubby despite being scaled down by a black shirt which made him look smaller than he appeared on screen – a little heavyweight when compared to the likes of Bowe and Lewis. After a long, slow shuffle, he reached the microphones near the VIP lounge, took his seat and sipped slowly from a glass of water.

As always on such occasions, we were treated to

interminable speeches, eventually including one from an ANC Youth Leaguer who reminded us about Chris Hani and we were all jolted back with a ripple of inhaled breath. This was followed by a collective effort to forget and focus, just for now, on the man of the moment. Ali, who no doubt had never previously heard of Hani, responded with what looked like real compassion, but perhaps I was projecting.

It was hard to know what to make of him in those first few minutes. He spoke in his painfully slow, quiet whisper – something about Allah, and about how for so long he'd wanted to make this trip but couldn't because of apartheid, and how grateful he was finally to get the chance. I was relieved at the appearance of lucidity but at the same time I thought he was doing no more than going through the pre-set motions. All that talk of the mind being fine, it's just the body and the tongue slowed down – I still wasn't quite won over. He looked exhausted. No dribble but, as yet, not much sign of inspiration. Where was the spark I'd read about?

And then, suddenly, it all changed. Muhammad Ali's eyes flashed and he smiled, knowingly. That famous twinkle was gently mocking and playful, but this time also full of pathos and acceptance. 'Let me take on one of your boxers now,' he whispered, and I noticed Dingaan Thobela seizing the moment, leaping to his feet to join his childhood hero. Dingaan was prepared because he was carrying a rose, as was his acquired custom, but Ali had something else in mind. His eyes flared again and he changed pace, springing to his feet without warning. He began pumping out his fists in surprisingly fast combinations, grinning broadly in his enjoyment at his own joke. The punches all stopped millimetres short of Dingaan's head. The lightweight fired back, and the heavyweight blocked in mid-air, sprightlier than any of us expected.

If you ever require evidence that the general intelligence supposedly measured by IQ tests is nothing of the sort just look into Ali's eyes for a few of those preciously animated seconds. Here is a man who, in his prime, consistently measured 78 on his Intelligence Quotient tests – 'moron' level – and yet, even more than the street suss, the witty doggerel, the mocking and self-parody, the intellectual coherence and debater's propensity of those brilliant early years, here was intelligence with the hint of real depth.

As he sat there sweating lightly he returned to a contemplative mode, but those few minutes were evidence enough for me that no matter how much the punches to his head and the Parkinson's disease had affected his speech and motions, his mind was as sharp as ever – sharper in some ways, because there was a look of wisdom behind the smile. These were not the eyes of a man whose thought processes were impaired. I'd seen my share of boxers whose powers of reasoning had been addled by the accumulation of punches – Riddick Bowe would soon be one of them – but not this Ali. I was immensely relieved and I was moved far more than I had expected. I had intended to get in a few words, but as I moved towards him, he smiled at me, and then for some reason my head filled itself with Chris Hani again. I had nothing to say, or to ask, and sat again, watching, smiling inanely while getting drawn back to a darker world.

To break the spell, I found Colin and raced back to the office and wrote up my Ali story, before cycling home in the early autumn heat, through the rapidly Africanizing city centre, past the simmering Inkatha hostels, to the welcome of my new wife Pat and our happy little bright-spark daughter Tessa and our tale-wagging pugnacious Staffordshire terrier Ben and his mate Brinjal in down-at-the-heel Malvern, to try to make sense of the day and the decade and my life.

And I'm ashamed to say that on that fateful day of 10 April 1993 my thoughts were more with the very much alive Muhammad Ali, whom I'd never before met in the flesh, than with my tragically dead comrade, Chris Hani. You see, Chris was part of a world I was running from – one I could no longer deal with satisfactorily on its own terms, and certainly not on my own. Ali was part of a safer world. For him, very real, obviously, but for me, fantasy, make-believe, removed but absorbing, self-contained and manageable. No longer merely an icon, but still less than real. I realized it then, on that autumn Johannesburg night. And I didn't really care.

Ali hung on for his week, getting mobbed in town-ships, touring the country, visiting Robben Island, receiving tickertape parades, but he had to scale back because for that week at least Hani's murder was even bigger than Muhammad. It had taken the joy out of the occasion, and replaced it with much mourning and some vigorous rioting, and more deaths.

Seven days later Muhammad was gone. Seven weeks later we were gone – off to England, leaving behind the Hanis and the Thobelas and the townships, the muggers, the carpetbagging former strugglers, the car thieves, the close friends and ex-lovers, the enemies new and old, the family, the mountains and the big skies and all the hope and all the fear for a new life as someone with a suspect accent, just for six months, which soon turned into six years, and more.

9

FIGHTING IN TEXAS, VOTING IN SEBOKENG

Braamfontein, Johannesburg, 5 June 1993.
PAGGGHHHH!!!! Or something like that. What I'm
reaching for with these entirely gratuitous exclamation
marks is the sound of cordite exploding a few feet from
my left ear and the simultaneous splattering of
buckshot around my shoes on a crowded pavement on
a sunny, early winter's afternoon. I skip, make a little
involuntary squeak and swing to my left – all in one
undignified motion – and then I see the cause of my
fright: a security guard, absentmindedly playing with
the trigger of his shotgun. We offer each other wide-
eyed looks of astonishment as we notice the circle of
indentations around our lucky feet.

Two seconds after the *paggghhh!!!* (or whatever) I
hear a man laughing loudly and rather gleefully behind
me. I swing around, irritated. 'Close one, hey,' says the
laugher, and I then notice he's Ken Oosterbroek, a long-
haired, Pulitzer-prizewinning photographer, packed
with the easy machismo that comes from regularly
leaping through hoops of fire. We've worked alongside

each other on many a story – long enough to develop a mutual appreciation – and I've seen him often of late because he's also the best buddy of my friend and *Weekly Mail* colleague Kevin Carter (another impossibly brave, tightly wired, Pulitzer-prizewinning photographer). 'Fuck you,' I say to Ken, because I can't yet see the humour in having my feet fired at on the day I'm walking out of South Africa, but Ken's smile is wonderfully reassuring.

'No, nought, man, don't get the wrong idea,' he says, still half-laughing. 'I wasn't taking the piss. No, no, fuck hey. It's more like, the situation, you know. Like for sure you've just lost one of your lives, but I'm down to my absolute fucking final last one. My nine are just about up, I *skeem*.' I raise a dubious eyebrow. 'No, next time you read of a photographer killed, you don't need to look further. *Ciao*, hey. Have a good one.'

I amble home after dropping off my 600-page political science thesis at Wits University. It's my last day of living in South Africa and I want to take it slowly. There are cases to be packed and goodbyes to be said, but I can't quite forget Ken's final words.

South Padre Island, 13 April 1994. 'Got a good one, got a good one,' says Texan Bubba, laughing before he starts. 'OK. OK. Bungu gets into the shower and he sees the walls covered in jissom. Now Welcome's just gotten out, see, so Bungu shouts at him: "Jeez, Welcome, you sure shot your wad here, boy. Next time you keep that big dick of yours under wraps when you're showering, bud." So Welcome turns round' – and Bubba flops a wrist – 'and he whispers to Bungu: "Sorry, but it's not my wad or my dick. I just farted." ' Bubba – the preferred name of the thick-set little trainer with a silly moustache, Terry Stotts – can't contain his own belly laugh. Vuyani Bungu, the chief sparring partner, tries to smile but he clearly doesn't get it. Welcome Ncita, the former world champion hoping to regain his crown, looks utterly bemused. Their manager, trainer and paterfamilias Mzi Mnguni shakes his head with the look of an indulgent parent. He'll let Bubba have his fun but his 'boys' know who's in charge.

It's my first minute in the giant corrugated-iron shed where Welcome is putting the finishing touches to his preparations for his return with America's Kennedy McKinney for his old IBF super bantamweight title, and I've just missed the sparring session. Bubba tells Welcome to step onto the scales naked. With four days to go he's only two pounds over the limit – perfect. 'Tell you what, Welcome,' says Bubba. 'We could get you back down to bantamweight.'

'No-o-o,' says Welcome, shaking his little boy's head. 'Ye-e-e-s,' says Bubba. 'Easy. We just chop off that big dick of yours and you'll make flyweight.' And all eyes focus on little Welcome's not-so-little penis. The boxer smiles shyly, suddenly aware of his nakedness, and not quite sure if his American trainer is joking or idly speculating.

Two more men enter the shed: Malcolm Garrett, cut man and all-round skivvy to the promoter Cedric Kushner, and John Lark, a broad-shouldered light-weight from Gary, Indiana, who also serves as Malcolm's helper, driver, odd-job man, sparring partner for Welcome, and now and then a decent fighter in his own right. Garrett, a tough little Chicagoan, is talking about his marriage and I catch the butt end. 'I say to her, "Babe: you got a choice. Either it's the big wedding and the little rock, or the big rock and Vegas." So she chose the fat diamond and we did it in Vegas drive-in style – in and out and no trouble and I didn't even have to dress like Elvis.' John, who'd collected me from the airport an hour earlier, laughs and rattles on about his woman of the hour. He talks so fast that you need to be a well-tuned local to pick up the specifics of his conversation, but whatever he's saying you can't help liking him. He's a warm and friendly regular guy, forever on the sniff in the most casual way, and from what I can see, always successful because his smile and his perfectly proportioned body make him irresistible, or so they say. Malcolm and John are tight.* In fact, they're all family, and for a week so am I.

Bubba sees Malcolm and John and once again says he's got a good one. 'OK, OK, Lark gets into the shower and he notices the wall covered in cum . . .' The boxers leave to shower, the rest of us make our way back to the Lonestar Motel lobby. Bubba, a cigar-puffing, hard-drinking man, former boxer, former US Olympic coach, a trainer of several professional world champions, entertains us with stories of his sparring sessions with the actor Mickey Rourke, whose status as a wannabe professional boxer is the running joke in the profession (everyone but Mickey knows that some of his fights aren't quite on the level). 'One day I'm letting him do his thing, and he can't box a lick so he sails out with his chin up in the air, and bam – man, I just can't stop myself – out pops my right and down Mickey goes, and

*When John gets gifted a fight for the world lightweight title against Kushner's South African protégé, Philip Holiday, a few years later, Malcolm refuses to serve in Holiday's corner, insisting his loyalty is with John. Kushner fires him on the spot.

out, and I mean lights *out*, man. *Oh shit*, I say to myself, and when Mickey comes round, I say to him, "Jeez, Mickey, I sure got lucky there." But he's worried, man, so I have to pump him up again. "No, Mickey, you was beating the crap outa me. You good man. You could be great. I just got lucky. Happens to the best of 'em – Joe Louis, Jack Dempsey." ' Bubba has our attention now – we're all waiting to hear the fate of the *9½ Weeks* man. 'So I let Mickey have his way you know for the next couple of sessions, and I tell ya, we're the best of friends. Anyway, a while later they need an opponent for Mickey, so who do you think they call? And this time I don't forget my role in life. Mickey taps me one on the chin' – and he thrusts it out, suggesting a willing target – 'and *Timber!* down I go.' Bubba rolls on his back, legs in the air, mouth open, and gives us a wink. 'And everybody's happy. Mickey thinks he can fight. Hollywood breathes again, and I get my money and the promise from Mickey of a part in his next movie. We's the best of buddies, I tell ya.'

Kushner's slick, Long Island promotional team sweep in, settle two pairs of eyes on me and ask if I'm up for judging a beauty competition that evening. I politely turn them down. Mzi smiles approvingly, motioning to me to join him. We walk out into the sunlight, down the main street, past a gay milkbar and an odd assortment of shops, chatting life and boxing, but it's hard to hear with the permanent loud buzzing of the phone and electricity lines above our heads. We can still hear the crackle when seated inside the coffee shop. South Padre Island is a one-act town on the Rio Grande Valley section of the Gulf Coast. It survives on students from the Texan mainland getting drunk and going mad during the spring break. For the rest of the year it relies on slim pickings from flower shows and beauty contests, so events like an international boxing bill make them jump and smile and 'Have a nice day, y'all' more than ever. Mzi is bemused. 'These Americans are a funny lot,' he says. 'I mean, look here: we have a choice of thirty coffees and they taste better than coffee anywhere else in the world, but how do they serve it? In a paper cup. They just don't get it.'

Mzi, a large, wise and avuncular middle-aged businessman, who never boxed himself, came into the game to help the poor kids from the massive, sprawling Mdantsane, near East London. The township had a long tradition of stick fighting, which was transferred into boxing through the success of a local hero, Nkosana 'Happyboy' Mgxaji in the 1970s. Mzi decided to capitalize on this tradition and started up the Eyethu Boxing Club in a small local hall and the children were soon squeezing in to join. 'Then, I didn't see myself so much as a trainer or manager but as a guardian. I was the one to organize the places to train and the gloves and things, but I realized my boys weren't getting the fights they needed, and so I began to do it myself.' Without the benefit of modern equipment he became Africa's most successful boxing manager, producing a steady stream of national and world champions and emerging as one of the most astute readers of fights and fighters in the game. Watching men like Bubba and Garrett, he also learnt how to train boxers, but his managerial style emerged from an older world. 'In our culture,' he explains, 'we respect the wisdom of age so the boys know who's in charge. I'm older than them and they must look up to me, and when they do, it works. So if you want to speak to my boys, fine, but first you speak to me. If they don't like it my way, fine, they can go somewhere else, but that's how it is in my gym. That's our way.'

We move on to the merits of his best lads and particularly Welcome Ncita, his first world champion, and Vuyani Bungu, his understudy. Bungu, the younger man, is *indoda* – a man – but Welcome, his older pugilistic mentor, is still something of an *inkwenkwe* – a boy – who says his Catholic prayers at night, goes to bed early, cries when he struggles to make the weight and laughs with the unaffected joy of a child when it all goes well. 'Ah, he's still a little kid at heart,' says Mzi, smiling indulgently. 'As soon as he comes home from a fight he kicks the football around and eats *vetkoek* [fried fatcake] with the teenagers.' Welcome has the speed, reflexes and punch but his problem is temperament. In his last title fight, in Sardinia in 1992, he was giving a beating to the much-favoured American Olympic gold medallist Kennedy McKinney, and he was well on his way to the seventh successful defence of his world title when he put in the finishing touches by dropping his man in the eleventh round. At that moment the dog in the American emerged, or perhaps it was just his cocaine-abusing past. Kennedy turned away and shook his head: enough. He wanted to go home and that should have been the end for the fight. But the American referee, Steve Smoger, had a little chat with Kennedy, who recalled his life's mission and decided to give it one last go. Welcome charged in to finish it and bundled McKinney into the ropes where the American met him with a desperation right that caught Welcome flush on the chin and put him down and out for the count. The question now is whether Welcome has the faith in himself to avenge his sole defeat.

It's night-time when I finally leave Mzi, still uncertain about the answer, and open the door to my motel room for the first time, although only after negotiating my way over a pile of sawdust, wood, tools and debris left behind by some workmen. The bad jokes and boxing stories, the buzzing lines, beauty competitions and now a broken ceiling form a persistent reminder of where I am, and more to the point, where I'm not: a rather important election is taking place in South Africa.

The Welcome–Kennedy show was originally set for the Carousel Casino, thirty miles north of Pretoria, just within the border of one of the bits and bobs of South African land calling themselves the Republic of Bophuthatswana. The idea was to link the event to the birth of the 'new' South Africa with fireworks and parading lions, elephants and tigers (yes, tigers, this being Africa) and then unfurl the new South African flag out of its wrapper for its maiden sporting display. But the American television network, ABC, which was screening the fight live and putting up most of the money, became edgy. For starters the people of 'Bop' had grown weary of their puppet dictator, Lucas Mangope, and rather violently asserted their right to rejoin the rest of South Africa – with the Carousel staff joining their general strike – and they got their way. Bop evaporated, but ABC – or rather its insurers – felt the country was becoming too wild, too dangerous, too likely to go up in smoke and down in blood, so at the last minute Kushner and Berman were ordered to relocate, and they found South Padre Island, Texas.

When I learnt this I felt irritated and frustrated. I was becoming agitated about the election, writing about it for anyone who'd take my copy, itching to go back. The Welcome fight was my ticket and I'd slung together a package of commissions from various British, American and South African magazines, newspapers, agencies and radio stations, some for the boxing, most for the politics and a few for a bit of both. But my motivations were more personal than professional. The sense of my country's destiny being decided was something I just couldn't miss, not after a decade or more working towards this end. I had to be there, to see it and feel it and live through it, and I felt utterly out of time and place landing in Texas.

The news I read on the flight over was dark. The British *Sunday Times* was particularly ugly – full of smug predictions of Armageddon. It was all going wrong because no-one was listening to Inkatha and the white right, they said. A succession of commentators was wheeled out on the opinion pages to vent their imaginations against the horror of an ANC election victory – mass genocide at best.* More rational voices were warning of the danger of a vicious civil war, pitting Boers and rural Zulus against the rest, unless a way could be found to bribe Mangosuthu Buthelezi's Inkatha movement into the process.

When I turn on the television in my motel room I surf the channels and finally settle on CNN: bombs, gun battles between township residents and Inkatha hostel-dwellers, right-wing terror, rumours of coup attempts

---

*The South African writer Rian Malan, for one, lurched from his perch on the American new right and flew to the old South African version by predicting a race war unless we accepted the racist solution favoured by apartheid extremists – including independence for white Boers (in an area where they represented less than 5 per cent of the population).

and earnest American commentators expecting the worst. After half an hour of this CNN switches to some other 'trouble spot' and I switch off and dial directory inquiries to locate my old friend Teresa, who is living in Austin. Teresa, a one-time cheerleader and lifesaver, was voted the 'best looker' in my Texan high school in 1978, but now she informs me she's become a tired ole Texan mamma with two jobs, a three-year-old son, no partner and parents who've disowned her because they belatedly discovered her dope-smoking past. We chat about old times and new, and it becomes hard to think that sixteen years have passed since we last shared a spliff, but when I finally say goodbye I feel even more disjointed. I don't want to be in Texas revisiting that little part of my past. I want to be back home where I belong. I just have to see and hear and taste it all for myself. In the meanwhile, however, there's a fight in the way.

Welcome Ncita was the last South African world champion of the apartheid era. More than any other boxer, his rise to the top, and his tenure once he reached it, was secured by sanctions-busting and bribery. The common link between the two was Bobby Lee, a former New Jersey cop turned president of the International Boxing Federation, and the 'Fatman' or 'Walrus' – Bobby's pet codenames for Cedric Kushner.

Let's start with Big Ced, a South African who personifies a version of the American dream. His calling card was the slow, plummy faux-Etonian accent he cultivated – well, that and his immense girth, his narcoleptic habit of falling asleep mid-sentence in astonishingly deep snore, and his walrus-like moustache. He once played a bit of rugby, he was capable of a decent game of tennis for one so large and he had a taste for the lewd, but all of this disguised the habits of a single-minded bachelor driven in the pursuit of recognition and fortune, or at least the sense of worth these things brought.

Having dropped out of school early, with no credentials, he left his Jewish Capetonian family in 1971 and worked his passage to America as a deckhand on a German freighter. He sweated away as a labourer in Boston, a swimming-pool cleaner in Miami Beach, a ferris-wheel operator in New Jersey and a messenger in New York but he always had an eye for the big chance and soon made his mark as a rock 'n' roll promoter – Steppenwolf, Bob Seger, Journey, Fleetwood Mac, the Rolling Stones, Rod Stewart – until his card was marked in 1982 when he received a criminal conviction and a five-year probation for price fixing. After that he turned to boxing, establishing a partnership with Rodney Berman and then going on to become one of the world's leading promoters, and an extremely wealthy individual, with a massive seaside pile in Long Island and, most of the time, no-one but himself to lavish attention on.

Bobby Lee's prominence and the IBF's existence owed a good deal to South Africa, or more specifically to the tight apartheid connections of the World Boxing Association, which inadvertently sired it. Lee challenged Venezuela's Gilberto Mendoza for the WBA presidency in 1983. Mendoza called in his white South African friends, who included Mr Justice H.W.O. Kloppers, a Bloemfontein judge, member of the Afrikaner secret society the *Broederbond* and president of the South African Boxing Board. As *Ring* magazine put it at the time, Kloppers's performance in controlling the voting from the chair was characteristic of 'what you'd expect from a South African judge' (and they weren't being complimentary). Mendoza survived thanks to Kloppers's casting vote, which prompted Lee to storm off in a huff, complaining that you could never make progress within an organization based on an alliance between Latin Americans and apartheid South Africans. Instead he formed the IBF, an organization whose American base guaranteed it instant recognition as one of boxing's big three international control bodies.

Lee had endured his fill of white South Africans after the failure of his WBA takeover bid and initially abided by the international sporting boycott, refusing to rank South African boxers, but Kushner had other ideas. He assured Bobby that as a political liberal he had no state connections, no racial agenda, no business other than business to conclude. All he wanted was a fair deal for his lads. 'I thought it was double punishment for our black fighters,' Kushner later explained, even though most of the South Africans he co-promoted at the time were white men. 'They were discriminated against in their country and they didn't get rated.' Of great help to Kushner were the whispers that Lee had acquired a taste for backhanders – more of a habit, actually – so it came as no great surprise when the former cop dropped his putative principles and sent his bagman C. Douglas Beavers to demand $20,000 to drop the boycott. The Fat Man haggled and they eventually agreed on $10,000 apiece for every South African rated. The payments continued for almost a decade – three or four times a year in exchange for ratings and other favours, with the price going as high as $100,000.

For what it's worth, Kushner's case was that this was

then the only way to succeed as a major-league American promoter. 'When you get approached and say, "I can't do it," then get repeated phone calls, you don't have to be too smart to realize if you don't pay it will impact on you.' He once told me influence-peddling went well beyond paying off the control bodies. 'Look at it this way,' he said. 'If I was involved in, say, tennis and I started wining and dining the umpires, offering their wives flights and accom-modation and so on, I would be thrown out of the game, but in boxing that's the minimum, and I certainly do it less than some. I can't defend it, but right now there's no alternative. It's the way of this world, and maybe it's better than the old days when fights were fixed, and boxers took dives, but I know it's not as it should be.' In a business of brigands he regarded himself as a man of honour, and most of his boxers agreed. 'Not screwing fighters is not something I want to be praised about,' he said. 'I want people to understand something about Cedric Kushner. If you do business with him, you're going to get a fair deal. Don't embrace him but trust him, because there's a genuine reason to trust him.' I never embraced him, and frequently criticized his boxers and his shows, but in a way I liked him – because he was a generous man who always paid for my supper and got me ringside seats, and also because he was quite an odd fish, who showed unintended traces of vulnerability behind the swagger.

Anyway, Welcome Ncita benefited enormously from the goodies Kushner purchased from his friend Bobby, and eventually came to deserve them. His start in the game was typical of Mdantsane lads – sparring with milk cartons on his fists because he couldn't afford boxing gloves – before wandering into Mzi's gym. He was a brilliant amateur and began his professional career as an 18-year-old flyweight of enormous potential – quick, flighty and hard to hit – but he had little chance of breaking out of the domestic market until Berman branched out into the world of black boxing. He settled on Mzi's promising stable and shared it with Kushner who made a 'passionate appeal' to Lee on Welcome's behalf – followed, no doubt, by a bribe. Within days Welcome was granted an IBF world ranking at super flyweight, and then jumped up two divisions and was granted a shot at the IBF world super bantamweight title, then held by France's Fabrice Benichou. They fought in Tel Aviv, three weeks after Nelson Mandela's release, and Welcome had no trouble jabbing and running his way to victory. A couple of easy defences followed as Welcome grew into his new division – until he was ordered to put his title on the line against Colombia's former world champion Sugar Baby Rojas in Aosta, Italy. Welcome's pitter-patter punches were ineffective and after being dropped he ran to survive. Survive he did, however, and I could come to no other conclusion than that he secured the decision solely through Kushner's relations with Lee – by any other standards he lost.

Welcome seemed to me like a fraudulent champion at that stage of his career, but then he turned it around. A top American trainer, Luthar Burgess, was drafted in and he changed Welcome's style and approach, and the frightened, skinny boy became a muscular, brave one. I was once again at the Sun City ringside to watch the return with Rojas and this time Welcome turned aggressor. For every minute of every round he fought his heart out to earn a split decision. A year later he was back in Italy to face another formidable former world champion, Jesus Salud. Welcome's left eye was banged shut in the third round which meant he lacked three-dimensional vision, so from then on he battled the brawler at close quarters, slipping and sliding while throwing punches in combinations of six and seven, and once again emerged victorious.

He relished the attention this victory brought. 'I bought me a six-room house, but it's still in Mdantsane, and my people appreciate that,' he said in a tone resonating with pride. 'I've been a hero here for ages but now it's the whole country. This is the first time that ordinary white teenagers are coming up to pat me on the back. I'm definitely starting to get recognition from white people.' Actually, his relationship with the people of Mdantsane was more ambiguous than he seemed to realize – or at least that's what the comrades told me. His 'defiance' of the embargo on international sporting competition meant that he incurred the mild disapproval of the ANC, and Mdantsane was a solidly ANC zone. This filtered down to the young lions – the youth and high-school students who were reluctant to embrace him. But there was no question that Welcome had arrived as a sports star with recognition beyond the confines of his own profession and that white South Africans were beginning to take notice.

My own approach to Welcome shifted from cynic to fan for more esoteric reasons: I drew closer to Rodney Berman, and by proxy his promotional stable, because we shared a common antipathy to and from Stan Christodoulou and his fiefdom. My own antagonism was rooted in politics. The existence of a white-dominated board appointed by an apartheid government in a black-dominated sport enraged me and I campaigned for licence-holders to be given a say in the control of their own affairs. The board had immense power, governing the destinies of everyone involved. Stan, a big, balding man of Greek Cypriot heritage whose own boxing history was limited to twelve amateur fights, effectively controlled its every breath through his Chief Executive Officer perch. He was an extremely efficient administrator, who appointed the referees and judges to handle the major fights and was able to dispense or withdraw patronage as he saw fit – creating a climate of fear and whispering among licence-holders. On top of this, through his role as a brilliant international referee, he had international connections that enabled him to act as a middle-man between white South Africans and foreign control bodies and promoters.

This was where Christodoulou's spell of antagonism towards Berman came into the picture. For nearly fifteen years his international focus had been concentrated on wooing the WBA. When this organization finally responded to American pressure by booting South Africa out, Christodoulou threw his lot into the breakaway Puerto Rican-based WBO – an organization that soon emerged as even more venal and blatantly corrupt than any of its counterparts but without the compensatory virtues of scale, reach and credibility. Stan backed them from the start, but once Kushner bought his way into the IBF, and bought rankings and title fights for the likes of Welcome Ncita, Stan ceased to be the sole avenue to the world and he seemed to resent it. He was helped by the fact that Judge Eddie Stafford, the board's cantankerous president, was blissfully ignorant about the intricacies of boxing and therefore clung on to Stan's every word on the subject. Stan stepped back and let Stafford rage when the ANC-supporting boxing groups proposed reform of the Boxing Board. The judge was then persuaded to employ the country's laager-like exchange control regulations to try to stop Berman from holding Welcome's fight against Salud in Italy. The board also tried to block another of Berman's leading boxers from taking part in a world-title fight, claiming he was not good enough, while at the same time doing their utmost to secure overseas title fights for lesser fighters from loyalist camps. When I interviewed the judge about this, he became incensed, praising Stan's suss, and adding for good measure, without provocation, 'I'm more liberal than that fucking Rodney Berman.' The resentment was palpable and it contributed to a spin-off effect that saw the ANC boxing lobby embracing Berman more firmly, while casting Stafford and Christodoulou into a reactionary, apartheid mould.

The issue became even more personal for me when I walked into the Nedbank central Johannesburg branch one autumn morning in 1992 and was ushered into an office by a manager. 'I thought I'd better let you know that the police were around here yesterday and they asked to see the details of your account to check whether you were illegally taking money out of the country,' he said. 'By law we had to let them see your account, and, of course, they left satisfied that you had done no such thing.' Assuming that this was a political thing, I prodded him for more details. 'I'm not sure I should say,' the manager said, 'but it was something to do with the Boxing Board. Does that make sense?' I nodded. 'It seemed someone on this board informed them you were taking money out of the country for some promoter, but you had no foreign transactions on

your account.' I left enraged. First there was Gerrie
Coetzee's attempt to bribe me, which I suspected was
being recorded for other purposes, and now this. It
looked like the Boxing Board was prying in this direction, bringing in the police to help them. It felt like old
times, and I reacted accordingly, rekindling the passion
I'd once expended on the struggle and focusing it
on the rather less pressing cause of justice for South
Africa's boxers.

From the time of my first boxing stories in the
mid-1980s my relationship with Stan had always been
combative. I would write something about him he
didn't like; he would call me and try to charm me into
his zone; I would repeat the offence; he might then
call my editor. But I was used to far stronger stuff
from the security police and, unlike other boxing
writers, I had editors who backed me the whole way,
so I kept snapping at his heels. After the Nedbank
incident I began to campaign more vigorously and
directly.*

The conflict became even more bitter later in 1992
when a white lightweight, Danny Myburgh – managed
and trained by Willie Lock – challenged the coloured
national champion Aladin Stevens, who was promoted
by Berman and trained by one of Stan's vocal critics,
Andries Steyn. I sat next to one of the judges, Warrant
Officer Abri Schutte, who volunteered: 'Danny's going

---

*For instance, I asked: 'Did the board help pay for that second top-of-the-
range Mercedes?' Yes. Then: 'Did the police interview you about corruption
in high places yesterday?' Yes, but only about others. He phoned me at
home, warning me that legal consequences could follow if I pursued this. I
went ahead. He phoned the deputy editor of the *Sunday Times* after another
interview, and tried to get the story pulled. The deputy editor called me in, I
convinced him of the facts, and the story ran.

to win tonight.' I pushed him on this, suggesting the world-rated Stevens was too experienced. 'No, Stevens isn't going to win. There's the winner,' he said, pointing to Myburgh while smiling like he knew something I didn't. Stevens outboxed Myburgh, dropping him in the last round to put it way beyond reach. Schutte looked across the ring, beamed at Lock, and then nodded at fellow judge and policeman Wally Snowball – by then a brigadier who headed the Hillbrow police station. They both overruled the black judge and made Myburgh the new national champion.* When I exposed this in the *Sunday Times*, Christodoulou appointed Schutte as the referee for the next major international fight. For my last months in South Africa the hostility between us was barely disguised by a kind of overpolite correctness.

More than sixteen months had passed before Welcome was granted his return with Kennedy McKinney, and during this time Berman had once again been without a world champion. Dingaan Thobela had lost his world title and several other Berman-backed South Africans had failed in their bids, so he was reliant on little Welcome, who'd picked up a couple of easy knockouts in the interim. Meanwhile McKinney had emerged as one of the stars of lighter-weight American boxing and he looked stronger and far more confident than first time around. 'I have a scenario which I go over and over in my head, like a tape, for three days before the

---

*Stevens, who had been on the verge of a world-title fight, was never allowed a return – the Board 'mislaid' his application to challenge – and he eventually returned to his previous existence as dealer and user of a terribly debilitating drug called Mandrax, and never fought again.

fight,' he told me. 'All I need to do is focus and relax. The night before, I have a nice dinner and then I re-run that tape through my brain. It starts with my entry into the ring, then the whole fight, move by move, then the announcement of my victory, all the way to the press conference.' He made a point of deriding Welcome for being 'terrified' of his right cross, while he also had a go at Bubba Stotts, who had once trained him, saying, 'Bubba was so useless we fired him.' Welcome smiled shyly and said nothing. This time he *knew* he was going to win. He'd even planned his victory speech: 'I'd like to dedicate this moment to our future president Rolihlahla Nelson Mandela.'

ABC Wide World of Sports picked up four million viewers for the fight and Kushner sold it to sixty-five other countries, which, he claimed, put me as one of something like ninety million people who watched it. As the moment approached I gave myself up to absorption, visiting Welcome in his changing room to wish him well and getting excited when Vuyani Bungu stopped his American opponent. By the time of the first bell the election at home was temporarily forgotten.

Welcome seemed quicker and sharper than ever, but also more skittish – the fear of that right making him wary of taking chances by applying too much pressure. He shaded the early rounds with his speed and then in the fifth landed a thudding right cross on McKinney's unprotected jaw. The American boxer fell heavily and dragged himself up at the count of eight, after which the referee took his time picking up Kennedy's gumguard, inspecting it, cleaning it and replacing it. Two seconds later the bell rang and that was the end of Welcome's chances. Early in the sixth McKinney closed

Ncita's left eye, and Welcome was unable or unwilling to chance the close-quarter tactics that had worked so well against Jesus Salud two years earlier. By the eighth the eye was completely shut and at the end of the ninth the ringside physician inspected the damage. In a bid to discover whether Welcome could see properly he showed three fingers and asked, 'How many?' Mzi said 'three' in Xhosa while Malcolm Garrett tapped him three times, and after they repeated the exercise with two fingers, Welcome was allowed to continue. He was outboxed over the next two rounds and then pounded and severely wobbled in the twelfth and was relieved to hear the final bell. The result was a win, by majority decision, for McKinney. Afterwards I consoled Welcome who promised he would be back. 'You see, Gavin, I had everything planned but maybe God didn't want me to win because I could hardly see at all, so I have no complaints but it will be different next time.'

Mzi assured me that it would indeed be different next time, but that it would be Vuyani Bungu who would make this difference. Bungu was the ideal citizen in Mzi's world – a model of fortitude, personal restraint, dedication and respect who had gradually shifted through Mzi's tuition and Welcome's example from brawler to boxer. 'Bungu will do it for us because he has the high-pressure style to beat McKinney,' said Mzi. 'Remember I told you that.' I went back to the motel, filed my copy, recorded my radio reports and turned on the television, to catch Nelson Mandela brusquely putting F.W. de Klerk in his place in a one-to-one debate. The fight faded into the background and I swelled with pride on seeing *my* leader doing the job on theirs. I was filled with expectation and, suddenly, a determination that it would all work out. When the plane took off – for Johannesburg via Heathrow – I felt an overwhelming sense of relief. I was going home.

The eleven months that passed between Ken Oosterbroek's ninth life and Welcome Ncita's second defeat seemed strangely unhinged. Travel always does that to me and thirty-two hours in the air and in airport terminals stripped me of perspective. I began to dream of my recent past, and then to dwell on it while half awake, the memories mixing with the dreams and jazz on the airline headphones. My thoughts kept returning to the last occasion I flew home alone – two and a half months after arriving in England.

That train of events started with the phone ringing in our cramped, income-support flat on the Haringey–Islington border. It was my father. His voice was halting, with long pauses. He was struggling for breath as his body was wasting away to motor-neurone disease but he had something he wanted to say as our conversation ended. 'I love you, my son, I love you.' A strange distaste for showing emotion to my parents prevented me from affirming my own feelings in the same straightforward way. Instead I spluttered uncertainly, 'And me you too.' Couldn't quite get the right words out, and they were the last I said to him: 'And me you too.' A week later there was a letter for me from my father. He asked me to send him some CDs: Beethoven, Glenn Miller, Simon and Garfunkel, and told me again that he loved me. The next day I bought the CDs and wrote back, with love, and posted the package.

We went off to Amsterdam for a happy week with an

old friend and then booked for an end-of-the-year return to South Africa. My father's prognosis had been reduced to 'six months to a year' but that seemed time enough. When we returned to London my mother phoned to say he was deteriorating and I should think of flying back sooner, and then another call to say, book a flight now, he might not last long. 'I asked him if there was any last thing he really wanted,' said my mother, 'and he said, "I want to see my son Gavin."' I booked, but then came the final call. 'I'm so sorry, Gavin,' my mother said.

My father was dead. I went into our bedroom, closed the door, and cried my first real, flowing tears since I lost my first amateur fight twenty-two years earlier. Tessa came in and I hugged her, and she asked Pat: 'Why's Daddy crying?' and Pat replied, 'He's sad because his daddy died.' And then I flew home to Cape Town, and saw his body at the funeral parlour, and was driven by my uncle to my mother's house, and later that morning the postman arrived with a letter and package from England – the CDs, and my letter, the one finally telling him I loved him, as always, too late.

His funeral was a triumphant occasion – he had chosen the music for us to say goodbye – and as the Trumpet Voluntary was piped through the organ, I was caught up with the celebration of it all. The sadness was blanked out for then and I spoke at the funeral – I wanted to and needed to. I spoke of his different sides, the bishop and the boxer, the Jew and the Christian. It was a kind of eulogy, to say I was sorry to have missed him. He was a kind and generous man who did his best, and as good a father as he could be, and I loved him and wished that I'd been able to tell him this.

A bomb, planted by the Pan-Africanist Congress,

418

exploded in a tavern across the road from my old Observatory house, the shrapnel killing a young, idealistic American woman, but I barely noticed it because all politics and boxing and everything else was blanked out for the week. My mother, Michael, Karen, their friends and mine – this is what mattered. On my last morning back in Cape Town I walked with my old friend Wanda and her dog in the Newlands forest, and I felt happy again, talking and walking and smelling the pine resin, but as the plane took off, I slowly, slowly began to absorb the realization that wherever he was, or wasn't, I no longer had a father.

It had, therefore, been a strange and disjointed eleven months, with moments of happiness within long spells of anguish, and now I was on my way back again, in a way to celebrate the death of an old way of life, and also to cover a birth, and by the looks of things it would be a bloody one; maybe even a stillbirth. The plane landed and I felt the first tinges of apprehension about what I would see, hear and find. As I made my way through customs I noticed an inspector reading the sports pages of the morning newspaper, the *Citizen*. Then he lifted it up and I saw the headline. 'Photographer killed in East Rand.' I remembered Ken Oosterbroek's last words, and had no need to look closer. The bullet with his number on it was not intended for him. He was shooting the war between Inkatha hostel-dwellers and ANC township residents in the East Rand, an area about twenty miles east of Johannesburg, when he was hit in the crossfire, and died instantly.

I arrived at the offices of my old newspaper, now called the *Mail and Guardian*, where I saw Ken's closest friend Kevin Carter sobbing uncontrollably. Kevin was a more intense character than Ken, tightly packed with inner demons he could barely contain, and he used his camera to direct this passion, which helped to make him one of the world's finest journalistic photographers. He had more physical courage than anyone I'd ever worked with, or perhaps it wasn't really courage but the absence of fear – never backing down, taking his beatings without flinching, putting his body in the line of fire to get the picture. I liked him and we got on well, going bungee jumping and combat shooting together, talking women and taking drugs, and working on stories on politics, boxing and life. He was very different from the university graduates and activists I usually associated with – direct, emotional and blissfully unaware of anything resembling feminist etiquette – and in a perverse way, I found this refreshing. Kevin was a handsome man, capable of great warmth, charm and kindness, but his inner turmoil was always close to the surface and Ken's death left him with nothing but despair. Everyone there seemed shaken that morning, not just by Ken but by the whole situation – the shootings and the bombings, the rising death toll and the prospect of far worse to come, with Inkatha acting more bellicose by the day while its prickly and paranoid leader, Mangosuthu Buthelezi, insisted on delaying the elections until his demands were met for the entrenchment of federalism. The final week of subjugation was looking like the start of a decade of war.

'Where would you like to work this week?' the editor asked after I said my hellos.

'The East Rand,' I said.

An hour later I drove off with a photographer for an

all-night visit to Thokoza, Sebokeng and Kathlehong, the prime war zones in the Transvaal. We drove past police and army roadblocks, past burning tyres erected by militant comrades and migrant-worker hostels patrolled by bandanna-wearing men wielding home-made spears, axes and army-supplied guns. We would stop and talk or rather listen and only once had we to make a getaway, because they all wanted their voices amplified, and the talk was of blood.

I visited the central Johannesburg headquarters of the Independent Electoral Commission the next morning. It was a place and institution full of little power struggles between competing fiefdoms and about to send a quarter of a million officials and monitors into 9,000 voting stations. As I was leaving, a cheering and ululating ripple spread through the building, as the news filtered through that Inkatha was laying down arms and joining the election.* Then the cheers subsided and the phones were frantically dialled to plead for 20,000 more officials and thirty million Inkatha stickers to be glued to the ballot papers. It

---

*Henry Kissinger and Lord Carrington had tried to seal a deal with Buthelezi, but failed dismally. Just when all seemed lost, one 'Dr' Washington Okumo, a rotund Kenyan father of eight, a born-again American prayer-breakfast Christian and self-proclaimed professor (who wasn't really a professor or a doctor), emerged. He was a long-time chum of Buthelezi's and managed to persuade the chief to see the light, or rather the darkness that would hit his own people, and his own future, if he refused to budge. After long moments of prevarication, ending in a flight that had to be turned around because of bad weather, Buthelezi backed down. I went to talk to Okumo, asking how he pulled off this miracle. 'Aah, it's an African solution to an African problem,' he said. 'There could be no deadlines. Kissinger was a very busy man and he wanted to set deadlines, which you can't do here. Mandela, De Klerk and Buthelezi are all Africans and all they wanted was someone they could trust. I just had to be very patient.'

looked like a major mess in the making, but a mess is better than a lake of blood.

The election was on and the bloodbath off and I wandered through the centre of Johannesburg feeling at home. I drew some money at a bank machine outside the Market Theatre, drank a beer in the autumn sunshine, greeted old friends passing by and then decided to walk the three miles to the house I was sharing with a trade unionist and her boyfriend. But as I ambled down busy Bree Street I felt that familiar sense of being followed once again. It was nothing specific but enough to make me remove my wallet from my moneybelt and surreptitiously stuff it down my undies. I kept to the middle of the road, to give me space to run, but I hit a bottleneck caused by too many pavement traders, customers and pedestrians, and was hemmed in. That's when they struck, three of them – a long knife slashing across my hips for the moneybelt, another slash for my empty little backpack and a grab for my sunglasses, and they were off, evaporating into the crowd. The traders, particularly the women, crowded round me, saying, 'Shame, shame,' which in South Africa usually means something like 'pity' or 'poor you', but I felt fine. I'd been wearing a leather jacket so my skin was protected, and I walked on for a bit, pleased about my money but pissed off about my sunglasses and my friend's keys. After about a minute my mood changed and I was overcome by a feeling of intense indignation. I retraced my steps and started making inquiries. 'Where did they go?' I asked, but the traders warned me to leave it. 'Better go home now, otherwise they will cut you or kill you.' I persisted with my foolishly futile quest until a young man arrived.

'Hey, *bra*, I can do you a deal. I can get your keys and

shades back, *bra*. But have you got the money? Follow me, *bra*. I know where they are, *bra*.'

'No, you follow me and I'll give you some money.' I walked to a lamppost outside a Kentucky Fried Chicken shop where there was room to move. 'OK, twenty Rand, but you got to get my keys and glasses back first, OK?'

Within two minutes he was back with the keys. 'Where are the shades?' I asked.

'Give me the money and I'll get them for you.'

I delved into my knickers, pulled out my wallet and gave him ten Rand. 'Ten Rand more when you bring the shades,' I said. At that moment he made a grab for the wallet and we pulled and pulled until I elbowed him away and he turned to run. At this point the three with the knives charged from the crowd and went for me, and I sprinted through the streets of central Johannesburg for a hundred metres or so until I seemed to have lost them. I walked another block, but then, from a side street, they rematerialized with another charge and this time they almost caught me. It was a close thing but I was wearing trainers and was fitter than them, and managed to open a gap of about fifteen metres by the time I finally made it to the Carlton Centre. I positioned myself next to a security guard and smiled at the knifemen as they walked away. Half an hour later I continued walking home. I'd been careless and idiotic but I had come through OK. I had my wallet and the keys and I could survive without my sunglasses. I felt lucky. All in all, it was a good day.

When I reached the front door I was met with the news that the white right had been on a bombing spree, hitting 'targets' in the centre of Johannesburg and around the country, killing several people. The next day the usual suspects were rounded up, and that was that. The election was safe. It was going to happen and we all felt this sense of overwhelming relief. Hour by hour I was becoming part of it again, getting sucked into the emotion of the last triumphant round, allowing myself to feel for my country again, blowing away those cobwebs of cynicism.

It all felt wonderful with the sun setting outside. I drank a Castle, shared a three-blade spliff with the trade unionist and her boyfriend and together we drove to the ugliest building in Johannesburg, the Civic Centre in Braamfontein, a long, thin, dark, monolithic slab of fatherland sterility. But just for that evening it was a place of beauty. We were there to watch the sad old orange, white and blue flag come down and be replaced for the first time by the gaudy new red, blue, green, yellow and white one. Never mind that the new one resembled a colourful pair of Y-fronts and was the product of an Afrikaner designer, chosen out of a pile of options by the ANC and National Party's chief negotiators in less than five minutes; it looked magnificent.

The combination of the dagga, the beer, the mugging, the sun and the passion of the occasion disorientated me. I sang *Nkosi Sikelel' iAfrika* with more feeling than ever as the Y-front flag shimmied up the pole, and then watched, dazed, as a swirl of people waved or winked or said hello, until the faces lost their identity and I was no longer quite sure who was who. I turned to a tall, friendly-looking man next to me. He said hello and I was relieved to recognize him, except that I couldn't quite place his benign, kindly face. I beamed back at him and said, 'Hey, howzit going?' He said he was having a wonderful time and was deeply moved by the occasion, and then asked me for my take on it all, which I provided in gushing detail. A few minutes later an old journalist colleague came up and said: 'Shew, Gavin Evans – Jon Snow' and I realized that my past with this friend was restricted to watching him on Channel Four every night. We smiled at each other again, and I wandered around the happy crowd, catching snatches of conversation from old friends, comrades, lovers and associates before drifting off again, unable to stop and talk but content to sample bits and pieces of this moment in history.

For the three days of the election I returned to the townships of the East Rand and watched hundreds of thousands of people waiting with a patience of 342 years to vote for the first time in their lives. They waited through morning and afternoon, hungry and thirsty and tired, but the ballot papers never arrived. 'I've waited over twelve hours and I'll wait another twelve, and I'll keep on waiting because I've waited my whole life for this moment,' an old man told me while waiting at Thokoza's Buhlebuzile High School. He waited eighteen hours and then went home. I watched an elderly, disabled woman being carried to the queue in a wheelbarrow by her son, but at the end of the day she too went home without voting. I shot off to the Inkatha hostels, where voting was proceeding according to plan, then to a polling station in the white part of Boksburg, where the queue doubled and then trebled in length because of the spillover from the closed polling stations in the black townships. 'Where did all these people come from?' whispered a bemused white woman at the back of the line. 'I've never seen so many of *them*.' I conducted another tour of the townships and saw the first mild ripples of anger. 'This is definitely apartheid,' said a young comrade. 'They don't want us to vote but they can't stop us.'

I rushed back to the ugly civic centre in Braam-fontein to cast my own two votes (national and regional) for the ANC – any other vote would have negated my thirteen years of activism, and anyway this was an election about a hopeful African future requiring a vote for the hopeful African party that delivered the death blows to white rule. An electoral official patted me on the back and said I was the six-thousandth person to pass through his hand-dye machine (to prevent double voting). It was a moment of delight but when I arrived back at the office my righteous fury returned. I was on the phone demanding ballot papers for this and that polling station from this and that electoral officer. 'Comrade, there are still no papers in Thokoza, Kathlehong and Sebokeng but there are piles of ballot papers gathering dust in the warehouses. Why? Why? Can't you fly them there in that helicopter of yours? When will they arrive? Comrade, the people are suffering in the heat.' It was no longer about the story – for a few days I felt like an activist again.

Eventually, by late in the second day, the old man and the wheelbarrow woman and everyone else were on their way to the front of a slowly moving line, and I watched with delight as they emerged beaming from the polling station after placing all their memories of the past and all their hopes of the future in that ballot box. 'It was beautiful,' 'It was lovely', they said. It seemed to be so deeply fulfilling without any sense of anticlimax. Even the coolest of activists found the occasion moving – like my stoical friend, the former UDF leader, Murphy Morobe, who was still smiling with unrestrained delight hours afterwards. 'It was an amazing feeling for me,' he said, 'and I became even more emotional after arranging for my mother to vote in Orlando East [in Soweto]. It was an absolutely big moment for her, and for me.'

Nelson Mandela talked of 'massive sabotage' in the distribution of ballot papers; there was largescale vote-rigging by Inkatha functionaries in Natal, and there were plenty of counter-complaints about the absence of Inkatha stickers on some ballot papers. Hundreds of polling stations failed to open, thousands of people were unable to vote and hundreds of thousands of ballot papers went missing, but in the end nearly thirty million people voted, most for the first time in their lives, and the election was justifiably declared free and fair. Ups and downs, lots of cock-ups, plenty of corruption, much confusion, enormous frustration, but also inspiring, hopeful and full of creative energy. This then was to be the way ahead: a kind of muddling through.

When it was over, and the news filtered through that the ANC had won 63 per cent of the vote, I felt exhausted contentment rather than ecstatic triumph. I had seen the future; it wasn't pretty, but in most places it just about worked. For a week I had swung from despair to euphoria, and finally settled on mild satisfaction. Yes, we were indeed the Rainbow Nation, we'd performed a magnificent miracle, but the three days of election watching pulled me back a bit. A new government, long on loyalty, short on experience, would soon be relieved of the frustration of serving by only standing and waiting, and would start having to solve real problems like creating one unified, non-racial education system out of sixteen separate, racial ones.

It had long been clear that when it came to grasping for solutions, there would be no more obeisance to the socialist haven we once envisaged. The new ethic owed little to the collective and the communal and everything to naked individual ambition, pursued through politics, bureaucracy, business, crime or any other means at hand. At its worst the old wars of caste, class, group and ideology would be replaced by vicious skirmishes of competing private fiefdoms, grasping for a declining surplus within a sea of poverty, brutality and disease. At its best, it would fire a vital entrepreneurial spirit and produce a brazen, bumbling frontier nation, well suited for dreamers, dealers and crooks of any colour, and for all that a healthier place for the poor, the weak and the downtrodden. A bit of both, I guessed, and flew back to England, wondering when I would return.

Once home to our tiny flat I hugged my daughter and wife and rushed to the television to watch the formal transfer of power. I placed my South African flag magnet on the fridge, and for a few more days, from the safe distance of 6,000 miles, allowed myself to be reinfected by what the narrator in Rushdie's *Midnight's Children* called the 'optimism disease' – along with the rest of the world. A while later I went with Pat and Tessa to see Nelson Mandela in Trafalgar Square. 'That's our leader, Tess,' I said.

'Is he a good man?' she wondered.

'Yes, and a great one – a giant,' I said.

'But he doesn't look that big.'

'Big enough, I think.'

The celebrations over, the euphoria spent, this most self-obsessed of nations moved off the centre of the world map. News from 'home' became sparse and idiosyncratic, usually linked to moments of great triumph or tragedy. The triumphs invariably were about reconciliation and forgiveness, usually from blacks to whites; the tragedies about violent death. Now and then, between breathless phone calls from friends who were feigning black humour at having AK-47s thrust down their throats as they were relieved of their cars and other possessions, there were stories that really hurt. People I liked were getting murdered – like one of my favourite boxers, Ginger Tshabalala, doing a favour for a friend by driving him to the centre of Johannesburg and being gunned down for his kindness, or the energetic activist, economist and businessman Dr Ronnie Bethlehem, shot dead in a carjacking. But the one that shook me most was only obliquely related to this killing spree: the suicide of my old friend and colleague Kevin Carter.

Shortly before I flew home Kevin talked to me about starting anew by reclaiming his Irish heritage and moving to Belfast, but either there were too many ties to break or he lacked the will to leave. Kevin's personal life was, as always, in a mess: he adored his young daughter, Megan, but couldn't see her as often as he wanted; he was forever falling in love but seldom securing the subject of his passion; and his drugs habit was becoming a problem. We'd often smoked dagga together and now and then he would offer me or sell me grams of cocaine, but then an Israeli photographer introduced him to heroin and he started 'chasing the dragon' with her in the darkroom. He offered it to me too, but I decided it was perhaps not the wisest move for a father of a two-year-old. I don't know whether Kevin was ever hooked but in no time heroin use

429

spread to other photographers. It started as a bit of a laugh for the lads on the edge – but some became addicts and it blighted their lives. He also sometimes added another drug to his dagga, called Mandrax, to make 'white pipes' – a powerful, highly addictive and thoroughly debilitating depressant that had long been the scourge of a section of the Cape coloured community. I think Ken's death, combined with the drugs, unleashed the inner turmoil that went back to early childhood, pulling him into a hellish world he couldn't escape. He sometimes expressed guilt about his Pulitzer-awardwinning picture, of a vulture beside a starving child – should he have helped, rather than shot? Then he lost his film after a southern African shoot and that seemed to tip him further over the edge. One day I opened the *Guardian* to read that Kevin Carter, Pulitzer-prizewinning photographer, father of Megan, had gassed himself to death in his car. He would go on to become the subject of a Manic Street Preachers hit song.

Once upon a time I fondly held the notion that the motions of South African professional boxing mirrored society more generally and it was easy to find parallels if you went looking. Take the career trajectory of my old *bête noire*, Stan Christodoulou. By the time we left for England the key ANC-aligned powerbrokers in black boxing, led by an astute activist turned business executive, Khaya Nqula, were moving decisively against Christodoulou and the board, blocking them at home and abroad. For a while they fought in retreat, but eventually Judge Stafford resigned while Stan realized the old game was up and a new one called for. Nqula, a wise man, persuaded his reluctant ANC

430

boxing allies that they had no option but to retain Stan in his position. As he explained it to me: 'Some of them said: "Are you crazy? How can we keep that so-and-so after all he's done?" So I asked them to suggest an alternative. Who's going to step forward? Then they understood because Stan had monopolized all the knowledge so there was no-one else who understood the job. I said to them, Look, it's different now, because we hold the power, not the white government, so they agreed to give it a try.'

Stan promptly dropped his old white coterie and served his new black masters with the same gushing charm as of old, while making friends with Berman again and handling it all with an archetypically white South African amnesia. And yet he continued to retain his exclusive administrative grip, which, I suppose, aptly reflected another wider truth in the changing-but-not-changing South Africa. He was also reinstated to his perch as one of the WBA's most respected referees and continued to travel the world, which was how I got to see him again a few years later in Newcastle, Australia, where we spent a week in the same hotel, before a fight he was judging and I was covering. Stan treated me like a long-lost chum and ally – constantly deferring to my opinion and pretending we'd never had a disagreement. He was like that – his enmities lasted only as long as the underlying cause and it was the same with his friendships. I decided I quite liked him.

However, some of his old white allies felt betrayed and found common cause with black licensees wanting their own slice of the financial action. Eventually they ousted Stan, after which the affairs of the board descended into chaos and corruption on a scale that came close to killing the game, leading to the full circle of direct government intervention again. Stan took the generous retirement package he'd negotiated for himself and became a boxing agent and promoter in Africa, still using his refereeing credentials to get business done.* Back home, however, boxing struggled to survive. Lesser local promoters ceased promoting. Others became no more than foreign agents, while the bigger promoters snapped up the best South African prospects and exported them.

Meanwhile in America one of Stan's former opponents, the transplanted Capetonian Cedric Kushner, was running into another spot of trouble. Bobby Lee and his bribers were caught out through a long FBI investigation that made a snitch out of his bagman C. Douglas Beavers. Together with the three other major American promoters Kushner became an 'unindicted co-conspirator' in Lee's trial. Undercover FBI tapes told of crisp hundred-dollar bills being stuffed into duffel bags handed from Kushner to Beavers to Lee. Kushner became a state witness and admitted his long history of paying kickbacks. However, he insisted that Don King, the biggest payer and player, was given preference. 'I always knew I was second fiddle, or fourth,' Kushner complained. 'No matter what happened, Fuzzy Wuzzy as he was called came first.' His admissions of guilt earned him immunity from prosecution but got him banned from promoting in New Jersey, suspended in Las Vegas and fined a total of $300,000.

In one sense Bobby Lee was less fortunate – after a five-month trial he was convicted of racketeering-

---

*In 2002 the Sports Minister appointed a new seven-man national boxing commission. Its seventh member was Stan Christoloulou.

related charges, tax fraud and money-laundering, sentenced to 22 months in jail and fined £25,000 – but he was also extremely lucky. Despite the first-hand evidence of bribery from several of the world's leading promoters, and extensive taped evidence backing this up, Lee was acquitted of receiving bribes, perhaps because jury members accepted his version that the IBF was a business rather than a world body and that the 'bribes' were therefore legitimate financial transactions for desired services, which perhaps says more about the state of world boxing than anything else.

I never asked Rodney Berman what he knew of Kushner's backhanders – in a sense I didn't want to know – but he defended his partner,* insisting this was the way things worked in world boxing, and that far from being the prime villains, Lee and the IBF were in fact the best of a truly terrible lot. In any event Berman was establishing an international bridgehead of his own, and again the pattern reflected a wider trend. His group, Golden Gloves, was snapped up by a major black-owned South African conglomerate, which made sterling multi-millionaires of Berman and his partners. Rodney, however, continued to run the show, this time as CEO, and with the group's capital behind him he set up a new promotional company in Britain, after an acrimonious break-up with his old partner, Frank Warren. The result was that the cream of South Africa's boxing talent began to fight primarily in Britain – an

---

*Like most alliances in politics and boxing, Berman's partnership with Kushner eventually ended in enmity. In 2002 Berman sued Kushner in New York for $10 million, claiming, among other things, that Cedric deliberately failed to pay him his share of a number of partnership deals. At the time of writing the case had yet to be decided.

exodus that mirrored a more general trend within the sport, with the best talent sucked from the peripheries and exported to the metropoles, with their efforts then blasted back through space to an international niche market. Which is where I return to the men I watched on a Texan island the week before the election: Welcome Ncita and Vuyani Bungu.

They grew up as near neighbours in the country's second biggest black township, Mdantsane, which was a labour reserve for the white town of East London but conveniently placed twenty miles away, just inside the border of the nominally independent 'homeland' of Ciskei. Both were raised in extreme poverty but Bungu's experience was harsher. His family of eight lived in a tiny shack with no electricity, no running water, no flush toilets and no guarantee of food on the table. His father, Tatiso, suffered from severe asthma and was unemployed. His mother, Lillian, was a domestic worker who earned R40 a month (£20 at the time) working twenty-five miles away, and was allowed to return home only once a month. 'Her wages were often all we had to survive on, so when she came home it was wonderful,' Vuyani once told me. 'It meant we could have some meat and vegetables, because otherwise it was just half a loaf of bread and a cup of tea.'

Vuyani was a dedicated student whose first ambition was to complete his schooling and train as a teacher to get his family out of the poverty trap. But the school boycotts and mass protests against the viciously repressive Ciskei government took priority, and for almost three years the schools were closed. His only other outlet was boxing, something of a family tradition. His two older brothers boxed, his father had been a champion stick-fighter and all the children worshipped 'Happyboy' Mgxaji – 'He would drive his Mercedes through Mdantsane and we'd all run behind him, and that was why so many of us became boxers.' At the age of twelve he followed his brothers to Mzi's makeshift gymnasium. 'I never dreamed I'd be very successful,' he said, 'but when the schools closed I thought, well, let me concentrate on this boxing thing instead.'

Soon after his twentieth birthday he turned professional, winning his first fight on a knockout. 'Yo! I remember, my mother was so proud of me that day,' he said. 'We bought all sorts of things – chicken, rice, potatoes, bread, paraffin and candles.' After thirteen wins he tried for the South African super bantam-weight title against the world-rated white boxer Fransie Badenhorst, but lost on points. Nine months later he got his revenge, showing the improvement that came from the daily grind of serving as chief sparring partner for Ncita. After Welcome won the world title in 1990, Vuyani followed him to Europe and America. There was not much money in it – he still lived in Mdantsane, struggling to support his girlfriend and baby daughter – but he refined his craft and closed the gap on his baby-faced mentor. 'All the time I was learning from Welcome,' he said. 'I started out as a brawler but I saw a lot of guys who just want to punch and they didn't last long, especially not if they train like me, six days a week, all year long, and sparring almost every time. So I concentrated on avoiding bombs.'

In August 1994, four months after the election, Kushner secured Bungu a world-title fight against Kennedy McKinney at the Carousel Casino. McKinney was approaching the A-list of American boxing, unbeaten in twenty-eight fights and coming up for his sixth world-title defence, but he did not take it seriously; after all, Bungu was merely Ncita's sparring partner, and he'd beaten Ncita twice. Bungu, however, knew what he was up against. 'I studied him so carefully in his two fights with Welcome and I noticed he couldn't fight going backwards, so I trained to put pressure on him.' This time Welcome was the sparring partner and Vuyani the main man, and by fight time there was no doubting who was the boss. Still, it was one of the major upsets of world boxing that year. Bungu routed McKinney, chasing him all over the ring to take the title, after which he made the speech that Welcome Ncita had rehearsed: 'I dedicate my victory to my president, Mr Nelson Mandela, to my people of South Africa – all of them – and to my country.'

Over the next four and half years he racked up thirteen world-title defences, beating McKinney again and two other former world champions before relinquishing his title with the aim of moving up in weight to become world featherweight champion. Bungu was Mzi's model of how to handle success: training hard all year round, teetotal, money wisely invested with a comfortably modest house, another for his mother and money to spare, and forever loyal to his trainer and promoter. He was never a national celebrity like Dingaan Thobela but in his understated way built a national profile as a sporting figure to be respected, and within his hometown he was revered in a way that Welcome never quite achieved. 'The kids just love Vuyani,' Mzi regularly told me. 'He came from terrible poverty, so it really is a wonderful story of what dedication, constant training and clean living can achieve, and the poor kids see in him something they can aspire to.'

Ncita's fortunes moved in the opposite direction. He waited a year for another fight, moved up in weight and was relegated to fighting at home on other men's undercards. Berman and Kushner adored Welcome, their first black star and the first boxer to win a world title for them, but there were bottom lines to fill, and Welcome was no longer internationally marketable. His speed and timing were dissipating and he had lost his edge, but like so many boxers he was the last to recognize it. After winning his world title he told me he would be out of boxing by the age of 28, and would study further or start a business. He had lived a life of frugal discipline, planning for this moment. 'The beautiful things will always be there so I don't need them now,' he said then. Boxing was just a means to this end and he was patiently waiting for the day he could hang up his gloves and spend more time on his real passions: playing and watching football, and beating his friends in squash. But that's not the way it turned out. He became obsessed with reclaiming what he thought was his to take. After that Texan defeat he would regularly phone Rodney at home, pleading for work, and once every six months or so the promoter would oblige but the relationship became strained. Welcome also wondered why Mzi wasn't doing more to promote his cause.

Finally, after one spell of almost a year without work, a rival Mdantsane boxing agent told Welcome that if he signed with Don King he could get him a world-title shot. Mzi said no. Welcome 'defied' him and travelled to Florida to fight for the vacant IBF featherweight title, taking a pounding from an American fighter he once could have beaten in his sleep. After retiring in his corner in the tenth round he should have known it was over. But still he thirsted for one more shot at immortality. Ten months later, in October 1998, he fought at home against Steve Robinson, a former WBO world champion, and again took a licking, only this time the local judges were unnaturally generous and awarded him with a draw. Thankfully, it was all the luck he needed. He realized then, at the age of 33, still with his baby face but now with sad, sad, eyes, that there was nothing left and downed gloves. He was still estranged from his life-long mentor. 'You see, in our culture, he must defer to me, and he stopped doing that,' Mzi explained to me. 'It wasn't only those fights where I said no and he did yes. He wanted to buy a steak-house franchise in white East London, and I am a businessman, so I know what can work, and I said no, a black man owning a steak house in a white area won't work yet. Better to start here in Mdantsane where you have a big name, but he did what he wanted and I was right. So it's up to him – he must come to me to say sorry because I am the older man.' Welcome tried his hand at various other ventures before settling on a career as a small-time boxing trainer, manager and promoter, producing the kind of fighters unlikely to make the leap over the ocean.

Bungu's career also ended in disappointment, but at least he seemed to know how to deal with it. Ever since I wrote a biography of Naseem Hamed in 1996, Bungu and Mzi had been telling me that they had the beating of the Prince, and we would argue on this point. Bungu had never before fought at featherweight, went thirteen months without a fight as he waited for Berman to finalize the deal, and at the age of 32 was showing signs of decline, but still he 'knew' he would do it. They fought in London in March 2000 and Bungu's confidence dissipated when his left hook bounced off Hamed's chin without effect, and it was drained when he felt the weight of Hamed's first body punch. He was knocked cold by a left in the fourth round. I hugged him afterwards, but all he could say was, 'I'm sorry, Gavin, I'm really very very sorry.' He went home to his girlfriend and two daughters and his seaside house with £300,000 in his pocket, and, for the moment, retired.

What will you do now? I wondered. He smiled, still embarrassed about his defeat. 'I always knew that my money from boxing had to keep me secure for life so I invested it wisely, and now with this big purse I can do what I want for the first time in my life. I want to help my community and my people because I came from them and they helped make me.' And what does that mean? How will you help them, I asked. 'It means I want to teach the children to box,' he said.*

---

*Sadly, however, the way it turned out was that teaching the children was not quite good enough for Vuyani. Yes, he knew all the dangers, but like most of the great, the good and the bad, he thought he could give them the slip. He wanted just one (or two, or three) last grasps at glory and so, in 2002, at the age of 35, he fought again, getting soundly outboxed by fellow South African Lehlohonolo Ledwaba.

10

GETTING REAL WITH BABY JAKE

Bethnal Green, London, 12 June 1994. 'Yeah, you can
'elp me, mate,' a man with a number-one haircut, two
tattoos on his neck and a third on his cheek says. He
beckons me closer to his head-butt zone. 'Know wha' I
want? I want *you* to gimme your money right now,
all-of-i', or I'll fuckin' 'it you.'

It's just past midnight and I am about to take the last
tube home. The station seems deserted except for the
pair of us. He has pulled his fist in a telegraphed
gesture that would not serve him well at Bethnal
Green's York Hall, where I've just watched Baby Jake
Matlala destroy some East End dreams. 'You go' money
on you, innit? So 'and it over. I mean it, mate. I'll
fuckin' 'it you. I'll fuck you up.'

For a microsecond I'm frozen by that adrenaline rush
that comes from alarm, but after momentarily contemplating applying the first-strike principle, I start
laughing because the situation suddenly seems extraordinarily funny. Not just that he's standing below me
on the escalator – not the smartest point to launch an
attack or absorb a counter – nor that the threat of a fist

seems a little lacking compared with the knifemen of Bree Street or the assassins of the CCB or the interrogators of John Vorster Square. The real hilarity is in the appearance behind the demand – my appearance, I mean. It crosses my consciousness that I must appear a pretty pathetic specimen for him to assume that the threat of a mere punch, from such a precarious position, should make me want to hand over my wallet. I try to look at myself from his position, and I can sort of see his perspective: let's just say that as boxing men go, I'm not exactly the hardest-looking specimen.

The would-be hitter is a bit taken aback, perhaps astonished that I haven't taken his threat the way it was intended. The genuine enthusiasm of my laughter seems to unsettle him and he mutters, 'Wha's the fuckin' joke, mate, wha's the fuckin' joke?' but by then I'm already moving on, pushing past him at the bottom of the escalator, walking and laughing, and he gives up and goes the opposite way.

I'd been sweating on this question of self-recognition for a while, you see. Less in the existential sense – though that too I suppose – than in the dramatic. Using my South African Equity card, I'd been conscientiously attending classes at the Actors' Centre in the West End for almost a year, and felt I was making steady progress until I ran into a television acting workshop a week after returning from the election in South Africa. We were taken the usual route from Stanislavsky to Strasberg, but this time I got it: to create a character real enough for a screen audience to suspend disbelief I had to find something of myself in that role. It had always seemed simple enough, but suddenly I realized I had no real clue of my own essence, of who I was or how I came across, even in the purely physical sense, and if I couldn't discover this, I couldn't really act.

I was pondering this question the following morning when I went off to audition for a theatrical showcase called the Casting Couch – the goal being three nights performing a ten-minute monologue at a West End theatre-pub, attended mainly by casting directors and theatrical agents. I reworked a short story by Barney Simon, a brilliant director and playwright I vaguely knew in Johannesburg. It was a piece I found deeply moving every time I read it – a white artisan telling the tale of a young girl being savaged by a pack of dogs. The accent was easy enough – I borrowed Gerrie Coetzee's plaintive monotone – but it required much more. I realized I had to find something of myself in conveying this emotion, particularly when it came to finding the real tears it demanded. Without any defined essence to draw from, I cherry-picked recent memory and settled on my father's death. The trigger worked: I was one of the chosen, and cried three nights in a row, and drew the applause I desired. But as I cycled home after the final night, I felt less certain. It was not that there was anything unacceptably profane in using my father's death as a cue, but rather that the experience of drawing from my own very real sadness and recycling it for something intrinsically unreal seemed to dilute those original emotions.

In a strangely superficial way, the man with the tattooed face at Bethnal Green tube station after the boxing match brought this home to me: obviously he'd got me wrong, but I also realized that the joke was on me – that I must have been getting myself wrong, at least when it came to the way I presented myself. Alone on the tube to Finsbury Park I thought some more about this question of image and essence. I realized I was having trouble finding the real within the layers of artifice. To throw away so lightly the few glimpses of real feeling I could mine seemed rash and even dangerous. I decided my indulgent search for dramatic reality was blunting the truth, and without that truth, acting and writing and everything else would be no more than fluff. By the time I arrived home I had resolved to suspend my fledgling acting career, perhaps for ever.

And so, on to Baby Jake Matlala, a boxer who, in so many ways, was not as he seemed. The most obvious element involved the relation between his size and his ability to fight. Officially, he's 4 foot 10, but actually even less and his opponents always outweighed him. He is not a dwarf but rather a truly tiny man – comically small, with a big, bald head and an old man's face that makes people laugh, and he seems to appreciate the joke. And often the joke has been on his opponents.

Earlier that June evening I'd watched him doing the business against the Ghanaian-born, East London-based Commonwealth champion Francis Ampofu, in defence of his WBO world flyweight title. Jake was not really a flyweight. His natural fighting weight was straw weight, two divisions lighter, while Ampofu was really a natural bantamweight, two divisions heavier, so by fight time the Londoner enjoyed an edge of around 13 pounds – a massive amount for boxers of that size. Ampofu was several inches taller with much broader shoulders, bigger arms and stronger legs, and when I saw them together the size gap looked frightening. But Jake nipped inside his opponent's hooks, absorbed a whopping head butt, and then got to work peppering the head and body with hundreds of light but impeccably timed punches. At the end of nine rounds the bigger, younger man had taken a comprehensive battering – down once, wobbling all over the place and no longer able to defend himself, until his compassionate corner pulled him out.

When we chatted in his changing room I asked Jake whether he'd followed a pre-conceived plan. 'It's always the same,' he said, with his disarming grin. 'They come out fast; I start slow, but with every round I step up the pace and the punishment, until I'm hitting them as hard as I can and as often as I can move my arms, and because I'm so short I concentrate on the body and I just work it over mercilessly until their resistance is gone.' He was indeed a merciless fighter and he was still beaming when he mentioned this absence of mercy, but the words and the face just didn't seem to fit, and here lay a second discordant note: it was hard to find the source of this brutality.

With most elite-level boxers I've known, I haven't had to look too hard for too long. Very occasionally I have encountered someone like Sheffield's world cruiserweight champion Johnny Nelson, who started as a timid coward and used boxing to develop confidence and self-respect, but many more at that level start as bullies – boys who just love to fight, to dominate and to hurt – and contrary to the myth that behind every bully is a coward, they are usually as brave as they come. Now and then boxers like Sugarboy Malinga find their early street brawling, alpha-male instincts absorbed by the nature of their profession and by maturity, but they are rarer than we like to think. Others are able to maintain an illusion, often to themselves too, that they are tomcat tigers inside the ring and warm-milk pussy-cats outside of it. They convincingly brandish the cliché about leaving their work at the office thanks very much, but I have learnt to remain sceptical, and often my doubts are confirmed by a rumour of a battered wife, a club brawl, a road-rage assault.

The truth is that boxers are men who come from violence and continue to live on the edge of violence through their work, dipping in and out every day they train, and many find it difficult to leave it there. Boxing demands the capacity to work without mercy to the point of victory or defeat. The best fighters are men driven to excel in a milieu that demands the constant giving and taking of exhaustion and hurt on a level that most of us never experience. It requires denial of the real – pain, weakness, fear, inferiority, deterioration – and their replacement with the opposite convictions. We don't blink if we hear a tennis player saying she has little hope of pulling off an upset, but with a boxer such talk is unacceptable. We expect him to believe he'll win because without that conviction, no matter how unrealistic, he can't really be expected to fight in the way we want. It is not a game that encourages self-questioning introspection.

And it is not only the boxers who are self-deluders. We, the people who make a living writing about this odd sport, are also quite a blinkered lot. We are not like writers on, say, football, rugby, tennis, golf or athletics; their sports are mainstream, establishment, universally accepted. Ours is different. It may still be capable of drawing the millions through terrestrial television ratings but it is under the hammer. Sooner or later most of us get to see a boxer or two killed while we're feeding on the sport from ringside, and anyway we know that it's a profession based on a pernicious paradox: demanding the extremes of health and yet at the same time damaging it in a way that leaves a permanent mark – brain damage, of course, but also kidney damage, eye damage, nasal damage, hand damage. Its morality is dubious – amoral doesn't quite cover it – and if we are to be honest the best defence we can offer is that, well, there are worse things in the world and better candidates for banning. Boxing is also more nakedly corrupt, venal and sleazy than 'real' sports, and its multiplicity of titles and control bodies makes it that much more diffuse and confusing. So it is hardly surprising that in the West at least boxing is now regarded as a fringe pursuit, and its writers fall into the same category. We respond like most people under fire and on the fringe, by clinging on to our sport with righteous fury, keeping our fights within the family and defending the family against outsiders.

This makes our relationship with the protagonists different from those in other sports. Most of us don't come from the same place as the boxers, and if we do, we've moved on. We're usually middle-class voyeurs who seldom hang out much with fighting men outside our working hours or working trips. We don't know them quite as well as we might like to think, but in subtle ways we crave their approval and feed off their largesse. We like to think of them as not just a brave breed but a noble one too, and therefore we resist asking them too many questions about their worth as people, rather than just as fighters, because we really know, or should know, that so many of the best fighting men get off on hurting and dominating and are prepared to take some hurt to achieve it, which is an integral part of what makes them so good at what they do. We can all cite this or that exception – enough to make an argument, but not quite enough to win it.

Jacob Matlala was certainly one of those I always cited as the exception that disproved the rule. He was my favourite example, and I really believed it because while he talked of being 'merciless' and of 'dishing out punishment' and boxed accordingly, I couldn't work out its source. It seemed out of kilter with everything else I knew about him as a human being. I was so confident in this view that I probed a bit. I tried out the notion that perhaps there was a little Napoleon lurking behind that perpetual smile, but Jake was so easy about his size; he never took offence. Was it always like this? I once inquired when chatting with him at his small four-roomed home in Meadowlands, Soweto. A bit of a scrapper at school, maybe? 'No, *never*. I never had a single fight at school or in any other place outside the ring,' he said, making him perhaps the only boxer in the world who could make that claim or even would want to. 'I didn't even come close to it because even before I was well known, nobody picked on me. Everybody just seemed to like me.' You couldn't help it, really. He was just so amiable and relaxed, and he was kind and considerate too. That evening, after I said goodbye, he was worried about my safety in driving home from Soweto, so he insisted on escorting me back to Johannesburg and then made the point of phoning to make sure I'd arrived home safely.

He was the only child of a Soweto family who were certainly poor by non-African standards, but not desperately so. His father was a driver, his mother a cook in a canteen, and they both sold fruit and vegetables on the side. 'I was an only child and they looked after their money so we had enough to get by,' he said. 'We certainly always had food on the table and I never thought of us as poor, but most of all I always thought of the three of us as a very stable family.' So his route into boxing was not motivated by that familiar fighting urge to escape deprivation, or by the lack of viable alternatives. He was top of his class in school and after matriculating eventually went on to graduate with a business diploma at Wits University and then a BComm. degree at the University of South Africa, placing him among the academic elite of black South African society, and along the way he acquired an impressive portfolio of shares and businesses.

Jake took to the game as a 10-year-old, 'just for fun', discovered he had a talent, and pressed on with it, enjoying himself thoroughly. He claimed he had 199 amateur fights, losing only one, before deciding he was good enough to use it for making a bit extra on the side. He chose as his trainer a former boxer, Theo Mthembu, who had tutored some of the finest black professionals the country has known. Theo once told me that Jake was by no means the most naturally blessed boxer he'd trained, but he was certainly the most dedicated. Jake settled into a lifestyle that he maintained six days a week over the next twenty-two years: up at 5.30 a.m. for his five-mile run, two hours a day in the gym, never smoking or drinking, always leaving parties early. At the age of 18 he won his first fight on points, then waited sixteen months for his second, which he lost on points. After seven more wins Theo decided he was ready to conquer the world, and began his quest in the hostile territory of Mdantsane, near East London, where he relieved the local hero, Mveleli Luzipho, of his South African title. With his size and his smile and his swarming style Baby Jake instantly achieved the kind of national name recognition that other little boxers could only dream of. Foreign opponents were imported and there was talk of world titles, but Jake had to wait.

Luzipho beat him in the return, and when they fought for the third time two years later the Mdantsane man was given a hometown nod. Jake then became the 'people's champion' but even this status was short-lived. Vuyani 'Wonderboy' Nene, a brilliant young boxer from Uitenhage near Port Elizabeth, arrived and obliterated both Luzipho and Matlala from the national scene. Jake tried again, and then again, and then again, but every time Nene was just too good. In their third fight Jake gave up in the eighth round, in their fourth he barely won a round.

Nene had the speed, reflexes and power to be one of the greats of South African boxing but he could never acquire the habits of discipline.* Jake, in contrast, pressed on, maintaining his daily routine even when there was no fight on the horizon, showing

---

*I once watched Nene's 'cousin-brother' manager, Alfred, trying to work a boxer's corner while drunk. I visited Nene's 'gym', which was really a male migrant-workers' hostel room no bigger than a small classroom, with only candles for light and precious little equipment. I talked to the boxer's mates who told me of their hero's disdain for training and his taste for dagga, and I marvelled that he ever made it so far. Nene eventually forfeited his national light flyweight title by coming in overweight, after which Berman secured him a shot at the IBF world super flyweight title – two divisions higher. Wonderboy didn't bother to train, convinced it would be another broken promise, but Berman's word held. An unfit Nene retired in his corner at the end of the third round, and was never the same again.

incremental improvement and eventually regaining his South African title. In 1991, shortly before his thirtieth birthday, his promoter Mike Segal gave him one of those take-it-or-leave-it offers. Ireland's Dave McAuley needed a last-minute opponent for his fifth defence of his IBF world flyweight title, did he want it? It meant travelling to Belfast for his first time outside of South Africa and moving up one in weight to take on a world champion with advantages of nine inches in height, ten in reach and an 11-pound weight edge by the time they stepped into the ring. Jake was knocked out in the tenth round, blaming this setback on Mthembu's mistimed signal to rise at the count of eight. Still, he said, it was a learning experience and his capacity to learn after twelve professional years was remarkable. The new Jake drew even deeper on his Promethean work ethic, pumping weights to build his strength and power, tucking his chin down even tighter and holding his gloves higher, working tirelessly on learning how to bob and weave his way inside and how to cut off the ring to corner an opponent and putting more focus on improving his accuracy and timing. The transition was remarkable.

Three weeks before I left South Africa, Jake travelled to Glasgow to challenge for the WBO version of the world flyweight title against the quick-footed local favourite Pat Clinton, who'd won 20 out of 21, was making the second title defence and was a favourite of the promoter Barry Hearn. Once again the size discrepancy looked ridiculous but Clinton struggled to make the weight and Jake had improved so much that after his customary slow start he delivered a brutally one-sided battering, working his way under Clinton's southpaw right jab and finding the Scotsman's body until he was finished. Clinton went down four times and remained on the canvas for five minutes.*

When Jake returned I noticed a different side to his personality – still charming and courteous but there was a steely edge I hadn't previously encountered. Now that he'd arrived Jake knew how to exploit his potential. Unlike most boxers he had a realistic view of what he was worth and he knew how to bargain for it. He was prepared to play hardball with his promoters and sponsors and with the advertising executives, and in the end most bowed to his demands. He was paid R37,000 (£8,000 at the time) to fight Clinton, but said that from then he would no longer accept anything less than £30,000, even if it meant never fighting in South Africa again. He didn't always get it, but he came close.

A week before I left South Africa the *Sunday Times* asked me to write a profile on Jake with a picture of him squaring off with the national heavyweight champion Corrie Sanders. Both boxers agreed. Jake said he would meet us in central Johannesburg, but Corrie didn't pitch up. I phoned Jake to rearrange it. 'Sure,' he said. 'But this time we'll do things my way. Last time I went out of my way to meet him and he didn't arrive. Now it's his turn. If Corrie wants his picture in the paper he must come to my house in Soweto.' Corrie had never been to Soweto before but there was no argument and when we made it to Matlala's cramped little house he was deemed to have passed Jake's respect test and was given a warm embrace by the boxer. I stood in the corner and watched while this huge white Afrikaner ex-cop in his skimpy shorts and

---

*Soon after, Clinton developed tinnitus in his ears, caused by boxing, and he ended up deaf.

451

Dr Scholl sandals was made to feel completely relaxed by little Jake, who was sitting back on the sofa in his designer tracksuit, with his three-year-old-son, Tsepo, on his lap, while his gospel-singing wife Mapule served an elaborate tea. When their chat was over Jake got up and gave us an escort back to Johannesburg. Perhaps I was reading too much into it, but I found something hopefully prescient in this moment: the self-assured little African man saying to the worried white giant, 'Look, we've done it your way and it didn't work out; now we're going to do it my way, on my terms, in my place and time', and the white man going along with this because he had no alternative, overcoming his fears about crossing over to the other side, and finding he was welcome.

With each title defence Jake's status grew, and he took over Dingaan Thobela's faded mantle as the country's most prominent cross-over sports star – one of the few who could bridge the racial divide. He moved to a large house in Johannesburg South but even then he remained a vital part of life in Soweto and continued to train in his own 15 by 60 foot gym, with no ring, no air-conditioning, no changing room, no shower and usually about twenty-five boxers squeezed in.* The gesture was hugely appreciated and every time you saw him in Soweto he was mobbed. 'Baby Jake's their hero,' said Theo Mthembu. 'He has his name painted on the side of the car so they would never carjack Baby Jake.'

He also worked hard on appealing to whites. He took out a share in a firm specializing in celebrity after-dinner appearances and motivational talks, and

*Towards the end of his career this was re-equipped and given a makeover by his sponsors and the government.

became a regular on this circuit, using his self-deprecating wit, easy charm and ability to switch from English to Afrikaans to woo his audiences, and they loved him for it. Sometimes he went well beyond the call of duty in his bid to come across as all things to all people. When the 1994 general election was called he was quoted as saying he would vote for Nelson Mandela's ANC on the national list, and F.W. de Klerk's National Party on the regional list. I didn't believe for a moment that a Soweto man as astute as Jake would really be giving half his backing to the party of apartheid and thought of it as a misguided attempt at currying favour. Still, Nelson Mandela never seemed to hold it against him and made it clear Jake was his favourite boxer, inviting him to his home on several occasions and giving him an extra-warm embrace whenever they met.

But South Africans can be fickle when it comes to fame. Jake would not be alone in the bittersweet discovery that some little sins produce sustained abuse while other larger ones are ignored because they are deemed to lack public resonance.

Early in 1995 I returned to South Africa for my fifth long visit since leaving less than two years earlier. We had a feisty, funny and already fiercely determined new daughter, Caitlin. I adored her and was delighted with the opportunity to show her off to my friends and family during our holiday tour of the country. I also had a Jacob Matlala fight to watch and a few political stories to cover. But the prime formal purpose was a *Playboy* commission to uncover one of the thousands of unsolved scandals from the apartheid era, involving the suicide of an apartheid cabinet minister eight years earlier.

John Wiley – a former Oxford cricket blue who opposed the idea of blacks on the beaches, in his church or in parliament – had cultivated the dual image of an incorrigible Lothario and a moral-majority crusader, calling for the castration of rapists, the return of the cat-o'-nine-tails and a ban on the 'most unhealthy' practice of men embracing on the sports field. But when he blew his brains out in 1987, using his son's pistol, there was a top-level clampdown, involving death threats, pressure on editors and frenzied intelligence service intervention, in order to curtail speculation on why he took his life. The clue came from the suicide or murder of his young friend David Allen, a gung-ho navy diver from Port Elizabeth, six weeks earlier. Allen had just been arrested for sexually assaulting two coloured teenage boys. Karen – my sister – and I traced Detective Sergeant Mark Minnie, the policeman who'd made the arrest, and he told us he had resigned from the force after death threats, intelligence service obstruction and direct government intervention. Allen, he said, admitted to him he was part of an elite paedophile ring with connections all over South Africa and London, which included three apartheid cabinet ministers, one of them Wiley. Minnie, whose story was backed up by several other sources, told us the ring used Bird Island, twenty miles off the Port Elizabeth coast, for parties involving rent boys. They were flown to the island by military helicopters, before being buggered and sometimes beaten up. Wiley, it appeared, killed himself because he feared his links with this ring were about to be exposed.

But my prime interest shifted to another apartheid-era cabinet minister, General Magnus Malan, the former military chief and 'defence' minister who was also a ringside regular. Every time I returned to South Africa I thought of how my friend David Webster would have relished working to make it a better place, and I found it hard to stomach the idea that the military men who murdered him could walk around with impunity. I assisted the attorney general with his investigation of David's assassin, Lieutenant Ferdie Barnard (later convicted of murder and jailed for life), but it niggled my sense of justice that Barnard's military overseers walked free. The man who personified their code was Malan. It was under his umbrella that men like Barnard did their dirty work. Forgiving and forgetting has never been my strongest point, and I wanted to see him going down.

I found allegations regarding Malan's dealings with Allen popping up all over the place, and eventually dug up an apartheid-era parliamentary question where he had acknowledged spending a couple of days on Bird Island in 1986. Others on the trip included Allen, Wiley and another friend of Allen's, the finance minister Barend du Plessis, and they were flown there by military helicopter at government expense. The purpose, Malan had claimed, was 'official business' but he acknowledged he had taken along his rod and tackle for some recreation, 'because when the minister of defence carries out a task he does it quickly'. I phoned Malan at his home and began to question him about his relationship with Allen. Taken by surprise and unaccustomed to interrogation he spluttered indignantly that, yes, he'd been aware of Allen's paedophilia at the time, but what of it? 'The next thing you'll ask is whether *I* was involved in paedophile activities,' he muttered. I left it there, and my story in *Playboy* and the subsequent South African media excitement over the details did the rest.

The story was wrapped and I flew from Cape Town to Johannesburg, feeling vindictively satisfied. The day I arrived I attended a dinner where Baby Jake Matlala was a guest of honour. Jake was to defend his WBO title for the fourth time five days later – against his toughest-ever opponent, a powerful and skilful Mexican called Alberto Jiminez, who was rated as one of the best little men in the world. When I saw Jake I was concerned by his appearance. His face looked drained, his smile was forced, he was walking slowly and seemed to be in pain. He told me that three weeks earlier he had been rushed to hospital after collapsing with 'terrible stomach cramps'. The diagnosis showed he had a severe intestinal infection that required imme-diate surgery. I was amazed Jake was even considering going ahead with the fight, but he said he was under pressure from his promoter and had been told he would be stripped of his title unless he fought. 'We'll just have to see how it goes,' he said weakly. 'I'm still not a hundred per cent and it's taken quite a bit out of me, but I'll take my chances and I'm sure I'll be OK.'

When we watch a fight on television we don't expect to see some intrepid cameraman entering the cham-pion's lavatory for a first-hand view, and we wouldn't want it either; it's more information than we need. We prefer the humdrummingly familiar pictures from space: the warm-ups, the soundbites, the histrionic announcements, the anthems, the smoke, the mirrors. These are the trappings of the ersatz gladiatorial arena of modern boxing, but for the young men at the busi-ness end of those shiny gloves, there's a far dirtier reality about what they do and it plays on their minds as the moment draws close. Pride of place goes to that toilet – there are few more vital determinants of a boxer's pre-fight well-being. I would guess that more fights are lost because a boxer was unable to get in that final dump after thirty hours of post-weigh-in carbo-loading (or because his nerves made him puke or gave him the runs) than through any other niggling ailment. It's integral to the lexicon of the game – boxers make their opponents 'shit off', they throw 'sickening' body blows, they 'beat the shit' out of each other – and there's a reality behind it. In the changing room, the ring and back again, mention of excreta is not always metaphorical. To enter the ring knowing you have a severe problem in this area – that for weeks you've been busting your gut with severe colitis and need an operation to begin the cure – seemed to me an act of folly.

And yet this was not immediately apparent. Once again Jake was dwarfed and the gap in power and strength looked prohibitive, so I was delighted to see Jake outboxing Jiminez. But when he returned to his corner at the end of the seventh round he complained of acute abdominal pains. He wanted out but Theo Mthembu persuaded him to give it one last try. The American referee came over, saw that Jake was in agony, and said: 'Son, if I notice you having the slightest problem, I'm stopping the fight.' I know a bit about stomach pain and my own approach is to monopolize the toilet and groan. Performing publicly in that kind of condition is an act of courage well beyond my resources. When performing involves being whacked in the stomach with the kind of punches that would put a normal man in hospital, and you still get into the ring, guts hardly covers it. And when you can take it no more and yet you still obey your trainer and answer the bell, we're talking heroic insanity. Jake held it together magnificently for as long as he could, jamming Jiminez's head back on his shoulders, until at the end of the round an intense wave of sickening stomach pain doubled him over, and he dropped down on one knee, hoping it would pass. The referee took one look and stopped the fight. 'I couldn't understand why he did that,' Jake said to me afterwards. 'I'm sure I could have come back to win, despite all that pain.'

But the South African press was having none of it. They turned on Jake, chewed on him and spat him out in disgust. He was a 'crybaby', a 'quitter', a 'chicken' and worst of all, considering what he'd been through, a 'gutless' loser. We were reminded how he had once shown the dog against Wonderboy Nene, and how about when he didn't get up in time against McAuley? Definitely something missing beneath the left tit. Retire, Jake, you sad old man, you let us down, they said. But Jake seemed utterly unaffected by it all. He had such a remarkably strong sense of self that it just didn't get to him. He smiled as infectiously as ever when I asked him, and said, 'Look, Gavin, don't worry about me, I accept criticism and I learn from it, and if the criticism is wrong then it's up to me to prove it wrong. I'll be back to win another world title, and then all this will be forgotten.'

When I flew back to London I thought a bit about the contrast between the two slapheads I'd encountered during my visit. Here was Jake, the apparently good little man, walking tall after being pilloried for a workplace crime he didn't commit – accused of cowardice when his sin was to take his body to the outer limits of physical courage. And there was Magnus, the big bad man, the apartheid general, brought low, I liked to think, by the innuendo of his own ill-chosen words after escaping any serious condemnation for running a machine that massacred thousands of southern Africans. I forgot about Magnus after that, but in time Jake too would have his turn at getting away with it.

For the moment, though, he was as good as his word. An observer at the Jiminez fight was another of Barry Hearn's protégés, Paul Weir, the WBO light flyweight champion who had also once held the straw-weight crown. They decided Jake was a soft enough touch with the kind of international name recognition Weir needed. So Jake dropped down a weight division and travelled to Glasgow to pick up his second 'world' title. But it was an unsatisfactory affair – a fifth-round technical decision victory, after the verdict went to the scorecards because of a tiny cut over Weir's eye caused by what the referee claimed was an accidental clash of heads but was in fact a five-punch combination.

Weir felt unlucky and had another try, in Liverpool in April 1996. I visited Jake in his changing room and found him as smiley and warm as ever. This fight was a little formality, he said. His real interest was Michael Carbajal, the Mexican American who was a three-time world champion and the world's highest-earning little boxer. I smiled politely, thinking that the chances of Jake getting a fight with Carbajal, let along beating him, were not even worth considering, and went off to watch the pipes and drums, played by a trio of Scousers in kilt and sporran and traditional weapons, followed by the Cape Town boxer Gary Murray, who was raised in Renfrew near Glasgow, yelling away in his Scots burr for his friend Jake, with his head covered in a Nelson Mandela latex mask.

This time Weir took Matlala extremely seriously, building his upper body through weight training while Jake looked even smaller, coming in, fully clothed, at a quarter of a pound over the 105-pound straw-weight limit. Weir tested his new-found power but seldom connected cleanly, while Jake pit-a-patted away with his non-stop tattoo, with each blow landing exactly as and where intended, most to the body but now and then reaching up six inches to clip the nose, eyes and mouth. Weir would reach with a right, Jake would slip it and catch the Scotsman with one of his own, its power doubled by Weir's forward momentum. In the tenth Jake decided it was time to close the show and landed six times in a row on Weir's face and head to drop him for a nine count. The Scotsman rose with his eyes betraying desperate, powerless victimhood. I've seen boxers show compassion when they have an opponent in that position – a step back and a pleading request for the referee to end it, but not Jake. He pounced, battering Weir's unprotected head with four perfectly placed head shots, and the former champion rolled over and remained prone for nearly ten minutes, before rising slowly and being escorted to hospital.*

'Hey! Gavin,' a beaming Jake called as I returned to his changing room. 'Man! I'm feeling so-o-o good. Haai! I did my job. I love to show that boxing is fun, that it's an art, that you don't need to get hurt.'

After their first Glasgow fight I missed the last

*He too was never quite the same again, and lost to men he once could have handled with ease.

train and without any accommodation plans ended up wandering the post-apocalyptic Saturday night streets of Britain's most unhealthy and violent city, hugging the shadows and watching furtively as little men produced puddles of blood by kicking the heads of other little men, while junkies spiked up in full view of bored cops, or shouted obscenities at me just because I was there, or vomited at my feet, until I could take no more and sat in the cold under a street light, waiting for the station gates to open, reading an appropriately bleak Raymond Carver short story while fretting that I was about to miss Caitlin's first birthday party. I didn't fancy a similar experience in Liverpool and asked Jake for a lift to the bus station. He sat next to me in the back, still smiling with delight, now and then holding my knee or touching my arm while telling me what he was going to do when he got hold of Carbajal, and as I hugged him goodbye I thought, *Yeah, couldn't happen to a nicer bloke.*

I made my way to the back of the coach in the hope of an uninterrupted night's rest and stretched out my legs as the seats filled. The engine coughed into action, the doors steamed shut and I closed my eyes, but just as we began to move I heard an insistent, angry banging on the side of the coach. The doors hissed open again and in stepped a pair of enormous, well-oiled, skin-headed lads with south London accents and they staggered their way to join me in the back. They were drinking Jack Daniel's but smelled of lager, and had all the hallmarks of the barking and burping jokers you find in squads of young males on the make, but this pair also carried an air of menace about them. I immediately concluded the wisest course was one of least resistance and pretended to fall asleep, as did just about everybody else on the bus. With the night still young, they started taking the piss out of whoever seemed vulnerable. After a few barks and bites they settled on an Ethiopian man who, fortunately, seemed oblivious to their malice and took everything straight, offering a convincing impression of being delighted by their interest, until, after half an hour, they grew bored and told him to fuck off.

Eventually the darkness, the motion of the bus and the Jack Daniel's lulled them into a different mood and they started talking quietly about more serious matters. They were AWOL squaddies on their way back to London, after which they planned to take off to France and then Thailand. But before leaving they had a few homegrown matters they needed to take care of: assaults, murders, stuff like that. The slightly smaller, uglier, stupider one had it in for a fellow he thought was messing with his former squeeze. He became morose over this and turned to his mate for advice. Soon they arrived at a plan. The rival needed to be taken out, of that there was no question. But how? They worked out the logistics as if it was a training exercise. The aggrieved squaddie would return incognito from Europe, garrotte the girl-messer to death, ''Cause garrotting leaves fewer clues, know what I mean?' and then return to his mate for some more drinking, fighting and carousing. Within about an hour they had it down to the intricate details: sorted.

They were now in a jolly mood, their malice dissipating, and they got to talking about boxing, which, it emerged, was their particular passion. Mike Tyson was their number-one hero and they competed with each other naming his opponents and chanting his praises, while expressing outrage about his trial and conviction for rape. They were particularly incensed about the recent allegations of his parole violations in a strip club. What a man! What a fucking fighter! 'Hey, hey, remember that Biggs fight,' said the thick one. 'Mike said he made him squeak like a woman,' and they laughed at the thought of making a man squeak, or a woman for that matter. The thick one felt the need to recreate the moment for his friend and stood up, knocking me without specific intent. I was forced to wake up when he put a paw on my shoulder, his face in front of mine, and amid a blast of stale whisky breath, shouted, 'Sorry, mate, huh-huh, just doing a Mike Tyson on him,' and just in case I missed the point, he did a slow motion version on me.

I decided to take the Ethiopian approach – complete oblivion to all that preceded this moment, and a fulsome appreciation of all they had to say or do. 'So what the fuck you doing in Liverpool, mate?' the larger, smarter one asked in a tone that was challenging rather than outright aggressive. I told him I had just been covering the Matlala–Weir fight. 'Baby Jake!' he barked. 'Seen his poster, mate. Who else d'you interview?' I said I was going home to complete a book on Naseem Hamed, and they were immensely impressed. They liked the swaggering little Prince. So what did I think of the Tyson rape thing? Innocent as they come, I lied. 'What about Tyson *v.* Lewis, mate?' said the thick one. 'Lewis will take him out,' I said, feeling more confident now. We argued that point but by then I knew it was OK. I was in, a fellow traveller. For the next five hours we talked boxing, women (theirs), and more boxing and by the end of the trip my back was well slapped and we were the best of chums, or so they thought. We arrived at Victoria bus station early on Sunday morning and said our effusive goodbyes.

Not long after that I was back in South Africa with the idea of finding out why it was that the apartheid South African equivalents of my garrotting chums so badly wanted to get their way with me. It was not just a narcissistic exercise: I wanted to test the lofty freedom-of-information guarantees in the new South African constitution. As I saw it, the standard was set in East Germany where the fall of the Wall enabled you to wander into the Stasi offices, draw your files and find out who'd been ratting on you. In South Africa, there were plenty of files to be drawn* but unlike Germany and more like Chile the old order had not entirely collapsed. It retained control over the military and a stake in the police and intelligence services. There was also another consideration: from my decade in the ANC underground, I had become aware of several apartheid spies who had re-emerged as ANC MPs, suggesting there were powerful forces in the new order who could be compromised by too much transparency.

My first stop seemed to confirm this reticence. When my brother, acting as my solicitor, applied to the National Intelligence Agency (South Africa's CIA), a senior, ANC-linked official told him my quest was not in the state's interest, and that the files might contain 'harmful information such as who had been sleeping with whom at the time'. As I had a fair memory of my small contribution to this score, I pressed on, eventually reaching the Director General Mo Shaik – a man I'd come across in the struggle days – at his

---

*A state document, leaked to me, stated that in 1990 the security police alone held files on 314,000 people.

Pretoria office. But by then the panic had subsided, replaced by obfuscation. 'Unfortunately, a substantial number of documents were destroyed,' he said, adding he was 'confident' my lot were 'in that batch'. Later, he wrote to tell me his agency was 'giving the matter the urgent attention it deserves'. No more was heard.

Next up was the former security police, and this time the result seemed encouraging, initially anyway. The minister involved, Sydney Mufamadi, had been a close 'comrade' – we had worked together for two years in an underground leadership cell – and although we'd subsequently had our differences, he immediately ordered the police commissioner to cough up. As a result, the manager of the police legal department supplied me with a computer file comprising edited versions of eighty-two reports on me from 1977 (my last year in secondary school) to 1985. All other files had been destroyed, the manager said, offering the straightfaced excuse that 'after 1990 the approach of the security police ceased to be ideological, so information on banned organizations and their members became irrelevant'. Still, these bowdlerized offerings provided a taste of the paranoia of the apartheid spooks, and left me with the queasy feeling of having been watched far longer than I'd imagined. Sixteen reports covered my stay in Texas as an exchange student and many more covered my university years. Some reports suggested the use of electronic and photographic surveillance, while spies supplied several accounts, usually comically inaccurate.

My final stop was the hard nut, military intelligence, the most powerful and savage agency in the late apartheid days, and the most obdurate since. Its agents

were responsible for hundreds of political assassinations as well as actively fomenting, sponsoring and
arming what they grotesquely termed 'black on black'
violence. Unlike the police, they were 'discouraged'
from opening up to Archbishop Tutu's Truth and
Reconciliation Commission and were allowed to get
away with this because of a pre-election pact between
Mandela and the generals to keep the peace. My
request was handed to a black army major who said
the computerized information held on me could not
be released without the minister's sayso. The minister,
Joe Modise, had been appointed on the recommen-
dation of the military so it was hardly surprising that
he refused. The major then suggested my only option
was to apply to the state attorney's office, and after
some vacillation an obsequious young legal jobsworth, Ben Minaar, suggested a meeting in Pretoria,
adding that I was being given permission to 'peruse'
the military intelligence files on me but not to take
them home because 'these documentation [sic] are
classified'. I prepared myself for an enlightening
read.

When I arrived Minaar pointed guiltily at a 6 foot 7
mortician from central casting, who extended a bone-
crusher hand the size of a bunch of bananas and
delivered a malign squeeze that was something other
than welcoming. More like, *I'm in charge here, boy, and
you're overdue for a bit of pain to help you get the point*.
No introduction, merely a sneer: 'Had any *perrrsonal*
experience of crime and violence since returning to this
new South Africa of *yourrrs*?' (Subtext: 'So this is what
you were fighting for?') I informed him that a friend's
Mini, which I had borrowed, was nicked in Johannesburg the previous day. He pursed his pencil-moustache

lip before responding with a knowing smirk. Minaar, the ingratiating jobsworth, then sat me down for a hand-wringing performance. 'Um, they've got scores of computer files on you, but it would be so time-consuming.' I reminded him of his previous commitment and he looked with due deference in the direction of the mortician who stamped his authority on proceedings. 'How do I know you are who you say you are? You *say* you're Gavin Evans but for all I know you *could* be Hannes Smit' (a 60-something Namibian newspaper editor).

'Are you seriously pursuing this point?' I asked, offering my identity document.

He waved it away: 'Just *making* a point.'

'I didn't catch your name.'

'Willem Adriaan van Deventer: brigadier.'

It sounded ominously familiar. 'Military Intelligence by any chance?'

'Ja, Military Intelligence and working directly in the office of the minister of defence, Mr Joe Modise,' he replied, giving me that sneer again.

Minaar changed tack. 'Perhaps you could give the brigadier more specific questions to narrow our search.' The mortician, however, was unaccustomed to interrogation. 'Hold it: I foresee problems. First, we in MI destroyed certain files in 1993. Second, there's legal complications.' I interjected; reminding him these had been resolved. 'Listen,' he continued, 'if we let you see those files, you may ascertain who was supplying this information on you, which could lead to criminal charges against members of the Defence Force – and we wouldn't want that.' Before I could say, 'Speak for yourself,' he completed his monologue with evident relish. 'Anyway, *Misterrr* Evans, the final decision on this matter rests with the minister of defence, and *I* report directly to *heeem*.'

A squirming Minaar suggested another meeting, a month later, but as a last sop he handed over a military file packed with 145 pages of press clippings on me (some of my own writings, others on me from MI publications and the mainstream press). The mortician hovered over me and began turning the pages quickly, until, noticing the source of his concern, I snatched away the file. Its flow continued seamlessly through to 1995, suggesting MI had continued keeping tabs on me for at least a year after South Africa's first democratic elections, when I was living in London. As I noted this down, he became flustered. 'I dunno how these got here. They shouldn't be in *this* file.' With that, he gave me another paw-paralysing squeeze, and sent me on my way.

One stolen Mini short of a ride, I walked to Pretoria station to take the train to Johannesburg. Along the way I passed Church Square, the site of a monument to Paul Kruger surrounded by smaller statues of his rifle-carrying Boer minions. As I drew closer I noticed these gargoyles were flanked by the real thing: fifteen white men in camouflage, their fingers stroking R1 rifle triggers as they watched five hundred black, militant trade union demonstrators, carrying banners like 'We demand a living wage' and 'We won't risk our lives for peanuts'. In the old days, of course, they would not have been allowed anywhere near the square, so some things had changed. But the impression that others hadn't was reinforced a month later when my solicitors received a fax from Minaar, refusing my request to see any more of the apartheid-era military files. 'We are not of the opinion your client is, in terms of the constitution, entitled to classified information,' he wrote.*

Soon after this, eight former military intelligence officers and policemen appeared before the Truth and Reconciliation Commission, pleading for amnesty for apartheid-era crimes. Staal, Slang, Chappie, Joe and the rest – still known by their rugger-playing, back-slapping, lager-glugging pet names – were all members of the CCB death-squad network that killed David Webster. In my case they applied for indemnity for attempted murder, basing their application on the commission's amnesty criteria that the crime was to be committed with a clear political purpose, ordered by their military superiors. (It had previously emerged that the strategy to 'eliminate' people like David, myself and hundreds of others was approved in principle by the State Security Council – a cabinet committee that included State President P.W. Botha and General Magnus Malan.)

The CCB officers said the 'priority list' with my name on it was put together through the compilation of 'various intelligence reports' from military intelligence and the security police. Their own intelligence officer, Captain Wouter Basson, said the computer file on me was nine inches thick. He claimed it included information that I had been 'observed' by an informer in Lusaka, working with one Hein Grosskopf (the scion of

*Not long afterwards military intelligence put together a clumsy plot to frame my old underground comrade Siphiwe Nyanda in a supposed coup attempt against Mandela. It was so crude that their intentions were instantly exposed and they were forced to resign along with their supreme military boss, with Nyanda himself emerging as the new chief of the Defence Force.

an Afrikaner establishment figure who had joined the ANC's military wing), planning bomb-planting. In fact at the time of the assassination plot I had neither met Grosskopf nor even visited Lusaka and my role in the 'armed' component of the struggle was limited to occasional recommendations of military 'targets' in coded reports. One of these targets was indeed bombed (fortunately with no-one seriously injured) and it is possible that the state was tipped off about my indirect connection through a mole at top of ANC's military pole. Not wanting to expose him, they decided to kill me and when they required a rationale they invented the Lusaka bomb-planning story, which collapsed under cross-examination. As a result of this lie and several others, each of the CCB officers was subsequently refused amnesty for the attempt on my life.*

When all this was happening Baby Jake was about to face his own moments of truth – first in the ring, and then in the moral arena. While I was busy trying to dig out old files he was being rather more successful in clearing away the impediments to his pugilistic destiny. He did this with a combination of ruthless efficiency and a huge smile. When his long-time promoter Mike Segal was unable to deliver Michael Carbajal, Jake dumped him and negotiated a deal with Rodney Berman. He then worked harder than ever before, doubling his quota of push-ups and pull-ups and sparring more rounds with greater intensity in his little Soweto gymnasium, and in July 1997 travelled to Las Vegas to take on the biggest-earning

---

*At the time of writing, Abram 'Slang' Van Zyl was launching a supreme court appeal against the commission's finding in his case.

sub-featherweight boxer in the history of the sport.*
Carbajal was a 29-year-old three-time world champion
who was eight inches taller than Jake, with jack-
hammer power and solid skills – an A-list American
fighter who appeared to be in a different league from
the 35-year-old Jake, and that was certainly the way
the bookmakers saw it, installing Carbajal as a 1–8
favourite.

One-sided it certainly was. Jake didn't bother with
the usual slow acceleration. He shifted into top gear ten
seconds after the first bell and drowned the American
in punches. Never before has one man thrown so much
leather per round: an average of 133 punches for each
180-second stanza. Carbajal was used to working at his
own pace from long range but Jake wouldn't let him,
and when he started bringing his punches up from the
body, the leathery face of the Latino hero began to mark
up until the skin opened and the blood was dripping
into both eyes. Early in the ninth round Nevada's
ringside doctor advised the referee to stop the fight and
it was over. After 1,115 punches Baby Jake had pulled
it off. 'I waited five years for this fight and I feel
fantastic,' he said. 'Carbajal is tough, sure, but I'm a

---

*Before Carbajal, little men fought their hearts out for promoters' spare
change and were ignored by the media. Carbajal changed all this by drawing
with him a huge Hispanic American following, which translated into the
first million-buck purse for his division, and set the path for the marketing
of Oscar de la Hoya. He turned professional after winning the silver medal
in the Seoul Olympics and in seventeen months was IBF world light
flyweight champion. After 28 wins he was ready for the first 'super-fight' of
his division, and unified the world title by knocking out Mexico's Humberto
Gonzalez, a boxer who had already attracted the sport's favourite epithet,
'legendary'. By the time of the Matlala fight – for the lightly regarded IBA
world title – his record stood at 45 wins out of 48, with 30 knockouts.

tough kid from Soweto.' Theo Mthembu was too old to put Matlala on his shoulders – he left that job to a younger cornerman – but he gripped the muscular thigh of the little bald man, wiped away a tear under his black-rimmed spectacles and shook his head in satisfaction. 'I feel so good for Jake,' he said. 'Everybody thought this was the end for him but, hey, he fought the fight of his whole life and look what he's done. He's succeeded in re-creating himself.' Then an idea crossed the mind of Jacob Matlala and his beam broadened. 'They'll all be tripping over themselves to get me now.'

And so they did. Every six months or so for the next few years Berman would give Jake another celebrity turn against someone not too threatening, and he would usually deliver in style, continuing until after his fortieth birthday. He finally retired with an impressive stoppage victory – his third in a row – in March 2002, with the actor Will Smith and his friend Nelson Mandela in attendance at ringside. His serious interest meanwhile shifted to his burgeoning business empire. There was Baby Jake's Diner – a fast-food chain – along with an ever-expanding range of Baby Jake products, from soft drinks to sports equipment. Nelson Mandela and everyone else who was anyone or who wanted to be someone would put him on their guest list and he was constantly in demand to front campaigns of various kinds. For instance, as a two-son family man who married his gospel-singing childhood sweetheart and had remained with her ever since, he was considered the ideal man to promote safe sex on television. People liked him and trusted him and believed him. But I was beginning to hear other stories from friends in Soweto that things were not quite as they seemed. 'He likes his women,' they would say, with a hand gesture or a wink, and I began to wonder where the truth lay. And then it all came out, or seemed to.

In January 1999 the front page lead of the country's biggest-circulation newspaper, the *Sunday Times*, screamed 'BABY JAKE IN BLACKMAIL DRAMA'. In the hands of a different subeditor it might have read, 'Baby Jake Confesses to Rape', and the truth lay somewhere between the two. The bald fact that everyone agreed on was that on 19 August 1998 Jake used a friend's Johannesburg townhouse to have sex with aspirant young singer Julia Ntla, then gave her R200, drove her home and refused to accept her subsequent calls. One question was whether the sex was consensual; another was whether it was a ruse for extortion.

Ntla's story was that she was trying to raise money for her dormant musical career and approached Jake for a loan. He agreed to meet up with her, picked her up at a local supermarket in his Audi A4 convertible and drove her to the townhouse, where he removed his pistol from the boot, and then gave her a tour of the house while discussing the music deal. When they reached the bedroom he stripped naked, which prompted Julia to remind Jake she was married and a Christian. He then placed his gun on the bedside table and pinned her to the bed, and although she tried to struggle and resist, he was too strong and raped her. Afterwards she said she felt 'embarrassed and dirty' and told Jake, 'You treated me like a prostitute.' Three days later she told her husband, Charity, and demanded an apology from Jake, which wasn't forthcoming. They contacted one Sergeant Mokwele Mailula, a policeman friend, and he contacted Jake to arrange a meeting at his office. Julia and Charity demanded R2 million as payment 'to compensate the lady what he did to her'. In Ntla's version Matlala admitted 'he was guilty and felt sorry' and wanted the matter 'settled the African way' because he didn't want to go to jail. He agreed to pay them R1 million and to attach his property as surety, and also agreed to sign a confession to the rape. The policeman agreed not to lay rape charges.

There was no dispute about the wording of the confession, which read: 'I, Jacob "Baby Jake" Matlala, pleaded guilty to allegations of rape of Julia Mnyamezeli, wife of Charity Ntla.' It goes on to state: 'I sincerely pleaded with the above-mentioned couple as witnessed by police officer Mailula on the 9th September 1998 . . . to withhold indefinitely the criminal charges against me on condition that I pay the couple an out-of-court settlement as arranged in our initial agreement bearing my signature.' Soon after Jake went to Rodney Berman and poured out his story. Berman contacted the Ntlas' attorney and managed to renegotiate the sum, settling on a R250,000 pay-off. The new agreement stated: 'Notwithstanding the allegations against Mr Matlala, this settlement is subject to your client warranting that other than the South African Police and yourself, no-one else is aware of the charge against Mr Matlala.' Berman, on behalf of Matlala, duly paid up and the Ntlas went on a wild spending spree around the country.

Jake's subsequent account was rather different. He agreed he signed the statement admitting to rape, but says he only did this because he 'was being black-mailed'. He acknowledged he had a one-afternoon fling with Julia but insisted it was entirely consensual. 'I took her to my friend's townhouse and she agreed to sleep with me.' He handed over the R200 she requested and thought that was the end of that. She phoned several times, asking for a job, but he refused. 'And still she kept on bothering me, and so I just ignored her, and then after a while she called me again to say she was going to lay a charge of rape.' He was then phoned by Sergeant Mailula who told him to come to the office and when he arrived he was confronted with the money-for-silence threat, which was given more meat when the policeman said: 'OK, if you don't agree with this I am going to lay a rape charge.' They then presented him with a pre-written statement, which he reluctantly signed as a way of avoiding the charge and the negative exposure. 'I know it wasn't a good thing to do, but at the time I wanted to avoid all that publicity because I needed to protect my family and my reputation.'

When I asked him about it a year later, he said it did not take him long to realize he had made a silly mistake. 'Five days after I signed that thing, I went along to the anti-corruption unit in Braamfontein and asked to lay charges of extortion against the three of them, but the police seemed very reluctant to do anything and I realized they were in on the whole thing. That's what I think now – that the anti-corruption police were part of the corruption.' The head of the unit later confirmed that Matlala had indeed laid a charge but said the state refused to prosecute because of 'scant evidence'. When I questioned Berman, he said: 'I'm not naive but I honestly think that whatever else went on, Jake was innocent of rape. This woman and her husband were just gold-diggers and he fell for the trap. I think I did the right thing and I'd do it again to help one of my boxers in such circumstances. The only problem was the *Sunday Times* got hold of it.' Jake reiterated this view, saying he was angry about losing his money. 'The only reason I signed was to keep it out of the papers, so when it went to the papers I should have got my money back. That's my main thing – I want to get my R250,000 back.'

Whatever the truth of the confessions and denials, they finally gave me a sense of the relation between the smiling charmer outside the ring and the man of brutality inside the ropes. This wasn't Jekyll and Hyde. There was no discord between the man who never had a fight outside the ring and the man who delighted in battering an already helpless man into unconsciousness. I've seen his kind in politics and business before, and I'm sure they prosper all over the place. For all his friendliness, kindness, humour and genuine warmth, Jake was, is, a man who likes to get his way – with money, with his reputation, with his career, certainly with his opponents and perhaps with his women too. He's a man driven to prosper, unencumbered by self-doubt, and if that requires him to be 'ruthless' and 'merciless' and to 'punish' the opposition, then so be it. He may not be a rapist, but he doesn't like taking no for an answer, and even if he has to go a few extra rounds he'll do everything he possibly can to get his way.

But the most disturbing element was that these revelations appeared to have no effect on Matlala's fortunes – the opposite in fact. The public response was a wave of sympathy for a man who made a tiny little mistake and was then caught in a web of blackmail threats by a bunch of unscrupulous chancers. There is, of course, another way of looking at it: here's a man who promoted safe sex and yet slept with a woman he barely knew, a woman who claimed he used force to get his way. He signed a statement, in front of a policeman, admitting he raped her and tried to buy his way out of it. But all this was neither here nor there for his millions of South African followers. His businesses thrived, he was invited for even more prestigious public appearances and was asked by the government to be an internal 'sports ambassador' whose role was to promote sport in the black townships with a view to future Olympic success.

I still warmed to Jake* whenever I saw him but I found the whole incident depressingly revealing about attitudes to rape in South Africa. Let's assume that Jake's version is the full truth. At best, he preferred admitting rape to the option of defending his honour in public. Even a year later he seemed far more concerned about the lost money than about the content of his confession, and sadly, there is nothing surprising in this. All available official statistics as well as academic studies and anecdotal accounts suggest that rape, which was already more common in South Africa than most other countries, has become significantly more prevalent over the last decade despite the advances of women in public life and the publicity given to women's concerns over the last decade.** To give a personal example, five of my past girlfriends and several other women friends told me they were raped, three of them by men they didn't know, but only one reported the crime to the police. They reacted in different ways – showing 'strength', trying to push it

*The last time we met, in September 2001, Jake was as friendly, courteous and warm as ever, despite my previous prying questions about his conduct in the blackmail saga.
**In one survey of young men in the Johannesburg area, nearly three in ten admitted to rape and one in ten thought gang rape was OK.

out of mind, acknowledging the hurt, going for counselling – but in each case it seemed to have a lasting effect on aspects of their self-confidence. It was and remains a big issue. But for far too many South Africans it seems to be simply accepted as a part of life: men rape; women get raped – what can you do?

And so Baby Jake, at best the philanderer who admitted rape to get out of a pickle, was allowed to prosper like never before. Two years earlier he committed the 'crime' of showing extreme courage in the face of insurmountable odds and was branded a coward. Now, if his version is to be believed, he showed moral funk in the face of a dilemma of conscience, and was hailed as a lovable old victim. Funny business, boxing. Funny place, South Africa.

11

MOVING ON

Carnival City, Brakpan, April 2001. 'We control the heavyweight champion of the world!' a raucous voice in front of me is yelling at the top of its pitch. 'South Africa owns the world heavyweight title!' The voice's owner, Terry, is on his feet trying to draw ringside attention to his message. 'I'm so glad,' he continues, getting even louder and bouncing up and down. 'Rodney and Cedric have the world champion.'

Terry, a man in late middle age, has long put me to shame when it comes to single-tracked obeisance to boxing. He named his daughter Dempsine, in honour of Jack Dempsey, and his son Driscoll, as a nod to Peerless Jim, the Welsh wizard, both of them boxers who made their mark early in the century. By his standards I'm just a fellow-travelling dilettante and this morning he takes a moment from his official praise-singing job for the South African promoters to rub this point in. More specifically he reminds me in a full-throated blast that I've been guilty of the sin of overrating the now former world champion, the sometime Briton Lennox Lewis. But his didactic message is a little more than I can take at this moment. I'm a bit shaken by the foolish demise of my favourite fighting man and so, as the crowd boos Lennox back to his changing room, I turn away, not wanting to acknowledge Terry's moment of vindication. Instead I offer a resigned wave to my friend, former ANC comrade and perennial ringside companion, Mark, who is sitting a few rows back. Mark raises his hands in a gesture of bewilderment.

We've just watched Lennox win three out of four rounds against Baltimore's Hassim Rahman, cut him up, batter him, and then get knocked cold with a single, massive punch. Now, all around me, spontaneous Sunday-morning celebrations are on the go. 'Thunder in Africa' – South Africa's first ever undisputed (or barely disputed) world heavyweight title bout, and Africa's second – has come to a thoroughly satisfying end for the local promoters and their many underlings. Out of the corner of my eye I see Johannesburg's Rodney Berman and his Cape Town-raised partner Cedric Kushner embracing each other and then 'their' world champion, while in the new champion's corner Nick Durandt – the trainer once dumped by his black boxers after the public airing of a bugged phone call containing racist chit-chat – is leaping up and down, trying to get a hand or a hug into the mêlée, with, a few steps behind him, Terry still bouncing and still hectoring British ringsiders with the view that South Africa now controls the world.

Oh yeah? I think – my irritation mixing with despondency – *You're missing the point.* The only flags these days are flags of convenience. That's how four white South Africans get to be jumping about at the triumph of a Muslim American over a Jamaican Canadian Englishman. I could add that promoters are

merely the middle men in this game, with the title and
its holder really 'owned' by the rival US cable television networks, HBO and Showtime, and anyway, you
just watch and wait, Lewis will get his revenge. But I'm
feeling too gutted to debate with the triumphalists, and
so I continue to avert my eyes and move away from
ringside. Mark joins me as I wander in the direction of
the post-fight press conference. It's a slow trip because
everyone from my boxing and political pasts seems to
be present. I bump shoulders with the strutting Winnie
Mandela (before being bumped by her minders), pause
for a few minutes to say howzit to a beaming Sugarboy,
wave to Welcome, smile at Baby Jake, offer a thumbs-
up to Vuyani Bungu, catch the scar-tissued eyes of
Pierre Coetzer, pass Stan Christodoulou with a polite
nod, snatch a glance at a face in the distance that looks
like Dingaan Thobela's, and avoid the eyes of the
provincial premier Popo Molefe – last time I spoke to
him was to help him move to a little flat in Alexandra
township, after which he went to jail for 'treason' and
emerged empowered – it's too much for a quick *hey!*

Eventually we take our seats and I'm struck by the
sense that everything seems topsy-turvy this morning.
We have an American world champion once more, but
this one winning his title in a far-flung periphery, when
for the past decade the flow has been in the opposite
direction – prospects from the sticks getting pulled or
pushed in the direction of the money, with the best
efforts of their finest sent home by satellite to be
watched at ridiculous hours of the night or morning.
And yet we're still at a ridiculous hour because American cable television viewers prefer it that way, and they
control the waves.

Lennox Lewis enters and says a few words to the

man who destroyed his legacy, and then Hassim arrives and tells us he will return 'home' to defend his title – home, he explains, being 'Africa and South Africa'. The last time I spoke to Lennox he too stressed his cosmopolitan credentials. 'When I'm in England people say I sound American. When I go to Canada they say I sound English. So I just say I'm mid-Atlantic. I'm someone who lives on planet Earth and wants to enjoy the planet.' This time he was after an affirming African experience, which is why, after a personal appeal from Nelson Mandela, he accepted this Brakpan gig against the wishes of his HBO sponsors. He'd been thinking of Muhammad Ali and the Rumble in the Jungle in Kinshasa twenty-seven years earlier but with each day in Africa his lot came to approximate something closer to George Foreman's.

He arrived at Johannesburg's rarefied altitude with barely a week to acclimatize and found, like Foreman, nothing was to his liking. He wanted to be an 'inspiration to the black youth and the underprivileged', to fight in front of the masses with the match shown on free television, but instead discovered he was to perform in a 6,000-seat tent, in a grotesque gambling complex on the edge of a mainly white, blue-collar town, with the fight shown only on subscription television, and the masses being charged even to watch his sparring sessions. He was pissed off and took it out on Rodney Berman, moaning that this wasn't the African experience he had in mind. 'South Africa is still oppressed in one sense,' he muttered before the fight. 'It is only six years or so since they came out of apartheid. They've come a long way but still have a long way to go.' And now he's an ex-champion whose only consolation will be Mandela's embrace.

The highveld sun is well up by the time we leave and I can finally see Sol Kerzner's Carnival City without the dazzle of the night-lights. It's one of those things that've moved on since I left South Africa – casino villages in every big town, providing jobs for the hundreds (while sucking at the pay packets of the millions) behind the rallying cries of Investment! Infrastructure! Construction! Employment! But under the confectionery garnishing of the Carnival City outer shell, you notice it's no more than just a few big circus tents decorated with fairy lights – and when you're exhausted and dispirited after your first night back in Johannesburg, and your favourite boxer has just been relieved of his crown, and you have a long Sunday ahead of you, it all seems a fitting metaphor for the relation between image and reality in this part of the world.

Every year I return to South Africa for a month or more – my annual fix: Johannesburg, Port Elizabeth, Cape Town, sometimes Pretoria, with occasional ventures inland, down the coasts and beyond the city limits. This visit – my eleventh in eight years – feels different. I arrived still in a state of chaos, the most immediate cause coming from my failure to check whether my passport was still valid (having perused everyone else's), which led to me watching an eye-rolling Pat, a sighing Tessa and a tearful Caitlin waving goodbye as I trudged back to the tube after being informed I had no chance of renewing my passport until Monday at the earliest (and this was Friday). An emergency number, a story from 'Dr Evans' – a title used only in moments of desperation – that my 'Irish' wife is ill, and I was on the plane on Saturday, clutching my restamped passport, and twelve hours later I was driving under the high skies and threatening clouds to Mark and Aspasia's leafy suburban home, feeling relieved but still foolish, for a week behind the electric fences. 'It feels like a prison,' said Pat. 'Yes,' said Tessa, 'but what a lovely prison.'

One of my little tasks in South Africa, this time around, was to show my friends and family the chapters of this book, or at least the ones where they feature. They were all so astonishingly gracious – no complaints, no requests for changes. And once they'd read, some wanted to say more, and ask more, and so we were drawn back into worlds left behind. David Hare once described his play *Plenty* – on the post-war decline of a behind-the-lines volunteer – as being about 'the cost of a life lived in dissent', and this was the question we invariably moved towards: have you had a good peace? We talked about our past lives of dissent and how we were coping with their passing, and the conversation meandered from the personal to impressionistically political and back again.

Some of my comrade friends joined me in a state of voluntary exile. Those of us who took this option lacked, and still lack, that quality of complete resolution in terms of our relationship with 'home'. We make instant judgements about the place that formed us. We change these judgements. We are always people with accents.

But most remained at home, watching, helping, in some cases hindering, the country's transition, unburdened by too much guilt. Among those I know and who survived, a couple entered the cabinet and a few became bureaucratic mandarins. One is a major-league drug dealer. Several became drug abusers or alcoholics. One is in jail for a bank robbery. Many became instant millionaires. Some struggled with mid-life poverty. But one way or another they made their acquaintance with normality. They had no option really. And the sunniest among them show a determination to find new meaning from living the new life and adjusting to its fresh demands, rather than dreaming of lives past and finding astonishment in the imperfections of the present, which is the disease of the émigré.

After Johannesburg we travelled to Port Elizabeth to spend a week with Karen and Mkhuseli – Khusta – and as always I relied on them to make me feel good about my old town and country. Khusta is the son of a single-mum domestic worker from a rural town. He was twelve before he owned his first pair of shoes, his schooling was patchy, and his prospects for work and further education were obliterated by the combination of his roles as a youth, UDF and consumer-boycott leader, as well as periodic spells of detention without trial (totalling six years). When the ANC was unbanned he and Karen relocated to Brighton, where he completed an economics degree at Sussex University, before returning home four years later to enter business.

Don't you miss the politics? I asked, as we talked over our bowls of cereal. 'In the struggle it was a question of throwing yourself with all your soul into the revolution, with no gain,' he reminded me. 'I thought of it as a patriotic call I had to obey. But when Mandela was released, I said, My goodness, I was in politics by default not design. I wanted a new challenge. I knew nothing about business but I thought I could create jobs.'

Within a couple of years he was employing a thousand people, mainly in construction, sometimes giving jobs to or helping out his former torturers and their families, and he found that the business of building houses and casino hotels and making money filled him with satisfaction and pride. 'When I was a child we were told that blacks were less intelligent than whites,' he said, 'and we thought it true because we were living in shacks, but now, under a successful ANC government, you can't tell that to my children. We are living everywhere.' I wondered what the future held. Well, he said, there were many problems in the country and the government hadn't always handled things well, but it was looking good. 'Success is never something that is guaranteed,' he cautioned. 'Still, I do have a lot of hope and what I hope is to have created a good life for us and our children, and also not to be worried about how it will be for Themba and Cayla, and for our country, when Karen and I are not around.'

The next day Khusta took us to meet Nelson Mandela at a civic function but Mandela didn't pitch up. 'Sorry, people, but you win some and you lose some with the old man – this time we lost, but we live in hope,' explained the regional premier. In Mandela's place the governor of the reserve bank was hauled in to say a few words, and he talked of the need for Aids education for young teenagers 'because by 16 it's often too late'. A middle-aged African man leapt to his feet and waved a pack of condoms, and I started to share Khusta's optimism.

They then took us to lunch at a complex adjacent to another of Sol Kerzner's new casinos, and as we were served Karen whispered, 'By the way, in South Africa waiters and waitresses are called waitrons these days,' and so I asked the young white Afrikaner woman what she called herself – waiter, waitress or waitron? 'I'm a waitron,' she proudly announced. 'I can't be a waiter because I've got a pair of these,' she said, cupping her breasts, 'and I'm not a waitress because our constitution forbids discrimination on grounds of race or creed or sex.' An hour later, still giggling about the logical leap of the waitron, I went for a long run through the wilds and everyone I passed, black and white, smiled and greeted me. And at a *braai* that night no-one mentioned crime and it all felt so good and clean and hopeful.

We ambled our way to Cape Town, detouring off to Addo to be confronted by a herd of elephants, setting off again to swim with a hundred dolphins in the surfer beaches of Jeffrey's Bay, and then getting roadblocked by a troop of baboons on the garden route to Knysna before finally settling in with penguins in Boulders. The sense of euphoria about animals and sea and scenery became overwhelming. I ran every morning along the beach road and the idea occurred once again that I could be so happy here. I knew it was where I belonged, ultimately, and the children reminded me of this at every opening.

My running, in preparation for the Two Oceans ultra-marathon, had a dual purpose – mainly a dying-of-the-light rage for me, but also a guilt-easing thrust to raise a bit of money, this one for a nursery school in Khayelitsha township where my mother teaches the teachers. She drove us there, to see the school, and I watched scores of 4-, 5- and 6-year-olds, sitting obediently at little tables, chanting slogans like this one: 'Learn! Learn! Learn! Otherwise no jobs, no home, no future. Then back to school to Learn! Learn! Learn!' I tried to speak to them in what remained of my forgotten Xhosa, and they came forward to shake my hand, touch Tessa and Caitlin, and stroke their hair. I desperately wanted to feel positive about their futures, to extend my sense of hope to their young lives.

But this tenuous sense of the positive drained away as soon as I stepped outside and saw again where they were coming from: hundreds of thousands of tiny shacks, put together from whatever came to hand – planks, pieces of corrugated iron, cardboard. No trees, no fields, no grass; rivers of mud in the winter; no protection from the sun in summer. Perhaps the government helped a bit – I'm sure it had: running water and streetlights and toilets in some zones where none existed under apartheid, and a few got to attend schools once reserved for coloureds or whites – but still, the picture just felt so terribly bleak. The teachers earned R9000 (today £65) a month and they were doing far better than average. They talked of unemployment rates of 60 per cent and of HIV rates growing exponentially by the year.

It was several years since I had last visited a large African township, and, anyway, the previous few times were near Johannesburg, where conditions were significantly better. But this was beautiful Cape Town, where you can always see the mountains and smell the sea and where black Africans are poorer than anywhere else and treated worse. The whites and coloureds, who now rule the city, really don't want to know. Cape Town was once known as the most liberal of South African cities, but now it is the most resistant to change and it is certainly not a place where black people are given reason to feel welcome.

On the way back from Khayelitsha we stopped off at Heathfield, as we always do, to visit our old char Maria, who was ill with heart disease and about to turn 74.

She hugged and kissed me and handed me a packet of Baumans Marie biscuits to take home to England, 'because you always loved those Maries – I haven't forgotten', and reminded me of her part in my early childhood, going back nearly forty years – 'Oh, Joan, do you remember his *bokkie* that was always hanging out of his mouth?' she said to my mother, 'and that blankie that he used to suck that I always had to wash quickly because he could never go without it,' and together they laughed about the old days. Maria's three surviving children arrived to say hello, and soon we were talking about Maria's grandchildren, who all had good jobs. Their lives were better. They were no longer subservient in status because of their skin colour. They had escaped the trap of poverty and were moving up in the world. And as we hugged and kissed goodbye a little of the morning's hope was resurrected.

But then as we drove back I watched little groups of young children, with no adults around, begging at the traffic lights, looking with pleading eyes. At the Hout Bay turnoff to Michael and Bridget's* house I noticed a group of young black men, sitting forlornly, waiting for someone to offer them a day's casual work. I turned away, the feeling of shame becoming overwhelming – shame about whiteness and wealth – because these were the people we struggled to liberate, and yet liberation didn't look like it had reached them. Not even close. I was struck by the unwanted thought that I really couldn't blame them if they robbed me or stole our hired car (except I also knew we had little to fear, because the gun-toting carjacking killers aren't begging children or job-seeking labourers but aspirant young

*My sister-in-law, the author Bridget Pitt.

men with suits and matric certificates and parents with jobs – lads on the make whose mission is not just to survive and certainly not to redistribute wealth but rather to buy designer gear, drive BMWs and have a bit of killing fun). As we drove off I caught the pleading look on a young man's face, and for a white guilt moment I wanted to throw all my clothes and money away, followed by an even stronger desire to run, to leave, never to return.

And so, a week later, and for the first time in my life, when I ran the self-proclaimed 'most beautiful race in the world' around the coast and across a mountain, the edge of this beauty was dulled by the human reality it framed. This coexistence of loveliness and misery was too much to take in – to relish the one, I had to ignore the other, and so I just concentrated on putting one blistered foot ahead of the other until I reached the finish line.

When the sun went down that evening we drove to Muizenberg for a *braai* at the seaside house of my friends Brett and Sarah. Brett is the former high-school classmate who tipped me off about the spy Billy van Zyl and once helped return me to my baby daughter after my mountain fall, and we have known each for more than a quarter of a century, although we had sort of glossed over the subject of how each of us has dealt with the changes we'd seen and experienced. But exhaustion and alcohol have their way of opening doors, and so we talked about how the peace had treated us.

A big, blond surfer, mountaineer and scientist, Brett went into exile in Zimbabwe after refusing to do his military service, only to be snapped up by the ANC and fast-tracked into an elite military officer's course in East Germany, followed by further training in the Soviet Union, a spell in an Angolan military camp and then the ANC's Lusaka headquarters. Along the way he seriously injured his back in a military exercise, almost died of malaria, and operated as one of the ANC's few white military commanders. He returned to South Africa full of joy after the ANC was unbanned in 1990 and resumed his studies but found himself becoming a recluse. 'Eventually I went to a psychologist who asked how I felt, so all I did was just cry for an hour – I couldn't stop. Then I realized I had problems. I had extreme difficulties adapting, with an enormous need to find people who'd understand what I'd been through,' he said. 'It's only now that I'm realizing that's not so important.'

He turned down a colonel's post in the new army and instead found meaning in life through marriage, fatherhood and a job transforming migrant-workers' hostels into flats. Later his rock-climbing background and fluency in Xhosa won him a 'dream passion' environmental job setting up a range of biodiversity projects in the Cape Town area, but still, he said, sometimes his past haunted him. 'If I think of the people I loved in exile who didn't come back, or who came back and ended up with nothing, I still cry a lot. Very few people skimmed the political cream. The others were left destitute or became criminals, alcoholics, drug addicts, strugglers, and it makes me sad.' I asked him how he copes with these feelings. 'Back to the sea. There's nothing more exciting than slipping into that screaming sensation of waves pouring overhead. If I can get a good surf on the weekend my week is made.' I wondered if escapism was his only answer. Did he hold any hope for his son

Kalai, and his daughter Saffron who was about to be born? '*Ja, ja*, I do,' he said, smiling a little sadly. 'My hope is that the next generation will grow up free from this apartheid psychosis. That's an enormous hope.'

On our final day in Cape Town another old comrade, Alan, popped around for a last visit and we spent a couple of hours alone in the playroom of my nieces, Joanna and Lara, chatting about old times. Alan, you may recall, was one of my premier boxing-watching comrade-chums – the trade unionist who helped me out after my brawl with Bokkie and Attie – and of all my friends he'd had the roughest ride. Freedom did not treat him right. His mother died, then a brother died of Aids, followed soon after by another brother from a heart attack. A lull in this sequence allowed him to study at Oxford and marry a Danish wife but after a year he was called home to salvage the ANC's doomed Western Cape election bid. While his comrades got rich, he turned down the chance to become an MP and scratched out a living as a trade union leader until tragedy returned. On the eve of the election, his 14-year-old son was partially paralysed by a riot police-man's dumdum bullet. Then his two-year-old stepson drowned in a swimming pool. Then his sister was killed in a car crash.

With all this trauma to deal with there was no time to adapt at a personal level to the disturbing changes. 'I found it very difficult,' he said. 'In the struggle there was no routine, no expectations, and we were always filled with fear, not knowing if someone was going to scrape you off the street the next day. I didn't get into serious relationships or acquire personal possessions because my lifestyle was organized around revolutionary activity, but I had a sense of purpose.

The structures were like family to me, though I always imagined that if I made it to old age I'd be sitting on a paint tin, calling the *lighties* to go borrow a cigarette because I couldn't afford it.' But democracy arrived far sooner and faster than expected. 'The personal questions started hitting me hard. How to adapt to this?' Eventually, though, he came to terms with it all, 'doing it right this time' with his wife and their baby daughter, and taking up the post as regional land commissioner, helping to redistribute the land stolen by apartheid.

'It's a massive struggle to fit into a normal society,' he reminded me. 'It's only now I'm starting to adapt.' And yet Alan, who was once classified coloured, had no hesitation in saying that for most people it's a far better place than ever before. 'For me there are a lot of positive features at a personal level,' he said. 'There's lots of things I can do now, and my *lighties* can do now, and I see my homeboys and black friends enjoying themselves in a way you wouldn't have imagined five or ten years ago. That is not insignificant – it's a helluva lot.'

For me, this visit, like all of them, brought fresh judgements, unmitigated by the erosion of perpetual exposure. There is forever that mix of hope and hopelessness, depending on the day's events – today a beach *braai*, tomorrow a mugging; here Khayelitsha, there the mountains. If I'm peering at the abyss, oh, I can just think of the friends I know who are among the country's five million HIV sufferers, and the culture of ignorance, denial, stupidity and buck-passing from the president down which assists its spread, or I can try to picture the people I have known who are among the 30,000 each year who are obliterated for the sake of a

car or a toolbox or a wallet, or I can just keep quiet and
listen to the sad tales from former comrades of the
spread of corruption from the top down and the bottom
up, and the way resources are squandered, and of the
widening gap between job creation and population
growth, and the paranoid centralization of political
power, and I don't need anyone to tell me of the lack of
real racial integration and the reluctance of whites to
share their wealth, and the way they moan about taxes
on their holiday homes and still talk about 'us' and
'them', and the way they still speak to their servants:
'Listen! You must . . .' See, it's quite easy to find
reasons to despair if you need them.

But then, when the sun is shining and the sea
sparkling, I can recognize the reasons for hope –
political peace when civil war was predicted, genuine
democratic debate in a region not known for tolerance,
primary health care, flush toilets, piped water, houses
where none existed before. And of the self-respect it
has given to millions. When I slammed the door of a
minibus taxi on my second day back in Johannesburg,
the black passengers admonished me in a tone that
would have been unlikely a few years earlier – the
barriers of deference finally being bridged, and it made
me feel much happier.

And so I still struggle with the duality of feeling
part of this adventure and retaining my distance.
I sometimes prefer to explain away my ambiguous
feelings as really having less to do with crime and
violence than a wariness about being lulled into in-
sidious apartheid rhythms which freedom has yet to
shift. Whenever I look back, which I do too often, I
see that even the happiest of childhood memories
are tainted by the realization that our suburban pasts

coexisted too comfortably with such a vicious social experiment. Much has changed, for good and bad, but the trappings remain: the expectation of service, the armies of servants and security guards, those slow voices of command.

We fly back to Johannesburg, where Mark and I experience the dubious thrill of Thunder in Africa, watching the South African-promoted American relieve the self-promoted citizen of the world of his world title at 6 a.m. The new champion, who talks of Africa as home, skips his meeting with Mandela to fly home to Baltimore where he dumps Kushner and Berman and defects to Don King's den* – so much for South Africa ruling the world. The old champion hovers, visiting Mandela, taking consolation and in-spiration from his hero's words of sympathy and encouragement and then, visiting a game reserve, still looking for that elusive African affirmation.**

Meanwhile we dozily drive back to Mark's house in one of the plush, razor-wired, electric-fenced, laser-alarmed suburbs of Johannesburg – a necessity after a string of burglaries and a carjacking where bullets were

---

*Kushner, who apparently had little faith in the ability of his charge to beat Lewis, negligently fails to pay Rahman $75,000 to extend his 'irrevocable' option to renew their contract before it terminated 10 days before the fight. Berman, however, bounces back. Eight months later, when Lewis is world champion again, he cuts a joint promotional deal with Lennox's company, which allows his South African and British boxers to fight on the Lewis-Tyson bill, and a pooling of resources and talent in both countries.

**Six months later, he finds it in Las Vegas, where he flattens Rahman in four rounds. A minute later the world champion shouts to the world: 'Madiba! The people of South Africa! Winnie! The blacks!' Finally, in June 2002, he confirms his legacy by destroying Mike Tyson in eight rounds in Memphis, Tennessee.

pumped into their family car after they drove into the driveway. A few hours later, after phoning through my jaded BBC report, I'm still thinking about Lennox's folly and Terry's hectoring vindication while making salads in preparation for a barbecue – an occasion to say hello and goodbye to old friends and comrades I've missed during our five weeks back.

But still I hover in the kitchen, mixing and minding my salads, not quite up to the business of meeting and greeting, kissing and hugging, and how's it been and you're looking sharp, and the grey hair suits you and she's definitely got your eyes – not quite recalling where we left off last time, not sure if I'll get stuck on the names when introducing my friends to Pat's or this old comrade to that ex-lover. But finally, bearing a drinks tray for security, I emerge, get drawn back, and the world I am about to leave swallows me for a while.

We tell each other our catch-up stories. Some are still working for the government, trying to hold on to their last threads of altruism; most have moved on, making mints in private; a few are finally talking of their first babies, a few more struggling to have their last. Several are relishing Johannesburg, ingesting its fresh energies, taking chances, doing deals, making killings, living by their wits and their imaginations; several others are in retreat, no longer reading the papers, no longer venturing beyond the malls and the office blocks after one carjacking or robbery or assault too many, and they feel to me like versions of something John Coetzee wrote about in *Disgrace* making the fraught compromises and diminishing accommodations they deem necessary for survival because they can't or won't move on.

When everyone else has left, and my eyes are starting to droop from beer and sleeplessness, an old underground comrade, now a senior central state mandarin, explains to me the intricacies of his job in impressive detail – the ins and outs of the politics and how he feels about it all – but this time I struggle to keep up. It's not just the tiredness. As he speaks I realize I've lost the thread. The names he spouts are no longer familiar; his passions and problems, the pain and the triumph, are no longer mine. I've moved on. I still care, but not quite enough, and my tired eyes keep shifting in the direction of the pool where Caitlin is teaching herself to swim with admirable success, with Tessa cheering her on.

Finally, everyone has left and I say goodbye to the last of the friends for another year, and then watch a re-run of Lennox Lewis's African demise, and for once I feel some light relief on departure as we drive to Johannesburg airport. For the first time I have the sense that it's no longer my problem, and with this I am freed, finally, from my defensive cynicism about nirvana's reluctance to arrive. Put differently, I'm happy to leave it alone.

Epilogue

WALKING WOUNDED

North London, August 2001. It's summer now and we're walking through the field that backs on to our little house – me and Caitlin and Tessa, and our dog Rosie. The robins and finches twitter in the trees while a gang of blackbirds is squawking as it descends for tea. The grass is sprinkled with little white flowers and little yellow ones and those white ones with the yellow middles and mauve ones too. The late afternoon sun is still high and the kite-flyers and dog-walkers are out in force. It feels a good time to be alive in London.

Caitlin, a child given to eccentric bursts of inspired determination – ever since she rose in the centre of our living room at eight months old and walked – is halting our progress by perfecting her dance routine while singing, 'Hit me, baby, one more time.' Between cartwheels Tessa is laughing and correcting, as big sisters do. Then Caitlin emulates her, throwing in ten push-ups just to show how strong she is. Stick-in-mouth Rosie is trying to coax me into a game of dodge.

Eventually we make it to the big tree, one designed by God for children to climb. With a little leap Caitlin, our sometime resident *kugel*, is performing pull-ups from a branch, demonstrating to us that for all her shoe fetishism, she's the most athletic in the family, and in no time she's up and settles safely in the middle branches, because she also appreciates the importance of self-preservation. Tessa, an adolescent whose intelligence and talent come in more considered, consistent packages, is a climber of steady progress and because it's summer and the tree is dry, she ventures to a branch higher than ever before. Then they turn to me. 'No, no,' I say, 'I've got to watch Rosie. We don't want her to get nicked, like James,' but unlike our stolen Jack Russell, our Labrador is content to chew her stick. The pleas turn to taunts, and it's summer and I love climbing trees, so up and up I go until the branches threaten to snap under me, and then, with my hand poking over the top leaves, I gaze out over the fields and on to the terraced houses, church steeples and tower blocks of north London.

Then, without warning, Tessa shouts up a question: 'Dad, why do you like boxing?' I could offer a hundred answers, really, but looking out of God's tree, with a kite-lifting breeze in the air, a gentle summer sun on my face and a clear view of our piece of London before my eyes, only one really comes to mind: 'No good reason, sweetheart.'

But let's go back a bit, because even questions without warning have their context.

Sheffield, England, December 2000. I am feeling extremely excited. My eyes are wide and my jaw is clenched in hopeful anticipation. A few more punches will take me into the territory of elation. I want to jump up, pump my fists high and scream, 'Yes! Yes! Yes!'

and 'Fuck him up, Mbulelo!' – stuff like that, but for the moment my screams are silent and my fist-clenching is restricted to my lap. I'm reporting this for the BBC, after all.

Mbulelo Botile, surrogate son of my friend Mzi Mnguni, has just drilled a trio of precision left hooks into the swollen bleeding face and jaw of the IBF world featherweight champion. Scarborough's Paul Ingle has been absorbing a sustained beating, ever since he was wobbled by a left hook in the opening round. Not the kind of biff-bang-wallop bashing that is quickly over and done, but rather the accumulation of pain – deep digs to the weight-drained body of a lager-drinking man who has lost too much too quickly, too many sharp jabs and hurtful, well-timed right crosses – until the last gasps of resistance are depleted and all that is left is the habit of courage. And now the Yorkshire Hunter, who entered the ring so jauntily to the sound of the England football anthem *Vindaloo!*, is down and struggling to pull his khaki and green camouflage trunks from the canvas. He staggers to his feet at the count of eight and the English referee Dave Parris looks into his glassy eyes, wondering whether to end it, when the bell rings. It saves him. Saves him for a final, desperate pep talk from a trainer in combat trousers. Saves him for the final round.

I know what's coming: the vindication of victory, and this time it will arrive with a little 3:1 perk from William Hill's because, for the first time in thirteen years, I've put some money on my prediction. But it's not really about the £75 at all. It's about, oh, so many things – poor African boys doing good I suppose, poor white boys doing bad, about a burglary and a thug and most of all about my place in a confusingly familiar

English world. So let me explain some more, the context within the context.

My office in north London is a room in a community centre, surrounded both by pretty parkland and by sinkhole estates, sometimes terrorized by gangs of aggressive male teenagers who move in packs and perform random acts of violence. When not mugging, breaking and entering, bullying or vandalising, they seem to get off on things like dragging pizza delivery men off their bikes, beating them senseless, joyriding for a bit and then burning the bikes, just for fun. At the time, they were also suspects in the murder of a 12-year-old Somali boy – the son of a former football star – in a park 150 meters from my office. The gang members chased him during a street festival and caught him. Then one of them stabbed him six times to the heart and liver, apparently because of a feud with the boy's older brother. He died in his mother's arms, saying, 'Hold me mamma, I don't want to die, I don't want to die,' according to those who witnessed the murder – most of them too scared to talk.* But the one who really got to me was a skulking skinhead who sneered and snarled and glared whenever he passed – usually followed by a pair of hooded lieutenants carrying long knives down the back of their trousers. If any of them spoke to me it was along the lines of 'What you fuckin' looking at, 'ey?' or 'Let's frow the fucker into the bushes for a laugh.' My response whenever I spotted

*18 months later, early in 2002, four of the thugs, aged 17 to 20, pleaded guilty to GBH in the Old Bailey and were sentenced to prison terms of between 12 and 40 months. The 16-year-old whom the judge found to have wielded the knife was deemed unfit to plead and placed in a mental hospital.

this dead-eyed young man and his fist-dragging coterie – threatening me on the street, casually vandalising the community centre, breaking bottles on the lawn – combined rage and fear: an urge to fight and an urge to run.

Shortly before the Botile–Ingle fight I discussed the gang's activities with David, a friend and author who shared my office after returning from New York. He lost his printer and mobile phone in the previous burglary. My losses included a CD-player, a knife, a bicycle saddle and a ring. We were both writing about men at the time – young English men in particular – and were ruminating over why it was that this lot, and so many others, were such scum. Was it their 'socialization' that made them so vile? No, no, we could do better than that. Perhaps they were products of Thatcher's 'no such thing as society' policies, along with the acquisitive logoland culture and the widening gap between rich and poor? Or was it a manifestation of the identity crisis of the young British male, as the young British female outperformed him? Maybe this perpetually reinforced collective hardness had more to do with the breakdown of family, neighbourhood and community – too many single mums and no-show dads, too few decent male role models. Or was this atavistic machismo the linear product of an older legacy of English, drinking-to-get-drunk male aggression, going back to *Clockwork Orange* Alex, to the Teddy Boys, and further, all the way to the burning, raping and pillaging squaddies of Agincourt and beyond? Ah, you can talk about this stuff for days without running dry, and so we ended up ruminating on how to protect our daughters from their rancid breath before tentatively speculating that what they really needed was a boxing club. Not a very impressive conclusion, I know, but at that moment the conversation was curtailed by the ringing of my phone, and David took the gap and waved goodbye.

It was the BBC World Service, asking me if I wouldn't mind rushing to the studio to do an interview on Mbulelo Botile, who was about to challenge Paul Ingle for the IBF world featherweight title. As it happened, at that moment Mbulelo, Mzi and Bubba Stotts were making their way from Heathrow to London. I reached them on their driver's mobile, which was passed from man to man, allowing me to catch up on the latest twists to their confusing story. And as I spoke to these men of professional violence I forgot the images of these gratuitously violent young Englishmen.

A bit more backpedalling then. Mbulelo was one of six children of a Port Elizabeth factory worker. Like most South African boxers he grew up in conditions that by British standards would be considered well below the zone covered by the word 'poverty'. Before his first birthday he was despatched to live with his grandparents in the township of Duncan Village, outside East London – just another makeshift matchbox house, with hammer-and-nail shacks at the back to accommodate the overflow from the extended family. Food was scarce, schooling sporadic, and day-to-day life harsh and brutal. Like so many boys in that part of the Eastern Cape he took to boxing and was immediately noticed as a lad with immense potential. At the age of 16 he lied about his age to get a professional licence but he struggled to get action and in 1992 decided to cross town and join Mzi Mnguni's thriving gym in Mdantsane.

Botile was given little chance when, after eleven

fights, he challenged the world-rated South African bantamweight champion Derrick Whiteboy – a veteran southpaw of nearly forty outings who'd not been beaten in six years. Mnguni, however, had always been a shrewd judge of styles and the youngster prevailed. This set him up for his sixteenth fight, against the big-hitting Colombian Harold Mestre for the IBF world title in 1995, and once again Botile pulled off an upset, knocking the champion cold with a right to the temple in the second round. He racked up five defences and looked to be the class of the division but it all fell apart when he defended against America's Olympic medallist Tim Austin in 1997. Botile struggled to make the weight and despite breaking Austin's jaw and dropping him he was stopped in the eighth. After the fight Mnguni informed him that his father had died three days earlier. 'I was very upset when I learnt,' Mbulelo told me at the time. 'It is terrible to lose my title and then to find that my father was dead made it much worse, but I decided to re-dedicate myself for the sake of my father.' The tragedies continued, however. Two of his brothers were murdered in township gang feuds within a month of each other. Then his closest friend was killed in a fight. Then he sustained multiple bruises and fractures when a car he was travelling in overturned. It took him months to recover, and the medical expenses almost crippled him financially.

In the meantime he moved up two divisions, picking up five wins, and through Cedric Kushner's influence became the IBF's top contender. He waited a year without a fight for his title shot and became frustrated and financially desperate. One day he failed to turn up to training and Mnguni discovered he was in the United States, enticed there by a local agent who promised him the services of Don King. When King didn't bite Botile wandered in the wilderness until he found his former American assistant trainer Terry 'Bubba' Stotts (whom Mnguni had fired three years earlier, alleging drunkenness) and they began working on a strategy to upset Paul Ingle. Immediately after the defection Mnguni told me he feared for the worst, complaining about Botile's lack of discipline and his partying habits – until the contrite prodigal returned with his tail between his legs and resumed service, begging for Bubba to be allowed back too. They all agreed to work together again. 'The way I see it now is that Mbulelo made a little slip on the road, he went down the wrong track, but that's in the past,' Mzi told me when I reached him on the mobile. Botile was gushing with expressions of guilt about his brief defection and of gratitude about being allowed back. 'I lost my mind for a bit and left Mzi and Rodney, but now I want to win to make it up to them,' he said. *Sure you do*, I thought. *Sure that's why you want to win*. They passed the phone to Bubba who said he'd never worked with a boxer who is more naturally talented. 'Botile is another Donald Curry,' he said, 'better than Ncita or Bungu.' The fight could have only one conclusion.

I locked up and raced off to the BBC's Bush House on my bicycle, feeling lucky for Botile and Mzi as I composed my words in my head. When I returned a few hours later, it was to find a window smashed and two doors battered down. A witness saw a white skinhead, followed by two others, running away. My laptop computer was gone and with it several of the chapters of this book (which reappear here in something that may resemble their original form). The police arrived with words of comfort. I told them about the gang and the dead-eyed leader with the number-one haircut and the three ear studs. They asked for a closer description and my eye was drawn to the calendar picture on my desk of Paul Ingle. 'A bit like him,' I said, pointing. A bit – the haircut and facial features were there but Paul's eyes were too alive and his expression too manic. It wasn't quite right. 'Oh yes, we know exactly who you're talking about,' one of the policewomen said, and implied to me the lad she had in mind could well be behind it. 'We have a lot of trouble with him. The thing is, he's not scared of us.' Should we confront him, if we see him? I asked. 'I wouldn't,' she said. 'Frankly, we don't, and I would certainly never approach him alone.' When they left I felt depressed, deflated and powerless.

My local paper ran a story entitled 'Author's Laptop Stolen . . . with his new book on it'. I put up posters offering a reward for its return, visited all the seedier cash shops and pawnbrokers in north London and made inquiries on the fringes of the underworld. The rumours eventually came in that it had been sold by the gang and wasn't coming back. My book was gone. So was David. He'd had enough and his place was taken by the parkland's environmental warden, who accepted the police offer of a self-defence and preservation course. I hesitated, then stayed after we hung heavier doors, wrapped the building in burglar bars and installed burglar alarms. I kept under my desk the steel claw-hammer left by the burglars, along with a Mace spray in my drawer, just in case. It all felt so South African, and I felt myself growing angry and fearful.

I was becoming obsessed with the dead-eyed young

man. His face – or the challenging gaze of sneering
contempt in his eyes – kept flashing in my brain and
I wondered what I should do about it. Look down
and scuffle past, or pull out that claw-hammer and
whack him one? I began to fall back on an older
mode of thought, going back to, let's say, my debut at
the Liesbeek Park gym all those years ago. Let him get
close, then a short underhand one in the balls and
maybe a head butt to the nose, and then grab his ears
and pull his head onto the right knee, yes, twice,
no, three times, and then an elbow in the back of the
neck and then stomp on his face. Or why not just two
jabs and a right cross, come to think of it. *No, just leave
it. These lads are young, armed, streetwise and never
alone, and if you make a mistake they'll hurt you –
they'll kill you. It's more than a decade since you've had
a proper fight. Anyway, this is pathetic. You're a father
of two. This is not your problem. If there's shit, call the
police. You believe in peace, in non-violence, in trust,
community and harmony. You want to be kind and good
and* real. *Drop it.*

But his face wouldn't go. And then I recalled where
I'd seen him before – or not him, but a dead ringer. Not
Paul Ingle, the bright-eyed, camouflage-trunked, skin-
headed, lager-loving, jug-eared world champion, but
one of his looky-likey relations, the last aggressive
young white Englishman to fill me with fear and loath-
ing.

So we go back in time a little further – Manchester,
April 1999. Another ringside, another world-title fight,
but this time with an unbeaten Paul Ingle in the
challenger's role. Two seats away from me, with his
chair a metre from Paul's corner, was another young
skinhead who grew increasingly agitated as the fight

approached. When the champion, Naseem Hamed, rope-flipped his way into the ring, the looky-likey could take it no longer, leaping up and yelling at full throttle: 'Fucking Paki, Naz, you fucking Paki bastard.' I knew racism had sullied British boxing history* but I also knew it had dissipated (reabsorbed within football or recast as bait-the-foreigner jingoism). This was, in fact, the first racial insult I'd ever heard at a British ringside. But not the last.

The skinhead went through a loop-the-loop of emotional responses. In the early rounds, when Hamed played with Ingle before dropping him twice, the young fan buried his face in his hands, sobbing, then leapt to his feet in a state of heightened exasperation, obscuring my view, with another 'Fucking Paki!' directed at the Yemeni-English tormentor. 'Paki' was the best he could do, and he did it several times. In the ninth round, fortunes changed. Hamed tired and Ingle got to work, driving the champion back, bloodying his nose, shaking him. Ingle increased his pressure in the tenth. The young man, still with his back to me, began pumping his fist in the air, shouting, 'Yes! Yes! Yes!' and 'Fuck him up, Paul, fuck him up!', forcing me to crane my neck to see the action. I wanted to tell him to sit down, I really wanted to pull him down, but frankly I was a bit afraid. He looked too wired. Best left alone.

In the eleventh Paul charged and Hamed flattened him. Out. Although I didn't care for Naseem as a specimen of humanity, I was delighted. It would sink

---

*From the ban on blacks fighting for British titles, which outlasted Hitler, to Alan Minter calling Marvelous Marvin Hagler 'nigger' (and the crowd following suit with chants and bottles).

the racist arsehole in front of me. What was he doing
there anyway? Why was he being left alone? Then he
turned around, and I realized who and why: a slightly
bigger version of Paul – the same face, just wilder, less
impish and far more insane. Clearly a close relation
– I'll save him the embarrassment of naming and
shaming. So then, a bit of misguided, thicker than
water, emotional passion. A family thing. Tourette's
Syndrome perhaps. I was looking for mitigating factors
when the skinhead turned and saw the former foot-
baller John Fashanu, on the other side of me, and could
no longer contain himself. 'Fucking nigger! Fucking
nigger!' he yelled, spitting hate. Fashanu met his
madman's gaze and glared, still, impassive, dignified,
but ready to spring. Skinhead picked up his chair and
flung it, then kicked out at no-one in particular and
started to move towards Fashanu when a security guard
finally materialized from one direction and an Ingle
family friend from the other. The friend got there first,
put the skinhead into a headlock, slapped his face a
few times and dragged him away.

It was the face of this family-fan I saw in the skinhead gang leader – and from him to Paul, with those
faux-army trunks and militarized corner and his
number-one haircut; the sins of one family member
visited upon another – not openly, but somewhere in
the corner of my consciousness. I knew there was
no real justification for this – khaki and too little hair
don't add up to 'Paki!' and 'Nigger!' let alone to office
burglaries. It was just one skewed image transposed
upon another, all the way to an illogical conclusion. I
knew this. Paul's trainer, Steve Pollard, assured me
Paul was a good-hearted fellow, a boy-next-door whom
every mother would love – one who gave generously to

community projects in his native Scarborough and raised funds for a special school for children with learning difficulties – but when I watched him bouncing back to win the IBF world title and then defending it at Madison Square Garden, those images of that ringside face, and that dead-eyed gang leader, kept repeating on me.

And then there was Mbulelo to think of. His brothers and best friend had died in township gangland violence, he hadn't fought for thirteen months, his last cents disappeared in medical bills, and his children needed the money that victory would bring. And my friend Mzi – his own son killed in a car accident a year earlier – he too deserved a good break from the prodigal Mbulelo. And even Texan Bubba, his belly even fuller with the residues of beer but still wearing a cheeky smile and a silly moustache, still angling for more money, still telling the same long tales and weak jokes, and still giving his all to a boxer he adored. I sat next to Mbulelo on the drive to the indoor arena in Sheffield. He looked calm, chatting away with quiet confidence, now and then flashing his gold-toothed smile. It was 16 December, Heroes Day in South Africa. I had used the family account to place my bet. I knew we couldn't lose.

So back to that twelfth round in the twelfth month of the third millennium. Botile glides from his corner with Mzi's words in his ear: 'Take him out, now!' He assumes his familiar pose in ring centre while Ingle shuffles towards him, futilely jigging and jogging, dimly aware that only a knockout can save his title, reputation and future fortune, but the combination of drastic weight loss and the accumulation of Botile's punches deplete his faculties of survival – reflexes, resistance, speed and strength. Mbulelo measures him with a few jabs and then blasts him twice with the right cross. Ingle implodes. His body slumps and falls on its side. His swollen eyes glaze and he lies awkwardly, making an effort to focus. Dave Parris counts to three, then shakes his head, crosses his hands above his head, and opens them. It's over.

'Yes! Yes! Yes!' Mbulelo shouts, raising his fist. 'Yes!' I whisper, pumping my microphone-holding right fist into my left palm, and then jumping out of my seat to make my way to the Botile corner. I'm smiling now. I'm happy. Mzi has just lifted his fifth major world title. Mbulelo's children will be fed. Bubba's faith has been vindicated. My family's joint account is slightly healthier. My side has won.

Mbulelo walks over to Ingle's still-prone body. The Englishman is conscious but clearly in a bad way. Mbulelo pauses for a few seconds, unsure what to do, and then turns, hesitantly raises his fist again, returning to the embrace of Mzi and Bubba and posing for the crowd. There are no more boos. For once, an English boxing crowd show their appreciation for a foreigner's job well done, even at the expense of one of their own, and offer up a polite, English clap. I am astonished.

I scramble up onto the ring apron, directly behind the new world champion. We both stand, transfixed, as medics place an oxygen mask over Ingle's face before strapping him to a stretcher and carting him off. Suddenly, my yes-yeses feel crass, my bet callous, and all those false images of mad relations and dead-eyed robbers seem imbecilically facile. I think about this for a few seconds and then follow Mbulelo and his entourage to the changing room.

Mbulelo is sitting on the bench while Bubba is removing the tape from his hands. His left eye is swollen, his eardrum burst and they are talking about whether to 'bleed' his other ear, but he seems more worried about Paul. 'I didn't want it to end like that,' he says in a quiet voice. 'I wanted Paul to be healthy. I wanted to wish him good luck for his future because, *tshew!*, he's a very brave man. I don't think his people should have let him out for that last round. Hey, man, I felt so very bad seeing him carried off on that stretcher. You know, I feel joy, but sadness too. I'm just hoping he'll be OK.'

Mzi and Berman also stress the folly of allowing the fight to continue into the final round* until the beaming Bubba joins the conversation, which returns to the subject of Mbulelo's brilliance, and for the moment Ingle is forgotten. They leave, laughing and joking, for Rotherham; I return to ringside to watch another fight. I am reabsorbed. Meanwhile, Paul Ingle is transferred from one hospital to another, while the surgeons wait with their scalpels to cut open his skull.

I reach Rotherham at 1 a.m. and settle down in the hotel pub for a Guinness and sandwiches with the remains of the Botile after-party. Mbulelo is sitting a couple of tables away, talking quietly to a friend, and I move over to join them. He mentions again that he hopes Ingle is recovering, and I realize he doesn't know yet. 'I'm sorry to have to tell you this, Mbulelo,' I say, 'but Paul fell into a coma and when I last heard was being operated on to remove a blood clot from his

---

* Although it later emerges that the blood clot appeared earlier in the fight, and might not have been noticed until too late had it not been for the manner of his defeat.

brain.' Mbulelo, the perennial party-partygoer, nods grimly, rises slowly to his feet making a sucking sound on his teeth and leaves the party to be alone in his hotel room. Rodney Berman follows him a minute later, but Bubba, Mzi and I remain – Bubba smoking cigars, getting drunk, pleading for more money, Mzi reliving the way Mbulelo was 'burying his fists in Ingle's body' before going to work on his head.

My daughter Tessa has seen the images of the fight on the television news and when I arrive home she asks me how I can watch a sport where this kind of thing happens all the time. 'Not all the time,' I reply, weakly. 'But, Dad, it's supposed to happen. Isn't the whole point to hit the other boxer's head?' Well, yes, and his body too. 'Oh, great,' she says. 'So that makes it OK then?' I shrug. There is nothing more to be said.

Mbulelo Botile is no Brian Mitchell. He can't just grit his teeth and carry on regardless. Too much partying, some say, but perhaps that's more symptom than cause, because it looks to me like he can no longer unload, that he's become scared of his own power. In any event he loses his title on a disputed points decision to an inferior American in his first defence.

And Paul Ingle? Well, at least he doesn't go the way of Jacob Morake and Brian Baronet. While his mother and brother pray and cry he eventually returns to consciousness and regains the use of his body and most of his brain. A few weeks after returning from my latest visit to South Africa I phone Steve Pollard, and as he puts it to me, 'They were both absolutely devastated when it happened, but you know the three of them are a very strong family and it was like they willed him to get better.' Never to box again, mind. Never quite the same again. His short-term memory still dodgy, at best. But at least alive, at least with some hope.

I am relieved after speaking to Steve, but when I think about it some more I begin to feel a little uneasy about the whole thing once again – or rather I feel bad about not feeling worse. Taking sides, taking bets, imputing the sins of one relative to another, playing out my own troubles through the medium of the fighting men – all this feels tainted, a bit cheap and nasty, and certainly unjust, unkind and immature. But the real question, which strangely enough I have never quite asked myself before, is why this enthusiastic absorption in a beating that came within a punch or two of ending a man's life?

In the past, friends had periodically expressed their intrigue and sometimes alarm at the depth of my fascination with boxing. Some rolled their eyes, most made allowances, but occasionally someone – usually a woman friend – would remark that it didn't seem to fit the rest of the picture of myself I presented, which I just took to mean they weren't receiving the full screen image. The difference now is that this is no longer 1985 with Jacob Morake, when I had just emerged from Sun City jail, or 1988 with Brian Baronet, when I was connected to an armed struggle, with death and killing all around me. My world has changed, and I like to think I have changed with it. For the first time my love of boxing seems totally out of focus with the rest of my life, my beliefs and my actions.

North London, June 2002. To give the barest sketch, so as not to dump on my own contemporary doorstep: we live in a cramped north London maisonette that backs on to acres of green fields, where, as I've said, we go for long labrador walks, usually with children in tow. We also go in for 'equal parenting'; each of us spending as much time as we can with our daughters who attend the local comprehensives down the road and around the corner. Most days are divided between writing and looking after my children while Pat is subediting at the *Guardian*. My prime diversion is to run in the heaths and forests. Once a month or so I test my worth in races, just to show I'm still alive. Now and then we venture off to a jazz club or theatre or exhibition or a walk along the Thames, but mostly we live a home-based, friends-visiting, wellies-in-the-park existence, and quite often I feel waves of gratitude that I can live in a place so full of stimulation and wonder.

I'm still fascinated by politics, and whisper to my children about the evils of consumerism and global capitalism, but whenever I feel I should do something I tell myself I should relocate to South Africa, and so I do nothing. I toss and turn about wealth distribution, global warming, gender identity, nature and nurture, Ireland, the Middle East, the supernatural, loads of stuff. I worry about divine purpose too, but I've lost my faith or energy for changing the world. I joined the Labour Party but in seven years attended one meeting, where the speaker didn't arrive. I abandoned it for a fling with Ken Livingstone's mayoral campaign, and then redirected my standing order to a green group. Now and then I indulge in half-politicized passions – the right of children to see their unmarried fathers was one, the anti-smacking campaign was another. Occasionally, when not being burgled by skinheads, I am motivated by a sense of obligation to help out at the community centre or to run for charity, but usually my goals are more parochial and inward-looking: say, to get a new personal best for the marathon, or to replace our mudpatch with grass, or to teach Caitlin to ride a bike – that kind of level.

Oh, yes, and as I've said, for a month or so each year I return to South Africa and enjoy it with a spirit of passive acceptance, watching it swirl and twirl with a glazed fascination between *braais* and runs and mountain climbs with friends who will be friends for ever. I still dream of it, and them, every night, and sometimes allow my conscious mind to flirt with thoughts of one day returning to Cape Town, to the people I love, but most of the time it doesn't pull quite as insistently as before. For a while I told myself and everyone else it was all about my English mother-in-law's health, and about the differences in school starting ages, but the excuses are wearing thin. Cape Town still pulls as strongly as ever, but I am starting to accept that South Africa may be fading a bit for me. I'm never quite satisfied in London, nor fully at home, but I am trying to live for the moment, to accept the reality of the present: I am married, with two English daughters I adore, and two dogs and a little home and a communal field, and an English family-in-law, and an Irish one, and this is where and how we live, for now. Give or take a thousand other details, that's about it.

So, not much time or place or conceptual space left for boxing then, but still it persists – the one reassuring continuum that has outlasted Jesus and Marx and South Africa and all the others, retaining its form while always willing to alter its meaning. After Paul Ingle's final fight I stayed away from the live ring for a few months, disgusted at my triumphalist reaction, but not long after, when my brother watched my animated observance of a Naseem Hamed television special, he said: 'Tshew. You're definitely worse than I am with cricket.'

On sunny days I like to think that some day I'll be contented enough with my relationships and my life and my place in the world to let boxing fade out of existence entirely, as a long phase I will look back on with a bemused 'now what was that all about?' twinkle. I would love to be able to conclude by saying I'd grown through it all and learnt some great lesson in life. But perhaps all I've learnt is that what comes around, comes around again and again. My revulsion faded and I drifted back and the best I can claim is that boxing has evolved into a beast of more manageable proportions.

I think I have it more in perspective now. I still write my columns and do my broadcasts, phone my fighting connections and scour the Internet sites, and I can't quite miss the really big ones, but I let the small ones pass, I can't name all the champions any more, and it's not on my mind most of the time. Then again, I still ponder about just one last little return to the ring and every day I shadow-box when no-one is looking.

Glossary

amandla – power
baas – boss
baaskap – master race domination
bakkie – small pickup truck
bobbejaan – baboon
Boer – farmer or Afrikaner
bom/die bom – bomb/the bomb
boytjie – lad
bra – brother, friend
braai – barbecue
breker – brawler or thug with a laddish swagger
Broederbond – brotherhood society (secret cabal of elite Afrikaner males)
casspir – police armoured car
chommie – chum
dagga – cannabis
Die Stem – old South African national anthem (The Voice)
donder/donner – fuck up
dood – dead
dorp – village
Fanigalo – African language hybrid, used for giving commands on the mines

519

fynbos – scrub vegetation indigenous to Western Cape

gatvol – pissed off (guts-full)

hippo – in this case, a South African riot police armoured vehicle

houtkop – idiot, literally 'wood-head' (also racist term used by whites about blacks)

indoda – man

inkwenke – boy

ja – yes

Joden – Jews

jol – party, fun, good time

jollers – party-goers, fun-lovers

jolling – partying, having fun

jong – literally young; colloquially mate or lad (pronounced something like 'yorng')

jurrah – wow!

Jus/Jussus – Jeez, Jesus

kaffir – 'nigger' (literally heathen)

kaffir boetie – 'nigger lover' (literally 'nigger brother')

kak – shit (pronounced cuck)

kugel – appearance-obsessed female, a 'princess' (literally a Yiddish pudding)

kwela – an urban African style of music, influenced by swing

labolla – African dowry, paid by the husband's family, usually in the form of livestock

larney – posh, posh person

lekker – nice

lighties – kids/children

Madiba – Nelson Mandela's clan name

makoti – newlywed woman

moer – beat up

moffies – cissies, 'queers'

moor – murder

muntu – person in Zulu (sometimes used in abbreviated form by whites in racist tone, i.e. 'that fucking munt')

muti – medicine

naai – fuck

Nkosi Sikelel' iAfrika – God bless Africa (national anthem)

nought – in this context, a negative expression to reinforce the 'no'

Ossewabrandwag – 'oxwagon sentinel' (pro-Nazi, Second World War Afrikaner military group)

ouk/oke – chap/fellow

panga – long, double-edged slashing knife, used for cutting corn

pantsula – a streetwise young man from an African township who wears loose pants

poes – cunt

potjiekos – farmer's pot stew

rooinek – limey (literally redneck)

senzeni na? – What have we done?

shaya umlungu – beat the white man

shebeen – illicit drinking establishment

siyabonga, vader – thank you, father (Zulu-Afrikaans hybrid)

sjambok – leather whip

skeem – think, consider

skinder – gossip

skop – kick

skrikking – scaring (verb)

slaan – hit

snor – moustache

spoek – spook or spy

Suid Afrika – South Africa

swart gewaar – black danger

toktokkie – ring-the-bell-and-run game

triomf – triumph

troepies – troops

tshotshaloza – manoeuvre (song sung by miners going to work by train)

tsotsie – young township thug

Umkhonto we Sizwe – Spear of the Nation (ANC military wing)

GLOSSARY

umlungu – white man
veld – bushland, countryside (pronounced 'felt')
vetkoek – fried fatcake
wenner – winner
zol – cannabis

Acronyms

ANC   African National Congress
AWB   Afrikaner Weerstands Beweging (neo-fascist paramilitary group)
BOSS   Bureau of State Security
CCB   Civic Co-operation Bureau (military death-quad network)
ECC   End Conscription Campaign
IBF   International Boxing Federation
Jodac   Johannesburg Democratic Action Committee
MI   Military Intelligence
NIS   National Intelligence Service
NP   National Party
PAC   Pan-Africanist Congress of Azania
PEN   Port Elizabeth News
RSA   Republic of South Africa
SACP   South African Communist Party
SADF   South African Defence Force

UDF   United Democratic Front
WBA   World Boxing Association
WBC   World Boxing Council
WBO World Boxing Organization
WBU World Boxing Union

GALLOWAY STREET

John Boyle

0 552 99914 8

BLACK SWAN

DON'T MEAN NOTHING

Susan O'Neill

'POWERFUL CHARACTERS, ORIGINAL STORIES . . .
SIMPLY MAGIC'
Larry Brown

In this remarkable début collection of interlinked stories,
written with subtlety and grace, Susan O'Neill – who
served a tour of duty as an army nurse in Vietnam –
offers a remarkable look at that war. Her fictional doctors
and nurses try their best to keep themselves together in
the middle of the madness. 'Don't mean nothing' is just
something they say, a throwaway phrase that keeps them
going when the bodies are piling up, when they clean the
operation room for the twentieth time in a day, when
their minds are shattered and they haven't slept for two
days. When they just want to be home again.

Don't Mean Nothing is a modern classic that, like Tim
O'Brien's *The Things They Carried*, extends the
possibilities of writing about war. Throughout, humour
and compassion wrestle with the inescapable fear and
sadness of the war. Powerful, provocative and,
amazingly, often very funny, this is a book that lingers
long in the memory.

'WE'VE HEARD THESE VIETNAM TALES BEFORE, BUT
NEVER FROM THIS POINT OF VIEW. SUSAN O'NEILL'S
DON'T MEAN NOTHING IS A VALUABLE ADDITION TO
THE LITERATURE'
Stewart O'Nan

'A NEW VOICE HAS RISEN TO JOIN THOSE WITH
STORIES OF AMERICA'S WAR IN SOUTHEAST ASIA.
SUSAN O'NEILL WRITES BRAVELY, WITH HUMAN
DECENCY AND COMPASSION'
Larry Brown

0 552 99975 X

BLACK SWAN

DANCE WITH A POOR MAN'S DAUGHTER

Pamela Jooste

'IMMENSELY MOVING AND READABLE'
Isobel Shepherd Smith, *The Times*

'My name is Lily Daniels and I live in the Valley, in an old house at the top of a hill with a loquat tree in the garden. We are all women in our house. My grandmother, my Aunt Stella with her hopalong leg, and me. The men in our family are not worth much. They are the cross we have to bear. Some of us, like my mother, don't live here any more. People say she went on the Kimberley train to try for white and I mustn't blame her because she could get away with it even if we didn't believe she would.'

Through the sharp yet loving eyes of eleven-year-old Lily we see the whole exotic, vivid, vigorous culture of the Cape Coloured community at the time when apartheid threatened its destruction. As Lily's beautiful but angry mother returns to Cape Town, determined to fight for justice for her family, so the story of Lily's past – and future – erupts. *Dance with a Poor Man's Daughter* is a powerful and moving tribute to a richly individual people.

'HIGHLY READABLE, SENSITIVE AND INTENSELY
MOVING . . . A FINE ACHIEVEMENT'
Mail and Guardian, South Africa

'TOUGH, SMART AND VULNERABLE . . . EMBLEMATIC
OF AN ENTIRE PEOPLE'
Independent

'I COULD HARDLY PUT THIS BOOK DOWN'
Cape Times

WINNER OF THE COMMONWEALTH BEST FIRST BOOK
AWARD FOR THE AFRICAN REGION

WINNER OF THE SANLAM LITERARY AWARD

WINNER OF THE BOOK DATA'S SOUTH AFRICAN
BOOKSELLERS' CHOICE AWARD

0 552 99757 9

BLACK SWAN

A SELECTED LIST OF FINE WRITING
AVAILABLE FROM BLACK SWAN

99915	6	**THE NEW CITY**	*Stephen Amidon*	£6.99
99914	8	**GALLOWAY STREET**	*John Boyle*	£6.99
99600	9	**NOTES FROM A SMALL ISLAND**	*Bill Bryson*	£6.99
77077	9	**THE STREAM**	*Brian Clarke*	£6.99
99926	1	**DEAR TOM**	*Tom Courtenay*	£7.99
99923	7	**THE MYSTERY OF CAPITAL**	*Hernando de Soto*	£7.99
99802	8	**DON'T WALK IN THE LONG GRASS**	*Tenniel Evans*	£6.99
99729	3	**TRUTH**	*Felipe Fernández-Armesto*	£6.99
99858	3	**PERFUME FROM PROVENCE**	*Lady Fortescue*	£7.99
99759	5	**DOG DAYS, GLENN MILLER NIGHTS**	*Laurie Graham*	£6.99
12555	5	**IN SEARCH OF SCHRÖDINGER'S CAT**	*John Gribbin*	£7.99
99987	3	**NO ONE THINKS OF GREENLAND**	*John Griesemer*	£6.99
77082	5	**THE WISDOM OF CROCODILES**	*Paul Hoffman*	£7.99
99958	X	**ALMOST LIKE A WHALE**	*Steve Jones*	£8.99
99757	9	**DANCE WITH A POOR MAN'S DAUGHTER**	*Pamela Jooste*	£6.99
14595	5	**BETWEEN EXTREMES** *Brian Keenan and John McCarthy*		£7.99
77133	3	**MY WAR GONE BY, I MISS IT SO**	*Anthony Loyd*	£6.99
99841	9	**NOTES FROM AN ITALIAN GARDEN**	*Joan Marble*	£7.99
99907	5	**DUBLIN**	*Seán Moncrieff*	£6.99
99901	6	**WHITE MALE HEART**	*Ruaridh Nicoll*	£6.99
99959	8	**BACK ROADS**	*Tawni O'Dell*	£6.99
99803	6	**THINGS CAN ONLY GET BETTER**	*John O'Farrell*	£6.99
99975	X	**DON'T MEAN NOTHING**	*Susan O'Neill*	£6.99
99928	8	**INSTRUCTIONS FOR VISITORS**	*Helen Stevenson*	£6.99
99638	6	**BETTER THAN SEX**	*Hunter S. Thompson*	£6.99
99891	5	**IN THE SHADOW OF A SAINT**	*Ken Wiwa*	£7.99